Mexico's Evolving Democracy

Mexico's Evolving Democracy

A Comparative Study of the 2012 Elections

Edited by JORGE I. DOMÍNGUEZ
KENNETH F. GREENE
CHAPPELL H. LAWSON
and ALEJANDRO MORENO

Johns Hopkins University Press

BALTIMORE

Johns Hopkins University Press
2715 North Charles Street
Baltimore, Maryland 21218-4363
www.press.jhu.edu

Library of Congress Cataloging-in-Publication Data

Mexico's evolving democracy : a comparative study of the 2012
elections / edited by Jorge I. Domínguez, Kenneth F. Greene,
Chappell H. Lawson, and Alejandro Moreno.
        pages cm
   Includes bibliographical references and index.
   ISBN 978-1-4214-1554-3 (hardcover) — ISBN 978-1-4214-1555-0
(electronic) — ISBN 1-4214-1554-2 (hardcover) — ISBN 1-4214-1555-0
(electronic)   1. Elections—Mexico.   2. Democracy—Mexico.
3. Partido Revolucionario Institucional.   4. Mexico—Politics
and government.   I. Domínguez, Jorge I., 1945–
   JL1292.M526 2014
   324.972'0842—dc23   2014011206

A catalog record for this book is available from the British Library.

*Special discounts are available for bulk purchases of this book. For more
information, please contact Special Sales at 410-516-6936 or
specialsales@press.jhu.edu.*

Johns Hopkins University Press uses environmentally friendly book
materials, including recycled text paper that is composed of at least
30 percent post-consumer waste, whenever possible.

Contents

Figures

Tables

Acknowledgments

We thank Mexico's Centro de Estudios Sociales y de Opinión Pública (CESOP), Cámara de Diputados, and Secretaría de Gobernación (Segob) for supporting the Mexico 2012 Panel Study. We are particularly thankful to Alejandro Poiré at Segob and to Gustavo Meixueiro at CESOP for making the panel study possible. We also thank the Instituto Tecnológico Autónomo de México (ITAM) for offering institutional and administrative support throughout the different stages of this research. We are appreciative and proud that Mexican institutions in the executive and legislative branches of government, as well as the ITAM, supported this scholarly endeavor.

We especially thank Harvard University's Weatherhead Center for International Affairs and its David Rockefeller Center for Latin American Studies for their institutional and financial support of an authors' workshop to prepare this book, as well as the Department of Political Science of the Massachusetts Institute of Technology, the Lozano Long Institute of Latin American Studies at the University of Texas at Austin, and the Woodrow Wilson International Center for Scholars for their support of our project. In addition, Kathleen Hoover and Lena Bae at Harvard provided splendid editorial assistance.

Contributors

Andy Baker is an associate professor of political science at the University of Colorado Boulder. He conducts research on Latin American politics, mass political behavior, and international political economy. He has written articles for the *American Journal of Political Science*, *World Politics*, *Latin American Research Review*, and several other journals. He has also published two books: *Shaping the Developing World* (Congressional Quarterly Press, 2014) and *The Market and the Masses in Latin America* (Cambridge University Press, 2009).

Kathleen Bruhn is a professor of political science at the University of California, Santa Barbara. Her research has focused on political parties, elections, and protest, primarily in Mexico and Brazil. Her latest book is *Urban Protest in Mexico and Brazil* (Cambridge University Press, 2008).

Ana De La O is an associate professor of political science at Yale University. She is also affiliated with the MacMillan Center for International and Area Studies, the Institution of Social and Policy Studies, and the Jackson Institute for Global Affairs. Her research relates to the political economy of poverty alleviation, clientelism, and the provision of public goods. Her work has appeared in the *American Journal of Political Science*, *Comparative Political Studies*, *Quarterly Journal of Political Science*, and *Annals of the American Academy of Political and Social Sciences*.

Alberto Díaz-Cayeros is a senior fellow affiliated with the Center for Democracy, Development, and Rule of Law at the Freeman Spogli Institute for International Studies at Stanford University. Among his publications are *Overawing the States: Federalism, Fiscal Authority and Centralization in Latin America* and the forthcoming book *Strategies of Vote Buying: Democracy, Clientelism, and Poverty Relief in Mexico* (with B. Magaloni and F. Estévez).

Alejandro Díaz-Domínguez is a lecturer at the Instituto Tecnológico Autónomo de México in Mexico City. His works have been published in *Política y Gobierno, Perfiles Latinoamericanos, Gaceta de Ciencia Política, Iberoforum,* and *Economía, Sociedad y Territorio,* among other political science journals, on religion and politics as well as elections.

Jorge I. Domínguez is the Antonio Madero Professor for the Study of Mexico at Harvard University. He was coeditor and chapter author for *Consolidating Mexico's Democracy: The 2006 Presidential Campaign in Comparative Perspective* (with C. Lawson and A. Moreno); *Mexico's Pivotal Democratic Election: Candidates, Voters, and the Presidential Campaign of 2000* (with C. Lawson); and *Toward Mexico's Democratization: Parties, Campaigns, Elections, and Public Opinion* (with A. Poiré). He was coauthor, with James McCann, of *Democratizing Mexico: Public Opinion and Electoral Choices.*

Edgar Franco Vivanco is a PhD candidate in the Department of Political Science at Stanford University. He has an MA in education from Stanford University. He collaborates as a researcher for the Program on Poverty and Governance at the Freeman Spogli Institute for International Studies at Stanford University.

Kenneth F. Greene is an associate professor of government at the University of Texas at Austin. He served as the principal investigator on the Mexico 2012 Panel Study and is author of *Why Dominant Parties Lose: Mexico's Democratization in Comparative Perspective,* which in 2008 won the Best Book Award from the Comparative Democratization Section of the American Political Science Association. His articles on democratization, political parties, and voting behavior have appeared in the *American Journal of Political Science, World Politics, Comparative Political Studies,* and *Comparative Politics.*

Chappell H. Lawson is an associate professor of political science at the Massachusetts Institute of Technology. He was the principal investigator for the Mexico 1997 City Panel Study, the Mexico 2000 Panel Study, and the Mexico 2006 Panel Study. He is the author or editor of three books and author of numerous articles on Mexican politics.

Beatriz Magaloni is an associate professor in the Department of Political Science and a senior fellow at the Freeman Spogli Institute for International Studies at Stanford University. Her publications include books such as *Voting for Autocracy: Hegemonic Party Survival and Its Demise in Mexico* and the forthcoming *Strategies of Vote Buying: Democracy, Clientelism, and Poverty Relief in Mexico* (with A. Díaz-Cayeros and F. Estévez), as well as articles in the *American Journal of Political Science*, *World Development*, *Comparative Political Studies*, *Annual Review of Political Science*, *Latin American Research Review*, and *Journal of Theoretical Politics*.

Eric Magar is a professor of political science at the Instituto Tecnológico Autónomo de México. His research primarily deals with how the interaction between institutions, parties, and elections shapes bargaining strategies in systems of separation of power. A sample of his published work includes "Gubernatorial Coattails in Mexican Congressional elections" in the *Journal of Politics*, "Partisanship in Non-Partisan Electoral Agencies and Democratic Compliance" (with Federico Estévez and Guillermo Rosas) in *Electoral Studies*, and "How Much Is Majority Status in the US Congress Worth?" (with Gary Cox) in the *American Political Science Review*.

James A. McCann is a professor of political science at Purdue University. His work on campaigns and elections in Mexico has appeared in many scholarly journals and edited volumes, including *Consolidating Mexico's Democracy: The 2006 Presidential Campaign in Comparative Perspective* (edited by J. I. Domínguez, C. Lawson, and A. Moreno) and *The Oxford Handbook of Mexican Politics* (edited by R. Camp). He is also coauthor, with Jorge I. Domínguez, of *Democratizing Mexico: Public Opinion and Electoral Choices* and is a coeditor of *Politics, Groups, and Identities*, the official journal of the Western Political Science Association.

Alejandro Moreno is a professor of political science at the Instituto Tecnológico Autónomo de México and director of public opinion polling at *Reforma* newspaper, both in Mexico City. His publications include *Political Cleavages*, *El votante mexicano*, *La decisión electoral*, and *Comportamento Eleitoral e Comunicação Política na América Latina* (coedited with H. Telles de Souza). He is the president of the World Association for Public Opinion Research (2013–14).

Simeon Nichter is an assistant professor of political science at the University of California, San Diego, and an academy scholar at the Harvard Academy for International and Area Studies at Harvard University. He has published articles in the *American Journal of Political Science*, *American Political Science Review*, *Comparative Political Studies*, *Review of Economics and Statistics*, and *World Development*.

Jorge Olarte has a BA in political science with honors and a minor in economics from Stanford University. He works as research assistant for the Program on Poverty and Governance at Stanford University's Center on Democracy, Development, and the Rule of Law.

Brian Palmer-Rubin is a PhD candidate in the Department of Political Science at the University of California, Berkeley. He studies interest representation, political economy, and ethnic politics, centrally in Latin America, combining field-based qualitative methods and the statistics of causal inference. He has published work in *Gestión y Política Pública* and in the Wilson Center report "Subsidizing Inequality: Mexican Corn Policy since NAFTA." His dissertation examines the participation of economic interest organizations in development policy in Mexico.

Mexico's Evolving Democracy

The 2012 Election in Context

CHAPPELL H. LAWSON

On July 1, 2012, a plurality of Mexicans cast their ballots for the presidential candidate of the once-dominant Institutional Revolutionary Party (PRI). Although Enrique Peña Nieto's victory had been widely anticipated for months, many observers still marveled that voters had selected a leader from the party that had served as the electoral arm of Mexico's erstwhile autocratic regime. Why had Mexicans rejected the center-right National Action Party (PAN), which had governed the country for the twelve years after democratization? And why had voters turned to the PRI, rather than to the candidate of the left, Andrés Manuel López Obrador (AMLO), who had lost the previous presidential election in 2006 by a tiny fraction of the vote? Finally, what does the return of the PRI mean for Mexico's still unproven democratic institutions?

This volume addresses these questions. It covers both party strategies at the elite level and voters' responses at the mass level, including the influence on electoral behavior of campaign regulations (Eric Magar, chap. 3), issues (Andy Baker, chap. 5), partisanship (Kenneth F. Greene, chap. 6), crime (Edgar Franco Vivanco, Jorge Olarte, Alberto Díaz-Cayeros, and Beatriz Magaloni, chap. 7), clientelism (Ana De La O, chap. 8; Simeon Nichter and Brian Palmer-Rubin, chap. 9), and salient campaign events (Alejandro Díaz-Domínguez and Alejandro Moreno, chap. 10).

This introductory chapter first summarizes the context in which the 2012 elections took place. It then provides a brief overview of the campaign, anticipating Kathleen Bruhn's more in-depth analysis in chapter 2. The primary purpose of these two sections is to ensure that the rest of the material in the volume is accessible to scholars with limited knowledge of Mexico and to remind those already familiar with that country of the state of play in 2012. But this chapter also puts the 2012 election in historical perspective by providing sufficient detail on how people perceived the parties and candidates. With this goal in mind, I draw primarily on voters' responses to questions about their impressions of the main parties and candidates over the past fifteen years that are intended to complement the more conventional survey items analyzed elsewhere in this volume.

The third section of this chapter summarizes why Mexicans voted as they did. In 2012, the mass public was dissatisfied with the state of the country and concerned about the future. This context made it extremely unlikely that the PAN could hold on to power. At the same time, AMLO had partly discredited himself by protesting the results of the 2006 election, and his base was limited both by the size of his party (the Party of the Democratic Revolution, or PRD) and the number of programmatically minded leftists in the population. Given that the PRI had chosen an appealing candidate with a reasonable track record, only a major blunder on Peña Nieto's part—or scandalous revelation about him— would have prevented his victory. Neither occurred; although his lead diminished somewhat, he won by a healthy margin (38.2% of the valid vote, compared to 31.6% for AMLO and 25.4% for PAN candidate Josefina Vázquez Mota). The PRI as a party did slightly less well than its candidate but nonetheless captured almost as many seats in the chamber of deputies and the senate as its two main rivals combined.[1]

Much of the analysis in this volume is based on the Mexico 2012 Panel Study.[2] This survey consisted of two waves, one in late April–early May (with 1,328 respondents) and one shortly after the election in July (with 923 respondents), as well as a smaller cross-sectional survey timed to coincide with the second panel wave (with 227 respondents). Like preceding panels during the 2000 and 2006 general elections and the 1997 Mexico City mayoral elections, the purpose of this panel was to understand why Mexicans voted as they did and how they reacted to campaign stimuli. As the data reveal, Mexicans remained highly persuadable by campaign messages; more than half changed their preference in the presidential race from the first to the second wave of the panel. They had many reasons for doing so, but as might be expected, voters with the weakest partisan attachments were most likely to switch (see Greene, chap. 6).

The fourth section of this chapter discusses the implications of the election for Mexico's political system more broadly, a decade and a half after the crucial electoral reforms that paved the way for a peaceful transfer of power from the PRI to the PAN. The PRI's victory inevitably conjured fears of a return to the old regime, and these concerns are to some extent reasonable, given the party's reputation. Nevertheless, a PRI victory may bring greater legislative productivity than in the past, which (as James A. McCann notes in chap. 4) could enhance Mexicans' perceptions of their government. Perhaps most importantly, democratic rules of the game are well enough established—and opposition parties powerful enough—to prevent authoritarian retrogression.

This book is in many ways a sequel to two previous edited volumes on the 2000 and 2006 elections, to which many of the authors contributed (Domínguez and Lawson 2004; Domínguez and Poiré 1999; Domínguez, Lawson, and Moreno 2009). As with those volumes, many of the chapters here focus on a single contest in a single country. But, as with its predecessors, this volume has a broader theoretical ambition. The final section of this introduction thus turns to the lessons from these studies for scholars seeking to engage the comparative literature on electoral campaigns, voting behavior, clientelism, and democratization.

The Context: The Old Regime and the New Three-Party System

For most of the twentieth century, Mexico was governed by a political system aptly described as the "perfect dictatorship" (Vargas-Llosa 1991). Formed in the wake of the Mexican Revolution, a protracted period of bloodletting that began in 1910 and continued into the early 1920s, the regime combined autocratic rule with a relatively liberal atmosphere in which opposition groups were allowed to participate at the margins of the system. The formalities of democracy were observed and, because reelection for executive office was prohibited, the people who ran the federal government did indeed change with each election.

The electoral arm of this regime was the Institutional Revolutionary Party. Originally created (under a different name) as a power-sharing device for the surviving leaders of the revolution, it became a mass-based organization with the incorporation of "sectors" representing organized labor, peasants (especially those on collective farms), and various other occupational groups. The PRI thus served as the vehicle through which those in power mobilized the population to cheer for visiting officials, attend campaign rallies, and vote for their chosen candidates on Election Day. In doing so, the PRI drew not only on its sectoral organizations but also on local bosses (known as *caciques*) who delivered votes from the sprawling settlements surrounding most Mexican cities (Cornelius 1975).

Opposition parties originally drew their support from the interstices of the system. Founded in 1939, the PAN tended to attract professionals, small businessmen, pious Catholics (in a political system long deemed hostile to the Church), and regional elites who had fallen out with the national establishment. Committed to electoral democracy, clean government, and civic participation (Calderón Vega 1992; Loaeza 2003; Mizrahi 2003; Shirk 2005), for most of its existence the PAN was basically a middle-class, Christian Democratic party[3]—but it was a middle-class party in a country where the majority of people were poor. This fact inevitably gave it an elitist tinge; a cynical observer prone to class-based analysis of politics might conclude that, if forced to choose, some PAN leaders would prefer to reach accords with the regime rather than press for authentic democratization that could unleash demands for redistribution. The PAN was generally tolerated by the regime: it secured representation in the lower house of congress (the Mexican Chamber of Deputies) starting in the 1940s and, in exchange for its support for president Carlos Salinas's neoliberal economic reforms, was allowed to win a number of state and local races throughout the country during his tenure (1988–94).

Leftist opponents of the regime faced a more complex set of challenges. Denied a strong base in organized labor, they drew support from new social movements, grassroots activists who challenged the political and economic establishment in their communities, factions of the sectoral organizations that attempted to defy their leadership, and the (non-Catholic) intelligentsia. The left was—unsurprisingly—heterogeneous, fragmented, and often not particularly interested in elections. Some leftists remained attracted to Marxist groups that had taken power in Cuba and Nicaragua or felt driven to radical action by an autocratic government. Others were willing to abandon the opposition and work within the system, given that the regime (1) promised progressive social action, (2) was willing to incorporate leftists into government, and (3) starting in the 1970s thoughtfully set aside some legislative seats for those willing to play in the electoral arena. It was not until Cuauhtémoc Cárdenas (son of a popular former president) and other prominent progressives defected from the PRI in the late 1980s that the left came together under a unified banner; this movement soon crystallized into the PRD (Bruhn 1997).

Given that opposition parties were destined to lose during the autocratic period, early joiners tended to be animated by ideological or principled considerations (Greene 2007, 2009; Magaloni 2008). Even as the PAN attracted widespread support from previously apolitical businessmen and others in the

1980s, it remained a "club" party of dues-paying adherents in which applicants had to be nominated by members and take weeks-long civics courses before they could join. And even as the PRD began to absorb ideologically flexible PRI defectors who had lost out in power struggles within their original party, most PRD activists continued to hold strong programmatic views (Bruhn and Greene 2009). Not surprisingly, PAN and PRD leaders tended to represent policy positions that were out of sync with the electorate (Bruhn and Greene 2009). They won increasing support in the 1980s and 1990s from Mexicans frustrated with the PRI, but not necessarily because of what they stood for.

By 1996—when President Ernesto Zedillo (1994–2000), the two main opposition parties, and a reluctant PRI leadership agreed to the electoral reforms that made Mexico a democracy—each of the three main parties had potential to grow, but each also had features that impeded its ability to connect with voters. The PRI continued to rely partly on machine politics in an era when ballot secrecy was guaranteed and the portion of the population represented by its sectoral organizations had shrunk. The PAN struggled to reach voters in Mexico's poorer south and most urban peripheral communities. The PRD remained an amalgam of disparate groups; it claimed significantly fewer adherents than either the PAN or the PRI, and it still suffered in some quarters from a reputation for radicalism. As with the PAN, support for the PRD had a pronounced regional basis; it dominated Mexico City and emerged as the PRI's primary adversary in many southern states, but it fared badly in the north and heavily Catholic Bajío region of the country.

Figure 1.1 displays Mexico City voters' responses to open-ended questions on what they liked and disliked about the three main parties in 1997.[4] For each party, negative comments are shown in italics above the party's logo; positive comments appear below. The font size for each descriptor is proportional to the number of respondents who offered that assessment (out of the number of positive or negative assessments of that party). Descriptors that could plausibly be interpreted as ideological or policy oriented are grouped on the right side of each party's symbol; descriptors that indicate reputational strengths or "issue ownership" (Petrocik 1986) are shown on the left; and global assessments are located in the center. (Terms used by only one or two respondents are excluded; they collectively constituted less than 5% of the total.) The term "ideology" captures both the specific use of that word and any responses that might conceivably have ideological content (e.g., "they stand up for the poor").

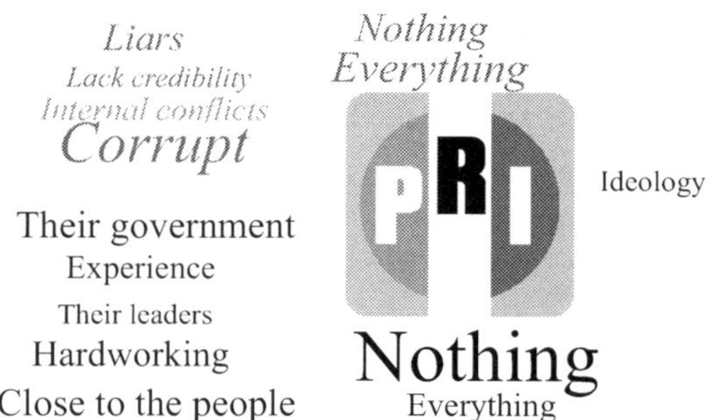

Figure 1.1. Impressions of the main parties among Mexico City voters, 1997

Perhaps the most important finding from these characterizations is the weakness of the linkages between the parties and most voters, either affective or programmatic. About half of respondents could not conjure up an assessment of *any* of the parties. Among those who did, global rejections—or, less commonly, embraces—dominated. And of the specific impressions that were offered, precious few could be considered ideological. In other words, the parties had not developed tight, policy-oriented ties to most citizens.

Another finding that jumps out is the relatively poor reputation of the major parties. None had a robust reputation for effectiveness in office. (The PRD's reputation in this sample is significantly more positive—and the PAN's much less so—than it would have been in a national sample, given the PRD's hold over the capital city.) The PRI in particular suffered from high negatives and a reputation for corruption; its best attributes were its experience in government and perceived closeness to the people (*cercanía al pueblo*), testimony to the party's long experience with retail politics. The PAN remained the party with the lowest ratio of negatives to positives (i.e., the proportion of respondents who answered "everything" to what they liked about the party and "nothing" to what they disliked about the party, compared to those who did the opposite). It also had a somewhat better reputation for clean government, but it was not viewed as particularly effective. And to the extent voters noticed, it was also not well served by its ideological orientation (at least in Mexico City).

How much the PRD deserves its reputation for being "aggressive" (which in Spanish has a purely negative connotation) remains intensely contested. The PRD did sometimes employ tactics that evinced, as one expert on the party put it, "a conscious acceptance of the possibility of violence"; for instance, when AMLO lost the 1994 Tabasco gubernatorial election amid allegations of fraud, his followers seized two dozen of the state's oil wells. At the same time, the Salinas administration and television broadcasters wildly exaggerated the PRD's radicalism (Lawson 2002).

The PAN won the 2000 presidential election by nominating a charismatic latecomer to the party, Vicente Fox, who made a point of being difficult to pigeonhole in programmatic or even partisan terms. Focusing his campaign relentlessly on the issue of "change," and creating his own parallel vote-mobilizing organization that freed him from reliance on the PAN, he drew support from a wide swath of voters disenchanted with the ruling party. PRI candidate Francisco Labastida, drawing on his party's continued organizational strength and ties to the federal government, finished second in the presidential race, retaining approximately 40% of the seats in both the senate and chamber of deputies. The 66-year-old Cárdenas—then running for the third time—suffered from a wooden image in what was now a television-dominated campaign environment, as well as from a weaker party infrastructure in most of the country; he trailed far behind the other candidates from the beginning of the campaign (Domínguez and Lawson 2004).

Voters' self-reports of why they cast their ballots for one candidate over another suggest what the election meant to them.[5] The reports shown in figure 1.2 are roughly analogous to figure 1.1, except that the question solicited only positive impressions (i.e., reasons for preferring a particular candidate). Any comments that conceivably had policy content are presented on the right-hand side; those that had no particular content of any kind are presented at the top; and those invoking candidate traits appear on the left. As figure 1.2 indicates, voters saw the race in the terms the candidates presented it: a referendum on the ruling party. Some voters, especially those who supported the left, mentioned policy proposals, but those rationales were normally quite general in nature.

Figure 1.2. What was the reason you voted for . . . ? (2000). *Photo credits:* Cárdenas, Eneas De Troya / Creative Commons; Fox, Ariel Gutiérrez Vivanco (Presidencia de la República) / Creative Commons; Labastida, Creative Commons

(That is, none of the respondents said anything to the effect of "he will prevent privatization of the oil sector," "he will make abortion legal," "he favors higher taxes on the wealthy," "I like what he says about social welfare programs," etc.) The PRI clearly depended on its machinery, legal and illegal, to generate votes for a candidate who had implausibly claimed to be a change agent, as evidenced by references to "custom" and "obligation" as well as by the higher percentage of respondents who could not articulate why they had supported him. In all three cases, candidate traits overshadowed partisan loyalties.

All told, most voters were discontent with the PRI and were searching for something different, even if they were not exactly sure what it would or should look like. They found Fox to be a better vehicle for ejecting the regime than Cárdenas, mainly on the basis of his personal appeal. As Alejandro Poiré and Beatriz Magaloni (2004) summarized their analysis of the role of issues in the

2000 campaign, "The mandate Fox received was to do better than the PRI at running the country. That was the powerful, unromantic, unpretentious message delivered by Mexican voters on July 2, 2000" (294).

Fox's actual performance in office (2000–2006) proved mixed: he retained and expanded a popular conditional cash-transfer program started by Zedillo and launched other welfare initiatives, thereby expanding the PAN's electoral base. Unlike its PRI predecessors, the administration also avoided an economic crisis. Economic performance was not stellar, however, and there was no serious investigation or prosecution of abuses and corruption during the autocratic period. With the old regime having been ousted, many voters who had supported Fox in the interests of kicking out the PRI felt prepared to entertain options other than the PAN. This set the stage for a highly competitive election in 2006, in which those without any partisan attachments continued to constitute the largest bloc of the electorate.

In that contest, the PAN returned to its purist roots by choosing party stalwart Felipe Calderón as their candidate in an internal primary. The old ruling party, factionalized and still recovering from its loss of control over the resources of the federal government, proved unable to identify a consensus candidate; it ended up with the unpopular former governor of Tabasco state, Roberto Madrazo, from whom many party bosses ultimately withheld their support. The PRD finally abandoned Cárdenas for AMLO, the popular mayor of the capital, whose image had benefited from the nationwide rebroadcasting of Mexico City news.

AMLO began the race with a commanding lead. Instead of running on his record in Mexico City, however, he campaigned on the slogan *Primero los pobres*, or "First the poor."[6] An astute campaign by Calderón—which focused on the risk of radicalism and populist economic mismanagement by the PRD— allowed him to close the gap on AMLO midway through the campaign (Domínguez et al. 2009). Meanwhile, Madrazo's campaign unraveled rapidly, dragging down the PRI's vote to its lowest level in history (Langston 2009).[7] In the end, Calderón eked out a narrow victory. AMLO's subsequent decision to challenge of the outcome of the race through months of street protests had no effect on Calderón's accession, but it did reinforce the PRD's reputation for "aggressiveness" among the two-thirds of the electorate who did not support it.

Aside from pronounced regional variation in partisan support for the PAN and the PRD, demographic factors remained only weak predictors of vote choice (Klesner 2004, 2007, 2009). In other words, despite the apparent polarization between right and left (represented by Calderón and AMLO), social

Figure 1.3. What was the reason you voted for . . . ? (2006). *Photo credits:* Obrador, David Agren / Creative Commons; Calderón, copyright World Economic forum, Remy Steinegger / Creative Commons; Madrazo, Gustavo Benítez (Presidencia de la República) / Creative Commons

cleavages at the mass level remained tepid. The same held for policy positions: despite pronounced ideological differences between the PRD and the PAN—one statist and the other pro-market—voters did not appear to choose on the issues (Greene 2009; see also chap. 5 in this volume for an opposing interpretation).

Again, open-ended responses by citizens to the question of why they voted for their preferred candidate convey a sense of how they saw the contest (see fig. 1.3).[8] Calderón's supporters believed the Fox administration had done a decent job and did not want to rock the boat; others supported AMLO because they found Fox's record disappointing or believed the candidate of the PRD would do better (Moreno 2009). These two groups were similar in size, making for a close election. Programmatic considerations and party affiliation did not loom particularly large; even AMLO voters tended to emphasize candidate traits as much as issues. The lone exception to this trend is the role of partisanship in support for Madrazo, a product of the fact that he ended up winning only the support of PRI loyalists, including those sufficiently ill informed or embedded in the party's machinery so as to believe, all polls to the contrary, that he would actually prevail.

Despite President Calderón's personal qualities and reputation for integrity, which ensured that his personal approval rating remained reasonably high, his tenure proved a challenging time for most Mexicans. Economic downturn in the United States, the destination for the bulk of Mexico's exports, threw Mexico into a deep recession. Although the economy had rebounded by 2012, most Mexicans continued to believe they were worse off than they had been a year before (Mexico 2012 Panel Study, Wave 1). Economic problems were exacerbated by a deteriorating public safety situation, as the administration's much-needed campaign against organized crime ended up triggering battles between drug cartels that the state proved unable to control. Drug-related homicides rose steadily, peaking in mid-2010 at 1,500 per month (Johnson 2011; Ríos and Shirk 2011). The grisly nature of the violence—severed heads rolled onto nightclub dance floors, mutilated corpses displayed in public places, large numbers of bodies found in shallow mass graves, and the like—conveyed an image of disorder that did not serve the government well.

One indication of public sentiment at the start of the campaign comes from an item included in both the 2006 and 2012 panels, which asked respondents to rate the urgency of various problems the next president might address.[9] Table 1.1

Table 1.1.   Perceptions of the state of the nation (in percentages), 2012

Problem	Perceive the problem as "very urgent" in 2006	Perceive the problem as "very urgent" in 2012
Crime	48	71
Corruption	45	68
Poverty	53	80
Jobs	50	77
Organized crime	n/a	72
Potable water	45	63
Education	48	68
Commercial relations with US	17	33

Note: Responses are from Wave 1 of the 2006 panel and Wave 1 of the 2012 panel, both of which were nationally representative. All differences between 2006 and 2012 are statistically significant at the 1% level. Organized crime was not included in the 2006 survey.

reports the percentage of respondents who rated a problem as "very urgent" (as opposed to "urgent" or "not very urgent"). For every issue included in both surveys, a much greater portion of respondents saw the situation as dire in 2012. This sentiment extended even to policy domains, where relatively little had changed in the intervening six years (water, corruption, etc.), indicating generalized concern about the state of the country and, possibly, frustration that long-standing problems were not being adequately addressed.

These perceptions set the stage for a rejection of the PAN. Given that AMLO's support appeared to be restricted to about a third of the electorate, a strong PRI candidate stood a good chance of recapturing the presidency.

The Campaign: Contesting the Inevitable?

In 2012, the PRI had solved the problems that bedeviled it six years before. As Bruhn's contribution to this volume (chap. 2) describes, the party came together around the attractive face of Peña Nieto, a 45-year-old former governor of Mexico's largest state who had begun announcing his accomplishments on the country's largest television network (Televisa) shortly after the 2009 midterm elections. Polls throughout 2011 showed him with a ten- to fifteen-percentage-point lead over all other contenders. With the Holy Grail of the presidency once again within reach, the PRI closed ranks, allowing Peña Nieto to run a highly disciplined, media-savvy campaign that presented him as the candidate of a younger, reformed PRI while at the same time mobilizing the party's machinery on his behalf.

PAN primary voters once again nominated a party stalwart over the choice of the incumbent president. Josefina Vázquez Mota inherited a difficult situation: running on a platform of continuity raised obvious problems, but distancing herself from the government posed a different set of challenges. Most serious contenders for the nomination—including Vázquez Mota—had served in the Calderón administration. Even more importantly, it was not clear what a PAN candidate could realistically promise to do differently. It seemed implausible that any reforms the PAN had advocated over the previous twelve years would magically pass in a new administration, given that the party could never hope to win a majority in congress, or that the party's nominee would be able to better execute the policies already in place. In short, Vázquez Mota's ability to appeal to independents was limited by the PAN's track record in office over the previous twelve years, and the PAN's base remained too small to allow her to win a three-way race.

One possibility is that Vázquez Mota could have done better had her campaign been more focused or clever. Certainly, there were low points: disputes in the party that had opened during the primary contest might have been better patched up; her relationship with the president suffered from her attempts to distance herself from the administration; she had to interrupt a speech to sit down after suffering a fainting spell in early April; and her team at times seemed disorganized. Undoubtedly, she could have garnered a higher percentage of the vote if her campaign strategy had been perfect and she had been better able to capitalize on the president's personal popularity. But there is also an undeniable element of Greek tragedy to her campaign: even after the fact, it is difficult to identify a winning strategy for the incumbent party.

Unfortunately for the PRD, AMLO failed to benefit from the PAN's perceived failings. His campaign call for a "loving republic" revealed an awareness that his polarizing postelectoral challenge in 2006 had not gone over well with large segments of the electorate. Nevertheless, he failed to convince most voters that he was a better choice than Peña Nieto. AMLO passed Vázquez Mota in the polls about a month into the official campaign season (which began on March 30, 2012), but he never took the lead.

As the clear front-runner, Peña Nieto's goal was to avoid making any major missteps during the campaign. Not surprisingly, he said as little as possible about the issues; where he did take positions, they were intentionally vague or moderate. He offered nothing particularly insightful or innovative on the drug war or on economic policy. Instead, his campaign highlighted his accomplishments as governor (particularly in completing public works projects) to project an image of competence. The overall message was simple: *I will do a better job.* This message was well suited to a fundamentally nonideological electorate; it was also sufficiently congruent with his record and image to be credible.

The principal opportunity for Peña Nieto to stumble was in the two legally mandated televised debates (held on May 6 and June 10, 2012). Presidential debates in Mexico have traditionally been major events: they temporarily catapulted PAN candidate Diego Fernández de Cevallos into the lead over Zedillo in the 1994 presidential campaign, allowed Fox to close the gap with Labastida in 2000, eliminated Madrazo as a serious contender in 2006, and boosted Calderón's fortunes in that same contest (Lawson 2004b, 2009). But in 2012 the front-runner emerged unscathed. None of his opponents produced damaging new revelations against him or appeared strikingly more competent. AMLO's performance was reassuring to those concerned about his potential radicalism, but he did not come across as an adroit policy thinker. Vázquez Mota held her own but failed to clearly outshine Peña Nieto. In the end, the most memorable moment of the debates proved to be the decision to employ a former Playboy model, clad in a skin-tight dress, to pass out slips of paper indicating the order in which the candidates would speak in the May debate.[10] Peña Nieto, himself married to a soap opera star, avoided ogling the hostess (a degree of gravitas that minor-party candidate Gabriel Quadri failed to display).[11]

To be sure, Peña Nieto suffered certain liabilities throughout the campaign. No one accused him of being a deep thinker: asked to name three books that had made an impression on him, he proved unable to do so.[12] (It was not a "gotcha" question—Peña Nieto was speaking at the International Book Fair in Guadalajara at the time.) But he was polished enough not to embarrass himself in stump speeches or conversations with journalists. One helpful inoculation tactic was Peña Nieto's decision to publicly surround himself with individuals of substance and to give indications about who would—and would not—be in his cabinet. The subtext was simple. *Even if I am not the world's most brilliant man, I will listen to competent people.*

Peña Nieto's liabilities, of course, extended to his party. As McCann documents in chapter 4, his support was not a product of nostalgia for one-party rule. Instead of praising the "good old days," Peña Nieto strove to reassure voters that he represented a new generation of PRI leaders willing to respect the rule of law. But there was no magic bullet for this reputational concern, and Peña Nieto's critics brought it up repeatedly in ads, speeches, and the debates. The only question was whether enough independents would be willing to submerge their distrust of his party enough to support him. In the absence of a smoking gun linking him personally to corruption, a sizeable minority appeared to be.

In this context, the campaign event that most threatened the notion of an inevitable victory was a student protest against Peña Nieto at the Ibero-American University. The heckling was unexpected and awkward for the candidate, but what gave it bite was the PRI's response. In an act of political autism, senior figures in the PRI denounced the protesters as outside agitators masquerading as students. In response, 131 Ibero students produced a homespun compilation of themselves holding their university identification cards. The video went viral, and reactions to the incident soon morphed into a spontaneous movement by Mexican youth denouncing Peña Nieto, the PRI, and Televisa, in which each participant volunteered to be counted as the 132nd protester.

The #YoSoy132, or "I am number 132," movement—the subject of Alejandro Díaz-Domínguez and Alejandro Moreno's contribution to this volume (chap. 10)—was potent because it reminded voters of the PRI at its worst: anachronistic, mendacious, dismissive of dissent, and still entwined in the same collusive relationships that had characterized its years in power. #YoSoy132 was also a novel feature in the Mexican political landscape—a spontaneous, nonpartisan movement driven primarily by social media. As Díaz-Domínguez and Moreno show, it revealed a division in public opinion that was somewhat different from the old regime's opposition cleavage of an earlier era (Domínguez and McCann 1995; Klesner 2004). Nevertheless, it was not enough to undermine Peña Nieto's lead in any fundamental or lasting way. After a dip in the polls, mainly to the benefit of AMLO, he recovered.[13]

Figure 1.4 shows the "poll of polls," comprising all surveys by reputable polling companies over the course of the race.[14] Because it combines data from organizations with different methods and biases, the results from one specific poll to the next are not necessarily comparable.[15] Nevertheless, there is a clear enough pattern to tell a coherent narrative about mass preferences during the campaign. Three trends stand out. First, Vázquez Mota's support began to slip as soon as the official campaign period began (March 30, 2012) and deteriorated

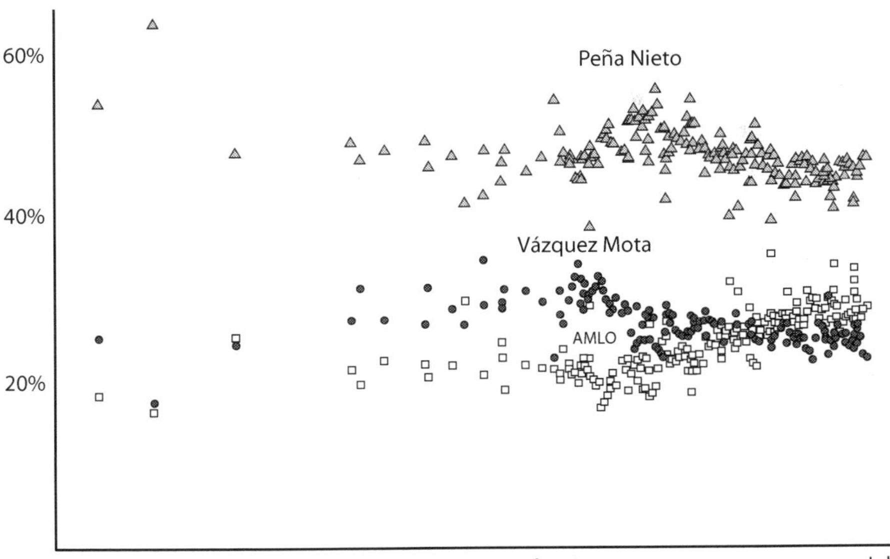

Figure 1.4. Poll of polls, 2012

steadily thereafter, though it never collapsed. Second, AMLO's support increased, especially in the first half of the race, peaking around the time of the #YoSoy132 protest and the first debate. Third, Peña Nieto's support declined somewhat, both in absolute terms and relative to his closest rival between the beginning and end of the campaign, but he was never in serious jeopardy.

What is less clear about the course of the campaign is whether AMLO continued to close in on Peña Nieto during the last two months of the race. The poll of polls has the gap holding steady, but the *Reforma* series (see Moreno and Díaz-Domínguez, chap. 10) has it growing slightly.[16] One plausible scenario, then, is that Peña Nieto's lead over AMLO was smallest in early May but then rebounded. If so, the panel data used in this volume, which first polled subjects in late April, would capture that latter trend; however, because of the timing of the first wave, it would not capture the fact that Peña Nieto's hold on the electorate had already declined in the period before early May.

These aggregate trends reveal significant changes in voters' preferences, but they do not capture the full extent of volatility within the electorate. As in 2006 (Flores-Macías 2009), at least half of potential voters changed their minds about whom they favored between early May and Election Day of 2012 (see Greene, chap. 6). In other words, a different outcome was theoretically possible. Voters were persuadable; they just were not persuaded that they had a better alternative than Peña Nieto.

Why Peña Nieto?

Writing on the 2006 presidential election, Jorge Domínguez (2009) argued that "Mexicans behave as democrats everywhere do" (303). Confronted by an incumbent administration that had failed to deliver positive results, they cast about in search of a reasonable alternative. What made Mexican voters somewhat different from their counterparts in most developed democracies was that the main parties had not yet forged durable links to much of the electorate on programmatic issues, and none had developed a convincing reputation for competence. This fact remained as true in 2012 as it had been in 2006, except that a much larger percentage of the population was unsatisfied with the state of the nation.

Figure 1.5 repeats the same sort of analysis for 2012 as for 2006. Even more than in the previous race, voters were not particularly impressed with their options: for two of the three main candidates, the most common response to the question "Why did you vote for X" was "I don't know." And, as in the past, issues and ideology did not loom large in voters' self-reports. "Proposals" and

Figure 1.5. What was the reason you voted for . . . ? (2012). *Photo credits:* Obrador, David Agren / Creative Commons; Peña Nieto, Chatham House / Creative Commons; Vázquez Mota, Creative Commons

"issues" are catchall terms in figure 1.5, comprising any response that might seem to have the slightest policy or ideological content. In virtually all cases, respondents simply said they had voted for the candidate because of his or her *propuestas* or *alternativas*, without specifying any particular element of their plan; respondents might well have been thinking of policy priorities and reputational competencies rather than stances on particular topics (e.g., how to handle drug-related violence). For instance, some of the statements grouped under the issues category include: "So things are cheaper," "So I have more money," "There's a lot of crime," "So that there are more jobs," and "To have accountability when they fail." For Peña Nieto, the contribution of purely shallow, image-based considerations is discernible even in self-reported responses; more of his supporters admitted casting their ballots for him because he was young or good looking than for his positions on specific policy issues. A number of Peña supporters frankly described him as the "least bad" rather than the "best" option, with the latter choice not necessarily being a ringing endorsement in the context of the 2012 race. Other less sophisticated explanations for supporting him included "Because he had the most advertising," "Because my husband told me to," "Because of his popularity," and (in a hint of machine politics) "Out of personal interest." One gets the sense of an electorate depressed about the state of the country and hoping, without necessarily much conviction, that things would improve under a new administration.

Was the 2012 election a "victory foretold" for Peña Nieto, as Kathleen Bruhn suggests in chapter 2? It seems unlikely that a PAN candidate could have won in 2012; however, it leaves open the question of whether AMLO could have prevailed over the PRI's nominee. As Baker points out in chapter 5, in a three-party system, a simple retrospective voting model does not provide insight into which of the two opposing candidates will win. Analysts must thus explain why Peña Nieto rather than AMLO prevailed.

This book suggests two main answers. First, as discussed above, voters found Peña Nieto to be a more attractive option than AMLO on the basis of his personal attributes. His appeal was more a product of his perceived ability to get things done than of his policy positions, which were (to put it mildly) not the main focus on his campaign. A second explanation is programmatic: at least some voters were attracted to (or repelled by) AMLO's progressive orientation. This interpretation is plausible given that issue-oriented or ideological voting seems to have been consistently higher for the left than for the PAN or the PRI. Consequently, changes in the number of leftists in the population would have affected his support. As Baker argues in chapter 5, Mexican opinion leaned more to the left in 2006 and 2012 than in 1994 and 2000, which might have made the PRD a more attractive option in recent contests. Nevertheless, committed leftists were far from a majority. AMLO could have defeated a weak PRI candidate in a three-party contest, just as he had finished thirteen points ahead of Madrazo six years earlier. Against Peña Nieto, the situation was different. There were not enough leftists or PRD identifiers to enable AMLO to win on his base, and Peña Nieto was able to win over a significant minority of independents.

What Ifs

A different question is whether the outcome might have changed if elements of the institutional context had been different. Three features of the 2012 landscape stand out: restrictions on campaigning, bias on television, and clientelism.

Clientelism was a staple of Mexican political life under the autocratic regime (inter alia, Cornelius 1975), and although electoral reforms undermined machine politics, scholars have continued to find evidence of vote buying and related tactics in the democratic era (Cornelius 2004; Díaz-Cayeros, Estévez, and Magaloni 2009). Many suspected the PRI was returning to its old tricks in 2012: violations of electoral law were the primary basis for AMLO's court challenge of the 2012 results, and credible evidence emerged of certain egregious examples (including the distribution of thousands of debit cards and gift certificates for a grocery store chain). In its ruling, however, the Federal Electoral Court made it clear that it did not find sufficient evidence to annul the election.

Chapters 8 and 9 both deal with clientelism, and they suggest the persistence of machine politics in some form or another in parts of Mexico. As Nichter and Palmer-Rubin report in chapter 9, 63% of respondents in the second wave of the 2012 panel believed that attempts at vote buying occurred in their community, and nearly 6% reported being offered a "gift." (A different method of eliciting responses about participation in clientelist exchanges suggests that as many as 22% of respondents may have received some sort of inducement from one of the parties.) The panel data also provide suggestive evidence of the targeting of gifts, indicating that brokers were indeed trying to use such items as part of an exchange. For instance, Nichter and Palmer-Rubin find that citizens who declared support for a party by posting propaganda outside their homes—an important signal for brokers in a context of ballot secrecy—were more likely to receive selective benefits from parties.

Consistent with the larger literature, Nichter and Palmer-Rubin find that clientelism in 2012 was unevenly distributed: in some communities, not a single respondent reported receiving gifts in either wave of the panel, whereas in others as many as 15% of respondents admitted to doing so. The two polling sites in which 90% of respondents "declared their support" were in small, poor, relatively remote localities in southern Mexico—precisely the type of community where old-fashioned clientelism is thought to persist.[17] Clearly, machine politics is not a pervasive practice; it persists in some places and has disappeared in others. The overall picture that emerges is one of islands of clientelism, mainly controlled by the PRI but sometimes by other parties, within a larger sea of modern campaigning (which includes local grassroots mobilization as well as political ads, television coverage, and social media).

How much did these islands of traditional politics contribute to Peña Nieto's support? The PRI's candidate was running well ahead of his rivals long before the party's machinery had been mobilized on his behalf. Moreover, because the PRI was not the only party to violate electoral rules, not all the clientelism that did occur benefited him. That fact makes it extremely unlikely that electoral irregularities put him over the top (Greene 2012; Simpser 2012).

A second what if concerns television coverage in a country where many media outlets have long been linked to the old regime, both politically and financially (Lawson 2002). Extreme and systematic bias on television has been overcome over the last two decades: all three major parties receive extensive coverage; visual tone was favorable toward all three major-party candidates in 2012; and verbal references to the candidates were relatively balanced. That said, the full extent of bias is difficult to measure with the sort of quantitative indicators employed by the Federal Electoral Institute (total time and positive versus negative verbal references) or even with more sophisticated measures of visual richness and tone (Lawson 2004a).[18] Even more importantly, news coverage occurs in a context; reporting that might appear neutral by any quantitative measure could be damaging or redemptive for a candidate, depending on what was on the minds of ordinary voters at that moment in the campaign.

Coverage of Peña Nieto on Televisa before the official campaign period began had the flavor of flattering visuals and commentary; in theory, such coverage could have helped him establish high name recognition and an early lead in the polls. Because no systematic content analysis of that period has been conducted, however, it is difficult to estimate the extent of bias or its effects. Once the campaign heated up, a more important source of bias appears to have been slanted coverage at potentially pivotal moments in the race; it was this sort of partiality that earned Televisa the ire of the #YoSoy132 movement. Such bias is not particularly pronounced in the aggregate measures of content conducted during the campaign, for the reasons noted above, but most observers perceived a clear pro-Peña tilt. Televisa's favoritism for the PRI's candidate led to widespread and persistent speculation that the two had reached some sort of private financial arrangement, which included the promise of additional time during regularly scheduled programming for "spin control" during the campaign, were it needed.[19]

Parsing the contribution of such suspected bias in news coverage to Peña Nieto's campaign is extraordinarily challenging. It was certainly *an* influence; Díaz-Domínguez and Moreno provide tantalizing evidence in chapter 10 that television viewers clearly preferred Peña Nieto, whereas users of social media flocked to AMLO. Judging from past contests in Mexico, however, the net effect of television bias is unlikely to have been powerful enough to explain Peña Nieto's margin of victory. In the 1997 mayoral race, the total impact on voters of Televisa's change in coverage during the campaign appears to have been between four and five percentage points (Lawson 2002, 163–65); in the 2000 campaign, the net effect of bias on Televisa in favor of Labastida appears to have been roughly the same (Lawson 2004a; Lawson and McCann 2005).[20] Assuming that media effects in 2012 did not exceed those in earlier contests, bias alone would not have been sufficient to account for Peña Nieto's 6.5-percentage-point victory.

A third what if concerns electoral rules. The 2012 contest took place under a new set of campaign regulations, which were put in place after the contested election of 2006. These controls were designed to rebalance the leadership of the Federal Electoral Institute (which oversees federal elections), prevent the sort of negative campaign that Calderón's camp had orchestrated against AMLO, eliminate the (already small) influence of private money, and reduce the cost of campaigns to the taxpayer. As Magar's critical assessment of these reforms makes clear (chap. 3), the result was one of the most tightly regulated campaign environments in history (see also Serra 2011, 2012).

What would have happened if the candidates had been permitted to air the sort of vituperative, factually challenged attack ads that characterize, for example, some US election campaigns? Peña Nieto's greatest vulnerability was undoubtedly the PRI's reputation for shady dealings. This topic received play in the debates, on social media, and even in some political advertisements, but it did not cost him the election. The question, then, is whether an even nastier and more relentless focus on those issues would have produced a different result.

Hesitations about the PRI were real. One signal problem with playing on those hesitations, however, is that no evidence tying Peña Nieto or anyone in his inner circle to corruption or transnational crime emerged during the campaign. Meanwhile, the PRI's candidate vigorously insisted that he would not reach an accommodation with the cartels once in office. As a result, more ferocious attacks by his opponents might not have stuck. Furthermore, it is not clear which opposition candidate would have been the beneficiary of such negative campaigning; had defectors from Peña Nieto split evenly between AMLO and Vázquez Mota, the PRI's candidate still would have won. Finally, in a negative free-for-all, Peña Nieto would have been able to retaliate against his rivals. The PRI has no monopoly on corruption, and Peña Nieto's campaign would have found plenty of fodder for attacks on AMLO from scandals during his tenure as mayor of Mexico City. It also would have been easy for the PRI's candidate to make hay out of the security situation in the country in order to discredit Vázquez Mota's competence on that issue.

Perhaps the most important challenge to consider, however, is the nature of the counterfactual. Should the rules of the game in 2012 be compared to those in 2006, which were already quite strict by global standards? Or should they be compared to a much less controlled environment in which private money plays a major role? In the latter case, the PRI would likely have had a distinct advantage over the PRD and possibly the PAN as well—from both legitimate and illegitimate sources. In other words, it is far from obvious that the institutional climate in 2012 advantaged Peña Nieto; there are many electoral regimes in which the PRI would have been better served.

Ultimately, it is impossible to parse the effects of campaign regulations, media bias, and machine politics. It seems likely that all of these factors, especially media bias, had an impact on the election, but it also seems unlikely that they altered the ultimate outcome, either singly or collectively. The roots of Peña Nieto's victory lie in voters' disaffection with the incumbent administration and favorable impressions of his competence relative to that of AMLO.

What the 2012 Election Means for Democracy in Mexico

Vicente Fox's victory in 2000 originally led to a flurry of predictions about the PRI's demise among both scholars and politicians. As one former PRI governor and cabinet minister put it succinctly on election night, after it became clear that Fox had won, "six years is a lot." His sentiments captured the concern among prominent PRI partisans—and hope among their opponents—that the party would splinter. These beliefs reflected the fact that the PRI was not held together by a coherent ideology but rather by its ties to the government, and it had lost access to the resources of the executive branch.

In retrospect, even twelve years out of power proved insufficient to shatter the party. It remained a force in subnational contests, and the PRI's performance since 1997 in federal legislative races has bounced between just over a quarter of the electorate and nearly 40%.[21] In short, the PRI's long secular decline that began in the 1960s has bottomed out in the last decade. Because Mexican voters are so volatile at the individual level, at least in presidential races, it does not make much sense to talk about a "natural" PRI share of the vote across different contests; however, the party clearly has a reliable partisan base, and it can win when it fields a strong candidate.

There are two primary reasons for the PRI's renaissance: (1) the inability of the PAN and PRD to consolidate their hold on those who lost faith in the PRI and (2) Mexican federalism. As discussed above, the first factor was a product of the failure of two PAN administrations (as well as various PAN and PRD administrations at the state and local levels) to systematically deliver on their promises of better government. Voter disillusionment with these parties reassured PRI leaders that they had a chance to return to power, which in turn kept most of them from abandoning their longtime home. The second factor concerns federal transfers to Mexico's thirty-one states and the federal district.[22] Because spending at the state level is not transparent, PRI governors have been able to use these monies to revive or re-create political machines, which in turn can be used to generate support for federal candidates (Langston 2003).

How does the PRI's return affect Mexico's political system? One concern is that federal resources will now be diverted to further rebuilding the PRI's old machinery. The result would be an expansion of clientelism, possibly to the point that it became a major force in Mexican electoral politics once again. Such a prospect is presumably unappealing from the standpoint of democratic accountability.

A related concern, of course, is corruption. The most salient fear is that a PRI administration would reach some sort of implicit or explicit modus vivendi with drug cartels, in which the latter were permitted to ply their trade in exchange for reducing the level of violence. Any such accommodation would be difficult for the administration to conceal, but it is undeniably a more likely outcome than it would have been under a PAN administration.

The same holds for less spectacular or scandalous forms of corruption. Peña Nieto has strong ties to the PRI's old guard: he joined the party in 1984, during the autocratic era, and his political mentor, Arturo Montiel, had been a leading contender for the PRI's presidential nomination in 2006. Campaign packaging aside, his actual political pedigree augurs poorly for clean government. On the other hand, as president, Peña Nieto confronts a different set of incentives than when he was governor of the State of Mexico and, later, the PRI's unity candidate. With an eye toward history, he could decide to avoid past PRI practices to protect his personal reputation and legacy. Which influence will predominate over the long run is impossible to ascertain from campaign rhetoric alone.

One salutary effect of a PRI victory is that Peña Nieto may prove more effective in enacting certain much-needed structural reforms (primarily in partnership with the PAN) than a PAN administration would have been. For programmatic reasons, PAN legislators are likely to support economic reforms on which the PRI and the president can agree, and PRI legislators should prove more disciplined when instructed how to vote by a president from their own party. As McCann shows in chapter 4, Mexicans remain strongly committed to democracy as a form of government but deeply disappointed by the way it has operated. Peña Nieto's victory, by itself, has not led people to feel better about their political system (Moreno and O'Neil 2013). But greater efficiency in government, if it is indeed realized, could alter their perceptions. Furthermore, if structural reforms in energy, education, taxation, competition policy, security, and criminal justice are implemented, the Mexican economy will be much better positioned for sustainable economic growth. Presumably, long-term improvements in living standards and public safety would in turn enhance the legitimacy of the democratic system.

One final issue concerns party politics. The 2012 campaign confirms that all three of the main political groupings are likely to remain potent players. Even in its most difficult hour, the PAN managed to capture a quarter of the vote—just as the PRI had managed to retain roughly the same portion in 2006. AMLO's decision to leave the PRD and found a new party may fragment the left, but the PRD has at least one potentially strong potential candidate waiting in the wings: former Mexico City Mayor Marcelo Ebrard, who has already demonstrated his ability to appeal to voters from all parties. Mexico could thus be in for a 2018 campaign in which three or four candidates all have a shot at victory. Regardless of what happens during the Peña Nieto administration, elections will remain competitive.

One benefit of a multiparty system is that no one faction will be able to claim the supermajority required to amend the constitution. (In fact, it remains unlikely that any party will be able to claim a majority in both houses of congress.) The opposition parties are simply too strong for a PRI administration to roll back the clock on two decades of political reforms. In short, electoral democracy in Mexico is not going anywhere. The only question is how transparent and effective it will be.

After 2006, the main parties chose to respond to their lack of popular appeal by further raising barriers to entry into the political market (see Magar, chap. 3). Independent candidacies were not allowed, and existing parties had a significant advantage in funding and access to the mass media. Even more remarkably, pre-2012 reforms gave party elites even more control over their rank and file than was the case in the past. The most serious risk, then, is cartelization of the electoral sphere, in which competition remains real but ordinary citizens have little say over who competes. (The extent to which a new set of electoral reforms, passed after the 2012 election, will reverse this trend is not yet clear.)

Lessons from Mexico

The Mexico 2012 Panel Study is the third major national panel survey in Mexico. Collectively, these three studies have produced a wealth of information on how ordinary Mexicans think about politics and why they make the electoral choices they do. Indeed, Mexico is one of the few countries in which such scholarly attention has been lavished on analysis of voting behavior; only American and perhaps British voters have been more thoroughly studied. And Mexico is the only new democracy in which more than one large-scale national panel study has been conducted. This fact makes the lessons from Mexico relevant for broader debates about voting behavior around the world.

The central contribution of the literature on Mexican electoral politics concerns the magnitude of campaign effects. Less anchored by partisan attachments and often disengaged from politics, Mexican voters are highly persuadable by the messages they receive. This fact provides the basis for significant changes in voter preferences over the course of the campaign, both at the individual level and in aggregate support for the main candidates. Such shifts altered the outcome of the 2000 and 2006 presidential elections; although the original front-runner still won in 2012, large numbers of voters nevertheless changed their minds during the campaign. The relative weakness of partisan attachments in most new democracies means that voters there look more like Mexicans than they do like Americans or Western Europeans; in other words, the findings from Mexico are likely to be more generalizable than those from the United States.

A second lesson from Mexico is that, in contests where voters are asked to cast their ballots for a particular individual, they focus overwhelmingly on their impressions of which person is most likely to perform well on "valence issues" (Stokes 1963); that is, topics on which all citizens agree, like economic growth, public safety, and clean government. Positional issues and parties play a role for some segments of the electorate, but they are secondary. This focus on candidates continued in 2012 and shows no signs of diminishing. Again, such a finding is likely to be the case in other presidential democracies.

Finally, analyses of Mexican voting behavior highlight the limits of the "mandate" that citizens deliver on Election Day. Like most of their counterparts around the world, Mexican voters are captives of the choices they are given. They are like patrons in a restaurant that serves a limited number of entrées: they get to pick a dish, but they cannot go into the kitchen and instruct the chef to prepare something else. They must order off a menu prepared by others or not eat at all, and in many cases they must order without knowing how the dish will actually taste. This fact places them in an awkward position when they dislike their government. They want something different, but the other options may be unappealing or untested. The challenge to democratic accountability becomes even greater if the leaders of the main political parties have successfully insulated themselves from internal competition and erected significant barriers to entry against new parties. Under these circumstances, the "mandate" of the electorate boils down to a plea for the next ruler to do better.

Some Mexican voters in 2012 did know what they wanted. They had enduring party loyalties, consistent preferences for one candidate over another, and even strong convictions about specific policies. But most voters did not. In a difficult economic and security situation, they struggled to identify the best alternative. By the end of the campaign, they remained divided on this question; the winner fell well short of a majority, and at least some of those who supported him did so reluctantly. The people did choose, and the electoral system functioned. But whether that outcome will render government more accountable to the people remains an open question.

NOTES

1. For official results, see the Federal Electoral Institute Web site at http://siceef.ife .org.mx/pef2012/SICEEF2012.html#.

2. For details on the 2012 panel, and to access the data, see http://web.mit.edu/clawson /www/polisci/research/mexico12/.

3. Some might describe it at certain points in its history as a Social Christian party instead.

4. These data come from the first wave of the Mexico City 1997 Panel Study. Open-ended reports of this kind from a national sample are not available for any year before 2000.

5. These data are taken from the final wave of the Mexico 2000 Panel Study.

6. López Obrador also used the slogan *Por el bien de todos*, or "For the good of all," which was the official name of his electoral coalition; however, the two slogans were nor-

mally combined as *Por el bien de todos, primero los pobres.* Another campaign mantra was "Smile, happiness is coming."

7. Calculating a party's share of the vote in legislative contests in Mexico is complicated by the fact that parties sometimes run in coalitions with other parties, and these coalitions may cover all districts or only some. The PRI-led coalition in 2006 won 28% of the vote in both the senate and the chamber of deputies; its coalition partner, the opportunistic Green Ecologist Party (PVEM), probably contributed no more than a couple of percentage points in that race. Madrazo himself won only 22% of the vote.

8. These data are drawn from the final wave of the Mexico 2006 Panel Study. Because this item is worded differently from the question used in figure 1.3, the results are not directly comparable.

9. This item is different from the standard open-ended question on the most important problem in the country, in that it explicitly asked about priorities for the next president to address and required respondents to separately evaluate each problem mentioned.

10. Televisa's main rival, Televisión Azteca, chose not to broadcast the debate at all and instead showed a soccer match. As its owner Ricardo Salinas-Pliego tweeted, "If you want a debate, see it on Televisa, if not, see the soccer on Azteca. I'll send you the ratings the day after" (de Córdoba 2012).

11. Quadri's covetous glances were mocked not only in Mexico but also as far away as the American television comedy show the *Colbert Report* (http://www.colbertnation.com /the-colbert-report-videos/414026/may-09-2012/mexico-s-debate-playmate, at 01:01).

12. Peña Nieto did name one book, but he misidentified the author; after a few embarrassing moments, he hit on the Bible as a further response. Characteristically, however, he remained unflustered throughout the entire episode.

13. A *Reforma* poll at the time placed López Obrador within striking distance of the PRI's candidate. Its publication provoked a good deal of criticism; however, in view of the final outcome, the poll looks much more like a reflection of actual public opinion at that point in the campaign.

14. To make the data as comparable as possible, the graphic omits all undecideds, nonvoters, and supporters of Quadri (who was never a serious contender), meaning that these votes are effectively redistributed among the three main contenders according to their existing share of the vote.

15. For a methodologically sophisticated treatment of these polling data, designed to compensate for some differences across polling firms, see Valle-Jones (2012). This treatment of the data does not take into account the strategic release of surveys by polling houses that are also (privately) working with particular campaigns or changes in polling houses' turnout filters and sampling methods over the course of the campaign. For these reasons, I simply report the raw results here.

16. *Reforma* was one of a minority of polling houses whose final survey predicted the actual outcome within the margin of error, and it was the only major polling house to predict the outcome of the legislative races within the margin of error. Virtually all major pollsters overestimated Peña Nieto's advantage over the runner-up, many of them by more than five percentage points (Moreno 2012). Because Election Day mobilization by the PRI was particularly vigorous, the extent to which those pollsters overstated Peña Nieto's lead before the election was probably even more pronounced.

17. Even in these cases, however, it remains difficult to discriminate between the effects of (1) sincere allegiances that have nothing to do with the provision of selective benefits; (2) the distribution of goods designed to curry favor with the electorate through legal means, as with constituency service and pork barreling; (3) the selective provision of

goods to voters, using government funds that should have been directed to other purposes, but without any explicit "contract" to buy votes; and (4) true vote buying. (Only the last two are illegal, and only the fourth would be considered a violation of electoral law.) One of the two communities in question is the hometown of two PRI governors of the state in question—a fact consistent with all four possible interpretations.

18. Content analysis conducted by the Federal Electoral Institute reveals that Peña Nieto received more airtime and more mentions that the other two candidates, though differences were slight. For instance, on the country's most watched nightly newscast (Televisa's *Noticiero con López Dóriga*), Peña Nieto received close to 37% of the airtime devoted to the three major candidates (about eleven hours and twenty minutes in total); Vázquez Mota received a little under 31%, and López Obrador a little under 33%. Content analysis of the main nightly news broadcasts on Televisa and Televisión Azteca (conducted by the author) reveals moderate bias in visual tone in favor of Peña Nieto, especially on Televisa. The score for "net positive images" (Lawson 2004a; Lawson and McCann 2005) was 50% for Peña Nieto, 47% for Vázquez Mota, and 38% for López Obrador.

19. In late June 2012, the English newspaper the *Guardian* published an article claiming that, as early as 2005, Televisa had commissioned videos promoting Peña Nieto and disparaging his rivals (Tuckman 2012). This article stemmed in part from an earlier investigation by Jenaro Villamil of the weekly newsmagazine *Proceso* (October 9, 2005), which first reported that Televisa and Peña Nieto had reached an agreement to improve his image in the run-up to the gubernatorial election in Mexico State that year; the arrangement supposedly continued with an eye to the presidential race. In a joint press release with Televisa in 2013, the *Guardian* acknowledged that the documents it possessed did not constitute "conclusive proof" (http://www.guardian.co.uk/gnm-press-office/inter active/press-releases-gnm-statement-february-2013), but it did not retract its reporting. All told, an arrangement along the lines originally asserted remains eminently plausible (*Proceso* 2012; Villamil 2012a, 2012b).

20. These estimates are based on the degree to which coverage on the main networks affected viewers of those networks, weighted by the portion of the population that reported watching the news on those networks.

21. Exact comparisons are difficult, because the PRI has sometimes run in coalition with the PVEM, and the terms of these coalitions (as well as the likely contribution of the PVEM) vary over time. The data do make clear that the PRI's best performance was not in the 2012 elections but rather the midterm elections of 2003 (when it garnered 41% in coalition with the PVEM). In 2012, the PRI won 32% of the proportional representation vote for the chamber of deputies. In the single-member district races, it won 38% of the total (combining the vote it received in districts where it ran without the PVEM and the coalition's share of the vote in districts where it ran with the PVEM). Adjusting for the likely contribution of the PVEM to their 2012 showing across all districts, the PRI fared about as well in 2012 as it did in 2000 (when it won 37% of the vote running without a coalition partner).

22. These come in two types: (1) constitutionally mandated transfers to state and local authorities and (2) discretionary transfers by the federal government, often in the form of funding for law enforcement. The latter have sometimes been used by presidents to attract the support of legislators in the chamber of deputies, many of whom owe their candidacies to the governor of their state. Because the PAN mainly courted support from the PRI, it made sense to direct such transfers disproportionately to PRI-run states (Langston 2010; Rosas and Langston 2011).

REFERENCES

Bruhn, Kathleen. 1997. *Taking on Goliath: The Emergence of a New Left Party and the Struggle for Democracy in Mexico.* University Park: Pennsylvania State University Press.

Bruhn, Kathleen, and Kenneth F. Greene. 2009. "The Absence of Common Ground between Candidates and Voters." In *Consolidating Mexico's Democracy: The 2006 Presidential Campaign in Comparative Perspective,* ed. Jorge I. Domínguez, Chappell Lawson, and Alejandro Moreno, 109–28. Baltimore: Johns Hopkins University Press

Calderón Vega, Luis. 1992. *Memorias del PAN.* Vol. 1–3. Mexico City: Editorial Jus.

Cornelius, Wayne. 1975. *Politics and the Migrant Poor in Mexico.* Stanford, CA: Stanford University Press.

———. 2004. "Mobilized Voting in the 2000 Elections: The Changing Efficacy of Vote Buying and Coercion in Mexican Electoral Politics." In *Mexico's Pivotal Democratic Elections: Candidates, Voters, and the Presidential Campaign of 2000,* ed. Jorge I. Domínguez and Chappell Lawson, 47–65. Stanford, CA: Stanford University Press.

De Córdoba, José. 2012. "Debate on Presidential Debate Riles Mexico." *Wall Street Journal,* May 2. http://online.wsj.com/article/SB10001424052702303877604577380313305142148.html.

Díaz-Cayeros, Alberto, Federico Estévez, and Beatriz Magaloni. 2009. "Welfare Benefits, Canvassing and Campaign Handouts." In *Consolidating Mexico's Democracy: The 2006 Presidential Campaign in Comparative Perspective,* ed. Jorge I. Domínguez, Chappell Lawson, and Alejandro Moreno, 229–45. Baltimore: Johns Hopkins University Press.

Domínguez, Jorge I. 2009. "Conclusion: The Choices of Voters during the 2006 Presidential Election in Mexico." In *Consolidating Mexico's Democracy: The 2006 Presidential Campaign in Comparative Perspective,* ed. Jorge I. Domínguez, Chappell Lawson, and Alejandro Moreno, 285–304. Baltimore: Johns Hopkins University Press.

Domínguez, Jorge I., and Chappell Lawson, eds. 2004. *Mexico's Pivotal Democratic Election: Candidate, Voters, and the Presidential Election of 2000.* Stanford, CA: Stanford University Press.

Domínguez, Jorge I., Chappell Lawson, and Alejandro Moreno, eds. 2009. *Consolidating Mexico's Democracy: The 2006 Presidential Campaign in Comparative Perspective.* Baltimore: Johns Hopkins University Press.

Domínguez, Jorge I., and James A. McCann. 1995. "Shaping Mexico's Electoral Arena: The Construction of Partisan Cleavages in the 1988 and 1991 Elections." *American Political Science Review* 89, no. 1: 34–48.

Domínguez, Jorge I., and Alejandro Poiré, eds. 1999. *Towards Mexico's Democratization: Parties, Campaigns, Elections, and Public Opinion.* New York: Routledge.

Flores-Macías, Francisco. 2009. "Electoral Volatility in 2006." In *Consolidating Mexico's Democracy: The 2006 Presidential Campaign in Comparative Perspective,* ed. Jorge I. Domínguez, Chappell Lawson, and Alejandro Moreno, 191–208. Baltimore: Johns Hopkins University Press.

Greene, Kenneth F. 2007. *Why Dominant Parties Lose: Mexico's Democratization in Comparative Perspective.* Cambridge: Cambridge University Press.

———. 2009. "Images and Issues in Mexico's 2006 Presidential Election." In *Consolidating Mexico's Democracy: The 2006 Presidential Campaign in Comparative Perspective,* ed. Jorge I. Domínguez, Chappell Lawson, and Alejandro Moreno, 246–67. Baltimore: Johns Hopkins University Press.

————. 2012. "¿Se compró la elección presidencial?" Paper presented at the Seminario Proceso Electoral 2012, Tribunal Electoral del Poder Judicial de la Federación, Mexico City.

Johnson, William Robert. 2011. "Data on Mexican Drug War Violence." *Johnson Archive*, February 28. http://www.johnstonsarchive.net/terrorism/mexicodrugwar.html.

Klesner, Joseph L. 2004. "The Structure of the Mexican Electorate: Social, Attitudinal, and Partisan Bases of Fox's Victory." In *Mexico's Pivotal Democratic Election: Candidate, Voters, and the Presidential Election of 2000*, ed. Jorge I. Domínguez and Chappell Lawson, 91–122. Stanford, CA: Stanford University Press.

————. 2007. "The 2006 Mexican Elections: Manifestation of a Divided Society?" *PS: Politics and Political Science* 40, no. 1: 27–32.

————. 2009. "A Sociological Analysis of the 2006 Mexican Elections." In *Consolidating Mexico's Democracy: The 2006 Presidential Campaign in Comparative Perspective*, ed. Jorge I. Domínguez, Chappell Lawson, and Alejandro Moreno, 50–70. Baltimore: Johns Hopkins University Press.

Langston, Joy. 2003. "Rising from the Ashes? Reorganizing the PRI's State Party Organizations after Electoral Defeat." *Comparative Political Studies* 36, no. 3: 293–328.

————. 2009. "The PRI's 2006 Presidential Campaign." In *Consolidating Mexico's Democracy: The 2006 Presidential Elections in Comparative Perspective*, ed. Jorge I. Domínguez, Chappell Lawson, and Alejandro Moreno, 152–68. Baltimore: Johns Hopkins University Press.

————. 2010. "Governors and 'Their' Deputies: New Legislative Principals in Mexico." *Legislative Studies Quarterly* 35, no. 2: 235–58.

Lawson, Chappell. 2002. *Building the Fourth Estate: Democratization and the Rise of a Free Press in Mexico*. Berkeley: University of California Press.

————. 2004a. "Television Coverage, Vote Choice, and the 2000 Campaign." In *Mexico's Pivotal Democratic Election: Candidate, Voters, and the Presidential Election of 2000*, ed. Jorge I. Domínguez and Chappell Lawson, 187–210. Stanford, CA: Stanford University Press.

————. 2004b. "Mexico's Great Debates: The Televised Candidate Encounters of 2000 and Their Electoral Consequences." In *Mexico's Pivotal Democratic Election: Candidate, Voters, and the Presidential Election of 2000*, ed. Jorge I. Domínguez and Chappell Lawson, 211–42. Stanford, CA: Stanford University Press.

————. 2009. "Introduction: The Mexican 2006 Election in Context." In *Consolidating Mexico's Democracy: The 2006 Presidential Elections in Comparative Perspective*, ed. Jorge I. Domínguez, Chappell Lawson, and Alejandro Moreno, 1–28. Baltimore: Johns Hopkins University Press.

Lawson, Chappell, and James A. McCann. 2005. "Television News, Mexico's 2000 Elections, and Media Effects in Emerging Democracies." *British Journal of Political Science* 35: 1–30.

Loaeza, Soledad. 2003. "The National Action Party (PAN): From the Fringes of Political System to the Heart of Change." In *Christian Democracy in Latin America: Electoral Competition and Regime Conflicts*, ed. Scott Mainwaring and Timothy R. Scully, 196–246. Stanford, CA: Stanford University Press.

Magaloni, Beatriz. 2008. *Voting for Autocracy: Hegemonic Party Survival and Its Demise in Mexico*. Cambridge: Cambridge University Press.

Mizrahi, Yemile. 2003. *From Martyrdom to Power: The Partido Acción Nacional in Mexico*. Notre Dame, IN: University of Notre Dame Press.

Moreno, Alejandro. 2009. "The Activation of Economic Voting in the 2006 Mexican Presidential Campaign." In *Consolidating Mexico's Democracy: The 2006 Presidential Elections in Comparative Perspective*, ed. Jorge I. Domínguez, Chappell Lawson, and Alejandro Moreno, 209–28. Baltimore: Johns Hopkins University Press.

———. 2012. "El desliz de la encuestas." *Reforma*, August 12, 12–13.

Moreno, Alejandro, and Shannon K. O'Neil. 2013. "El malestar democrático en México." *Foreign Affairs Latinoamérica* 13, no. 1: 41–47.

Petrocik, John R. 1986. "Issue Ownership in Presidential Elections: A 1980 Case Study." *American Journal of Political Science* 40, no. 3: 825–50.

Poiré, Alejandro, and Beatriz Magaloni. 2004. "The Issues, the Vote, and the Mandate for Change." In *Mexico's Pivotal Democratic Election: Candidate, Voters, and the Presidential Election of 2000*, ed. Jorge I. Domínguez and Chappell Lawson, 293–320. Stanford, CA: Stanford University Press.

Proceso. 2012. "Loret confirma contubernio Peña Nieto-Televisa, como documentó Proceso." *Proceso*, June 8. http://www.proceso.com.mx/?p=310137.

Ríos, Viridiana, and David A. Shirk. 2011. "Drug Violence in Mexico: Data and Analysis through 2010." San Diego: Trans-Border Institute, University of California.

Rosas, Guillermo, and Joy Langston. 2011. "Gubernatorial Effects on the Voting Behavior of National Legislators." *Journal of Politics* 73, no. 2: 477–93.

Serra, Gilles. 2011. "La Reforma Electoral en México: ¿Un Retroceso Democrático?" In *Caleidoscopio de la Innovación Democrática en América Latina*, ed. Yanina Welp and Laurence Whitehead, 75–95. Mexico City: FLACSO.

———. 2012. "The Risk of Partyarchy and Democratic Backsliding: Mexico's 2007 Electoral Reform." *Taiwan Journal of Democracy* 8, no. 1: 93–118.

Shirk, David A. 2005. *Mexico's New Politics: The PAN and Democratic Change*. Boulder, CO: Lynne Rienner.

Simpser, Alberto. 2012. "Did the PRI Buy Its Electoral Result in the 2012 Mexican Election?" Unpublished manuscript, University of Chicago.

Stokes, Donald E. 1963. "Spatial Models of Party Competition." *American Political Science Review* 57: 368–77.

Tuckman, Jon. 2012. "Mexican Media Scandal: Secretive Televisa Unit Promoted PRI Candidate." *Guardian*, June 26. http://www.guardian.co.uk/world/2012/jun/26/mexican-media-scandal-televisa-pri-nieto.

Valle-Jones, Diego. 2012. "Final Poll of Polls." *Diego Valle-Jones* (blog), June 27. http://blog.diegovalle.net/2012/06/final-poll-of-polls.html.

Vargas-Llosa, Mario. 1991. "Mexico: The Perfect Dictatorship." *New Perspectives Quarterly* 8, no. 1: 23–24.

Villamil, Jenaro. 2012a. "Televisa Asume la Defensa de Peña Nieto (Primera Parte)." *Proceso*, July 22. http://homozapping.com.mx/2012/07/televisa-asume-la-defensa-de-pena-nieto-primera-parte/.

———. 2012b. "Televisa Asume la Defensa de Peña Nieto (Segunda Parte)." *Proceso*, July 23. http://homozapping.com.mx/2012/07/televisa-asume-la-defensa-de-pena-nieto-segunda-parte/.

2

Chronicle of a Victory Foretold

*Candidates, Parties, and Campaign Strategies
in the 2012 Mexican Presidential Election*

KATHLEEN BRUHN

Cuando despertó, el dinosaurio todavía estaba allí.
When he woke up, the dinosaur was still there.

AUGUSTO MONTERROSO, 1959

There was never much suspense about the outcome of the 2012 Mexican presidential election. Well before the official start of the campaign—or even the selection of candidates—polls consistently showed the eventual winner, Enrique Peña Nieto (EPN) of the former ruling party (Partido Revolucionario Institucional, or PRI), with a commanding lead over all rivals. The only surprise was that the once-vilified PRI, whose demise many prematurely predicted after it lost the presidency in 2000, was back in charge after only two terms out of power.

Although the campaign did not lead to the defeat of the early front-runner, as had the presidential campaigns of 2000 and 2006, it did have a significant impact on the margin of victory, the balance of power in the legislature, the order of finish of the candidates, and turnout rates, particularly among the young. The election was no mere formality; it had to be won, and it was fiercely contested.

Campaigns are also a key moment in the functioning of democracy. Close observation of campaigns in any democracy can lay bare the extent to which the political system offers voters clear and meaningful choices, provides them with the necessary information to decide which of these choices best represents their own preferred policies, allows them to make their choice without coercion or intimidation, and ensures that their votes are counted honestly. These are precisely the criteria on which experts determine whether a country may be legitimately classified as a democracy at all. Campaigns are the first link in the chain of representation that begins with the selection of representatives and ends with the implementation of policy (Domínguez and Lawson 2004; Lawson 2000).

What does the 2012 presidential campaign tell us about representation and democracy in Mexico? All is not well. The parties are stable on the surface but hollow at their core. Electoral institutions functioned smoothly, but voters seem increasingly alienated. The greatest excitement of the entire campaign had little to do with the candidates or the outcome, but focused on a more or less antipolitical Internet movement that disappeared after the election almost as quickly as it had emerged.

Four facets of the campaign deserve particular attention. First, the campaign turned almost entirely on the personal competence of the candidates. The top two issue priorities for Mexicans were clear: jobs and economic growth on the one hand, and crime and public insecurity on the other. But rather than engage in a spirited debate about the proper policies to address these priorities, as in the US presidential campaign of the same year, Mexican presidential candidates simply claimed they were the best individuals to do the job; *how* did not really matter. Yet it should, in fact, matter whether a president plans to resolve the problem of public insecurity by strengthening courts, militarizing the country, or making pacts with criminal networks. And it should matter whether candidates intend to raise revenues by taxing the wealthy or the poor, and by spending money on universities or elementary education.

In this first step in the chain of representation, therefore, the campaigns gave voters incomplete information about the future policy consequences of their choice. This failure was not because the candidates lacked access to media; parties had unprecedented media access in 2012. Over the course of a three-month campaign, more than forty million ads aired on radio and television, leading some to call 2012 the most media-centric campaign in Mexican history (Urrutia and Martínez 2012, 12). The candidates simply did not use this time to explain their policies in detail. Although some information was provided, in ads and through the two presidential debates, the candidates focused more on competence than policy substance.

Second, voter alienation found expression in an Internet movement, organized through social media, which opposed the leading candidate and eventual winner as well as the traditional mass media (especially the main television network, Televisa) but refused to endorse any other candidate, propose an alternative political agenda, or support any specific set of policies to address the issues of the day. While the movement does help explain the narrowness of the winner's margin of victory, the surge of Andrés Manuel López Obrador (AMLO) to second place, and perhaps higher turnout among young voters, it may have no lasting impact on the political system, and it certainly has not repaired the breach between existing parties and many voters.

Third, the persistence of efforts by all three parties to "buy" votes by promising material rewards in exchange for support, regardless of whether it worked, indicates that candidates and parties feel uncertain about their ability to win votes through programmatic appeals or loyalty alone. Losing US presidential candidate Mitt Romney may have called universal health care a giveaway that Obama used to buy victory, but there is clearly a wide gulf between the provision of nondiscretionary entitlement programs or public goods and trading a bag of cement for a vote. The fact that Mexican presidential candidates believed that these exchanges would work, and that they were necessary, suggests an underlying sense of insecurity about the ability of parties to connect to voters.

Finally, parties mattered for outcomes, but not in the expected sense of providing policy platforms or the organizational structure necessary to run a successful campaign. Rather, parties acted as spoilers. They could hurt their candidates—sometimes badly—but rarely added much. Trust in and support for individual candidates routinely exceeded popular trust in and support for their parties. The strange irrelevance of parties in presidential campaigns reinforces the suspicions raised by the importance of personalistic media images and the candidates' use of particularistic exchanges: that the representative linkages between parties and voters in Mexico are dangerously weak, despite apparent stability in voting patterns. To the extent that voters feel represented in government, their affective, emotional linkages are to individuals, not institutions or parties. The same trend in the rest of Latin America has often led to party system collapse and growing electoral volatility. This is not a hopeful sign for democratic consolidation.

The rest of this chapter introduces the three principal candidates as well as their assets, liabilities, and opening strategies. Next, I discuss two major turning points in the campaign: the onset of negative campaigning in mid-April, and the Internet youth movement #YoSoy132 in mid-May. Finally, I analyze the role played by the parties.

Enrique Peña Nieto: *Yo sí cumplo*

Enrique Peña Nieto's main task lay in convincing voters to trust the PRI with the power of the presidency again. After all, just twelve years earlier, jubilant voters carried papier-mâché coffins labeled "PRI" through the streets and celebrated the end of the PRI's seventy-year rule. Should he distance himself from the PRI and its baggage? Or should he try to reshape the PRI's image and sell it as a reformed and democratic version of its former self? Could that even be done?

On a personal level, Peña Nieto had all the right stuff. He was a young, handsome man with a glamorous TV-star wife, born into a prominent political family with enviable connections in the business and the political world, and, to top it off, a former governor of the most populous state in Mexico. To be sure, he did not always seem like the smartest guy in the room. When he attended the International Book Fair in Guadalajara—a venue where he might legitimately have anticipated questions about his taste in books—he found himself unable to name even three books that had influenced him. But given that 43% of Mexicans have never visited a library, only 27% had read at least one book in the previous year, and 24% owned no books, EPN's inattention to the printed word probably seemed less scandalous to voters than it did to journalists (Conaculta 2010).

Culturally conservative voters might have been troubled by EPN's admitted adultery during his first marriage (when he fathered two illegitimate children). Leftists denounced his role as governor in ordering the repression of popular protests. Working-class voters might have wondered why—à la Mitt Romney—Peña Nieto did not know the price of tortillas (a problem he chalked up to the fact that he was "not the lady of the house") or the minimum wage. But most of these failings were either already known or of limited relevance.[1] Mexican voters cared more about the policy failings of the incumbent administration than the personal failings of Peña Nieto. Eight out of ten Mexicans believed that the economic situation had deteriorated in the previous year and that the Calderón administration was worse than the previous presidential term, also governed by the PAN. Eight out of ten Mexicans felt that violence had increased in the previous three years and that violence was the top problem in the country by far (Consulta Mitofsky 2013, 3). The year 2012 was a good one for challengers.

Still, Peña Nieto's status as the early front-runner was no fluke. He began crafting his 2012 presidential campaign even before the 2006 presidential election, when he decided to run for governor of the State of Mexico. As the PRI lost its grip on power in the 1990s, governors became increasingly powerful players, controlling as they do important subnational resources. In 2000, all three major presidential candidates had previously served as governor (counting Mexico City as the equivalent of a governorship). Thus, in running for governor, Peña Nieto implicitly declared his interest in a future presidential bid. His campaign also prefigured his later presidential campaign in one particularly significant way: as he visited municipalities throughout the state, he took the unusual step of signing commitments—*compromisos*—before a notary public, usually to build a bridge, extend a roadway, or create some other public work. Each completed project was meticulously documented as a "promise kept." Efforts to project Peña Nieto's image nationally also date to before 2006. According to a report released by the British newspaper the *Guardian*, Peña Nieto began paying Televisa for this purpose as early as 2005 (see the appendix to this chapter, June 7).

These two themes, relentless self-promotion and a carefully sculpted reputation for keeping campaign promises, became the centerpiece of EPN's 2012 presidential campaign. His earliest campaign slogans were *tu me conoces*—or "you know me," using the familiar form, *tu*—and *yo sí cumplo*, or "I deliver." One of his first official ads shows him in casual clothing, against touristic backdrops, even dancing in a plaza with a young woman—familiar (*tu*), energetic, and approachable. Not to appear too frivolous, however, he then tours several factories, talks about the problem of crime, and promises to reduce violence and "defend happiness." The ad concludes with the phrase "that's my commitment, and you know I will do it" (appendix, March 30a). The word *compromiso* deliberately evoked his record in the State of Mexico. As he visited other states in 2012, he signed new commitments tailored to the location, again verified by a notary public.

With respect to the PRI, rather than distancing himself, Peña Nieto selectively emphasized the PRI's positive contributions: economic growth, political stability, and social peace. Like many former ruling parties in Eastern Europe and elsewhere, the PRI had already begun to try to romanticize its past as a period full of major accomplishments and one or two regrettable errors best forgotten. Its slogan in the 2009 midterm legislative election sums up this aspiration: "Today's PRI: Proven experience, New attitude" (El Universal 2009). The widespread public perception that two successive PAN administrations had failed to deliver on their promises made this message more compelling.[2]

Peña Nieto's youth (aged 45, the youngest of the candidates) extended this claim to the candidate himself. In the 2006 campaign, PRI presidential candidate Roberto Madrazo could not have played the part of a traditional PRI dinosaur with greater gusto; Peña Nieto, in contrast, at least tried to suggest that the PRI under his leadership could be trusted to govern democratically. It seems likely, however, that Peña Nieto won fewer votes among those who believed in the PRI's reform than among those who thought the PRI looked pretty good in the first place. As James A. McCann notes in chapter 4 in this volume, voters with positive retrospective evaluations of the PRI regime were significantly more likely to support Peña Nieto in both waves of the survey. Interestingly, once these retrospective evaluations were taken into account, younger voters were *more* likely to support Peña Nieto in the April (preelection) wave of the survey than older voters—a remarkable reversal of past trends. By the end of the campaign, however, this advantage had vanished. The #YoSoy132 campaign, discussed below, is almost certainly the culprit.

Andrés Manuel López Obrador: *Por una república amorosa*

In stark contrast to 2006, Andrés Manuel López Obrador of the leftist Partido de la Revolución Democrática (PRD) began the 2012 presidential campaign in a distant third place, roughly twenty-five points behind EPN, according to polls. The main challenge confronting AMLO in 2012 was trying to convince voters that he was not as radical as he seemed. In the aftermath of his excruciatingly narrow loss to Felipe Calderón of the National Action Party (PAN) in the 2006 presidential election, AMLO accused the PAN of fraud and took his protest to the streets. His supporters camped out along Paseo de la Reforma, one of Mexico City's main streets, blocking traffic through the heart of the capital and occupying the central plaza, or Zócalo, where AMLO held increasingly frenzied rallies. Inciting his supporters to declare him "legitimate president of Mexico," he established a "shadow government," promised continued resistance to the government of the "usurper" Calderón, and famously proclaimed "to hell with your institutions." His erratic and extreme behavior seemed to confirm the PAN's accusations during the campaign that he posed a "danger to Mexico" (see Domínguez, Lawson, and Moreno 2009, especially chapters 6, 9, 11, and 13, by Bruhn, Greene, and Moreno).

These actions left a lasting mark well into the start of the 2012 presidential campaign. In early April 2012, a *Reforma* poll found that 38% of voters would "never" vote for AMLO, far more than the 23% who would never vote for the PAN's candidate or the 20% who would never vote for EPN (Everdy Mejía 2012). Even the two commissioned polls used by the PRD in November 2011 to decide whether AMLO should receive the PRD nomination found that AMLO scored worse than his rival Marcelo Ebrard (AMLO's PRD successor as mayor of Mexico City) on the question "For whom would you never vote?" (Romero and

Román 2011, 2) More people also expressed a positive opinion of Ebrard than AMLO.

Nevertheless, López Obrador scored higher on all three questions about which candidate respondents would prefer to see as president.[3] Ebrard gracefully conceded defeat and accepted AMLO as the party's nominee. But López Obrador began the campaign at a significant disadvantage. His first job was to try to reshape his negative image. The day after Ebrard's concession, he announced a new goal: to make Mexico a *república amorosa* (loving republic) in which love and respect would take the place of confrontation. A few weeks later, he ended his campaign of resistance against the Calderón government. He scheduled a series of meetings with business groups and church leaders, declaring them vital partners in the transformation of Mexico.

His early ads continued this message. One ad presented him not as the disheveled firebrand who slept in a tent in the Zócalo, but as an impeccably groomed silver-haired statesman in a nice office, wearing a suit and tie. This gracious, polite man offered the audience his hand in friendship and expressed his sincere desire for reconciliation with "those who might have been affected by my determination to fight for democracy and peace." He asked former opponents to collaborate with him in the goal of creating a more prosperous, just, and brotherly society. He did not apologize or promise not to do it again—he insists to this day that his actions in 2006 were necessary to prevent violence by his outraged supporters—but did offer a truce, saying "I will put the past behind me if you will." The ad concludes with one of AMLO's 2006 slogans: "Real change is in your hands" (appendix, March 30a, March 30b). A second early ad also echoes the 2006 campaign, but without any reference to reconciliation or compromise (appendix, March 30c). Instead, the viewer sees a series of black-and-white shots of the Mexican Revolution, followed by still photos of PRI and PAN governments that "betrayed" the revolution. The ad fades into color at an AMLO rally with another reference to "real change." Apart from one ad referring to AMLO's term as mayor of Mexico City and his successful reduction of crime rates (appendix, April 3), the thrust of AMLO's early ads amounted to a reprise of 2006: real change.

Instead of developing a sophisticated media campaign, like his rivals, AMLO emphasized a grueling series of rallies *a ras de tierra* (at ground level), taking buses and commercial airlines and even the subway. These rallies offered him the freedom to connect personally with his base, from which he drew strength, but did not help him reach out to independent voters or to those who had been alienated by his actions in 2006. Perhaps as a result, polls released around April 9 showed a mild deterioration in his already weak position.

Josefina Vázquez Mota: *Diferente*

Josefina Vázquez Mota (JVM) began the general campaign in second place, with a comfortable lead over AMLO but a significant gap to reach EPN, roughly fifteen percentage points. Where Felipe Calderón overcame a 10% deficit with three months left in the campaign and ultimately won the 2006 election, however, Vázquez Mota's peak popularity began to decline as soon as the campaign started (Parametría 2006).

To be sure, actually winning the presidency would have been a long shot for any PAN candidate. President Calderón had the lowest approval ratings of any of the past four Mexican presidents (starting with Carlos Salinas) in his final year of office. For much of 2012, including some campaign months, Calderón's approval stood at less than 50%, compared to roughly 60% for Vicente Fox at the same point in 2006 (Consulta Mitofsky 2013, 16). Yet Vázquez Mota managed not only to lose the presidency, but also to stumble so badly that, according to the Instituto Federal Electoral (IFE), the PAN lost over a quarter of its district seats in the national legislature (from seventy to fifty-two) and slipped to third place behind the PRD despite the latter's self-destructive behavior after the 2006 election (IFE 2006). The scale of her defeat deserves explanation.

Vázquez Mota had two key structural problems. She had to deal with Calderón's policy failures and his lack of personal popularity. To handle the first problem, she could have tried to distract voters by focusing on the PAN's more positive achievements. Despite popular perceptions of failure, the Mexican economy grew by 4% in 2012, faster than the much-lauded Brazilian economy (Central Intelligence Agency 2013); moreover, more could have been made of some of the popular social programs promoted by the PAN governments.

Handling the second problem, a president's individual lack of popularity, was the purpose of having a single-term president in the first place: to purge the system of accumulated grievances without disturbing the party in power. Any failures were the fault of the man rather than the party. Mexican electoral law even made it easy for candidates to avoid those awkward photo ops by prohibiting sitting presidents from campaigning with or fundraising for co-partisans. Josefina never had to invite Calderón to a rally or appear in an ad with him. But she did need his supporters in the party to work for her, and early on she found it difficult to accept their help. Alone among the major candidates, Josefina

Vázquez Mota faced internal competition for her party's candidacy. In the PAN's internal election, she ran against Calderón's choice of successor (Ernesto Cordero), and although she won a decisive victory, the process pitted her supporters against those of Calderón. In the immediate aftermath of the primary, her supporters were not inclined to cede any positions of inside influence on her campaign team.

She therefore began the campaign having distanced herself not only from an unpopular president but also from his network, which was neither necessary nor helpful. To distance herself from the unpopular policies of the Calderón administration, she chose as her initial campaign slogan the unspecific: *Vázquez Mota: Diferente*. Presumably, voters were intended to insert whatever meaning they preferred. Instead, voters seemed to be confused. How is Vázquez Mota "different"? Different from what, or from whom? Different in what way? Different good, or different bad?

For example, one early ad raises the key issue of violence while leaving the distinction between Vázquez Mota and Calderón frustratingly vague. The dark imagery of the ad and its ominous portrayal of children in danger and faceless men with weapons seem odd, only encouraging the fear of violence that Mexicans negatively associated with the PAN. Vázquez Mota then proposes to create a police force that protects Mexicans and inspires confidence and trust rather than fear (appendix, March 30a). Alas, Calderón had already made the creation of a new police force one of his initiatives, and Mexicans blamed Calderón for the violence in the first place. So what would Vázquez Mota do "differently"? There were alternative ways to address the issue of violence—and she would hit upon some of these alternatives later in the campaign—but by then many voters were no longer listening.[4]

In a stroke of bad luck, on the fourth day of her campaign, Vázquez Mota became dizzy during an appearance announcing her security program and had to sit in order to read her remarks. Her press team gave confusing explanations of her sudden illness—it was the heat, she had a cold, she suffered from low blood pressure, she had been thrown off balance by a minor earthquake shortly before her talk—but the variety of responses only added to concerns that her campaign was hiding something about her health. Her opponents expressed gentlemanly concern while implying that a woman was not up to the rigors of campaigning, much less the stress of being president.[5] Peña Nieto made a point of telling reporters that while he sympathized with the exhaustion produced by an electoral campaign, campaigning was an invigorating and useful experience for him, an opportunity to meet people and learn about their problems. He sent his best wishes to Josefina: "I hope that it's nothing, and that if it is something, that she recovers quickly" (Vargas 2012a, 9). Vázquez Mota was different all right—different weak.

Vázquez Mota also found her own résumé limited by the record of the two PAN administrations. In her ads, Vázquez Mota claimed credit for welfare programs and public works delivered while she was the secretary of social development (SEDESO) under President Fox and referred to her experience as secretary of education under Calderón as proof she could fix Mexico's disastrously inefficient educational system. Some of the PAN's welfare programs have been quite popular vote winners. Unfortunately, Vázquez Mota got a few numbers wrong. PRI ads, in response, claimed she had exaggerated her accomplishments as SEDESO and called her a liar (appendix, April 10b). The ads were dropped. In any case, ministers administer budgets passed by legislatures that the PAN did not control, and thus had few genuine opportunities for credit claiming as individuals.

Her tenure as secretary of education was even less rewarding, limited by the opposition of the powerful teachers' union (the Sindicato Nacional de Trabajadores de la Educación, or SNTE) and its "leader for life," Elba Esther Gordillo. Even presidents have found themselves unable to control Elba Esther and the armies of teachers she could mobilize against reforms that threatened her empire. Vázquez Mota had little to show for her time as secretary but photos of her with Elba Esther Gordillo making nice in public.

After one week of campaigning, Vázquez Mota held an emergency meeting and announced a shakeup in her campaign team, this time incorporating Calderón allies. Still, on April 8 she felt she had to reassure the public by announcing that she did not intend to resign her candidacy, a remarkable sign of weakness. By April 9, all of the main national polls showed Vázquez Mota slipping and Enrique Peña Nieto at over 50% of national preferences (appendix). Vázquez Mota would never recover from these early stumbles. Between the ineptness of AMLO and Vázquez Mota, Enrique Peña Nieto coasted during the first weeks of the campaign.

Negative Campaigning in the 2012 Election: *Campaña de Contrastes*

The idyllic period was not destined to last. The brevity of the campaign (limited by law to three months) gave candidates little margin for error. Mistakes had to be corrected immediately. Thus, by mid-April, López Obrador brought new communications experts into his campaign team to make his ads more dynamic and attractive. And Vázquez Mota—newly reinforced by Calderón insiders—turned to the same strategy that had turned around Calderón's 2006 campaign: attack. On April 10, the national PAN leadership announced what it called a "campaign of contrasts," which would aggressively dispute EPN's claims to have kept those famous commitments in the state of Mexico (Urrutia and Muñoz 2012).

In principle, the 2007 electoral reforms were supposed to prevent such negative advertising. López Obrador claimed, not without reason, that the PAN's 2006 ads unfairly smeared his character, and that the IFE failed to protect him as the law even then required. The 2007 law therefore prohibited defamatory advertising and gave the IFE power to order the parties to withdraw any ads it found to violate this prohibition.

As in 2006, most of the negative advertising targeted the front-runner and came from the campaign team of the second-place candidate. As in 2006, negative ads did not feature the presidential candidate of the sponsoring party, but rather were anonymously sponsored or sponsored—in small print—by the party's legislative candidates. And, as in 2006, the IFE did little to block the transmission of negative ads. Instead, the IFE interpreted defamation quite strictly, trying to walk the fine line between permitting blatant slander and limiting free speech. As one IFE councilor noted, "if there is no serious accusation against a candidate, or indication of a crime, there is no reason to take the spot off the air. Not every criticism deserves to be withdrawn" (Urrutia, Martínez, and Olivares 2012).[6]

The new law did affect campaign strategies in two ways. First, it encouraged parties to release proposed ads on the Internet while simultaneously submitting them to the IFE. The IFE's monitoring responsibilities did not include the Internet. Many negative ads, including some that were subsequently withdrawn, debuted on YouTube before appearing in traditional mass media (and are still available there). It is notoriously difficult to censor content on the Internet, even in highly repressive countries. Whereas parties could be held directly responsible for the content of an ad on television or radio, the ability to post rumors or innuendos anonymously on the Internet led observers to predict that the Internet would become the leading edge of negative campaigns.[7] All of the candidates used false accounts, "bots," and "trolls" to artificially inflate the number of likes and positive comments their candidates received, or to place negative comments on the pages of rival candidates. Independent citizen monitoring groups in June 2012 estimated that 30–40% of Twitter accounts devoted to the campaign did not represent real people.[8]

Second, parties used the IFE's monitoring power to refute attack ads indirectly. By registering complaints that a given ad constituted calumny (and announcing this to the press), parties tried to leave the impression that an ad was untrue when in fact neither they nor the IFE presented evidence to verify its truth.

Yet the new law did not fully sanitize or civilize the campaign. All of the candidates used negative ads at least occasionally, though the PAN's use of negative ads was by far the most frequent and indiscriminate. Less than two weeks after the start of the campaign, the PAN launched a series of ads with the theme *Peña no cumple* (Peña does not deliver). Viewers saw images of unfinished projects in the State of Mexico, attached to a *compromiso* EPN had listed as met. The PRI, predictably, appealed to IFE to quash the ad, but the spots continued apace. The PAN also established a Web site, www.penanocumple.com, where people could go for further information, and set up a traveling exhibition of "evidence" that Peña did not keep his promises. The other major theme of the PAN's attack ads linked EPN to corruption and drug violence by proxy. Playing on EPN's campaign slogan, "you know me," the PAN showed pictures of Peña Nieto with some of the other people that he "knew"—prominent members of the PRI accused of taking money from drug cartels. A later ad, referring to Peña Nieto's "new PRI," ends with the line, "they say that in the PRI of Peña, there is no longer room for corruption (*ya no caben corruptos*). Of course— because it's already full of them (*porque ya está lleno*)" (appendix, May 29c).

Peña Nieto refused to respond to the PAN's accusations relating to corruption and drug trafficking. In one ad, in late April, he appears in his campaign office, looking serious in a suit and tie and saying that he will not respond to the "dirty war" against him because he refuses to divide Mexico or Mexican families, "as happened six years ago" (appendix, April 21a). But he did respond immediately and effectively to the PAN's efforts to undercut his record as governor. The first *Peña no cumple* ads appeared on YouTube on April 10. On April 15, a new series of ads titled *Compromisos Cumplidos* appeared on YouTube. In contrast to his earlier ads, which made new promises to additional states, these ads highlighted completed commitments in the State of Mexico—the same commitments that the PAN said were unfinished. The initial ads covered infrastructure, a second series covered education, and a third series covered health (appendix, April 15, April 21b). In each set of ads, EPN concluded by promising to extend these accomplishments to the rest of Mexico. On April 16, he announced the creation of a new Web site, www.penasicumple.com, to counter the PAN's Web site; the site went live on April 18.

The PAN offensive had some effect. By the end of April, support for Enrique Peña Nieto had declined modestly to just below 50%, but he retained a commanding lead in most major polls. Worse yet, from the PAN's point of view, Josefina's support had not improved at all. Instead, shifts in voter preferences primarily benefited López Obrador, bringing him into a virtual tie with JVM for second place.

AMLO sensed momentum swinging his way and began to increase the critical tone of his media campaign. Two ads exemplified this shift. The first, uploaded May 1, compared support for EPN and JVM to "paper support"— with images of their campaign posters blown away by the wind—contrasted to the "real" support earned by López Obrador in huge rallies (appendix, May 1a). A second ad showed a young man sitting down on the hood of a blue Volkswagen Beetle (one of the most popular working-class cars in Mexico) painted the color of the PAN and creaking ominously. The young man says, "I really need a change" (*me urge un cambio*). The car magically begins to turn red and green (the PRI colors) and acquires a hood ornament (mimicking the hairstyle of Enrique Peña Nieto?). Then the bumper falls off and the car sags to the ground. Andrés Manuel says, "don't be fooled. For a real change there is no other way" (appendix, May 1b).

During the first two months of the campaign, neither Vázquez Mota nor López Obrador suffered significantly from negative ads. López Obrador himself admitted that the dirty war was less severe in 2012 than in 2006, although he characteristically gave himself the credit: "they have already attacked me too much and it didn't work" (Muñoz 2012). A more impartial observer might have argued that, as the third-place candidate, he simply posed no threat.

Not until the beginning of June, when AMLO passed Vázquez Mota and began to close the gap with Peña Nieto, did the PAN and the PRI turn their attention to negative ads against AMLO. They had, of course, an enormous stock of embarrassing AMLO footage to draw upon. The PAN went with the theme, "some people never change," using pictures of AMLO in full rant, Paseo de la Reforma during the 2006 street blockade, and AMLO declaring, "to hell with your institutions" (appendix, June 5d). The PRI (of all parties!) called AMLO corrupt, showing video of a 2004 bribery scandal involving one of his closest collaborators (appendix, June 5a), and claimed that AMLO did not believe in democracy (appendix, June 5b).[9] As icing on the cake, the PRI argued that nobody supported AMLO anyway (showing images of empty stadiums at AMLO rallies) and that Peña Nieto would surely win (appendix, June 20b).

These negative ads had an effect on voters: they stopped AMLO's steady rise in the polls. At the end of the campaign, all of the major candidates had substantially higher negative ratings than at their peak popularity, and negative campaigning contributed to that result.

#YoSoy132: Social Media and the Youth Vote

On May 11, the campaign of Enrique Peña Nieto, which had until then progressed virtually without a hitch, suffered its first serious setback. Peña Nieto's team scheduled him to make a speech at the Ibero-American University (commonly known as the Ibero). The speech was something of a risk because the university—a private, Jesuit school on the outskirts of Mexico City—was not only the alma mater of former president Vicente Fox and Josefina Vázquez Mota, but also university authorities had publicly criticized then-governor Peña Nieto's decision to use force to suppress popular protests against the construction of a new national airport in San Salvador de Atenco in the State of Mexico. The speech had been postponed twice before EPN finally appeared. Predictably, a small but vocal group of students showed up to protest his presence, mostly denouncing the violence in San Salvador de Atenco, but also taking up the theme raised earlier by Andrés Manuel López Obrador, that EPN was little more than a media creation, with signs declaring *Televisa te Idiotiza* (Televisa makes a fool out of you [the citizens]).

Though EPN's abrupt and unceremonious flight from the campus made a delicious headline in the next day's paper, candidates have been heckled before. What turned a small protest into a movement that changed the course of the campaign was, first, the ham-fisted attempt by PRI leaders to discredit the protesters and, second, the use of social media by students, at the margin of candidates and parties, to spread their message questioning Peña Nieto's qualifications.

In classic authoritarian fashion, the knee-jerk impulse of party leaders, most notably PRI president Pedro Joaquín Coldwell, was to claim that the protesters were not students at all but outside agitators, paid by the PRD and AMLO to cause trouble for EPN (appendix, May 12). Two days later, 131 Ibero students who had participated in the protest filmed themselves with their student identification cards and posted the video on YouTube (appendix, May 14).[10] The video went viral. Soon students from other universities (and nonstudents in solidarity) joined the chorus denouncing Peña Nieto and the bias of the mass media. They would eventually call themselves "I am number 132," or #YoSoy132.

On May 15, AMLO jumped onto the students' bandwagon, posting a new ad on YouTube that contrasted his own reception at the Ibero with that of Peña Nieto (appendix, May 15). On May 16, Peña Nieto finally responded, albeit with some ambivalence. On the one hand, he accused AMLO of encouraging the protests (Vargas 2012b). On the other hand, he endorsed the students' right to disagree with him, vowed to be the president of all Mexicans, including his critics, and praised those young people who "demand, and rightly so, a better today" (appendix, May 16).

But it was already too late. By May 18, the Twitter hashtag #MarchaYoSoy132 ranked among the top ten trending topics in the world, and the students' video had been reproduced over 850,000 times (García Hernández 2012). On May 19, an anti-EPN march in Mexico City attracted thousands of supporters. As #YoSoy132 continued to use social media to publicize his movements and call for flash protests, Peña Nieto's press team began to conceal his schedule or change it at the last minute, creating a sense of disorganization and anxiety that the campaign had not previously felt. Security was also increased, including metal detectors at the candidate's appearances. Peña Nieto was the only candidate to skip a debate sponsored by #YoSoy132. Finally, his advertising made a pronounced shift toward images of young people. A new series of ads called *Interviews* featured young people explaining why they supported him. Despite these efforts, EPN never managed to win back the youth vote.

Instead, the main beneficiary of #YoSoy132, almost accidentally, was López Obrador (for analysis of these findings, see Díaz-Domínguez and Moreno, chap. 10, this volume). Although #YoSoy132 never endorsed any candidate, its hostility to Peña Nieto and complaints about the partiality of the television networks dovetailed perfectly with AMLO's critique—from the beginning of the campaign—that Peña Nieto was *producto chatarra* (junk food), an empty suit sold to the public just as cynically as if he were a brand of soft drink. After #YoSoy132, AMLO began to urge his supporters to use social media to counteract the bias of the main TV networks. His ads started featuring a soundtrack of rap music (appendix, May 28). By May 31, he had passed Josefina in the polls and come within four points of Enrique Peña Nieto (appendix, May 31).

The PAN, in contrast, barely mentioned #YoSoy132 in its campaign or propaganda. Criticism of EPN was welcome, of course, but the incumbent party could hardly endorse complaints about lack of media freedom or censorship. If these problems existed, the governing party could not escape blame. Moreover, the preference of many participants for AMLO discouraged the PAN from embracing the movement. Thus #YoSoy132 failed to help (or hurt) Josefina Vázquez Mota.

The (Ir)relevance of Political Parties

Parties in Mexico are typically viewed as relatively strong. Party leaders control vast sums of money and have significant influence over nominations. Party discipline in the legislature is high, and partisan affiliation is a stronger predictor of vote choice than any other variable. Yet when it comes to presidential campaigns, parties exert less influence, largely because the presidency is unlike any other office. If their candidate gets elected, even the highest-ranking party leaders and office holders of the party know that their immediate political future depends on their relationship with the candidate. Governors, mayors, senators, and legislators cannot be reelected. Party leaders must rotate out of office or serve at the pleasure of the president. And the president is the largest source of patronage in the country. It simply would not do for any party member to be other than cooperative with the presidential candidate, at least to the degree that the candidate seems to have a reasonable chance of success. If some sector of the party dislikes a specific candidate so much that they just cannot bring themselves to help him or her (or if the division is so deep that they can expect no future favors from that candidate regardless) the responsible thing to do is nothing at all—no help, but no harm that might provoke actual retaliation. As a result, presidential candidates have a fair amount of leeway to design and implement their own campaign strategies. The extent to which they get help from the organizational structure of their parties depends first on the quality of the organization and second on its unity behind the candidate. For Peña Nieto, both factors worked in his favor. On Election Day 2012, the PRI governed twenty of Mexico's thirty-two states (thirty-one plus the Federal District). The PRI remains the only Mexican party with a truly national presence that can draw upon resources in every state during an election campaign.

In addition, as Eric Magar points out in chapter 3 in this volume, the 2007 electoral reform that gave the parties free airtime and prevented them from buying more left parties with a considerable amount of leftover money, and parties spent it in other ways. Some of it went to old-fashioned campaigning, the small-town rallies and personal appearances supposedly made obsolete by modern mass media. Peña Nieto benefited the most from the renewed popularity of in-person campaigning. His good looks and charisma maximized his ability to use these events to create a personal connection with voters, and, more importantly, when married to his mass media campaign, served to emphasize EPN's rock-star popularity and the inevitability of his electoral victory. The "Campaign Tour" (*Gira*) series of ads that ran throughout the month of May showed clips of EPN amid cheering crowds with the theme, "So many people can't be wrong. Mexico wants a change" (appendix, April 30). The ads were supplemented in June with poll data and the conclusion, "we're winning" (appendix, June 2).

Still, one can only spend so much on rallies. The PRI supplemented its already substantial advantage in organization by paying workers to canvass house by house prior to the election and to mobilize the vote on Election Day. The potential effectiveness of such efforts is increasingly acknowledged even in established democracies like the United States, where Republicans attributed their 2012 loss in part to the superiority of Obama's ground game in key battleground states. The tactic is not entirely new in Mexico, either; the PRI used paid vote-promoting teams in the 1991 federal elections, for example, and the PRD had the paid "Sun Brigades" in 1997. Tellingly, however, both of these were midterm elections. The cost of paying for a national media campaign had previously tended to reduce the resources available for national canvassing.

In 2012, these limitations were looser. On June 25, the PRD asked the IFE to investigate the PRI's alleged distribution of nearly 10,000 Monex debit cards for such canvassing work. The PRI issued an immediate denial of any connection to Monex. Two days later, the IFE confirmed that the PRI had in fact channeled money to its campaign workers via Monex. The PRI would eventually admit using paid campaign workers, though denying it was illegal.

Peña Nieto could also count on a PRI unified behind his candidacy. In 2006, significant sectors of the PRI so strongly opposed the party's eventual standard-bearer, Roberto Madrazo, that they first formed a committee, Everybody United against Madrazo, to try to block his nomination, and then refused to campaign vigorously for Madrazo in many of the states governed by the PRI. Peña Nieto had far fewer enemies and was the clear favorite overall to win the presidency.[11] After twelve years out of power, it would have taken a lot more than the disappointed ambition of potential rivals for them to oppose Peña

Nieto and risk spoiling the PRI's big comeback. Thus EPN had his pick of the best strategists and advisors. Perhaps even more important, he had the full support of his co-partisan governors and mayors to make his campaign go smoothly and ensure that the PRI's state-level party machines were successfully mobilized on Election Day.

Vázquez Mota was not as fortunate. The PAN historically enjoyed a reputation as the most coherent, disciplined, and well organized of Mexico's political parties, though it lacked the national presence of the PRI. Yet twelve years in power had taken their toll on the PAN's famous collegiality. Some top PAN leaders had become embroiled in corruption scandals or accusations of incompetence. Others felt insufficiently compensated for their years of loyal dedication and self-sacrifice with top government posts or positions on the party's electoral list.

These internal divisions contributed to the organizational deficiencies of Vázquez Mota's campaign team, plagued from the beginning by constant logistical problems. The candidate repeatedly showed up late to rallies, appeared to improvise campaign stops without informing local activists, and occasionally mixed up her agenda so badly that she showed up to a rally in the morning that was scheduled for the afternoon or vice versa. Her initial exclusion of Calderón insiders, who had more experience in presidential campaigns and broader national contacts, did not help. Once she did include the pro-Calderón camp, continued miscommunication and mistrust among her top advisers slowed the creation of an effectively coordinated ground campaign. One hardly need add that party unity was shaky as well. Vázquez Mota publicly blamed the party's internal tensions for her rocky start, and complained that Calderón had failed to support her.[12]

Far more damaging, however, were public declarations by former president Vicente Fox (2000–2006) barely two weeks into the campaign that it would take "a miracle" for Vázquez Mota to make a comeback and that, in his view, Peña Nieto was sure to win the election (Ballinas 2012). Fox later promised to support Vázquez Mota as a fellow member of the PAN, then changed his mind and offered to help Peña Nieto. Party leaders—even those lukewarm in their support of Josefina—were horrified. Many PAN leaders had never truly trusted Fox (and vice versa). Fox was not one of them—not a PAN stalwart of long standing who had joined the party in the dangerous years. He forced himself on the PAN as a presidential candidate in 2000 by building an irresistible popular network outside the party—the so-called Friends of Fox—that made his candidacy the most promising way to beat the PRI. He never paid proper respect to the PAN leadership (in their opinion). Nevertheless, Fox was the public face of the PAN to a far greater degree than Calderón or Vázquez Mota. Fox was the man who brought down the PRI. Fox was the hero of democracy. His de facto endorsement of Peña Nieto and his dismissal of Vázquez Mota as a loser did incalculable harm to her prospects. There was virtually no way for her to rebut his attack: in matters of opinion, Fox's view would inevitably carry more weight with voters.

PRD presidential candidates have rarely enjoyed either organizational strength or party unity, and they have never had both at once. Organizational strength and coherence in particular have yet to emerge. From the PRD's earliest days as a loose coalition of movements and small parties, it has favored autonomy over centralization, freedom over discipline, with the result that party decisions are only weakly enforced and implemented at lower levels of the organization. The PRD has also governed fewer states than either the PAN or the PRI, reducing its geographical reach. The notable exception is Mexico City, which the PRD has governed without interruption since 1997. In addition to Mexico City's dense population, which offers a large number of votes, its place as the center of national power and its media allow the PRD to project itself onto a national stage out of proportion to the resources it actually controls. In 2012, AMLO ran his campaign less through the PRD than through his own Movimiento de Regeneración Nacional (MORENA), a civil society organization created specifically to support his presidential candidacy. The logic of this choice became even clearer in September 2012, when AMLO resigned from the PRD and announced his intention to turn MORENA into a political party.

Strangely, neither the PRD nor the PAN seems to have used public financing to replace volunteers with paid workers in areas of party organizational weakness, a sort of "rent-a-party" strategy. We do not yet have enough information on the PRI's use of Monex workers to be sure exactly how and where they were deployed. It may be that parties primarily use paid workers as a way for party brokers to reward clients and build their networks. Alternatively, the use of paid workers may require a minimal level of existing infrastructure (offices, functioning party committees, etc.) to train and monitor them.

As for unity, the PRD's famously contentious internal politics have led its own members to refer to it as a party of tribes, or "savage democracy" (Wuhs 2008). Even in moments of peak unity behind a popular candidate with prospects of winning, like AMLO in 2006, tensions and conflict are seldom far below the surface. In 2006, for example, former presidential candidate Cuauhtémoc Cárdenas was feuding with AMLO and essentially sat out the presidential campaign. AMLO had to name an internal rival, Jesús Ortega, as the head of his campaign committee, which meant the campaign committee had little influence over the candidate and vital shifts in campaign strategy were fatally delayed. In 2012, in contrast, the PRD did not expect AMLO to win. So they let him choose his own campaign committee, with the result that the chair of the committee was not even a member of the PRD. But PRD leaders did not actively undermine AMLO's campaign. Because much of the PRD base still loved AMLO, PRD leaders thought that starting a fight would weaken their chances of putting party leaders in legislative seats, which they definitely did care about.

So far, political parties appear to have played a minor role in the 2012 presidential campaign. They did not take the lead in designing campaign strategies. The PRD stayed out of choosing AMLO's campaign team altogether; Vázquez Mota—to her later regret—omitted members of the faction closest to the sitting president; and the PRI simply gave EPN whatever he needed. Party organization mattered mostly in terms of geographical reach, particularly when co-partisan governors with resources could help a presidential candidate. Curiously, parties do not appear to have used the resources available through public subsidies to compensate for organizational problems by "buying" organizers in areas where their own parties had weak structures. If anything, they used paid workers to supplement party volunteers in regions where they were already strong. Finally, the impact of parties seemed greatest in a negative sense. Parties could hurt candidates either deliberately (as in the case of Fox) or unintentionally (as in the PRI leaders' response to #YoSoy132).

We have not yet discussed, however, the most important alleged function of political parties in electoral campaigns: providing an informational shortcut to voters. Because parties last longer than any individual politician—especially in Mexico's now-you-see-them, now-you-don't, no-reelection system—parties give voters an ideological platform and a track record in office from which voters can predict the likely future performance of a candidate. Mexican political parties do seem to offer voters relatively stable ideological frames compared to other Latin American party systems (admittedly, a low bar), but in the 2012 election, neither the candidates nor the parties chose to strongly highlight their policy differences. All of the candidates claimed to be different in one way or another (e.g., EPN's "Mexico wants a real change"; JVM's "Josefina: *Diferente*"; AMLO's "Real change"), but without going into detail. The key issues in the campaign, crime and the economy, turned mostly on candidate competence rather than on differences in policy approach. Two of the presidential candidates (EPN and AMLO) even issued an individual electoral platform separate from the platform registered legally with the IFE by their coalition.

Moreover, all of the campaigns engaged to at least some extent in vote buying, defined as an attempt to persuade voters to support a specific candidate in exchange for a material resource, such as a bag of cement or a food basket. The most famous example is attributed to the PRI, which gave out thousands of debit cards to potential voters, issued by the electro-domestics store Soriana. Ana De La O (chap. 8, this volume), Simeon Nichter and Brian Palmer-Rubin (chap. 9, this volume) address the questions of how prevalent such tactics were, whether they affected the election results, and what impact they had on democracy overall.

From the perspective of understanding campaign strategies, however, the big story is not that the PRI is corrupt (old news), but that the PRI, despite its monetary and media advantages over its rivals, its telegenic candidate, and its lead in the polls from start to finish, thought that such tactics were necessary to win. Something is wrong here. Despite its many advantages, the PRI's political strategists saw voter loyalties as so weak and programmatic appeals as so inadequate to the task of winning elections that votes had to be bought. Vote-buying schemes may indicate trouble for Mexican democracy, not because they reveal parties as corrupt but because they reveal parties as weak.

Conclusion

The 2007 electoral reforms tried to reduce the rather large campaign and media effects observed in previous Mexican elections (e.g., Domínguez and Lawson 2004; Domínguez et al. 2009). The law shortened campaigns, favoring those with an early lead; sanitized and routinized campaigns by prohibiting negative advertising and offering free media access; curtailed the influence of private money; and cut public subsidies in half. On the surface, the reforms succeeded. The man who led in the polls at the start of the official campaign (by an average of 47%) won the presidential election, albeit with only 39.2% of the vote.

And yet, when we take a closer look at the campaigns, a more complex and nuanced picture emerges. As in many democracies, the images produced in mass media influenced perceptions of the candidates and trends in their popularity, even though the outcome did not change. Social media became an increasingly influential element, not as controlled by candidates as traditional mass media.

And parties—like in many presidential democracies—were less important in designing strategy and organizing campaigns than the candidates themselves.

The 2012 campaigns differed from those in more established democracies, however: first in the notable absence of any real effort by the candidates to distinguish themselves from one another on policy grounds, and second in their troubling efforts to trade material gifts for electoral support. Policy differences may exist at the elite level (Bruhn and Greene 2007) but, at least in 2012, the candidates did not seem eager to highlight them for voters. Perhaps the very polarization of the 2006 election and its aftermath made them reluctant to risk a second such confrontation. For voters, however, the result was a campaign that offered relatively little information about the policy implications of their choices, and thus a government that could not reflect the policy preferences of the electorate.

One final thought: It is unlikely that vote buying was practiced on a large enough scale or with a high enough success rate to alter the results of the election. It is even possible—as Nichter and Palmer-Rubin tantalizingly suggest in chapter 9 in this volume—that vote buying was primarily used to reward party supporters and not to win over new voters at all. A scenario in which parties have to buy off their own supporters in order to prevent defections is even worse for the future of parties than one in which they spend scarce resources in order to expand their support. It is hard to view this as a hopeful sign for democracy in Mexico.

APPENDIX: CAMPAIGN TIMELINE

March 28   *Reforma* poll shows EPN at 45%, JVM at 32%, and AMLO at 22%. Consulta Mitofsky (March 27) has EPN at 38%, JVM at 29%, and AMLO at 23%.
Buendia and Laredo (March 26) has EPN at 51%, JVM at 28%, and AMLO at 20%.
Average of polls in March of 2012: EPN 47%, JVM 31%, and AMLO 21%.
See http://gruporeforma-blogs.com/encuestas/wp-content/uploads /2012/06/capsula_01_ok.png and http://www.parametria.com.mx /Estudios/Images/images/Diapositiva3.GIF.

March 30   **Official start of the campaign.**
Thirty percent of airtime for spots is distributed equally among candidates, 70% according to each party's performance in the most recent congressional election (2009).

	Peña Nieto gets 40% of funds, Vázquez Mota receives 28%, and López Obrador gets 21%.
March 30	First ads appear:
(a)	http://latimesblogs.latimes.com/world_now/2012/03/mexico-presidential-election-campaign-ads.html;
(b)	http://mx.ibtimes.com/articles/23138/20120321/spots-presidenciales-pri-pan-prd-ife-viedo.htm; and
(c)	http://www.youtube.com/watch?v=2Idn5wybRbw.
April 1	AMLO complains about high levels of campaign spending by EPN.
April 2	JVM nearly faints while delivering a speech on public security.
April 3	AMLO says he can bring security to Mexico because he did it in Mexico City: http://www.reformas.sdpnoticias.com/nacional/2012/04/03/amlo-lanza-nuevo-spot-sobre-seguridad.
April 5	JVM has an emergency meeting and makes changes to campaign team, including the incorporation of advisers close to Calderón.
April 6	JVM begins to air the first of many ads with the slogan *no voy a pactar con el crimen organizado*. A lower-level consultant to EPN says this backfired because many people care only that the violence stops, not necessarily how.
April 8	JVM announces that she does not intend to drop out of the presidential race.
April 9	EPN proposes national gendarmerie, a "civil police force" made up of military men (it is unclear whether current or former military men are implied).
April 9	Parametría shows EPN with 51%, JVM with 28%, and AMLO with 19%.
	Grupo de Economistas y Asociados—Indagaciones y Soluciones Avanzados (April 10) shows EPN with 51%, JVM with 30%, and AMLO with 18%.
	Buendia and Laredo (April 11) shows EPN with 52%, JVM with 28%, and AMLO with 19%.
	See http://www.parametria.com.mx/Estudios/Images/images/Diapositiva4.GIF.
April 10	**Start of the negative campaigns.**
	At a press conference, the PAN national leadership announces the initiation of new *campaña de contrastes* attacking EPN aggressively as a liar who did not deliver (as governor of the State of Mexico) what he claimed he had.
April 10 (a)	First of a series of ads uploaded to YouTube with the theme *Peña no cumple*: http://www.youtube.com/watch?v=nGlozW9ceyg.
April 10 (b)	PRI ad says JVM lied in a previous spot about the number of *pisos firmes* (concrete floors) installed while she was SEDESOL under Fox:

	http://www.mediosyciudadanos.com/2012/04/inician-pan-y-pri -guerra-de-spots-en-tv.html.
April 11	PRI national leadership announces it will appeal to the IFE to quash *Peña no cumple* ads as violating law against defamation.
April 12	EPN meets with business leaders and reiterates his support for private sector participation in PEMEX.
April 12	Former president Vicente Fox says he thinks EPN will win, and that "only a miracle" could save JVM's candidacy.
April 15	EPN ad *Compromisos cumplidos* emphasizes his achievements in the State of Mexico. First ads focus on infrastructure: http://www.youtube .com/watch?v=LDJyPxFoAmE.
April 16	EPN announces a new Web site, www.penasicumple.com (to counter the PAN's penanocumple.com), where voters can find evidence of his achievements. Activated April 18.
April 18	PAN sends a formal complaint to IFE that EPN has violated campaign spending limits.
April 21 (a)	EPN ad states he will not respond to PAN attacks because he does not want to divide Mexico: http://www.milenio.com/cdb/doc/noticias 2011/afcd0043d9189dc4f452f148579d4bff.
April 21 (b)	Additional ads highlight EPN's achievements in the State of Mexico with respect to infrastructure (http://www.youtube.com/watch ?v=3ZXwtbUgNvM), education (http://www.youtube.com/watch ?v=dA2dBdiWCiU&feature=endscreen), and health (http://www .youtube.com/watch?v=JdYsVyhqqb4&feature=endscreen).
April 23	According to Parametría and Covarrubias, JVM and AMLO are in a virtual tie for second place; Covarrubias has AMLO ahead (27% to 25%), while Parametría has JVM ahead (25% to 23%). EPN retains a commanding lead of at least twenty percentage points. See http:// www.parametria.com.mx/Estudios/Images/images/Diapositiva4.GIF.
April 24	PAN ad ending *Peña no cumple* highlights issue of violence: seven out of ten murders are committed by organized crime occurred in states governed by the PRI. See http://www.youtube.com/watch ?v=Gxhf6WgboD4.
April 25	*Reforma* poll has EPN with 42%, JVM with 29%, and AMLO with 27%: http://gruporeforma-blogs.com/encuestas/wp-content/uploads /2012/06/capsula_01_ok.png.
April 27 (a)	Shift in JVM's campaign strategy to *La mujer tiene palabra* starts heavily targeting women. Focus groups apparently suggested this: http://mexico.cnn.com/nacional/2012/04/27/vazquez-mota-lanza -nueva-estrategia-de-campana-en-su-gira-por-mexico.
April 27 (b)	EPN appears, wearing a green tie and PVEM logo, in an ad endorsing the Partido Verde proposal to issue government "vouchers" for medicines good at any pharmacy if government clinics do not have

	the appropriate medicine available: http://www.youtube.com/watch?v=JVIy2BnLPk8.
April 30	EPN releases first in a series of "Campaign Tour" ads: EPN with large, enthusiastic crowds and the voiceover saying, "So many people can't be wrong. Mexico wants a change." See http://www.youtube.com/watch?v=w2-caPzj4XE; www.youtube.com/watch?v=r9t7pHOTwcE.
May 1 (a)	AMLO ad compares rival candidates' support to *apoyos de papel* contrasted with AMLO's large groups of "real" supporters: http://www.youtube.com/watch?v=hhoLUz1wwTw&feature=endscreen.
May 1 (b)	In an AMLO ad, a blue (PAN color) Volkswagen Beetle changes to red and green (PRI colors), neither of which work. For a real change, call AMLO. Paid for by the PT. See http://www.youtube.com/watch?v=r9hNYVa36PU&feature=endscreen.
May 6	First debate. There is no clear winner. All attack EPN. The biggest hit of the night: the scantily clad assistant to the moderator (and 2008 Playboy Playmate).
May 10	Mother's Day. JVM calls EPN a deadbeat dad (for not supporting his illegitimate son): http://www.jornada.unam.mx/2012/05/11/politica/010n2pol.
May 11	**Enrique Peña Nieto is booed at the Ibero-American University.**
May 12	PRI president Pedro Joaquín Coldwell states that protesters were paid provocateurs, hired by AMLO to cause trouble: http://www.jornada.unam.mx/2012/05/12/politica/007n1pol.
May 14	One hundred and thirty-one of the Ibero protesters post a video of themselves with identification cards proving they are enrolled and legitimate students: http://www.youtube.com/watch?v=cT5E3SqAHKI.
May 15	AMLO issues a new ad contrasting his reception at Ibero with that accorded to EPN: http://www.youtube.com/watch?v=Kqf5qICZfd4&feature=player_embedded.
May 16	EPN accuses AMLO of promoting protests against him; also says he respects freedom of speech.
May 16	*Un Presidente que escuche, respete, y gobierne para todos.* New ad says EPN would be president of all Mexicans, including those who disagree and specifically young people: http://www.youtube.com/watch?v=9ypsxlk_u54.
May 18	The Twitter account #MarchaYoSoy132 is among the top ten trending topics in the world, and the student video has been reproduced over 850,000 times.
May 19	Thousands of people march in Mexico City against EPN and the PRI.
May 20	Covarrubias puts EPN at 40%, AMLO at 30%, and JVM at 26%. All other major polling organizations continue to show EPN in the middle to upper forties and AMLO and JVM in a near tie between

	May 11 and May 28. See http://www.parametria.com.mx/Estudios /Images/images/Diapositiva4.GIF.
May 28	Young people (graffiti artists) support AMLO; in the background the rap song "A Poco Crees" says nothing will change with PRI or PAN; AMLO is real change: http://www.youtube.com/watch ?v=nVCGNhiIIJw.
May 29 (a)	EPN launches a series of "Entrevista" ads in which (mostly young) people say that they are voting for him. Ads run through June: www .youtube.com/watch?v=U1kx5PRvGE8.
May 29 (b)	PAN announces it will air ads criticizing both EPN and AMLO. A sample ad poses a choice between the corrupt, repressive Mexico of the past which pacted with criminals (picture of EPN) or the Mexico that is intolerant, violent, and *con rencores* (picture of screaming AMLO). "Let's choose a safe and stable Mexico." See http://www .youtube.com/watch?v=G5EUvgzhjEU&feature=player_detailpage.
May 29 (c)	"Dicen que en el PRI de Peña ya no ćaben los corruptos. Por su-puesto, porque ya está lleno." Also says PRI wants to ENRIQU-Ecerse más. Paid for by PAN candidates for legislature: http://www .youtube.com/watch?v=IqYQsf1K-IA.
May 29	The president of the Consejo Coordinador Empresarial says that the left is no longer a danger to the country and that AMLO is more moderate than he was in 2006.
May 31	*Reforma* poll shows AMLO only four points behind EPN: EPN at 38%, AMLO at 34%, and JVM at 23%; other polls record a 15% difference or more. See http://gruporeforma-blogs.com/encuestas/wp -content/uploads/2012/06/capsula_01_ok.png.
June 2	Another set of ads in the "Campaign Tour" series debuts with a new twist—polls with EPN twenty points ahead—and adds *vamos ganando*: http://www.youtube.com/watch?v=LoX9XRd3Sho&feature=player _detailpage.
June 5	PAN and PRI announce that new negative ads will target AMLO. In the case of the PAN, the emphasis shifts to AMLO over EPN.
June 5 (a)	First PRI ad shows a portion of the *videoescandalo* involving Rene Bejarano as well as an audiotape saying, "now it's happening again." The ad questions AMLO's honesty and says Mexico deserves better: http://www.youtube.com/watch?v=gkuezCyjYoA.
June 5 (b)	Second PRI ad shows a clip of AMLO saying *al diablo con sus institu-ciones* and the 2006 *Reforma* blockade. "No cree en la democracia. Eso quieres para Mexico? Tu decides." See http://www.youtube.com /watch?v=jC8XQnLyGXE.
June 5 (c)	JVM shifts to *La mejor* as the primary campaign slogan: http:// sedena1.wordpress.com/2012/06/06/spot-la-mejor-opcion-es-josefina -vazquez-mota-tu-decides/.

June 5 (d)	The first PAN ad, "Algunas personas nunca cambian," shows clips of AMLO in 2006 saying "to hell with your institutions," the *Reforma* blockade, and a May 2012 speech where he appears to call "the armed path a possibility to achieve the transformation of the pueblo." IFE would later fine the PAN for defamation, because what AMLO actually said was that while he respected those who believe that the armed path is a possibility, he remained committed to a peaceful path. See http://www.youtube.com/watch?v=8qlIV2J37So&feature=player _detailpage.
June 5 (e)	A second PAN ad says AMLO will ruin the economy, while PAN will keep it stable: http://www.youtube.com/watch?v=8C6Ia9jJqzU& feature=player_embedded.
June 7	The *Guardian* publishes evidence of contracts between EPN and Televisa in 2005: http://www.jornada.unam.mx/2012/06/08/politica /007n1pol.
June 10	Second debate: JVM dismisses EPN and AMLO as two faces of the same authoritarian past; once again there is no clear winner.
June 10 (a)	AMLO says not to believe the lies of his opponents. They are afraid only because their candidates are sliding in the polls. See http://www .youtube.com/watch?v=TctDtUxUEZc.
June 10 (b)	Mexico City Mayor Marcelo Ebrard appears in an ad saying that as Secretario de Gobernación he will work with AMLO to make Mexico safe and peaceful: http://www.youtube.com/watch?v=v1gXfUAcdco.
June 11	An AMLO ad shows masked figures of EPN, JVM, Fox, Elba Esther, and Carlos Salinas all saying *tengo miedo*. Then the EPN figure takes off his mask and says, *Yo ya no tengo miedo*—"Do not let yourselves be fooled. Real change is in our hands." Vote PRD. See http://www .youtube.com/watch?v=rMVstx6KOLk.
June 11	A group of artists post a music video, "La Bamba a Andres Manuel," as a "gift" to the candidate, endorsing him as "real change": http://www .youtube.com/watch?feature=player_embedded&v=S5ZqabSGekA.
June 17 (a)	Father's Day. JVM runs an ad wishing a happy Father's Day to men who support, love, protect, and respect women: http://www.youtube .com/watch?v=opjETK2MCLs.
June 17 (b)	AMLO ads start emphasizing momentum of the "millions" who support AMLO: http://www.youtube.com/watch?v=7bviPcJSfVY.
June 18	Ads begin to ask each AMLO supporter to convince five more voters to support him: http://www.youtube.com/watch?v=g_v4Fsq Fug8&feature=endscreen.
June 19	#YoSoy132 hosts debate; EPN declines to participate.
June 19	*Reforma* shows EPN recovery to 42%, AMLO decline to 30%, and JVM stagnant at 24%: http://grupreforma-blogs.com/encuestas/wp -content/uploads/2012/06/capsula_01_ok.png.

June 20 (a)	New ad from PRI says few people follow López Obrador (showing scenes of empty stadiums); seven out of ten Mexicans do not trust him: http://www.youtube.com/watch?v=VVcjR7-5pVI.
June 20 (b)	Meanwhile, AMLO releases his own version, showing huge, cheering crowds with the slogan *SOMOS MILLONES*: http://www.youtube .com/watch?v=LtTwU78HWPE&NR=1&feature=endscreen.
June 20 (c)	Second PRI ad says AMLO manipulates elections and twists democracy (*se burla de la democracia*) and shows a clip of the Clara Brugada in Iztapalapa debacle, where AMLO tries to explain the trick to a crowd: http://www.youtube.com/watch?v=Fi3j8tkjsHE.
June 25	PRD asks IFE to investigate PRI's use of Monex cards; PRI denies connection.
June 26	PAN sends out letters to members asking them to convince thirty more voters each.
June 27	IFE confirms a connection between Monex and PRI.
June 27	*Reforma* poll shows EPN at 41%, AMLO at 31%, and JVM at 24%: http://grupoforma-blogs.com/encuestas/wp-content/uploads/2012 /06/capsula_01_ok.png.
June 27	**Campaign ends.**
June 28	PRD coalition accuses PRI of distributing Soriana debit cards in a vote-buying scheme.
July 1	**Election Day: EPN wins 39.2% of the vote, AMLO receives 32.4%, JVM receives 26.0%, and Gabriel Quadri receives 2.3%.**

NOTES

Epigraph. This quotation, which constitutes the entire text of a "micronovel," came to represent in Mexico the predictability of PRI electoral victories during the era of its hegemony.

1. His adulteries, for instance, were public at least two years earlier. The protests in San Salvador Atenco received national and international attention at the time. And in most middle-class households the *muchacha*—the servant girl, not the lady of the house—would buy tortillas.

2. Specifically, 65% of voters thought that Vicente Fox (2000–2006) had kept "few" or "none" of his campaign promises, while 58% thought that Calderón had kept "few" or "none" of his (Consulta Mitofsky 2013, 34).

3. The three questions were (1) "Sí los candidatos a la Presidencia en 2012 fueran los siguientes (presentaban cinco nombres), usted ¿por quién votaría?"; (2) "¿A quién de los cinco personajes que aparecen en la tarjeta preferiría usted como presidente?"; and (3) "¿Entre Manuel López Obrador y Marcelo Ebrard, a quién preferiría como presidente de la República?" (Romero and Román 2011).

4. Later ads would more successfully separate violence from the PAN government, pointing out that most of the violence occurred in states governed by the PRI, and even blaming the PRI's supposed "collusion" with drug traffickers for the failures of the drug war.

5. Public commentary about the episode echoed the same theme: "si no aguanta las bajas presiones, menos va aguantar las altas que significa ser presidente de la república" (if she can't stand low [blood] pressure, even less will she stand the high [pressures] that being president of the republic means). (See Avilés and Cruz Sánchez 2012.)

6. Citing IFE Consejero Lorenzo Cordova (Urrutia et al. 2012).

7. Concern about this mismatch between IFE authority and the freedom of the Internet led to the formation of a citizens' group to monitor Internet propaganda, with funding from the United Nations (Muñoz Ríos 2012).

8. The organization Citizen Observation and Monitoring, formed specifically to fill the gap created by lack of IFE oversight of the Internet, made these observations in June 2012 (Poy Solano 2012).

9. In the first version, the PRI simply used the same clips of the 2006 *Reforma* blockade and "to hell with your institutions." A more picturesque version of "AMLO isn't a democrat" referred to AMLO's attempt to manipulate the electoral process to put a political ally into power as *jefe de delegación* (a position similar to a mayor, for a borough within Mexico City). AMLO's preferred candidate had lost the PRD primary, but rather than accept the winner as the PRD nominee, AMLO endorsed a candidate from the rival Partido del Trabajo with the understanding that upon being elected, this candidate (so-called Juanito) would resign in favor of the PRD candidate who lost the primary. The video in question shows AMLO trying to explain this byzantine maneuver at a campaign rally, saying "Juanito's the candidate, but he's really not the candidate, it's really Clara and the PRD" (appendix, June 20a).

10. As of June 2013, the video was still available on YouTube: http://www.youtube.com/watch?v=cT5E3SqAHKI. It begins with images from the original protest, where the voice of a Green Party representative can be heard in the background (the Green Party ran in coalition with the PRI) saying that the protesters were trained and planted by López Obrador (see also Olivares Alonso 2012).

11. The main problem for Madrazo was his despotic style as the president of the PRI after Fox's victory. He repeatedly made promises to secure support, and then later broke those promises in a public and humiliating way. No one had any confidence that he would keep promises made in a presidential campaign once he became president. Pena Nieto wisely stayed out of party leadership.

12. In April, she claimed that having to fight in a primary (which her PRI and PRD rivals did not have to do) had consumed a lot of energy and aggravated internal party divisions. She demanded that the PAN leave behind these conflicts to support her candidacy (Herrera Beltrán 2012; see also Saldierna 2012).

REFERENCES

Avilés, Karina, and Armando Cruz Sánchez. 2012. "Pálida y temblorosa, Vázquez Mota niega cualquier malestar." *La Jornada*, April 3, 7. http://www.jornada.unam.mx/2012/04/03/politica/007n1pol.

Ballinas, Victor. 2012. "Peña Nieto plantea alianza entre gobierno e industria para potenciar el desarrollo." *La Jornada*, April 13, 10. http://www.jornada.unam.mx/2012/04/13/politica/010n1pol.

Bruhn, Kathleen, and Kenneth F. Greene. 2007. "Elite Polarization Meets Mass Moderation in Mexico's 2006 Elections." *PS: Political Science and Politics* 40, no. 1: 33–38.

Central Intelligence Agency. 2013. "World Factbook." https://www.cia.gov/library/pub
    lications/the-world-factbook/geos/br.html; https://www.cia.gov/library/publications
    /the-world-factbook/geos/mx.html. Accessed October 18.
Conaculta. 2010. "Encuesta Nacional de hábitos, prácticas y consumos culturales." http://
    www.conaculta.gob.mx/encuesta_nacional/.
Consulta Mitofsky. 2013. "Evaluación Final de Gobierno: Felipe Calderón, 2006–2012."
    Mexico City: Consulta Mitofsky. http://consulta.mx/web/images/evgobierno/2013
    /evaluacionfinalcalderon.pdf.
Domínguez, Jorge, and Chappell Lawson, eds. 2004. *Mexico's Pivotal Democratic Election.*
    Stanford, CA: Stanford University Press.
Domínguez, Jorge, Chappell Lawson, and Alejandro Moreno, eds. 2009. *Consolidating
    Democracy: The 2006 Presidential Campaign in Comparative Perspective.* Baltimore: Johns
    Hopkins University Press.
El Universal. 2009. "El PRI: Entre la experiencia probada y la nueva actitud." *Ciudad Posible*
    (blog), July 1. http://www.ciudadposible.com/2009/07/el-pri-entre-la-experiencia-pro
    bada-y-la-nueva-actitud.html.
Everdy Mejía, Luis. 2012. "¿Por cuál de los candidatos a la Presidencia nunca votarías?"
    ADN Politico, April 3. http://www.adnpolitico.com/encuestas/2012/04/03/por-cual-de
    -los-candidatos-a-la-presidencia-nunca-votarias.
García Hernández, Arturo. 2012. "Logran las protestas resonancia mundial en Twitter."
    La Jornada, May 19, 5. http://www.jornada.unam.mx/2012/05/19/politica/005n3pol.
Herrera Beltrán, Claudia. 2012. "Familiares del presidente Calderón, en el nuevo equipo
    de Vázquez Mota." *La Jornada*, April 10, 5. http://www.jornada.unam.mx/2012/04
    /10/politica/005n1pol.
Instituto Federal Electoral. 2006. "Instituto Federal Electoral, 1996." http://siceef.ife.org
    .mx/pef2012/SICEEF2012.html.
Lawson, Chappell. 2000. "Mexico's Unfinished Transition: Democratization and Au-
    thoritarian Enclaves." *Mexican Studies/Estudios Mexicanos* 16, no. 2: 267–88.
Monterroso, Augusto. 1959. *Obras completas (y otros cuentos).* Barcelona: Editorial Anagrama.
Muñoz, Alma E. 2012. "Todo indica que el IFE tiene un candidato preferido, dice AMLO."
    La Jornada, April 20, 14. http://www.jornada.unam.mx/2012/04/20/politica/014n2pol.
Muñoz Ríos, Patricia. 2012. "Grupo ciudadano dará seguimiento en redes sociales a prác-
    ticas de *guerra sucia* electoral." *La Jornada*, April 19, 8. http://www.jornada.unam.mx
    /2012/04/19/politica/008n1pol.
Olivares Alonso, Emir. 2012. "No somos porros ni acarreados, responden alumnos de la
    Ibero que increparon a Peña." *La Jornada*, May 15, 11. http://www.jornada.unam.mx
    /2012/05/15/politica/011n1pol.
Parametría. 2006. "Carta Paramétrica: Felipe Calderón aventaja a López Obrador (May
    06)." http://www.parametria.com.mx/carta_parametrica.php?cp=4017.
Poy Solano, Laura. 2012. "Las redes sociales, secuestradas por profesionales del rumor y
    la intolerancia." *La Jornada*, June 6, 11. http://www.jornada.unam.mx/2012/06/06
    /politica/011n1pol.
Romero, Gabriela, and José Antonio Román. 2011. "López Obrador, virtual candidato a
    la Presidencia." *La Jornada*, November 16, 2. http://www.jornada.unam.mx/2011/11
    /16/politica/002n1pol.
Saldierna, Georgina. 2012. "En la cúpula de Acción Nacional dan por hecho que perderán
    la Presidencia." *La Jornada*, May 19, 8. http://www.jornada.unam.mx/2012/05/19
    /politica/008n2pol.

Urrutia, Alonso, and Fabiola Martínez. 2012. "Finalizan las campañas electorales más mediáticas de la historia mexicana." *La Jornada*, June 28, 12. http://www.jornada .unam.mx/2012/06/28/politica/012n2pol.

Urrutia, Alonso, Fabiola Martínez, and Emir Olivares. 2012. "Rechaza Leonardo Valdés que se esté reditando la *guerra sucia*." *La Jornada*, June 7, 3. http://www.jornada.unam .mx/2012/06/07/politica/003n1pol.

Urrutia, Alonso, and Patricia Muñoz. 2012. "Difundirá el PAN promocionales más agresivos, en especial contra Peña." *La Jornada*, April 11, 10. http://www.jornada.unam .mx/2012/04/11/politica/010n2pol.

Vargas, Rosa Elvira. 2012a. "Peña Nieto fustiga las cuentas alegres del jefe del Ejecutivo." *La Jornada*, April 4, 9. http://www.jornada.unam.mx/2012/04/04/politica/009n1pol.

———. 2012b. "No caer en provocaciones de quienes van abajo en preferencias, pide Peña a priístas." *La Jornada*, May 17, 12. http://www.jornada.unam.mx/2012/05/17/politica /012n1pol.

Wuhs, Steven T. 2008. *Savage Democracy: Institutional Change and Party Development in Mexico*. University Park: Pennsylvania State University Press.

3

The Electoral Institutions

Party Subsidies, Campaign Decency, and Entry Barriers

ERIC MAGAR

The 2012 presidential and congressional races took place under a different set of rules than in 2006. Although most of the electoral institutions of interest to political scientists (e.g., the translation of votes into seats) remained unchanged, Mexico imposed new campaign finance regulations and new limits on television and radio advertising. This chapter offers a description of and commentary on institutional changes that go to the heart of how modern campaigns are run.

In the last three presidential elections, each major party has seen its candidate finish a distant third at some point: Cuauhtémoc Cárdenas of the Partido de la Revolución Democrática (PRD) in 2000; Roberto Madrazo of the Partido Revolucionario Institucional (PRI) in 2006, and Josefina Vásquez Mota of the National Action Party (PAN) in 2012. And in all of these elections, the front-runner's lead has eroded significantly—enough to turn the tide in 2000 and 2006. These facts indicate how weak the links between Mexican parties and the electorate remain, despite decades of heavy subsidies and institutional protection from competition.

With parties unable to anchor themselves firmly in the mass public, campaigns have been key to making Mexican democracy work (Domínguez and Lawson 2004; Domínguez, Lawson, and Moreno 2009; Moreno 2003, 2009). By affecting the legal architecture under which competition for office is conducted, changes in campaign rules can have a great impact on electoral politics. This chapter argues that significant increases in public subsidies to the parties and the adoption of strict controls on campaign advertisements further insulated party leaders from potential challengers, both outside the party establishment and inside their own parties. Ultimately, this outcome tends to constrain the choices available to voters and does little to encourage closer linkages between the parties and the electorate.

I begin by revisiting the context under which the electoral reform was negotiated and highlighting two key elements of the reform package. The first is the expansion of subsidies to the parties: total transfers including indirect subsidies in election years went up by 20% in the 2009 midterm and by 120% in 2012. As a result of these subsidies, spending per vote in 2012 stood at $13 (compared to $18 per vote in the US presidential election that same year, and less than $2 per vote in France, both countries with several times the per-capita gross domestic product of Mexico). The key datum here is that, comparing 2012 to 2006, approximately a dozen times more campaign advertising was broadcast during an official campaign season that was half as long. Meanwhile, legal voluntary donations to parties were restricted to at most 5% of major party spending, ensuring that party leaders controlled messaging during the campaigns.

The second concerns rules on campaign advertisements: Mexican electoral authorities now control who can say what and when on radio and television for campaign purposes. The "who" in this case stands for the registered parties only; the Federal Electoral Institute (IFE) distributes time among the parties during the campaign season according to rigid, bureaucratic criteria. The "when" is also strictly enforced; campaigns have become drastically shorter, especially for primaries, and all attempts by candidates to advertise before the official campaign became illegal. Even the "what" is now strictly regulated; the IFE has the authority to verify campaign message content in order to remove attack advertisements from the airwaves. Although court rulings limiting these powers and lax censorship standards by the IFE allowed some "contrast" advertising to seep into the race, what American political actors would regard as freedom of speech remains a matter of regulatory discretion in Mexico. This chapter closes by showing how changes in campaign rules have added new entry barriers to the party system and further raised those already in place.

Origins of Reform

Electoral reform was the political elite's response to the 2006 fiasco, when candidate Andrés Manuel López Obrador cried foul, refused to concede, and mobilized supporters for weeks in an attempt to force a recount that would legally invalidate the presidential election. Mexico's main parties embraced the notion that campaigns dominated by the sort of attack advertisements that characterized the 2006 race—caricaturing López Obrador as a dangerous Hugo Chávez copycat or portraying Felipe Calderón's in-laws as white-collar criminals—lay at the root of political polarization. In their zeal to prevent negative ads and elevate political discourse, reformers prohibited any statements that would "denigrate" candidates. And in a radical attempt to redress the problematic relationship between parties and broadcasters, they abolished the market for political advertisements, replacing it with a direct allocation of time from the IFE to the parties. Finally, they further raised entry barriers against outsiders. All told, the reform gave precedence to equitable competition among existing parties, to "decency" over freedom of speech, to parties over other social actors, and to party leaders over the rank and file.

Party leaders and President Calderón stitched together the proposal in the second half of 2007. Political observers knew it was coming, yet few details leaked to the press. Submitted to the senate and sent to committee on August 31—the eve of Calderón's first state of the union address at the start of the congress's regular session, with all eyes turned at what López Obrador's supporters would do to protest the event—the constitutional reform was reported to the floor and approved, without amendment, by a nearly unanimous vote on September 12. It cleared the chamber of deputies two days later, again with no amendment and with the vote of every major-party representative save one. Smoke-filled-room negotiations, speedy adoption, and unanimous consent left a distinct scent of universalism, in which parties turned a blind eye to unpalatable requests in exchange for having their pet proposals included in the final bill. In fact, Calderón may have been aware that several items would hurt his party's chances in 2012 and accepted the reform anyway in exchange for the PRI's support for modest new federal taxes (Magar and Romero 2008).

What Changed?

The changes adopted were all encompassing. Nine of the constitution's 136 articles were amended, and most of the federal electoral code was rewritten (see IFE 2008 for text comparison). Of the 300 articles in the old code, only half survived substantively unchanged. The rest were rescinded or more or less amended, and many new points were added. The new code has 31% more articles and 35% more words than the one it replaced.

This chapter's focus is on a subset of reforms most intimately connected to campaigning.[1] The reforms of interest here fall in two groups, each of which matches a key stated objective of the reform. One of these was achieving "significant cuts in electoral campaign spending"; it involved four changes to the status quo regarding party financing:

1. The "ordinary" public subsidy to parties, used for party-building activities, was made proportional to the number of registered voters instead of the number of registered parties as an attempt to contain costs.
2. The supplemental campaign subsidy (additional public funding that can be spent during the legal campaign season) was reduced relative to the ordinary subsidy.
3. Party access to the mass media was based exclusively on allocations from a stock of television and radio time controlled by the IFE, an off-the-books subsidy that grew exponentially.
4. The ceiling for legal private donations to parties and candidates was lowered significantly, pushing this source of funding into relative insignificance.

Preventing "actors outside the electoral process from interfering with campaigns and outcomes" was another stated goal, and five reforms focused on establishing tighter control over political advertising:

1. The sale and purchase of advertising on radio and television aimed at "changing electoral preferences" was prohibited.
2. The legal campaign season was shortened significantly, to ninety days for a general election, and candidates were forbidden from "self-promoting with electoral aims" before the official start of the campaign.
3. All government advertising, in which the incumbent administration or other federal or state agencies might report their accomplishments, was suspended during the campaign season.
4. Negative advertisements were prohibited, and the IFE was authorized to order the summary suspension of advertisements deemed unlawful.
5. Harsh penalties, such as half-million-dollar fines for corporations that ran electoral ads and a ban from running for public office for anyone advertising on television before the legal beginning of the campaigns, were set for failure to comply with the new restrictions.

Granting the IFE powers "to overcome limitations with which [it has] been confronted" was the third general goal of the reform; though important for Mexican politics, these reforms are beyond the scope of this chapter.

Barely Dropping Cash Subsidies

The reform, proponents claimed, would halve the subsidy for general elections (when the president and all members of both houses of congress are elected) and reduce it by 70% in midterm elections (when the lower house of congress is replaced in full). These targets were not attained. A review of official reports shows that cash transfers to the parties in the 2009 and 2012 elections dropped by much smaller percentages. When the six-year cycle from one presidential race to the next is considered as a whole, the drop in cash transfers was a mere 2%.

Excessive campaign spending (however defined) is a problem, if at all, for those paying the bill. In the United States, private donations from citizens and interest groups primarily finance political campaigns. Questions remain about the adequacy of the regime to guaranteeing equal representation (Olson 1965), but those contributing do so willingly, making the scope of spending per se unproblematic. In Mexico, taxpayers foot the bill, and it has grown in constant prices nearly every fiscal year.

Since 1996, public subsidies have predominantly financed Mexican parties. Some room remained under the status quo for private campaign contributions, but they were capped at less than one-tenth of overall receipts, making public transfers the parties' dominant source of funding. Although the size of the subsidy was defined in statute, the IFE retained some discretion. Total funding "for sustaining parties' permanent ordinary activities," to which I refer as the ordinary subsidy, was set by a formula relating directly the legislative seats to be elected (fixed constitutionally), campaign duration (fixed in the election code), and the number of registered parties. An abstract "minimal cost of a congressional campaign" multiplied all these terms to determine the total amount. The IFE established the minimal yearly cost, and calibrating it gave the regulator scope to influence the amount of public subsidies that the chamber of deputies earmarked in the annual budget. The rule for distributing these funds—and most other subsidies for the parties since the late 1970s—was that 30% went to registered parties in equal parts, and the remaining 70% was allocated according to the vote share each party received in the last election for the chamber of deputies. The ordinary subsidy was then doubled in federal election years to finance campaign spending.

Reformers pushed through several changes. The subsidy formula became simpler. The total yearly subsidy for ordinary activities since fiscal year (FY) 2008 equals the number of registered voters multiplied by two-thirds of the minimum daily wage in Mexico City. This approach indexes parties' awards to inflation and removes most of the IFE's former discretion; it would need to meddle with voter registration in order to effect changes in the subsidy. It also bought federal deputies (only the lower house of congress passes appropriations) leverage to exert pressure on the IFE through cuts in its yearly budget—as occurred in 2006 and 2008—with no fear that the regulator might try to absorb part of the shock by cutting parties' public subsidies proportionately.

The 30/70 distribution remained unchanged, but incentives changed with the introduction of a formula that no longer takes the sheer number of parties into account. Registered parties have a greater incentive to prevent the creation of new parties in order to preserve their slice of a fixed pie.

In addition, each party received an extra 50% of its ordinary budget for presidential campaigns (30% for midterm elections), instead of the former 100%. Proponents' claim of public transfer cuts through reform was based exclusively on this provision, ignoring that the ordinary subsidy was also redefined, leading them to mischaracterize the reform. Figure 3.1 reports public transfers to the parties in constant 2012 prices. (Inflation was corrected in pesos, and the 2012 exchange rate was then used to produce figures in dollars.) Topping most bars are six-year percentage changes in public transfers to the parties. The allotment, then and now, of more generous subsidies in election years makes first differences inappropriate, and six-year changes pit more comparable years against one other than three-year differences. Without the white, dotted portions topping postreform columns for years 2009 and 2012—corresponding to noncash transfers that require some elaboration—the trend is clear: subsidies increased between 1% and 9% before the reform, except in 2007. Figures in parentheses at the foot of each bar report the number of registered parties eligible for public funding. The spike in 2003 (which 2002 would parallel had the series started earlier) was particularly acute owing to new entrants: eleven registered parties pushed the total subsidy upward. Five of those failed to clear the threshold to reregister in 2004, explaining the 7% drop observed in FY 2007.

Postreform changes are interesting. Figures in 2010, 2011, and 2013—all nonelection years, when campaign subsidies are not allotted—show that when all adopted changes are factored in, transfers grew despite the fact that the number of parties stayed roughly the same (one more or one less than six years before). With the change in ordinary subsidy formula, transfers in both 2010 and 2011 were up 24% and up 6% in 2013. In election years, cash transfers did recede compared to levels six years before, down 42% and 5% in 2009 and

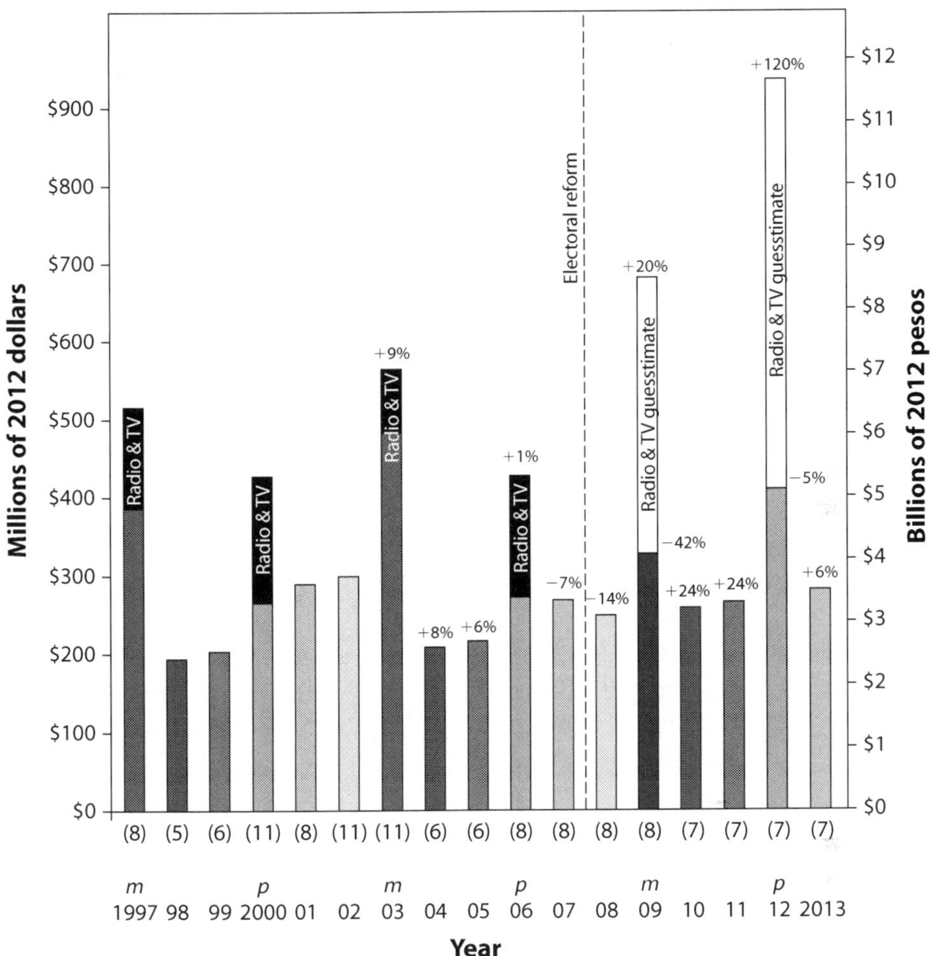

Figure 3.1. Parties' yearly public subsidy. *Note:* Letters *p* and *m* in the *x* axis indicate presidential and midterm election years, respectively. Columns report yearly total (ordinary and campaign) subsidies to parties. The black portions of columns in election years show the amount of total subsidy corresponding to radio and television advertisement spending by parties in 1997, 2000, 2003, and 2006. The white dotted portions of columns for years 2009 and 2012 report an attempt to valuate unaccounted advertisement subsidies. The numbers in parentheses below columns report the number of registered parties eligible for subsidies, and the numbers atop columns beginning in 2003 report the six-year percentage change in total subsidy. The exchange rate used is $1 = 12.50 pesos.

2012, respectively, but much less than the 70% and 50% drops announced by reform proponents.

Ballooning Total Public Subsidies

A more important element of the new law was the massive increase in a form of subsidy that was relatively small under the status quo: free time for the parties on radio and television. Once this element is accounted for, total public subsidies to the parties were actually 20% (in midterm elections) and 120% (in general elections) larger after the latest electoral reform.

In an attempt to address long-standing complaints about the relationship between parties and broadcasters (discussed below), reformers prohibited the sale and purchase of campaign advertising in the electronic media. Access to the mass media for election purposes is now allocated centrally by the IFE. Regulation of mass media franchises under the status quo was adapted to implement this key element of the reform. In addition to the corporate tax, broadcasters must grant the federal government thirty minutes of daily coverage on every station, free of charge. Rules adopted by executive order in 2002 formalized payment in kind of another 25% tax on commercial franchisees of government activity, such as broadcasters, the federal executive thus receiving eighteen minutes of free daily coverage on average between 6:00 a.m. and midnight.[2] It does not take long after a television is turned on to experience the so-called "official time"—recurrent federal government announcements from 6:00 a.m. to midnight. Under new electoral rules, however, the IFE administers 12% of official time (five minutes and forty-five seconds daily on every TV station) in off-election years, and its entirety (forty-eight minutes) in federal election years. From the start of primary season (known as the "precampaign") through Election Day, the IFE controls and allots to parties and electoral authorities advertisement spots adding up to between two and three minutes every hour on every channel and radio station nationwide. The party portion is split according to the 30/70 rule. In election years, parties receive advertising time totaling eighteen minutes daily during the primary season, and forty-one minutes daily during the official campaign season—enough for eighty-two thirty-second spots on every station in the country on a daily basis.

Perhaps more striking than its gargantuan proportions is the hidden nature of the subsidy. The claim that the new scheme saves taxpayer money rests implicitly on the premise that this advertising time is free. The IFE's claim in party finance reports, by leaving this huge item off the accounting books, rests explicitly on the same premise (México Evalúa 2013). Of course, opportunity costs do not vanish by giving television-advertising time to parties free of charge. The finance ministry, for example, foregoes revenue when it swaps the 25% tax on profitable networks for airtime, which is in turn given to campaigning parties. And this is just a small portion of the official time.

I therefore offer a conservative guesstimate of the monetary value of the advertising "ghost subsidy," using party reports of amounts purchased in 2006 (when they last went to the campaign advertising market) to compute an average unit price that can be projected to the 2012 campaign.[3] Not counting radio, parties acknowledged the purchase of more than 28,000 spots in their 2006 campaign spending reports. Most went to the major parties. The PRD-led coalition topped the ranking, reporting the purchase of 10,514 television spots (37% of all); the PRI-led coalition trailed with 7,723 spots (27%); and the PAN came in between them at 8,491 (30%). Smaller parties purchased about 6% of television spots altogether. The total bill for electronic media advertisement sums to nearly $140 million at the time, but parties rank differently than with amounts: the PAN and the PRI coalition reported similar figures of about $49 million (35% each), and the PRD reported about $36 million (26%). Not all spots are created equal: prices are higher for times and stations with better ratings, and the left seems to have purchased more but also cheaper spots. The PAN, and especially the PRI, did the opposite. These disbursements for communicating with voters through electronic media consumed much of parties' campaign resources, constituting three-quarters of the overall 2006 campaign subsidy and one-third of the total subsidy. Coalitions were able to keep the proportion spent on advertisement below the PAN's, which ran solo—and whose media bill nearly ate up its entire campaign subsidy. This is so by virtue of the "30" part of the 30/70 subsidy split rule. Each of the seven registered parties was worth 4.3% of the campaign subsidy distributed, plus the part proportional to its size in votes. Teaming up with the Green Ecologist Party in 2006, the PRI received 38% of the overall campaign subsidy instead of 30%; the left got 30% instead of 17% for the PRD alone.

Parties typically underreport campaign spending in order to evade legal limits, which would be desirable information to include in the figures used for the estimation. One study (IFE 2006) of all broadcasting from January 19 to June 28, 2006, on the 150 highest-rated television stations nationwide sheds light on the scope of underreporting. Out of 40,000 presidential television spots the study identified, about 12,000 went unreported. My projection therefore relies

on the monitored figures. There were 224 hours of paid campaign advertisements by the PAN, 256 by the PRD coalition, 368 by the PRI coalition, and
seventy for one minor party—918 hours in total. These figures pale by comparison to what parties would have received in these 150 stations under the
new system: more than 9,000 hours over a ninety-day campaign period, a tenfold increase from 2006 to 2012. The allocation is thirteen instead of ten times
larger if the primary season period is also considered; I chose to exclude
them owing to restrictions for the use of advertisements by parties nominating candidates other than by primary elections. Factoring in that the 2012
campaigns were nearly half as long (discussed below), the increase is even more
striking. Voters were incessantly bombarded with spots during the 2012
campaign period.

Dividing the reported total spent in advertisements in 2006 ($139.6 million)
by the hours paid (918) yields an average price of $152,000 per advertisement
hour. This figure is not far from costs reported for a controversial spot in support
of a write-in candidate (Víctor González Torres, aka Dr. Simi) heard by the Federal Electoral Court (technically known as the Tribunal Electoral del Poder Judicial de la Federación, or TEPJF, but commonly referred to by its previous name,
the TRIFE). Dr. Simi purchased one full minute during several news programs.
Reported prices for broadcasting for four consecutive days fluctuated greatly:
$3,000 around lunchtime, $11,000 during the morning news, and as much as
$20,000 during the evening news (TEPJF 2006). Translated to dollars per hour,
the $173,000 average price Dr. Simi paid was not far from the projection.

From another angle, however, projecting this average price linearly to 2012
would seem to overstate value. New rules homogeneously allocate the generous airwaves subsidy from 6:00 a.m. to midnight on every station, regardless of
audience density and demographics. A network specializing in children's car-
toons, for instance, is not excluded from airing party advertisements. It is unlikely that campaigns would express interest in many of the low-rated slots included in the award, if offered at the average price. Having them in the award
is certain to lower the average price, and discounts for purchasing such massive amount of commercials would certainly apply. To be conservative, I divide
the average price by three, leaving it at $50,000 per hour of advertisements,[4]
which can be used to value the ghost subsidy.

The approximate price tag affixed to the formidable gift that parties received in 2012 (and, one-third smaller, in 2009) is $465 million in 2006 dollars,
or $535 million in 2012 dollars.[5] Compared to a similar exercise carried out by

México Evalúa (2013), my guesstimate is indeed conservative. Their price tag on parties' "indirect" subsidy in the airwaves is three times larger, a staggering $1.5 billion in 2006 dollars or $1.75 billion in 2012 dollars. The magnitude is easier to appreciate when the unaccounted subsidy is plotted along with reported subsidies in figure 3.1, represented by the white, dotted portions of the 2009 and 2012 columns. With some variance, revised totals now drop markedly in all off-election years of the time series. Of more relevance, contrary to the official accounting, the six-year differences in federal election years surged markedly after the reform when the ghost subsidy was considered. Considering the approximated value of the television advertisements, party subsidies are actually 20% higher in midterm campaigns and 120% higher in general election years.

The regulator felt confident to "state categorically that Mexicans today spend less money in election campaigns . . . the aim of the reform was accomplished" (IFE 2010, 8). For this claim to be sound, the largest election-year source of funding must be omitted. When it is not, the explicit goal of saving money failed dramatically, contrary to the official line.

Spending per Vote

Federal campaign spending oversight was concluded in July 2013. The IFE audits revealed substantial amounts in excess of legal limits, and parties and coalitions were fined accordingly (Baños 2013; Córdova 2013; Cristalinas Kaulitz 2013). The finding that López Obrador's campaign spent $3.7 million above the nearly $27 million legal presidential candidate limit (nearly 15% more), but Peña Nieto's was right on target, captured most headlines (Vázquez Mota's campaign underspent $9 million). Because, under the argument that campaign spending has spillover effects, by law parties have the discretion to reclassify up to half the monies disbursed for their presidential campaign as congressional campaign spending (and vice versa), focus on presidential candidates masks much of what actually took place. Possibly in anticipation of judicial invalidation, the PRI-Green coalition opted to shield its presidential victor by reporting huge amounts as congressional campaign spending: in 149 of the 199 federal deputy campaigns they ran in tandem, and twenty-eight of the 101 where the PRI fielded candidates solo, spending surpassed the legal limit. The left coalition chose the opposite accounting strategy, consolidating the near-totality of overspending in the presidential campaign report (just nine of their 300 deputy campaigns exceeded the spending limit). When all federal campaigns are considered, the PRI-Green coalition surpassed the legal limits by $4.7 million and was penalized with $16 million in fines. The left coalition fines added to $11 million, and half a million for the PAN.

Looking at parties' spending reports in comparative perspective is revealing. Dividing all presidential candidates' reported monetary spending (nearly $85 million) by the valid votes they received (49 million) equals $1.73 per vote. Compared to the $18.35 per vote (or $8.81 per vote when super–political action committee [PAC] expenditures are subtracted; see Boaz 2013) that Barack Obama and Mitt Romney spent in the United States, the Mexican quantity looks small. And it is not far from the $1.65 per vote spent in both rounds of the French presidential race the same year (Commission nationale des comptes de campagne et des financements politiques 2013). But take the noncash media subsidy into consideration, and spending in the Mexican presidential race rises to $12.63 per vote. While still below spending by American presidential candidates, the data for Mexico exclude primary campaign spending and radio advertising. Because virtually all spending is public, the parties in 2012 extracted considerable rents from Mexican taxpayers. All told, reformers left the size of the public subsidy to the parties nearly untouched. Freed from the need to devote the bulk of their campaign subsidy to the purchase of television advertisement in 2012, parties had vast amounts to spend on ground operations.

Less (Legal) Private Money

If cutting party public subsidies was the goal reformers sought, the removal of caps on private campaign donations was one obvious way to achieve it. But campaign finance liberalization in Mexico has been anathema for decades. Reformers further limited private campaign contributions, choosing instead to confront the problem by tightening cash subsidies (with little success) and removing legal campaign spending opportunities.

By limiting small campaign donations from citizens and noncorporate, nonreligious groups for each party to at most 10% of the overall ordinary subsidy, the preform regime guaranteed that the public subsidy dominated private money in party funding. Using the pooled subsidy to quantify the cap effectively made the legal belt much tighter on larger rather than smaller parties. To illustrate, assume that all parties had enough private donors to reach the legal preform limit for 2007. The PAN, PRI, and PRD could have added an extra 36%, 52%, and 60%, respectively, to their ordinary public budget. The same figure ranged from 125% to nearly 200% for minor parties. Smaller parties would presumably find it harder to persuade strategic private contributors than larger parties (Cox and Magar 1999). But the scheme kept the door open for political entrepreneurs outside the party establishment to compete by joining forces with minor parties. By changing each party's legal limit to one-tenth of the previous presidential campaign expenditure ceiling, reformers drastically restricted private campaign contributions. Private donations will be capped at $2.7 million until 2018, when the IFE sets a new presidential campaign spending limit. To offer some comparative perspective, ninety donors contributing the yearly American individual donation limit to parties ($30,800) would surpass that amount; Jeffrey Katzenberg's super-PAC alone spent $2.6 million on behalf of the Obama campaign in 2012. Applying the new (inflation-corrected) rule to 2007 would have allowed major parties to add just 4–6% to their ordinary subsidy, and 12–19% for minor parties.

A system with mostly private campaign donations changed overnight in 1996 to one with predominantly public funding.[6] Reformers in 2007 continued the trend, bringing limits much further down. The new regulations have now virtually eliminated the market for political advertising; the purchase of spots survives only in off-cycle subnational contests and special elections, when official time may be insufficient and the IFE is entitled to purchase more for state parties and local election regulators.

This policy is unlikely to curb the influence of powerful private interests in politics, its alleged rationale. Lower limits to total private money have pushed such donations to the black market; the new policy did not prevent large private contributions to the 2012 campaigns, it just made them illegal. In one instance, federal police caught officials aboard a Veracruz government plane in January 2012 carrying bags full of cash totaling $2 million—three-fourths the total legal limit for a party—allegedly for Peña Nieto's campaign (though this relationship was never proven). A system that embraces legal private money in campaigns, with proper limits on individual contributions rather than attempting to expunge the influence of organized interests by making donations illegal, makes the relation between private interests and politicians easier to map (Romero 2012).

Furthermore, placing the great bulk of campaign spending in the hands of party leaders makes them more powerful actors, who inevitably have interests of their own to protect. Businessmen are at least social actors. To the extent that elected representatives dance to the tune of actors in a position to make or break their careers, it is not clear that party apparatchik are preferable pipers than oligarchs.

Much Shorter Campaigns

Reformers hailed the new system as creating a "new communication model between society and the parties." The time allocated to parties for political advertising is one element of this equation, but other provisions were adopted to control campaign message timing, messengers, and even message content. The changes tightening the regulator's control of political advertising were at the time much more controversial than party and campaign finance. Their adoption raised concerns that central tenets of liberalism were being sacrificed for equitable competition and decency in campaigns (Cantú 2009; Roldán Xopa 2010; Sarmiento 2007). The crowd of enthusiasts who welcomed these elements of the proposal was quick to dismiss such arguments as veiled attempts by powerful vested interests—two main television networks in particular—to defend the influence and immense profits earned under the oligopolistic status quo (Córdoba 2008; Dresser 2007; Murayama 2009; Salazar 2008). They may have been right about their opponents' motives, but the dangers that these opponents identified were real.

Defining the official duration of campaigns is not new to Mexican election law, but enforcement has been problematic. Decreeing an end point to campaigns by statute was quite straightforward: to ensure a period of national "reflection," mass rallies and public events by candidates and the parties were prohibited three days before the election, and for eight days prior to the election, no polling results could be published. (The reform reduced this time to three days but raised the penalties for violation.) With politicians in permanent campaigns to stay in office—campaigns that simply become more active and visible with approaching elections—enforcing a certain date for the start of the campaign was much harder. Delimiting the start and end of campaigns acquired new meaning with the adoption of strict controls on advertising, especially centralized allocation of radio and television advertisement.

Reformers broke campaigning into two distinct, nonoverlapping periods: primary season (the "precampaigns," when "pre-candidates" vie for nomination) and official campaign season. A precampaign can legally last up to sixty days in presidential election years and forty days in midterms, ending at most the day before the primary election. Precampaigns must start the third week of December before a presidential election and the fourth week of January otherwise. Because federal elections are held in early July, the latest a primary can take place is the last week of February. Such details would be trivial had reformers not also prohibited all pre-candidate advertising before the precampaign period officially starts. The penalty for not complying is ineligibility to run for public office, enabling enforcement of the new rules. Once candidates are selected, the official campaigns then last exactly ninety days in presidential election years (sixty in midterms). This change halved the length of presidential campaigns, clearly a substantial reduction. But it is really in precampaigns that the bite of duration limits was felt: formerly unregulated intraparty competition went from essentially continuous to limited.

Controlling Who Can Say What

Strict controls of election advertisement content complemented the centralized allocation of radio and television spots by the IFE. The explicit driving force was an attempt to guarantee equity in electoral competition. Reformers echoed faithfully the TRIFE ruling of September 5, 2006, reprimanding President Fox's "undue interventions" before, during, and after that year's presidential campaign. An incumbent campaigning on behalf of her party, if not on behalf of herself, is considered normal, even expected, in democracies such as Chile, France, or the United States. But the fact that outgoing presidents in Mexico once picked their own successors and because of the fear that incumbents would manipulate Mexico's federal apparatus have made the public leery, even normal campaigning by the outgoing president is generally perceived as inappropriate, especially among the elite (Lawson 2009, 11).[7] In the judges' unanimous opinion, Fox's use of such terms as "the Messiah," "the Enlightened," and "populist" when lampooning López Obrador, although ultimately not decisive for the outcome and therefore not warranting an invalidation of the election, "did affect the freedom of voting and the race's equity." In that spirit, reformers prevented the government from "including names, images, voices or symbols implying the personalized promotion of any public officeholder" in any advertisement. Limitations on citizen and interest group access to media for political goals follow the same general understanding that "outsider" actors—i.e., outside the party establishment—easily manipulate voters.

Content control went much further. Reacting to the negative campaigning that occurred in the 2006 race—a degree of negativity that would have been fairly typical in the United States—standards of decency in advertisements were adopted. Attack advertisements are now explicitly prohibited; parties and candidates are obliged to abstain in radio and television advertisements from using expressions that "denigrate institutions and political parties or slander any person." The term "denigrate" is ambiguous enough to leave ample discretion for regulators to interpret which messages are lawful and which are not. Enforcement was also strengthened. In addition to imposing fines, the IFE now has the authority to summarily order broadcasters to suspend any advertisement that it believes violates the decency standard. Censorship was thus adopted—a drastic measure to prevent campaigning that many believed pushed Mexico dangerously to the brink of violence in 2006. Survey evidence never warranted such interpretation; polarization in 2006 was largely confined to the elite, not the general population (Domínguez et al. 2009; Moreno 2009).

When the new campaign rules were first tested in the 2009 midterm campaigns, parties, business organizations, and even op-ed writers went to court to roll back some parts of the reforms on advertising. They sometimes won. TRIFE rescinded IFE-imposed penalties on the Green Ecologist Party for purchasing, with private money, television spots promoting its legislative achievements. A federal judge also granted individual exceptions to the ban on purchasing electoral spots in the mass media. The IFE dropped sanctions against broadcasters that, contrary to regulation, grouped party ads in three-minute blocks and interrupted popular soccer games with a sarcastic "we can't help it (*ni modo*); we are going to cut to ads from the IFE." It also chose to not rule on the difficult case of thinly veiled self-promotion by various mayors and governors—Governor Peña Nieto of the populous State of Mexico in particular—in the form of nightly infomercials on highly rated news programs. Reform enthusiasts denounced such actions as a de facto counterreform (Salazar 2009). Although the judges often argued their rulings in bizarre ways, and the principles of jurisprudence they invoked sometimes contradicted basic tenets of separation of power (Murayama 2009), the rulings testified eloquently to the tension between strict controls of political communication and fundamental rights of freedom of expression. With these in mind, Casar (2009) saw a "reform of the reform" as imminent.

Against such a background, the IFE proved more flexible in interpreting the law throughout the 2012 campaigns. The censor made little use of its authority despite the fact that campaigns featured a significant amount of negativity. Instead of subjecting messages to ex ante screenings, as done in the 2009 legislative races, the IFE chose to immediately send spots to the networks, and to react to party complaints instead. As a result, campaign advertisements could be broadcast three days after their delivery to the regulator. Still a far cry from allowing immediate reaction in the campaigns, it nonetheless represented a substantial improvement over the five to seven days that ex ante screening would otherwise have taken.

Just as important as the removal of red tape was the high bar for messages to qualify as "denigrating." Forty complaints regarding breach of communication rules were filed with the IFE between April 2 and June 30, 2012. In only four did the IFE order the summary removal of the offending piece from the airwaves: three by the PAN and one by PRI. (It once opted to fine the party without removal.) Attack advertisements were thus present to some degree in the 2012 campaigns without being thwarted by the IFE.

Partyocracy Reloaded

For critics, administrative controls on the eligibility, timing, and content of advertisements boded ill for the capacity of campaigns to invigorate the electorate. Devoid of negativity, presidential campaign messages ran the risk of turning into empty slogans incapable of mobilizing segments of voters with the least interest in politics (Lau, Sigelman, Heldman, and Babbitt 1999). The exponential growth in time devoted to such televised campaign spots available during much shorter periods seemed like a formula for losing the audience's attention. The audience for any television channel was bombarded with rigidly scheduled party spots (using the 30/70 rule) between 6:00 a.m. and 2:00 p.m. in a portion of the official campaign (see ancillary figure available at www.press .jhu.edu). Much shorter campaigns also removed opportunities for voters to assess candidates by watching them live on the campaign trail (Popkin 1991). And the process of bureaucratic verification of compliance by political advertisers threatened to remove the capacity of campaigns to respond rapidly to unfolding events and opponent mistakes.

Things went much better than expected. Turnout in the presidential election was the highest in the democratic era: 65% of registered voters, compared to 64% in 2000 and 59% in 2006. And, against all odds, the campaigns had effects on voters (a theme that Chappell Lawson and Kenneth F. Greene elaborate in chaps. 1 and 6, respectively, this volume). Peña Nieto won the presidency as expected (see Kathleen Bruhn, chap. 2, this volume), but the PRI's performance disappointed its enthusiasts. Although four out of five pollsters with national media coverage had reported a lead of more than twenty points for Peña Nieto throughout the campaign, the actual margin of victory on July 1 was less than seven points, just one-third of the preelection poll average. As Lawson notes in chapter 1 in this volume, *Reforma* polls were much closer to target than the modal pollster: *Reforma*'s predicted margin, consistently smaller than most measurements from start to end, stood at ten points in the last preelection survey at the end of June. Campaigns failed to move vote intentions quite as much as in the 2000 and 2006 campaigns, but its effects remained noticeable. The winner did not come from behind, as Fox did in 2000 and Calderón in 2006, but Peña Nieto lost two-thirds of his edge over the leading rival. Of even greater consequence, the PRI failed to capture the congressional majority that pundits had anticipated—a failing that may have caught even Peña Nieto by surprise, judging by his lackluster victory speech on election night.

Yet problems raised by the new electoral institutions remain. In political advertising, the IFE's tolerance of negativity is a matter of discretion. Nothing in the new law or the constitution prevents a U-turn if the IFE and especially the parties that indirectly control it (Estévez, Magar, and Rosas 2008) deem it necessary. Court rulings could make this lenient approach to censorship more robust. In the United States, Federal Election Commission policy since the 1970s and Supreme Court rulings more recently have excluded soft money (not used to pay for advertisements that promote a specific candidate) and independent expenditures (made without coordination with parties or campaigns) from contribution limits established in the law. Such a legal interpretation by the Mexican Supreme Court remains theoretically possible.

Reformers encouraged the partyocracy—as the party establishment is known in political commentary—to new extremes. Actors outside the party establishment have been handicapped for decades in the contest to influence policy. The status quo erected entry barriers of all sorts, from public subsidies for parties and fund-raising impediments for organizations without party registration to ineligibility to run for public office without a party nomination. But political entrepreneurs had never been prevented, as they now are, from buying airtime, which is arguably the cornerstone of modern campaigns. The ban raised barriers against groups seeking to mobilize support for new initiatives, react to government encroachment, or challenge the establishment. Potential buyers of television spots for those causes will no doubt argue that their efforts are not aimed at changing electoral preferences. Again, this view is a matter of perspective, and the regulator can order the removal of all advertisements it deems unlawful. It can also fine offenders with amounts set in statute at \$2,500 for individual citizens infringing electoral regulation, \$25,000 for interest groups, and \$500,000 for corporations.[8] Networks in violation of the prohibition to sell advertising for electoral purposes may also face an embargo on selling any advertising for periods of one to thirty-six hours—blank screens with text explaining the IFE's penalty are mandated instead. The use of these remarkable powers is discretionary.

In addition to shifts favoring parties against social actors, the reform had distributive consequences within parties. The new balance favors party leaders against the rank and file. Prohibitions of personal promotion and impediments against buying advertisement spots affected incumbents with access to government televised communication (such as members of the cabinet, governors, and legislative party leaders) much less than other ambitious politicians. Although they are barred from explicitly campaigning before precampaigns start, the former can improve their name recognition through official advertisements (as well as in the ordinary course of their jobs). Governor Enrique Peña Nieto was particularly adept at circumventing the legal prohibitions on campaigning with nightly infomercials on major networks presented as official advertisements of the State of Mexico.

Conclusion

How strong Mexican parties appear depends on one's perspective. The party in power looks robust. Members of congress routinely toe the party line. Between 2006 and 2012, 99%, 98%, and 93% of PAN, PRI, and PRD federal deputies voted cohesively on typical roll call votes, respectively, with negligible drops when only votes pitting half or more of one party against half or more of another are considered; the latter are relatively rare (Magar 2012). Legislative parties represent different interests from each other, expressed in systematic differences in members' apparent policy positions (Cantú, Desposato, and Magar 2014) and attitudes (Estévez and Magaloni 2000). This assessment of the Mexican party system accords with Mainwaring and Scully's (1995) classification of Mexico as one of Latin America's institutionalized party systems.

The party in the electorate looks much less impressive, as Lawson (chap. 1), Greene (chap. 6), and Jorge I. Domínguez (chap. 11) demonstrate in this volume. Volatility in vote intentions across three presidential races, and also during each of them, remains much more pronounced than in established democracies. Two-fifths of interviewees in *Reforma*'s quarterly polls, and often more, are self-declared independents.

And herein lies a paradox of insulation, exacerbated by the electoral reforms of 2007. Failure to grow solid roots in society has led the parties to further insulate themselves from competition. Entry barriers to the party system have waxed and waned since the mid-twentieth century (Molinar 1991). The public subsidies and limits on private money adopted in 1996 began a new trend toward higher barriers; the new ban on paid advertising has built upon them. But preventing competition hardly seems like a formula for stronger parties in the longer term.

As Estévez (2007) pointed out, the perhaps most puzzling aspect of the 2007 reform is how politicians appear to have willingly abdicated their right to challenge party leaders in the future. The effects of blocking vertical mobility inside the parties would be felt more intensely as the new institutions age. Recent hopefuls rose to prominence in politics under the status quo, but next generations will be muzzled by and financially dependent on party leaders. Against all odds, the Pacto por México between major party leaders and president Peña Nieto to push major legislative reforms achieved historical change in 2013 by removing the eight-decade-long ban on immediate reelection for legislators and mayors. While many crucial details of the new electoral reform remain undefined, this major change promises to contribute greatly to the reversal of trends toward partyocracy discussed in this chapter. Incumbents and mayors in their districts now have incentives to pay systematic attention to the interests of core constituents, and not just to party leaders at the state and national level. As a result, examination of whether campaigns in Mexico continue to be shaped by a heavily regulated system dominated by party leaders who rely on large public subsidies or start being shaped more distinctly by local forces will open an exciting area for research in 2018, when the first set of elected officers will face no single-term limit.

NOTES

1. Important changes of less relevance to this volume were also adopted. See Casar (2009), Langston (2009), Serra (2012), and Woldenberg (2008) for comprehensive analytical descriptions of the reform, and essays in Córdoba and Salazar (2008) for detailed changes at the constitutional and statutory levels.

2. The executive order also allows networks that do not receive federal executive spots for broadcasting to use the corresponding time as they see fit. The president can thus raise or lower network taxes at will. The Interior Ministry's bimonthly reports of official time usage for 2010 and the start of 2011 (at http://www.rtc.gob.mx/NuevoSitio /tiempos_oficiales.php) reveal that, in nonelection years, the size of "state time" (thirty minutes daily) relative to "fiscal time" (up to eighteen minutes daily) varies widely. On average, the latter add to 31%, down substantively from the 37.5% it could weigh if the executive were extracting the full extent of the tax. In election years, however, the working breakdown mandated by Article 59 of the *Ley Federal de Radio y Televisión* and the

Decreto presidencial of October 10, 2002, is less important, as networks are forced to grant exactly forty-eight minutes daily to the IFE, who also instructs them what to broadcast.

3. These calculations are available from the author upon request.

4. Computing a rating-weighted average price with Dr. Simi's produces the following: Reported broadcasting prices between April 25 and 28, 2006, were 33,240 pesos ($3,022 on channel 4, 3:18 p.m., news), 120,000 pesos ($10,900 on channel 4, 9:27 p.m., *Noticas con Adela*), 123,000 pesos ($11,182 on channel 4, 8:25 a.m., *Cristal con que se mira*), 144,900 pesos ($13,173 on channel 2, 6:20 a.m., *Primero noticias*), and 222,500 pesos ($20,227 on channel 13, 8:40 p.m., *Noticias de 7 a 9*). If two high-rating, three medium-rating, and thirteen low-rating television hours are assumed between 6:00 a.m. and midnight, with prices per four daily minutes at 200,000, 100,000, and 25,000 pesos, respectively, the average hourly cost is 854,000 pesos, or about half the original average. The volume discount would be a further 33%, yielding a final figure of 555,000 pesos or $50,000.

5. The figures were corrected for inflation (5.1 billion 2006 pesos are 6.7 billion 2012 pesos), and the actual exchange rates (11 to 1 in 2006, 12.5 to 1 in 2012) were used to obtain the figures reported in the text.

6. No attempt to estimate the public subsidy to private donations ratio before the 1996 reform could be found. Yet public subsidies were far from generous at the time, sufficing maybe for the survival of minor parties who routinely nominated the PRI's presidential candidate and needed fewer campaign funds. The medium (PAN) and large (PRI) parties needed funds from supporters, and private donations were unregulated prior to 1996 (Prud'homme, Morales, Apreza, and Villavicencio 1993, 85). So it is fair to infer that private money (legal or not) was the dominant party-funding source at the time.

7. A national telephone poll taken within days of the TRIFE's decision revealed that 45% of respondents considered the reprimand to be an insufficient penalty for Fox's interventions, versus 41% who saw it sufficient (*Reforma* 2006).

8. Article 354.d of the Federal Electoral Code also contemplated an additional fine, double the price paid by citizens and corporation for spots purchased. The Mexican Supreme Court invalidated this provision in 2008.

REFERENCES

Baños, Marco Antonio. 2013. "Las claves del dictamen." *Voz y Voto* 241: 19–22. Boaz, David. 2013. "Dollars per Vote in the Presidential Election." *Cato at Liberty* (blog), January 17. http://www.cato.org/blog/dollars-vote-presidential-election.

Cantú, Francisco, Scott Desposato, and Eric Magar. 2014. "Consideraciones metodológicas para estudiantes de política legislativa mexicana: Sesgo por selección en votaciones nominales." *Política y Gobierno* 21, no. 1: 25–53.

Cantú, Jesús. 2009. "El tribunal cancela la libertad de expresión en la propaganda electoral." In *Democracia sin garantes: Las autoridades vs. la reforma electoral*, ed. Lorenzo Córdoba and Pedro Salazar, 107–24. Mexico City: Universidad Nacional Autónoma de México.

Casar, María Amparo. 2009. "Anatomía de una reforma electoral." *Nexos* 382: 68–73.

Commission nationale des comptes de campagne et desfinancements politiques. 2013. "Home page." http://www.cnccfp.fr/.

Córdoba, Lorenzo. 2008. "Las razones y el sentido de la reforma electoral de 2007–2008." In *Estudios sobre la reforma electoral 2007: Hacia un nuevo modelo*, ed. Lorenzo Córdoba and Pedro Salazar, 47–70. Mexico City: Tribunal Electoral del Poder Judicial de la Federación.

Córdova, Lorenzo. 2013. "Ficción contable." *Voz y Voto* 246: 17–21.

Córdoba, Lorenzo, and Pedro Salazar, eds. 2008. *Estudios sobre la reforma electoral 2007: Hacia un nuevo modelo.* Mexico City: Tribunal Electoral del Poder Judicial de la Federación.

———. 2009. *Democracia sin garantes: Las autoridades vs. la reforma electoral.* Mexico City: Universidad Nacional Autónoma de México.

Cristalinas Kaulitz, Alfredo. 2013. "Tope y rebase." *Voz y Voto* 246: 22–25.

Cox, Gary W., and Eric Magar. 1999. "How Much Is Majority Status in the US Congress Worth?" *American Political Science Review* 93, no. 1: 299–309.

Domínguez, Jorge I., and Chappell H. Lawson, eds. 2004. *Mexico's Pivotal Democratic Election: Candidates, Voters, and the Presidential Campaign of 2000.* Stanford, CA: Stanford University Press.

Domínguez, Jorge I., Chappell H. Lawson, and Alejandro Moreno, eds. 2009. *Consolidating Mexico's Democracy: The 2006 Presidential Campaign in Comparative Perspective.* Baltimore: Johns Hopkins University Press.

Dresser, Denise. 2007. "País feudal." *Reforma,* September 24.

Estévez, Federico. 2007. "Ulises Criollo y el canto de las sirenas." In *Reforma constitucional en materia electoral 2007: Diversos enfoques para su estudio,* ed. Alberto Benítez and José Roldán Xopa, 67–78. Mexico City: Partido Nueva Alianza.

Estévez, Federico, and Beatriz Magaloni. 2000. "Legislative Parties and Their Constituencies in the Budget Battle of 1997." Working paper, Department of Political Science, Instituto Tecnológico Autónomo de México, Mexico City.

Estévez, Federico, Eric Magar, and Guillermo Rosas. 2008. "Partisanship in Non-Partisan Electoral Agencies and Democratic Compliance: Evidence from Mexico's Federal Electoral Institute." *Electoral Studies* 27, no. 2, 257–71.

IFE. Federal Electoral Institute. 2006. *Elecciones federales 2006: Equidad y transparencia en la contienda electoral.* Mexico City: IFE.

———. 2008. "Anexo 2: Cuadro comparativo de Reformas al Código Federal de Instituciones y Procedimientos Electorales." Mexico City: Centro de Desarrollo Democrático del Instituto Federal Electoral y Centro de Capacitiación Judicial Electoral del Tribunal Electoral del Poder Judicial de la Federación.

———. 2010. "El IFE y el costo de la vida democrática en México." Mexico City: IFE.

———. 2012. "Financiamiento público a Partidos Políticos 1997–2012." Mexico City: IFE. http://www.ife.org.mx/docs/IFE-v2/DEPPP/PartidosPoliticosyFinanciamiento/DEPPP-financiamiento/financiamientopublicopartidosnacionales/FinanPublico-PPNs1997-2012.pdf.

Langston, Joy. 2009. "Las reformas al COFIPE, 2007." *Política y Gobierno* theme volume 2009: 245–72.

Lau, Richard R., Lee Sigelman, Caroline Heldman, and Paul Babbitt. 1999. "The Effects of Negative Political Advertisements: A Meta-Analytic Assessment." *American Political Science Review* 93, no. 4: 851–75.

Lawson, Chappell. 2009. "Introduction." In *Consolidating Mexico's Democracy: The 2006 Presidential Campaign in Comparative Perspective,* ed. Jorge I. Domínguez, Chappell Lawson, and Alejandro Moreno. Baltimore: Johns Hopkins University Press.

Magar, Eric. 2012. "Roll Call Votes in the 60th and 61st Legislatures of the Mexican Chamber of Deputies." http://ericmagar.com/data/rollcall/dipFed/README.

Magar, Eric, and Vidal Romero. 2008. "México: Reformas Pese a un Gobierno Dividido." *Revista de Ciencia Política* 28, no. 1: 265–85.

Mainwaring, Scott, and Timothy Scully. 1995. *Building Democratic Institutions: Party Systems in Latin America.* Stanford, CA: Stanford University Press.

México Evalúa. 2013. "El costo de las elecciones presidenciales de 2012." Mexico City: México Evalúa, Centro de Análisis de Políticas Públicas.

Molinar, Juan. 1991. *El tiempo de la legitimidad*. Mexico City: Cal y Arena.

Moreno, Alejandro. 2003. *El votante mexicano: Democracia, actitudes políticas y conducta electoral*. Mexico City: Fondo de Cultura Económica.

———. 2009. *La decisión electoral: Votantes, partidos y democracia en México*. Mexico City: Porrúa.

Murayama, Ciro. 2009. "Reforma para la consolidació democrática vs. contrarreforma desde el interés privado." In *Democracia sin garantes: Las autoridades vs. la reforma electoral*, ed. Lorenzo Córdoba and Pedro Salazar, 1–27. Mexico City: Universidad Nacional Autónoma de México.

Olson, Mancur. 1965. *The Logic of Collective Action*. Cambridge, MA: Harvard University Press.

Popkin, Samuel L. 1991. *The Reasoning Voter: Communication and Persuasion in Presidential Campaigns*. Chicago: University of Chicago Press.

Prud'homme, Jean François, Rodrigo Morales, Inés Castro Apreza, and Lorena Villavicencio. 1993. "Alternativas para la regulación y el control del financiamiento y gasto de los partidos políticos en México." In *Dinero y partidos*, ed. Jorge Alcocer, 15–145. Mexico City: Nuevo Horizonte.

Reforma. 2006. "Encuesta: Avalan resolución del TEPJF." *Reforma*, September 5, 12.

Roldán Xopa, José. 2010. "Libertad de expresión y equidad: La Constitución contra sí misma?" Cuaderno 38, Documentos de trabajo del Departamento Académico de Derecho. Mexico City: Instituto Tecnológico Autónomo de México.

Romero, Vidal. 2012. "No más financiamiento público a partidos políticos." *ADN Politico*, November 18. http://www.adnpolitico.com/opinion/2012/11/17/opinion-no-mas-finan ciamiento-publico-a-partidos-politicos.

Salazar, Pedro. 2008. "La reforma constitucional: Una apuesta ambiciosa." In *Estudios sobre la reforma electoral 2007: Hacia un nuevo modelo*, ed. Lorenzo Córdoba and Pedro Salazar, 73–94. Mexico City: Tribunal Electoral del Poder Judicial de la Federación.

———. 2009. "Una corte, una jueza, y un réquiem para la reforma constitucional electoral." In *Democracia sin garantes: Las autoridades vs. la reforma electoral*, ed. Lorenzo Córdoba and Pedro Salazar, 29–57. Mexico City: Universidad Nacional Autónoma de México.

Sarmiento, Sergio. 2007. "Nueva censura." *Reforma*, September 24. http://busquedas. gruporeforma.com/reforma/Documentos/DocumentoImpresa.aspx?Valores Forma=914888-1066,sarmiento%20nueva%20censura&_ec_=1.

Serra, Gilles. 2012. "The Risk of Partyarchy and Democratic Backsliding Mexico's 2007 Electoral Reform." *Taiwan Journal of Democracy* 8, no. 1: 31–56.

Tribunal Electoral del Poder Judicial Federal. TEPJF. 2006. "Dictamen relativo al cómputo final de la elección de presidente de los Estados Unidos Mexicanos, declaración de validez de la elección y presidente electo." Mexico City: Tribunal Electoral del Poder Judicial Federal. http://www.te.gob.mx/documentacion/publicaciones/informes /dictamen.pdf.

Woldenberg, José. 2008. "Estampas de la reforma." In *Estudios sobre la reforma electoral 2007: Hacia un nuevo modelo*, ed. Lorenzo Córdoba and Pedro Salazar, 27–43. Mexico City: Tribunal Electoral del Poder Judicial de la Federación.

4

Time to Turn Back the Clock?

*Retrospective Judgments of the Single-Party Era and
Support for the Institutional Revolutionary Party in 2012*

JAMES A. McCANN

No model of voting choices in any national context would be complete without taking into account citizen evaluations of government performance. Since the last round of elections, have officeholders presided over a growing economy? Is the crime rate falling, and is there less fear of being victimized? In general, has the country been going on the right or wrong track? Such assessments are ubiquitous in academic survey instruments because they are thought to correlate closely with electoral preferences. Of course, many other factors contribute to the voting calculus, and the effects of government performance judgments have been found to vary considerably across countries or across subpopulations within countries (see, e.g., Alcañiz and Hellwig 2011; Anderson 2007; Duch 2001; Fiorina 1981; Gomez and Wilson 2006). Nevertheless, as Lewis-Beck and Stegmaier (2007) note in their review of the scholarly literature on retrospective voting, it is beyond question that when times are good in a democracy, incumbent parties tend to be returned to office following an election. In bad times, they are liable to be cast out. This verdict has undeniable normative appeal. When times are tough, incumbent parties *should* be on the defensive.

In this chapter, I consider a dimension of performance evaluation that has not received nearly as much scrutiny but could be relevant for voters in newer democracies with some partisan carryover from the pretransition period. Many transitions to democracy involve a clean break with the past, with a ruling party or authoritarian figure being completely discredited, removed, and replaced with a fresh partisan configuration. But in a number of other instances, one of the candidates or parties competing for votes has an actual or symbolic connection to the former hegemonic party or ruling clique; this has been a common experience in former Communist Europe but also in countries as diverse in their posttransition circumstances as Chile, South Korea, and Taiwan. In these cases, comparisons between two different forms of governing arrangements or regimes may become salient for voters. In addition to asking whether the country has become better or worse off under the incumbent administration—the conventional retrospective performance judgment—citizens might also consider whether times were better or worse in an earlier era, before the move to competitive multiparty politics. In the recent past, when power was not dispersed across different branches of government or divided among rival parties, was the country in better shape? Was the economy better managed? Was there more opportunity? More stability, less social unrest, and more unity of purpose? The grave economic challenges that many democracies faced during and following the 2008–9 global recession could make "pretransition/posttransition" comparisons of this sort particularly accessible. Even without referring directly to governing accomplishments in the pretransition period, the candidate with links to the former ruling party or clique could appeal to voters who believe that trying times call for bolder and better orchestrated leadership reminiscent of that earlier era.

This form of retrospective voting may imply a troubling loss of faith in basic democratic principles among citizens, and might serve as a harbinger of a return to single-party rule. Without widespread support in both good times and bad, a system of multiparty pluralist representation premised on the checking and balancing of competing interests cannot last long (Dahl 1956, 132–33; Taylor-Robinson and Ura 2013). It does not necessarily follow, however, that voters who perceive flaws in the fledgling multiparty policy-making environment and support a candidate with ties to the pretransition system will also wish to turn back the clock, which would surely be a radical step. Such a voting choice could instead stem from a belief that officials should act in a more efficient and coordinated—but still publicly accountable—way to solve major national problems, or from simple feelings of nostalgia for a bygone political era, rather than a wish to revive an authoritarian state.[1]

I examine these themes in the context of the 2012 elections in Mexico, a time when the transition to competitive multiparty democracy would still have been fresh in the minds of adult voters. During the campaign, Enrique Peña Nieto, the presidential nominee of the former ruling party, took an early lead over his main rivals, Josefina Vázquez Mota of the National Action Party (PAN) and Andrés Manuel López Obrador of the Party of the Democratic Revolution (PRD), and ultimately won nearly four out of ten votes, a marked improvement over the Institutional Revolutionary Party's showing in 2006 and a sufficient margin to make him the plurality winner. The party also garnered over 40% of the seats in the chamber of deputies, retaining the plurality margin it had won in the 2009 midterm elections and nearly doubling the size of its share following the 2006 campaigns. To what extent were these victories a reflection of dissatisfaction with posttransition politics?

The Mexico 2012 Panel Study offers much analytical leverage to address this question. The results indicate that a substantial portion of the public believed that times were indeed better when a single party was in control, and that Peña Nieto and the PRI benefited from this judgment. Reassuringly, however, retrospective voting in this mold was not accompanied by a marked downward shift in support for democratic governance. The ideals of democratic representation continue to resonate with most Mexicans, even if many believed on the day of the election that the new multiparty system was not as successful in some respects as the Institutional Revolutionary Party of yesteryear. In the following sections I develop these points, beginning with an overview of voting choices during this transitional stage in Mexican politics.

Theoretical Background

Within Mexico, the systematic examination of voting behavior began in earnest in the 1980s, when large-scale scientifically sound surveys of the Mexican electorate first became widely available to scholars. Initial studies confirmed that assessments of economic performance, presidential approval ratings, evaluations of candidates, and issue stances could all shape electoral choices to a significant extent. In many respects, Mexican voters in the 1980s and 90s resembled the citizens of established pluralist democracies. Yet in this pretransition era the principal divide within the electorate was over the soundness of the political order itself and the desirability of multiparty democracy (Domínguez and McCann 1996; Molinar Horcasitas 1991; Moreno 1998). Is the dominant-party system still uniquely suited to govern the country? Would there be an increase in social unrest if the PRI were to lose control? Would economic performance suffer if the country moved toward more open multiparty democracy? Answers to such questions differentiated to a considerable degree those voters who backed the ruling party in spite of its well-recognized faults from those who moved toward one of the opposition partisan camps. Mexican citizens are portrayed in this literature as pragmatic and somewhat risk averse (Cinta 1999;

Morgenstern and Zechmeister 2001). Barring major doubts about the viability of the dominant-party regime, they remained with it.

This mind-set among voters in the 1980s and 90s was in keeping with the founding mission of the PRI. Although the Mexican Constitution, drafted in 1917 in the final stages of the revolution, formally separates political power across the branches of government and recognizes the rights of parties to organize and compete in elections, the PRI became the sole focal point of politics in Mexico for most of the twentieth century. In the 1920s, national governing institutions were unstable and political violence was rampant, particularly during elections. In an attempt to end the bloodshed, former president Plutarco Elías Calles and other leading figures created a single extraconstitutional partisan organization in 1929 to manage disputes among regional strongmen and factions. Order was maintained by incorporating in machinelike fashion as many significant economic and political groups as possible, and offering ambitious office seekers an internal path to power, with the presidency being the ultimate goal. For decades, the PRI routinely won elections with only token opposition (Gillingham 2012).

As challenges to the PRI rose in the late 1990s, however, many analysts anticipated a day when beliefs about the governing system would matter less for voters. Electoral outcomes would instead depend more on evaluations of incumbent officeholders, ideology and issue positions, and partisanship. Following the watershed elections of 2000, it appeared that evaluations of the former dominant-party arrangement would soon become irrelevant. After all, there was no longer any doubt that a president from outside of the PRI could manage the executive branch; nor did divided government necessarily lead to unrest and economic crisis. Models of electoral behavior in 2006 seemingly confirmed this expectation (Beltrán 2009; Benton 2009; Domínguez, Lawson, and Moreno 2009; Moreno 2009). Partisanship, ideological positioning, perceptions of the major party candidates, evaluations of governmental performance in the recent past—these criteria and others that we would expect to find in any democracy loomed large in the minds of voters in Mexico.

But these attitudes do not yet constitute solid "anchors" in Mexican public opinion. Over the course of major national campaigns in this posttransition environment, partisan ties, candidate preferences, and political evaluations have been subject to change (Camp 2013; Greene 2011; McCann and Lawson 2003; see also Kenneth F. Greene, chap. 6, this volume). At the same time, one of the constants within Mexican politics has been the centrality of the Institutional Revolutionary Party. Even though the party lost the presidential race in 2000 and 2006, its organizational apparatus remained strong in all parts of the country, its connections to major media outlets continued to be quite close, and it governed approximately two-thirds of the states as of early 2012. Views of the party and its legacy might well have remained salient for much of the mass public years after the transition to multiparty competition. In the 2012 campaign, the phrase "You Know Me" came up frequently in the political advertising of Enrique Peña Nieto. While voters were almost certainly better acquainted with the figure of Andrés Manuel López Obrador, who had run for president once before and nearly won, there is no doubt that Peña Nieto's party would have been a common reference point in Mexican politics.

In a time of grave national challenges and uncertainty—certainly a description of the policy-making environment in Mexico in 2012—the fact that the PRI was more of a known quantity would likely have been an asset for risk-averse voters.[2] The bloodshed and economic hardship that characterized the presidential administration of Felipe Calderón of the National Action Party would have contrasted with the image that the PRI promoted about itself, namely, that for generations it has been uniquely equipped to govern. Because the Party of the Democratic Revolution was formed much more recently, in 1989, and was closely identified with the new multiparty governing system—an arrangement that many Mexicans in 2012 might have judged to be ineffective—the PRD may not have been a plausible alternative to the PAN.

Tucker (2006) posits similar decision-making dynamics in the multiparty elections that took place beginning in the mid-1990s in the emerging democracies of Eastern Europe. In the years following a transition away from one-party rule in the former Soviet bloc, Tucker argues that voters who suffer under the new political system "are likely to want to avoid putting parties into power whose primary identity is with the transition . . . if the voter is particularly concerned about the current state of the economy, then she knows at least one type of party that in the past—at least on the surface—ruled in a period of time without the current economic difficulties. Even if a return to the past is not explicitly desired, the voter may still be more likely to have confidence in Old Regime parties to address the current economic ills than any of the other parties" (46).

The above discussion suggests two hypotheses regarding public opinion and voting decisions in the 2012 Mexican elections. First, in the crisis environment of these campaigns, we would expect Mexicans to exhibit rather well-developed judgments concerning the legacy of the PRI as well as how the older dominant-party governing framework compared to the new multiparty system. Second, these evaluations were likely to have been relevant for voters as they went to the polls, even after controls were in place for more commonly used measures of incumbent government performance (e.g., presidential approval ratings), evaluations of the Mexican economy, partisan identifications, ideological stances, and other socioeconomic and demographic factors that have been linked to electoral behavior in this context. I consider these hypotheses below.

Empirical Findings

The preelection wave of the Mexico 2012 Panel Study, which was fielded in April of that year, included one item to capture evaluations of the dominant-party era: "When the PRI controlled the federal government, conditions around the country were better. Do you agree or disagree with this statement?" Respondents had little trouble offering opinions on the legacy of the former system. Only 8% were unsure or could not answer the question.[3]

Not surprisingly, opinions on whether Mexico was in better shape when the PRI was in charge overlapped quite strongly with identification as a *priísta*, which approximately 30% of the sample did in April, and beliefs about Enrique Peña Nieto's personal leadership abilities (the extent to which he could manage the economy effectively and reduce unemployment, corruption, and crime). The correlations in these cases surpass .30. As one would expect, attitudes toward the pretransition governing system also correlate with presidential approval ratings for Felipe Calderón, perceptions of Mexican economic performance over the last twelve months, and evaluations of government policies to fight crime. These latter correlations tell us that judgments regarding the policy-making legacy of the PRI are not set in stone, but respond to the ebb and flow of contemporary successes and failures in government. While we do not have data on how Mexicans evaluated the "old regime" before the shock of the global recession and the escalation of violence around the country, it is likely that relatively few respondents in a relatively tranquil period would have looked more favorably on the dominant-party system in comparison to the posttransition political environment.

As shown in the first column of figure 4.1, at the early stage of the 2012 general election campaign the public was split nearly evenly on whether the country was in better shape when governing institutions were unified under a single party. One out of five respondents strongly agreed with the statement,

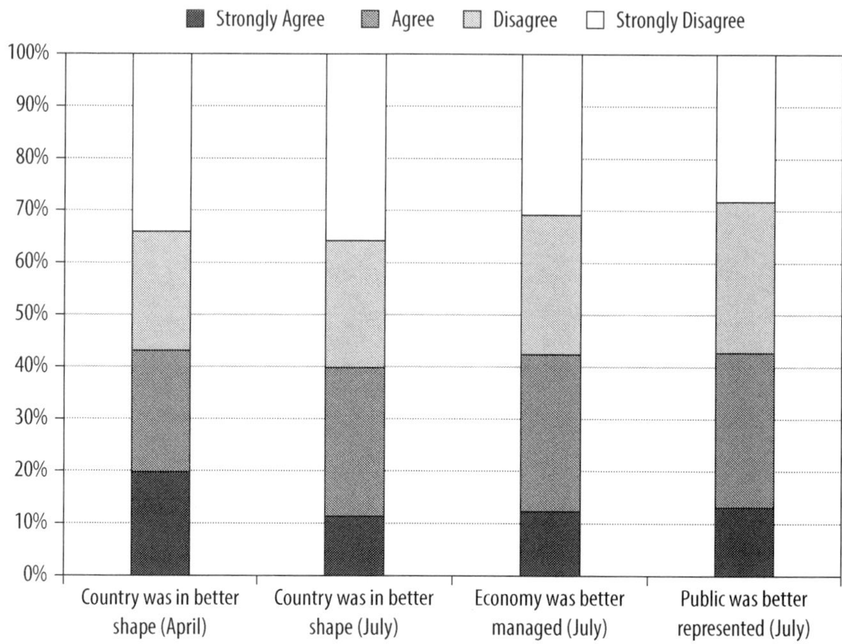

Figure 4.1. Agree or disagree: When the PRI controlled the government, the . . .

and another 23% agreed but not strongly. This division persisted over the remainder of the campaign. In the second wave of the panel study the same item was put to respondents along with two fresh retrospective questions: whether the economy was better managed under the PRI, and whether the Mexican public had been better represented.

Following the election the aggregate distribution of opinion on "whether the country was better when the PRI controlled the federal government" was essentially what it had been in April. Somewhat fewer respondents strongly agreed with the statement, but this was balanced by the slightly greater number that simply agreed. Responses to the two new items in the postelection wave mirror these patterns. Approximately 40% agreed that the dominant-party regime did a better job of managing the economy and representing the public.

The consistency of these attitude responses suggests that opinions about the pretransition PRI had become fairly hardened by the time of the April survey, and that when rendering judgments about this era Mexicans do not differentiate finely among the various tasks of government. The number of respondents stating that the PRI did a better job in its day of managing the economy is approximately equal to the proportion believing that the general public had been better represented as well, implying that the impression one had of the former system and its capability to govern was quite general, reflecting an overall disposition toward life under a dominant-party state vis-à-vis the current divided and polarizing multiparty system.

This characterization of retrospective dispositions can be examined more fully through an individual-level structural equation model, where the three items from the postelection wave are factor analyzed and the continuity in responses is gauged. If Mexicans possess a meaningful general orientation toward unified versus divided government, it should be evident in the factor loadings and the stability coefficient. The results from this structural equation model are given in figure 4.2.[4]

The paths linking the three items from the postelection wave to the underlying factor are quite high, indicating that a general latent disposition shaped responses to these questions. To believe that the country was in better shape when the PRI was in control implies also a belief that the ruling party had done a good job representing the interests of the general public and that the economy was better managed. The standardized continuity coefficient of .50 indicates substantial stability in these judgments. The campaigns had a relatively modest impact on these retrospective attitudes. This level of stability from one wave to the next is comparable to that for partisan identifications, and is slightly higher than that for presidential approval ratings and perceptions of leadership capabilities for the three main presidential contenders.

The findings in figure 4.2 suggest that in the political environment of the 2012 campaigns, beliefs about the "old" and "new" governing systems were salient for voters. The degree of salience can be probed further by examining the impact of these retrospective assessments on voting choices. If respondents who saw the PRI in a positive light relied on these attitudes at the ballot box on July 1, we would expect significant effects at both the presidential and legislative levels. Simple bivariate analyses show that views of the PRI regime aligned closely with support for Peña Nieto and PRI candidates for the chamber of deputies. The correlation between a summary index of the three retrospective items in the second wave of the survey and voting for Peña is a strong .59; the correlation between this index and support for a PRI legislative candidate is an even stronger .77. Clearly, on the day of the election if we knew how citizens viewed Mexican politics before the transition to multiparty democracy, we could predict with a great deal of accuracy whether they voted for the PRI—not

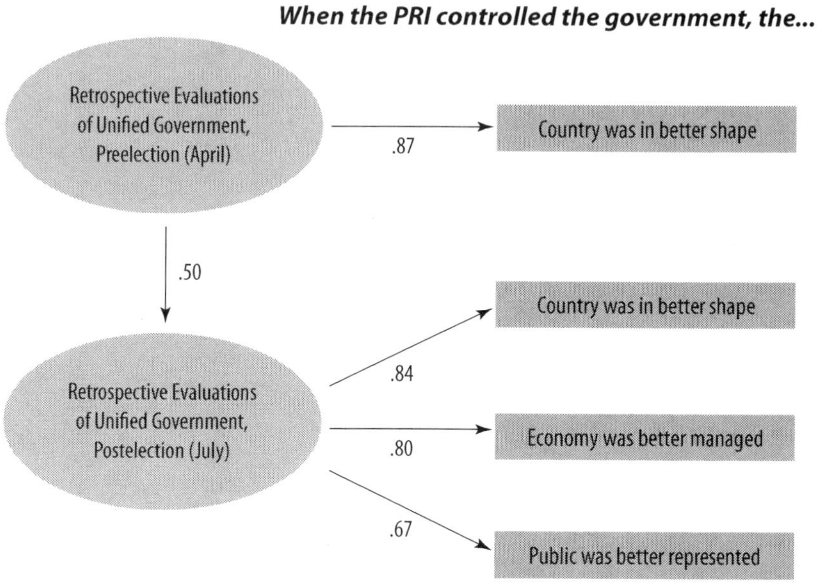

When the PRI controlled the government, the...

Figure 4.2. Evaluations of unified government under the PRI: Measurement models and stability from April to July

just for the most visible leader of the party running for the presidency, but the ensemble of politicians who comprise the party as an institution.

Because evaluations of governance in the pretransition period overlap with many other variables that also explain the vote, however, it is necessary to estimate multivariate models. Based on the literature on electoral behavior in Mexico, the most relevant variables to take into account are those mentioned above as correlates of retrospective evaluations of the PRI—partisan identification, presidential approval ratings, perceptions of economic performance, changes in one's personal finances in the recent past, performance evaluations for the Calderón administration in the fight against crime, and ratings of the leadership qualities of the three major presidential nominees—plus general ideological orientations and several socioeconomic and demographic traits (gender, age, level of education, household affluence, and religious attendance). These various controls could be considered the "standard model" of voting choices in Mexico (McCann 2012; Moreno 2009).[5] Screening out their effects will considerably lessen the estimated impact of beliefs about the PRI regime on voting choices.

The ancillary appendix to this chapter (available at www.press.jhu.edu) gives the coefficients from two multivariate regression models. Because the dependent variables are presidential and congressional choices, I utilize a multino-mial logistic regression specification.[6] The coefficients from these regression models and their respective standard errors are relegated to an ancillary appendix because they are not of great substantive concern. The more relevant quantity of interest is the partial impact of retrospective evaluations of policy making under the PRI on the probability of supporting Peña Nieto and the legislative candidates from his party. These effects are statistically significant ($p < .05$) and undeniably noteworthy, as illustrated in figure 4.3. When calculating these fitted probability forecasts, all of the control variables from the "standard model" are fixed to their mean values.

In the case of presidential voting, respondents who disagreed that conditions were better, that the economy was better managed, and that government was more representative when the Institutional Revolutionary Party was in control are estimated to have had only slightly more than a one-in-four chance of backing the PRI standard bearer. In the legislative elections, this probability drops even further. At the other end of the evaluation scale, the multinomial regression models point to more than a 50% chance of supporting candidates from the PRI, with the probability being particularly high for legislative races.

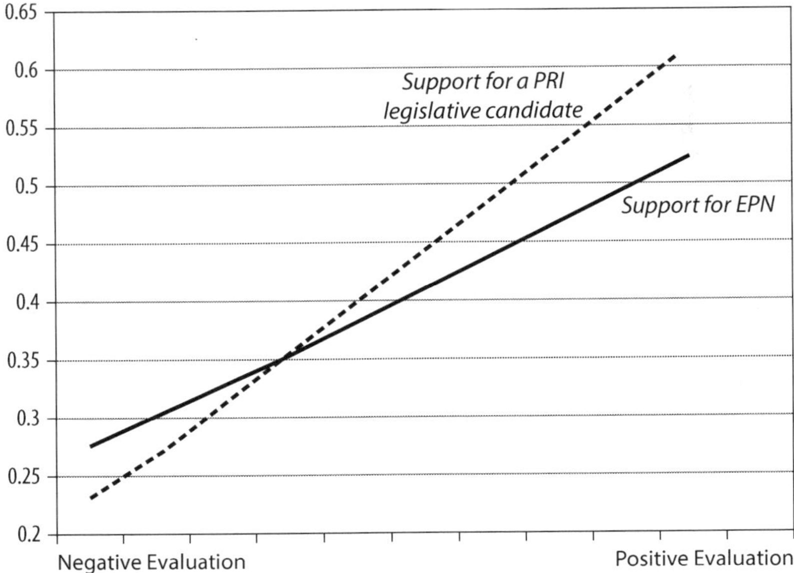

Figure 4.3. Predicted probability of voting for the PRI by retrospective evaluations of policy making under the dominant-party system

The legacy of the former ruling party shaped to a profound degree the scope of the PRI victory in this era of multiparty democracy.

To simplify the presentation in figure 4.3, voting choice probabilities for the two other presidential contenders and congressional candidates from the PAN and PRD are not drawn. None of these candidates was forecasted to do well among voters who thought that times were comparatively better under the PRI. For those respondents who did not believe that the pretransition system served the country well, voting preferences tended to be split roughly equally between the PRI's two rival parties. As in voting models estimated in the pretransition period (Domínguez and McCann 1996; Greene 2007), this dimension of choice provided a strategic advantage to the PRI. The National Action Party and the Party of the Democratic Revolution competed for support at the "multiparty governance is better" end of the evaluation scale, while among citizens who had a more positive view of unified governance in the earlier era the former ruling party garnered the lion's share of votes in both the presidential and congressional races.

To place the effect of this retrospective dimension in the context of the other predictors in the multivariate regression models, figure 4.4A displays the changes in expected probability of support for Peña Nieto and PRI legislative candidates as the value of each predictor moves from its lowest to highest score.[7] As with the probability estimates presented in figure 4.3, these differences are calculated from the findings in the ancillary appendix (www.press.jhu.edu). Statistically significant predictors are indicated by an asterisk ($p < .05$).

Regarding support for Peña Nieto, the most striking effects are for leadership trait evaluations and personal identification with the PRI. All else equal, the multinomial logistic regression model implies that a respondent with the most positive impression possible of the PRI standard-bearer would be over 80% more likely to vote for him compared to Mexicans who had the most negative view. While this difference is huge, it is not surprising. In many democratic systems around the world, perceptions of candidate qualities can loom large in the voting calculus. Such effects may be particularly pronounced in younger democracies (Costa Lobo 2006). Identification as a *priísta* also shaped the vote for Peña Nieto to a considerable degree. The difference in probabilities in this case, where PRI identifiers are compared to political independents, surpasses .60. This large effect is not unexpected either, however. In any model of the vote, partisanship is typically among the strongest predictors. When these factors and others are held constant, we see that retrospective evaluations of the old system of dominant-party governance in the pretransition period mattered as much in shaping the vote for Peña Nieto as personal impressions of Vázquez Mota and López Obrador did in moving citizens away from the PRI nominee. Approval ratings for President Calderón, evaluations of government performance on fighting crime, and beliefs about the trajectory of the Mexican economy mattered relatively little in comparison to views of the PRI regime.

Turning to the model of support for PRI legislative candidates, figure 4.4B indicates that party identification was by far the most consequential predictor, followed by the coattails that Peña Nieto offered. In each case, the swing in probabilities of PRI support is over 50%. According to the model, the third-strongest factor in shaping the congressional vote for the PRI is evaluation of the previous single-party system. The impact of this predictor again trumps the effects of the more conventional measures of retrospective performance evaluations.

Taken together, these findings demonstrate that a large portion of the Mexican electorate was fed up with "business as usual" to the point that politics in the pretransition era was more attractive by comparison. These frustrations helped propel Peña Nieto and PRI congressional candidates. In a less crisis-ridden decision-making environment, it is likely that such retrospective judgments would not have been as relevant for voters.[8] The high level of stability in these attitudes suggests, however, that opinions crystallized early in the campaign. In fact, if the single item from the first wave of the survey on whether "times were better when the PRI controlled the entire federal government" is entered as a predictor into the multinomial regression models in place of the composite index of retrospective assessments from the postelection wave, the findings are not substantively altered.[9]

If Mexican voters gravitated toward the PRI in part because life under a dominant-party system seemed more attractive than current conditions, does it signify a loss of faith in liberal pluralist democracy? Given the major institutional changes that have taken place in Mexico since the transitional election of 2000, it is exceedingly unlikely that Peña Nieto would ever be able to re-create the old regime at the national level. Nevertheless, if this were possible, would the Mexican electorate approve of such a monumental restructuring of politics, a change that would place Mexico again in the ranks of semidemocratic or authoritarian nations?

A

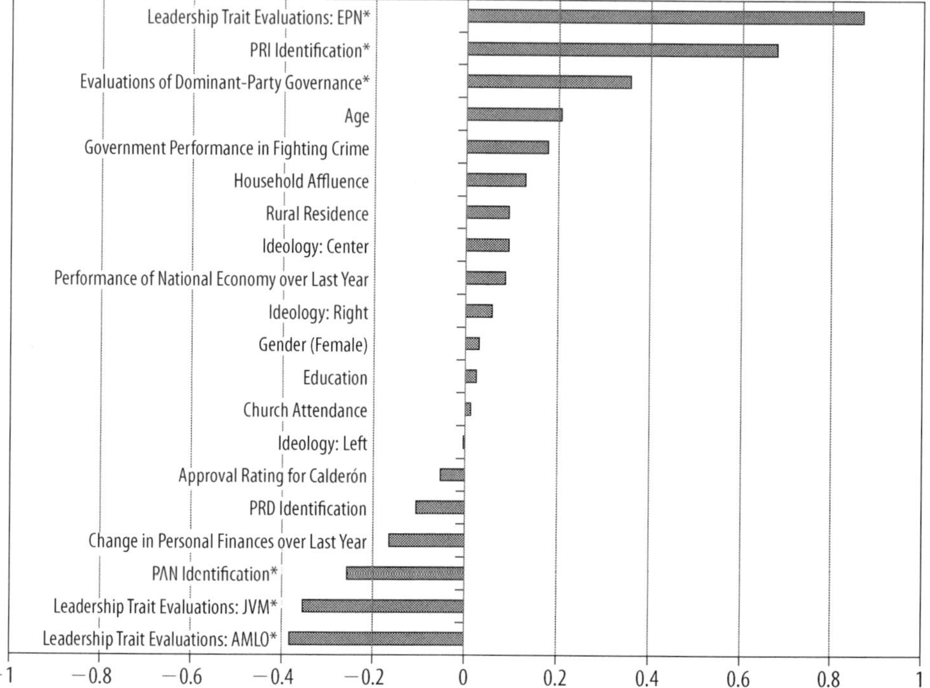

Figure 4.4. Changes in the probability of supporting the PRI in the 2012 elections: Differences between high and low values for each predictor

In a recent essay on the elections, Flores-Macías (2013) sees the electorate as ready for such an authoritarian turn: "the meager achievements of the last twelve years—not enough economic growth but considerable violence—have created greater openness to nondemocratic alternatives" (137). Mexican historian and commentator Lorenzo Meyer voiced a similar view in an interview three weeks before the elections. "There is a kind of longing for the 'good old days' . . . [Mexicans are saying] let us return to the good old days of efficient authoritarianism" (Miller Llana 2012).

Certainly, beliefs about the "good old days" played an important part in Peña Nieto's victory and the success of the PRI in its legislative races. To address whether this is symptomatic of a reemergence of an antidemocratic mind-set in Mexican political culture, however, requires further analysis. The

B

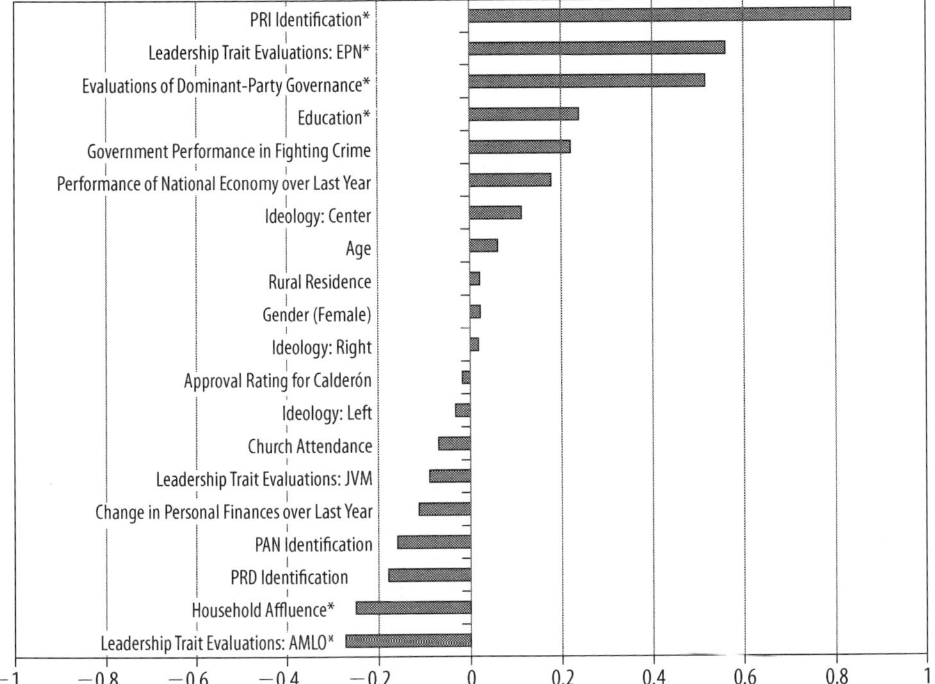

Mexican electorate may have yearned for more efficiency in government, as Lorenzo Meyer writes, but not necessarily a rebirth of an authoritarian state.

Survey data drawn from the Latin American Public Opinion Project (LAPOP) at Vanderbilt University can shed additional light on whether disappointments with policymakers led to a more general rejection of democratic principles. Every two years between 2004 and 2012, LAPOP affiliates in Mexico conducted interviews with large representative samples of respondents to track attitudes toward government officials and representative institutions. The findings from these surveys show that over this eight-year period, Mexicans became appreciably more pessimistic about the workings of multiparty democracy (Moreno and O'Neil 2013; Parás García, Olmedo, López, and Seligson 2011). When asked on the eve of the 2006 elections how proud they were of living under the current political system, nearly 60% of citizens expressed at least a modest amount of pride. In two related items, respondents reported how much respect they felt toward political institutions in Mexico and how much confidence they had in the national congress; approximately 60% of the sample also felt respectful and confident. Similar levels of pride, respect, and confidence are evident in the 2004 LAPOP survey. Such results prompted Parás and López (2007) to write that "Mexico has a stable and comparatively robust democratic culture that can contribute to the consolidation of its democracy" (491). Unfortunately, later surveys conducted after the economic crisis found significantly less pride, respect, and confidence. The level of disappointment with policy-making institutions gauged in the 2012 LAPOP study essentially mirrors what the Mexico 2012 Panel Survey detected when respondents compared the current political system to the pretransition period.[10] Mexicans had become much more pessimistic about governing authorities and institutions.

Along somewhat different lines, the LAPOP questionnaires also included an item that tracked the desirability of democratic systems in principle, without touching on performance evaluations for democratic institutions and officeholders: "With which of the following phrases do you most agree? (A) For people like me, it doesn't matter whether a regime is democratic or non-democratic; (B) Democracy is always preferable to any other type of government; or (C) Under some circumstances, an authoritarian government can be preferable to a democratic one." In contrast to the questions on pride in the workings of the contemporary political system, respect for governing institutions, and confidence in the legislative branch, responses to this item show practically no change over time. In 2004, 74% of the Mexican public saw democracy as most preferable under all circumstances. This margin dropped by a trivial amount in the 2006 sample (73%), rose but also by a trivial amount in 2008 (75%), dropped more significantly in 2010 (66%), but then nearly returned in 2012, just weeks before the official start of the general election campaign, to the levels recorded in 2004, 2006, and 2008 (70%).

A related survey question on support for democracy that appeared on LAPOP instruments in these five years was worded as follows: "On some occasions, democracy does not work. When that happens, there are persons who say that we need a strong leader who does not have to be elected through voting. Others say that even if things do not function, democracy is always best. What do you think?" The percentage believing that democracy is "always best" was high in 2004, 83%, and remained high in the later samples: 88% in 2006, 85% in 2008, 79% in 2010, and 82% in 2012. On the basis of these distributions, a case could be made that Mexicans grew somewhat disenchanted with democratic ideals in

2010 relative to the three previous LAPOP surveys, but by 2012 the democratic political culture appears to have been on the mend. These trends show that it is possible to lose confidence in and respect for democratic policy-making institutions—to be so disappointed that the pretransition regime looks more attractive by comparison—without losing faith in democratic governance itself.

Another perspective on authoritarianism and voting choices can be gained through a battery of items on childrearing preferences that appeared in the second wave of the Mexico 2012 Panel Survey. Should children be taught to be obedient? Should they be reared to be altruistic rather than self-centered, and to be independent? Such questions are frequently utilized to capture an authoritarian disposition in Mexico, the United States, and other democracies (Hetherington and Weiler 2009; Merolla and Zechmeister 2009).[11] Authoritarians favor bringing up children who are obedient, not independently minded, and community oriented rather than self-centered.

Based on responses to these items, one-quarter of the Mexican public espouses authoritarian values. At the other end of the scale, 17% could be considered "anti-authoritarians"; that is, they wish children to be independent and would not emphasize obedience or self-sacrifice. The rest of the public, just over 40%, may be labeled authoritarian to a degree. This index of authoritarian values correlates negatively with education level and household affluence but positively with religious attendance ($p < .01$ in each case). Authoritarianism is also positively correlated with the age of the respondent, though this relationship is not as significant ($p < .05$). There is also a slight correlation with presidential voting choices, with less authoritarian respondents preferring Andrés Manuel López Obrador and the more authoritarian tilting toward Vázquez Mota or Peña Nieto. Importantly, however, this relationship is not particularly striking or statistically significant. While Mexicans are divided over which values are most appropriate to teach children, and these attitudes overlap with socioeconomic and demographic traits that have historically been linked to an authoritarian disposition in Mexico and elsewhere (Almond and Verba 1963), the implications of this cleavage for electoral politics are minor. There is no evidence that an authoritarian mind-set was behind PRI successes in 2012.

Conclusion

One day after being sworn in as president, Enrique Peña Nieto and leaders of the PAN and PRD signed a "Pact for Mexico," whereby the three major parties pledged to collaborate on sweeping reforms in the areas of "rights and freedoms," "economic growth, employment and competition," "security and justice," "transparency and accountability," and "democratic governance." The aims put forward in this pact range from general aspirational goals (e.g., fostering respect for multiculturalism and diversity) to specific program objectives (e.g., placing laptops in fifth- and sixth-grade classrooms). It is too early to tell whether this pact will ultimately reduce gridlock and polarization within governing institutions. Early signs suggest that the major political parties will continue to clash over the issues that dominated debates during the campaigns. For its part, the Mexican public does not possess strong opinions about this agreement. One nonpartisan poll conducted nationally in March 2013 found that the majority of Mexican citizens were unaware of the pact. Among those who had an opinion, most saw the move as benefiting the political parties more than the country as the whole (Parametría 2013).

While Peña Nieto's outreach to the two rival parties may fail to reach a genuine working consensus, his attempt to act in this manner immediately after the inauguration is understandable in light of the findings presented here. Twelve years after the fall of the dominant-party regime, Mexican voters expressed significant doubts about policy making under the current multiparty system. The electorate in Mexico is hardly unique in this regard. Frustrations over a lack of responsibility in government and weaknesses in dealing with the daunting challenges of the day are commonly aired in many democracies. Yet in contexts where the transition away from authoritarianism is relatively recent, any moves to concentrate power in the hands of an executive or a partisan clique cannot help but raise red flags for some. Others may welcome more vigorous governance.

In practice, the line separating bold presidential leadership in the Hamiltonian tradition from authoritarian overreaching may not be clear. But the signals sent from the Mexican public can be read with clarity. Voters want a democratic system that works. For many citizens the historic legacy of the PRI, and the narrative that party leaders promoted about its capabilities during the campaign, made it the best available option to deliver. At the same time, the elections of 2012 did not confer a mandate to turn back the clock to authoritarianism.

ACKNOWLEDGMENTS

The author thanks Steve Ansolabehere, Frances Hagopian, José Kaire, Michael Lewis-Beck, Tom Mustillo, Katsuo Nishikawa, Bert Rockman, Elizabeth Zechmeister, and the participants at the Weatherhead Center for International Affairs workshop on the 2012 Mexican Elections—particularly Jorge I. Domínguez—for helpful comments on this chapter. He also wishes to acknowledge the Latin American Public Opinion Project—whose major sponsors are the US Agency for International Development, the United Nations Development Programme, the Inter-American Development Bank, and Vanderbilt University—for making its surveys available for general use.

NOTES

1. On the desire to increase the power and decision-making authority of officials in democracies around the world to make these systems more resilient, see Naím (2013).

2. Under Calderón's watch, economic growth had been far less than impressive, with an average annual increase of only 1.5% over the first five years of his term. As the elections approached, the majority of Mexicans (51%) were said to be living in poverty, and drug-related violence was a lamentable part of daily life across many states. Policy analysts spoke of governmental mismanagement, a lack of coordination among officials, persistent corruption, and "failed states" in the north and west of the country. See, for example, Hale (2011) and Rubio (2013).

3. Missing responses to this item did not correlate with age or whether respondents lived in a state where the PRI remained the leading political party, which underscores how the PRI of the pretransition period was a familiar point of reference for Mexicans, even for citizens with less direct personal experience living under PRI governance.

4. The estimates reported in figure 4.2 were calculated through maximum likelihood estimation. To identify the model, the unique variance estimates for the item on whether the country was in comparatively better shape under the PRI were constrained to be equal in both survey waves. When fitting structural equation models, the goal is to articulate a specification that comports with the covariance matrix for the items. In this case, an appropriate fit was obtained; $\chi^2_1 = .94$, $p = .33$.

5. Party identification was coded on a three-point scale (0, did not identify with the party; 1, weak identification; 2, strong identification; cf. McCann and Lawson 2003). Approval ratings for Calderón are based on a five-point scale ranging from strong disapproval to strong approval. Retrospective assessments of the national economy and one's personal financial well-being over the last twelve months are also measured on a five-point scale ranging from much worse to much better. Perceptions of leadership qualities for each of the major party candidates are based on summary indices for four items—ability to manage the economy, reduce poverty, fight crime, and lessen corruption—each of which was measured on a four-point scale. Ideological orientations are dummy coded. All of these attitude items were drawn from the second wave of the panel study.

6. In the model of presidential voting choices, the dependent variable takes on four values: voted for Peña Nieto, voted for Vázquez Mota, voted for López Obrador, or did not vote for one of the major party candidates, a group that includes both nonvoters and supporters of a minor protest candidate. If this fourth category is omitted from the analysis, the findings are substantively unchanged. Congressional-level voting choices were coded using a similar format. When estimating the coefficients, all available cases were taken into account; missing values were imputed via Amelia software.

7. When simulating a difference for a given predictor, all of the other independent variables are fixed to their mean values. In the case of partisanship, the estimated changes in probabilities are based on comparisons between Mexicans who were "pure independents" versus those who strongly identified with a given party. For political ideology, comparisons are between respondents who did not report any ideological leaning at all versus those who took a particular stance.

8. Comparable instrumentation on the policy-making legacy of Mexico's single-party system does not appear in any publicly available surveys conducted during the 2006 campaign, the first election after the transition to genuine multiparty competition at the presidential level. Consequently, it is not possible to examine whether a less crisis-ridden electoral climate would have featured the same type of divide in public opinion that is uncovered here for the 2012 contest. But the first wave of the panel study permits us to explore whether such considerations might have been salient in the previous election cycle. In this survey, respondents reported their presidential voting choices in 2006. These recall measures are undoubtedly contaminated by various errors in measurement; accurately stating preferences from an election that occurred six years in the past would have been a challenge for many survey participants. With this caveat in mind, when the recall measure is substituted in as the dependent variable in the multinomial logistic regression model of presidential choices, replacing presidential preferences from 2012, retrospective evaluations of the PRI regime do not account for past voting preferences to any significant degree. The choice between Roberto Madrazo, the PRI nominee in 2006, Andrés Manuel López Obrador of the PRD, and Felipe Calderón of the PAN rested on a wide array of factors (Domínguez et al. 2009; Moreno 2009), but judgments concerning the effectiveness of the former governing regime do not appear to have been relevant.

9. These additional findings are available upon request.

10. The 2012 LAPOP survey in Mexico was fielded in early February, approximately six weeks before the first wave of the Mexico 2012 Panel Study.

11. In the panel survey, a list of ten qualities that children might be encouraged to learn was presented to respondents, and they were asked to pick up to five that are most important. The three qualities analyzed here cohere well in a factor analysis and were summed to create a four-point additive index indicating the number of authoritarian views that a survey participant offered.

REFERENCES

Alcañiz, Isabela, and Timothy Hellwig. 2011. "Who's to Blame? The Distribution of Responsibility in Developing Democracies." *British Journal of Political Science* 41, no. 2: 389–411.

Almond, Gabriel, and Sidney Verba. 1963. *The Civic Culture*. Princeton, NJ: Princeton University Press.

Anderson, Christopher J. 2007. "The End of Economic Voting?" *Annual Review of Political Science* 10: 271–96.

Beltrán, Ulises, ed. 2009. "Elecciones en México." *Política y gobierno* thematic volume 16, no. 1.

Benton, Allyson, ed. 2009. "Elecciones en México." *Política y gobierno* thematic volume 16, no. 2.

Camp, Roderic Ai. 2013. "The 2012 Presidential Election and What It Reveals about Mexican Voters." *Journal of Latin American Studies* 45: 451–81.

Cinta, Alberto. 1999. "Uncertainty and Electoral Behavior in Mexico in the 1997 Congressional Elections." In *Towards Mexico's Democratization*, ed. J. I. Domínguez and A. Poiré, 144–202. New York: Routledge.

Costa Lobo, Marina. 2006. "Short-Term Voting Determinants in a Young Democracy: Leader Effects in Portugal in the 2002 Legislative Elections." *Electoral Studies* 25: 270–86.

Dahl, Robert A. 1956. *A Preface to Democratic Theory*. Chicago: University of Chicago Press.

Domínguez, Jorge I., Chappell Lawson, and Alejandro Moreno, eds. 2009. *Consolidating Mexico's Democracy*. Baltimore: Johns Hopkins University Press.

Domínguez, Jorge I., and James A. McCann. 1996. *Democratizing Mexico*. Baltimore: Johns Hopkins University Press.

Duch, Raymond M. 2001. "A Development Model of Heterogeneous Economic Voting in New Democracies." *American Political Science Review* 95, no. 4: 895–910.

Fiorina, Morris. 1981. *Retrospective Voting in American National Elections*. New Haven, CT: Yale University Press.

Flores-Macías, Gustavo. 2013. "Mexico's 2012 Elections: The Return of the PRI." *Journal of Democracy* 24, no. 1: 128–41.

Gillingham, Paul. 2012. "Mexican Elections, 1910–1994: Voters, Violence, and Veto Power." In *The Oxford Handbook of Mexican Politics*, ed. R. Ai Camp, 53–76. New York: Oxford University Press.

Gomez, Brad T., and J. Matthew Wilson. 2006. "Cognitive Heterogeneity and Economic Voting: A Comparative Analysis of Four Democratic Electorates." *American Journal of Political Science* 50, no. 1: 127–45.

Greene, Kenneth. 2007. *Why Dominant Parties Lose*. New York: Cambridge University Press.

———. 2011. "Campaign Persuasion and Nascent Partisanship in Mexico's New Democracy." *American Journal of Political Science* 55. no. 2: 398–416.

Hale, Gary J. 2011. "A 'Failed State' in Mexico." Policy Briefing Report. Houston, TX: James A. Baker III Institute for Public Policy, Rice University.

Hetherington, Marc, and Jonathan Weiler. 2009. *Authoritarianism and Polarization in American Politics*. New York: Cambridge University Press.

Lewis-Beck, Michael, and Mary Stegmaier. 2007. "Economic Models of Voting." In *The Oxford Handbook of Political Behavior*, ed. R. Dalton and H. Klingemann, 518–37. New York: Oxford University Press.

McCann, James A. 2012. "Changing Dimensions of National Elections in Mexico." In *The Oxford Handbook of Mexican Politics*, ed. R. Ai Camp, 497–522. New York: Oxford University Press.

McCann, James A., and Chappell Lawson. 2003. "An Electorate Adrift?" *Latin American Research Review* 38, no. 3: 60–81.

Merolla, Jennifer, and Elizabeth Zechmeister. 2009. *Democracy at Risk*. Chicago: University of Chicago Press.

Miller Llana, Sara. 2012. "Is Mexico's Leading Presidential Candidate a Retreat from Democratic Progress?" *Christian Science Monitor*, July 8. http://www.csmonitor.com /World/Americas/2012/0608/Is-Mexico-s-leading-presidential-candidate-a-retreat -from-democratic-progress

Molinar Horcasitas, Juan. 1991. *El Tiempo de la Legitimidad: Elecciones, Autoritarismo y Democracia en México*. México City: Caly Arena.

Morgenstern, Scott, and Elizabeth Zechmeister. 2001. "Better the Devil You Know than the Saint You Don't? Risk Propensity and Vote Choice in Mexico." *Journal of Politics* 63: 93–119.

Moreno, Alejandro. 1998. "Party Competition and the Issue of Democracy: Ideological Space in Mexican Elections." In *Governing Mexico: Political Parties and Elections*, ed. M. Serrano, 38–57. London: Institute of Latin American Studies.

———. 2009. *La Decisión Electoral.* Mexico City: Miguel Ángel Porrúa.

Moreno, Alejandro, and Shannon K. O'Neil. 2013. "El malestar Democrático en México." *Foreign Affairs Latinoamérica* 13, no. 1: 41–47.

Naím, Moisés. 2013. *The End of Power.* New York: Basic Books.

Parametría. 2013. "Carta Paramétrica: El Pacto por México." http://www.parametria.com.mx/DetalleEstudio.php?E=4523.

Parás, Pablo, and Carlos López. 2007. "Auditoría de la Democracia: México 2006." *Política y Gobierno* 14, no. 2: 491–512.

Parás García, Pablo, Carlos López Olmedo, Dinorah Vargas López, and Mitchell A. Seligson. 2011. "Cultura Política de la Democracia en México, 2010." LAPOP working paper. Nashville, TN: LAPOP. http://www.vanderbilt.edu/lapop/mexico/2010-culturapolitica.pdf.

Rubio, Luis. 2013. "In the Lurch between Government and Chaos: Unconsolidated Democracy in Mexico." Washington, DC: Regional Migration Study Group, Woodrow Wilson International Center for Scholars, and the Migration Policy Institute. http://www.wilsoncenter.org/sites/default/files/lurch_between_government_and_chaos.pdf.

Taylor-Robinson, Michelle, and Joseph D. Ura. 2013. "Public Opinion and Conflict in the Separation of Powers: Understanding the Honduran Coup of 2009." *Journal of Theoretical Politics* 25, no. 1: 105–27.

Tucker, Joshua A. 2006. *Regional Economic Voting: Russia, Poland, Hungary, Slovakia, and the Czech Republic, 1990–1999.* New York: Cambridge University Press.

5

Public Mood and Presidential Election Outcomes in Mexico

ANDY BAKER

Who wins elections and why? This question seems straightforward, and political scientists should certainly know enough to provide plausible answers. In scholarship on the United States, there is a cottage industry in explaining and forecasting aggregate election outcomes, and plausible answers abound (Campbell 2012). Most such models and theories have settled on one overriding cause: the health of the macroeconomy (Lewis-Beck and Rice 1992). The incumbent party does well on Election Day when the economy is booming, while the opposition party is likely to perform well when the economy is sluggish. This standard retrospective economic voting model has taken firm root in scholarly understandings of Latin American election outcomes as well. There is now an impressive body of evidence demonstrating the importance of valence issues and reward-and-punishment orientations in Latin American voting behavior (Remmer 1991; Singer and Carlin 2013). It seems that Latin American voters vote out incumbent parties that oversee poor economies, and they reelect ones that govern during times of economic growth.

This chapter does not take issue with the core of the retrospective voting claim—it is simple yet explanatorily powerful. Instead, I argue that it is incomplete for the Latin American, and especially Mexican, case. Quite simply, it is quiet on the question of where anti-incumbent voters go in a multiparty system. The theory is whole in the two-player world of the US party system, because voters in an anti-incumbent mood during tough times have but one option. But Latin America's proportional representation systems feature at least three-party competition in the vast majority of presidential elections.

To fill this gap in scholars' understanding of the causes of aggregated electoral returns in Latin America, I introduce a new dimension alongside the standard valence or performance evaluations: positional issue voting. In particular, I argue that there is positional issue content to not just the opposition vote but all voting in Mexican elections. Voters' "mood" or aggregate central tendency toward important policy and positional issue debates of the day can help to explain which parties perform well in Mexico's presidential elections. Mexican voters, I find, were in a liberal, market-friendly mood in 1994 and 2000 when the National Action Party (PAN) was the leading opposition party (1994) or outright winner (2000) and the left-leaning Party of the Democratic Revolution (PRD) was marginalized to also-ran status in third place. In contrast, voters were in a more statist mood in 2006 and 2012 when the left nearly won and the centrist Institutional Revolutionary Party, or PRI (2006), or rightist PAN (2012) were more marginalized. All told, I conclude that public mood is a fruitful line of research in thinking about Mexican and Latin American elections.

The Importance of Policy Mood

Retrospective voting theory has been applied with some success to Mexican elections, giving scholars a solid understanding of trends in aggregate returns and party success. The PRI's steady decline through the 1980s and 90s was almost certainly due to economic turmoil. The debt crisis of 1982, the subsequent lost decade, and the peso crisis of 1995 all played a role in chipping away at the PRI's credibility as an able economic manager, leading to a gradually decreasing vote share for the PRI and eventually its first presidential loss in 2000 (Magaloni 2006, chap. 2). The drying-up of patronage resources for the PRI to divvy out also contributed to its graduate demise (Greene 2007). The 2012 outcome likewise has a nice retrospective-voting ring to it: rising cartel violence soured voters on the twelve-year incumbent PAN, so voters abandoned it in droves, consigning it to third place.

But these narratives leave crucial questions unanswered. Why was it the PAN's Vicente Fox, and not the PRD's Cuauhtémoc Cárdenas, who most profited from the anti-incumbency mood in 2000? Arguments that Cárdenas was an unattractive candidate or was not seen as viable are post hoc or even tautological, especially considering his surprising second-place performance in 1988. Similarly, why was it the PRD's Andrés Manuel Lopéz Obrador (AMLO), and not the PRI's Roberto Madrazo, who received the bulk of the anti-incumbent vote in 2006? Arguments that voters were tired of the PRI or that it had lost its credibility because of poor economic performance in the

1990s are belied by its return to power in 2012. To answer these questions about aggregate election outcomes, I turn to the concept of Mexican voters' public mood.

James Stimson defines public mood as a society's "general disposition" toward a set of conceptually related positional (i.e., controversial or divisive) political issues of the day (Stimson 1991, 18). As a concept, mood can be thought of as the central tendency of opinions held by all individuals over a set of related policy issues. In practice, this central tendency is defined and calculated over two levels of aggregation: survey respondents and positional issues. It is not, however, aggregated over time (at least no more than annually), meaning mood is allowed to shift temporally. Indeed, many of the interesting findings from mood emerge from seeing how it shifts through time. Analysts looking at the United States, for example, speak of the public being in a "conservative mood" in one presidential election and then a "liberal mood" in the next. The simple notion of a conservative mood evokes an average opinion within an entire electorate over a large swathe of political issues that can be characterized as having a conservative position and a liberal position.

Do Mexican voters have policy moods? Scholarship to date has not provided an answer to that question. Some vague references to the notion exist. For example, a *New York Times* article on the 2006 election referred to a "populist groundswell" (Rieff 2006). For Latin American electorates as a whole, there has been vague talk of "reform fatigue" and a "post-neoliberal age" (Hershberg and Rosen 2006; Lora, Panizza, and Quispe-Agnoli 2004; Roberts 2008; Samuelson 2002). In general, however, there is no scholarly research on the topic, save an analysis of regionwide trends by Baker and Greene (2011).

For the Mexican case, this oversight stems in part from a certain skepticism about the relevance of positional issues to voting behavior. In their classic work on the 1988 presidential and 1991 legislative elections, Jorge Domínguez and James McCann conclude that "these Mexican elections were not about the issues" (Domínguez and McCann 1995, 41). In another analysis of the 2000 election, McCann and Chappell Lawson argue that "the notion that citizens might base their voting decisions on candidates' issue positions seems implausible at best" (McCann and Lawson 2003, 75). Finally, of the 2006 election, Greene (2009) concludes that candidate images, not positional issues, drove vote choice.[1] To the extent that there has been any research on the impact of aggregate opinions, it is on performance assessments—of the economy, of crime, of the political system—and their movement through time (Buendía 1996; Buendía

Laredo 2001; Magaloni 2006). This is not mood in the Stimsonian sense, as these are valence issues, not positional ones.

Furthermore, most analyses of Mexican voting behavior focus on single elections and use individual-level data (Domínguez and Lawson 2004; Greene 2011; Lawson 2002). The predominant scholarly approach has been one of estimating individual-level covariance between vote choice and causal factors such as performance evaluations, issue positions, campaign attention, and so on (e.g., Domínguez and McCann 1996; Moreno 2009). These studies are highly valuable for their expressed purpose: explaining what kinds of people vote for each party. But individual-level analyses on a single election (even with panel data) cannot provide convincing answers to questions about which party did better or about changing party fortunes from one election to the next. Fundamentally, these are questions about an aggregate process that, while rooted in individual-level decisions, cannot be satisfactorily answered by merely discerning the kinds of individual-level factors that are correlated with vote choice. Many questions central to comparative and Latin American politics (Why did the left rise? Why did some Latin American party systems collapse?) can only be answered with at least some focus on national- or multinational-level factors. In short, this chapter makes the case for not ignoring aggregate data and trends (Kramer 1983).

Measuring Mexican Mood

To estimate Mexican policy mood, I use the Stimson (1991) algorithm to recover estimates of mood from a set of repeated survey items that query respondents' opinions about different but conceptually related positional issues. Policy mood is a latent variable that takes on different values at each interval t. For my purposes, the interval is annual. To recover these annual values, the analyst first compiles as many time series of repeated positional issue survey items as possible and calculates the percentage of individuals in support of the rightist (or leftist—the choice is arbitrary) position on each one. For inclusion, any given time series needs not be complete; that is, there can be years in which the question was not asked. The issues queried by the survey items should all be interrelated in the sense that respondents' positions on each one are partly informed and constrained by a singular, underlying political philosophy, core value, ideology, predisposition, meta-orientation, or ascertainable source of constraint. Respondents' self-placement on these positional issue items need only be partly informed by this underlying source of ideological constraint. Mood can exist when a substantial portion of mass thinking about different policy elements is "morselized," or unconstrained (Baker 2009; Converse 1964; Lane 1962).

The first choice in calculating mood, therefore, is to pick a meta-dimension, meaning an issue dimension that could underlie a set of technically distinct but conceptually related policy debates or elements. In the Mexican case, at least four such meta-dimensions are plausible. The first is the statist–liberal divide, a dimension that exists in seemingly every Latin American, North American, and European society to at least some extent (Gunther and Hsin-chi 2007). (Throughout this chapter I use "liberal" in the classical liberal sense of free market and capitalist advocacy, not in the sense of leftism or progressivism as is often used in the United States.) In Mexico, debates over privatization, free trade, fiscal policy, and government antipoverty programs have been highly salient in elections and party competition for at least thirty years, ever since the government began a dramatic policy shift from state-led development to a more market-oriented model in the mid-1980s. Numerous specific policies and policy debates—such as those over the North American Free Trade Agreement (NAFTA), the opening of Pemex to private investment, the privatization of the electricity sector, the establishment of fiscal programs such as the Programa Nacional de Solidaridad and Oportunidades, and the nature of fees for public university students—all can be characterized as having a statist position and a liberal promarket position.

A second potential meta-dimension for Mexico is the regime cleavage first pinpointed by Domínguez and McCann (1996). Political debates around the pace and nature of democratization, which were deeply intertwined with opinions of the long-standing partisan sponsor and beneficiary of hegemonic-party authoritarianism, the PRI, were central in Mexican voters' minds up through the PRI's first presidential loss in the 2000 election. Perceptions of the depth of voter fraud committed by the PRI, the transparency of government agencies, security and stability in a potential post-PRI political system, and opposition parties' capacity to manage the economy were among the more specific policy debates and concerns that were shaped in part by this underlying regime dimension. (See James A. McCann, chap. 4, this volume.)

The third potential dimension is religious and moral. Mexican parties and voters are divided on a broadly defined religious–secular meta-dimension that is associated with a number of more specific policy issues—abortion rights, access to contraception, same-sex marriage—that have been part of political contestation for decades (Kitschelt, Hawkins, Luna, Rosas, and Zechmeister 2010; Magaloni and Moreno 2003). The final meta-dimension is anticrime policy, with opinions falling on a continuum ranging from the *mano dura* approach of repression and overwhelming state force to the more conciliatory approach of treating the underlying socioeconomic causes of criminality and negotiating with organized criminal gangs. (See Edgar Franco Vivanco, Jorge Olarte, Alberto Díaz-Cayeros, and Beatriz Magaloni, chap. 7, this volume.)

In the end, I focus exclusively on the statist–liberal dimension for both theoretical and practical reasons. On the theoretical side, evidence is abundant that this is the primary meta-dimension and political cleavage in the Mexican party system, with the three major parties falling roughly on the statist center-left (PRD), the mixed economy center (PRI), and the pro-market center-right (PAN). Support for the importance of this dimension comes from a variety of sources. Wiesehomeier and Benoit (2009) asked experts in 2006 and 2007 to rank the importance of eleven different issue dimensions to parties in Mexico. Three of the four most important dimensions were privatization (first), regional economic integration (third), and globalization (fourth).[2] By contrast, a crime policy dimension ranked fifth in importance, and a dimension loosely related to the regime cleavage (on the desired extent of government regulation of party financial and campaigning activities) ranked second to last. Another bit of evidence comes from Kitschelt et al. (2010, chap. 2), who find an economic redistribution dimension to be one of two primary cleavages among parties in the Mexican national legislature. In contrast, a political regime dimension barely registered as significant. Finally, Baker and Greene (2011) analyze mass opinion data from across Latin America and find the main cause of partisan waves—and particularly the rise of the left in the 2000s—to be mass shifts in beliefs about the Washington Consensus. Changes in mass attitudes on other dimensions, including criminality and democratization, mattered little. In short, these various pieces of evidence point to the statist–liberal divide as being more important than both the crime and regime dimensions.

Admittedly, however, some of these same sources of evidence point to the religiosity dimension as being just as important as the statist–liberal one. Wiesehomeier and Benoit's (2009) expert coders ranked the religious dimension—the role of religious versus secular principles in politics—as the second-most important in Mexico's party system.[3] For their part, Kitschelt et al. (2010) found a religiosity dimension to be slightly more important and divisive than the economic redistribution dimension in the Mexican legislature. The three major parties fall on the secular center-left (PRD), the moderately religious center (PRI), and the conservatively Catholic center-right (PAN).

Ultimately, the choice to maintain an exclusive focus on the economic dimension and ignore the religious dimension, despite the latter's importance, comes down to a practicality. The data demands for constructing policy mood are high, and available survey data on religious and moral policy issues come nowhere close to meeting these demands. Time series constructed from equivalently worded, repeated survey questions on homosexuality, abortion, contraception, and religiosity are choppy and few. For example, the annual Latinobarometer surveys have only asked questions about abortion in three years and about homosexuality in four years.

By contrast, the set of survey questions asked of Mexicans that relate to the statist–liberal debate is far richer and more voluminous, as illustrated by figure 5.1. The raw materials that go into constructing annual measures of

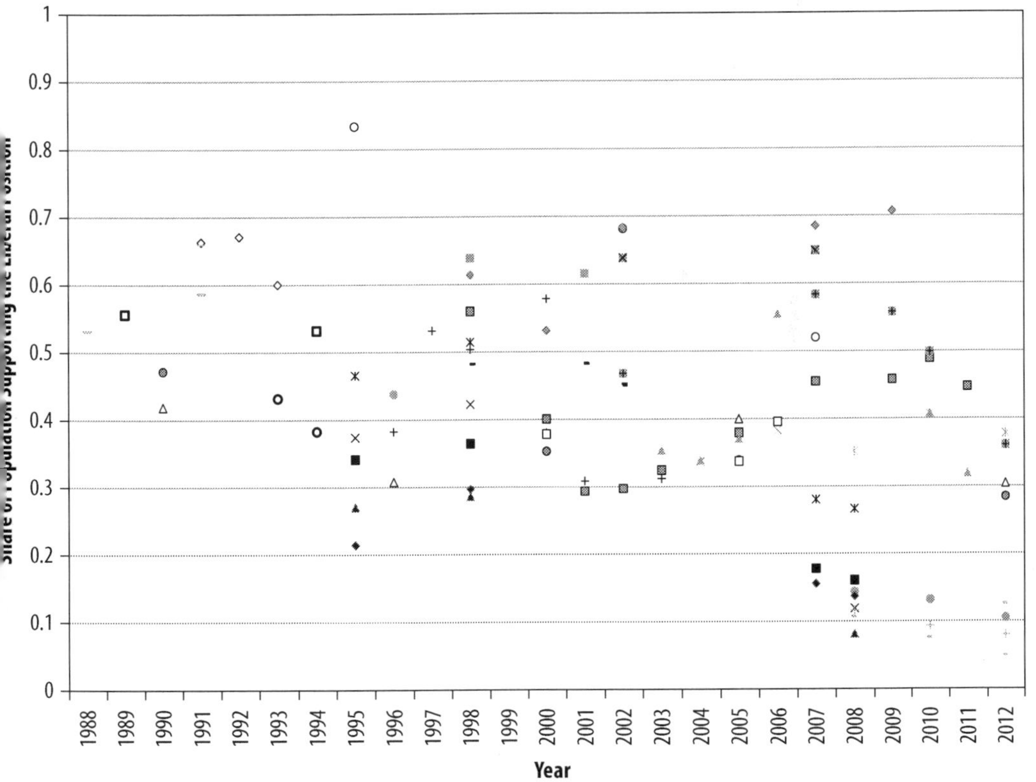

Figure 5.1. Observed percentages in favor of a liberal stance on twenty-six different statist–liberal survey questions, 1988–2012

policy mood are the proportion of liberal responses to relevant survey questions (asked in nationally representative surveys) that are repeated at least once in a later year (and ideally much more than once; see Stimson 1991).[4] Figure 5.1 plots the raw materials of my policy mood estimates, showing the simple proportion of Mexican respondents that supported the economically liberal side of twenty-six different survey questions between 1988 and 2012. Each series has its own distinct symbol or marker, although (given the clutter) the point of the figure is less to convey individual series trends than to display the raw data and thus the intuition behind mood calculation. Some of these questions were asked only twice, while the most complete was asked in ten different years. The total number of item-years, or observed points, is ninety-six. The questions come from a variety of sources, including Latinobarometer, World Values Survey, the Latin American Public Opinion Project, the Mexico 2006 Panel Study, the Pew Global Attitudes Survey, Office of the Technical Advisor to the President of Mexico, Gallup Mexico, and a few others. Questions fall into one of four types: (1) attitudes toward privatization, (2) attitudes toward foreign investment, (3) attitudes toward NAFTA and international trade, and (4) diffuse values about the market and capitalism. (All question wordings are reported in an ancillary appendix available at www.press.jhu.edu.)

A naïve approach of estimating policy mood would take a simple average of the observed percentages in each year, and a slightly less naïve approach would take a moving average or calculate a central tendency based on some other kind of smoother. The problem with these approaches is that they are highly sensitive to data availability in any given year. In years when only trade-related attitudes were measured, for example—trade being a highly popular measure (Baker 2003)—mood would seem to be liberal. In years when only questions about privatization, a far less popular measure, were asked, mood would appear to be statist. Obviously, these observed changes in mood would be largely due to instrumentation and the arbitrariness of data availability, not to changes in the true latent variable itself. To improve on this method, the Stimson algorithm uses the information on changes through time within series of repeated questions to estimate changes in the latent national mood. The main drawback of the Stimson approach, relative to the naïve approaches mentioned above, is that mood has no metric. One cannot say that $x\%$ of the population was in a liberal mood in 2000. Instead, the analysis simply focuses on the relative movement of mood through time, although one can point to the marginal percentages in some of mood's constitutive elements to provide something of an anchor.

The algorithm is similar to a factor analysis. It first calculates pairwise correlations among all the series, and then it extracts a latent dimension based on this correlation matrix. From there, it calculates each series' loading on the underlying dimension. Annual estimates of policy mood are then generated on the basis of these loadings and their associated factor scores. Although the algorithm is less sensitive to data availability than the alternatives, its estimates of mood can still be fickle and highly uncertain in years with few or no data points.[5] (For example, relatively little data are available from 1988 to 1994 for Mexico; see fig. 5.1.) I proceed with this caveat in mind.

Results

Figure 5.2 shows the estimates of Mexican policy mood from 1994 to 2012. Although the few data points available from 1988 to 1993 were used, mood estimates for this *sexenio* are not reported because they are based on such sparse information. The estimates are scaled so that higher values equate to eras of more liberal, pro-market moods and lower values to more statist moods. On the basis of these estimates, figure 5.2 divides Mexican mood into four eras: an era

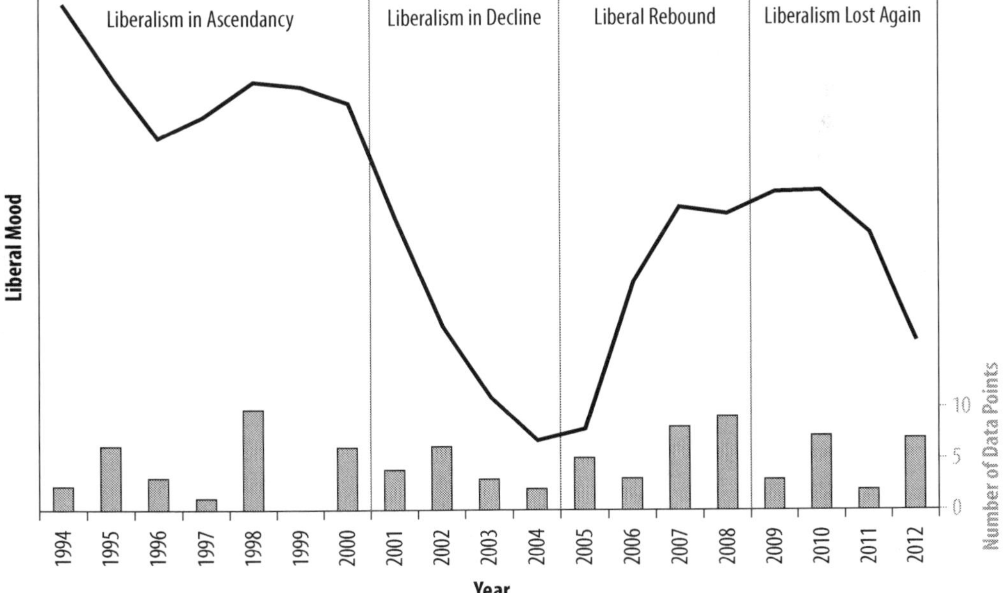

Figure 5.2. Liberal policy mood in Mexico, 1994–2012

of liberal ascendancy from 1994 to 2000, an era in which liberalism was in decline from 2001 to 2005, a short-lived era of liberal rebound from 2006 to 2009, and an era from 2010 to 2012 in which liberalism lost the ground it had gained in the previous era. The grey vertical bars (scaled to the right *y* axis) report the number of observations in each year.

Mexicans were in their most liberal mood during President Ernesto Zedillo's *sexenio* (1994–2000), which is somewhat surprising given the political upheavals of NAFTA's first year (i.e., the Colosio assassination and Zapatista uprising), the peso crisis of 1995, and the discrediting of the market-friendly ex-president Carlos Salinas de Gortari after he left office. Nevertheless, Mexicans remained enthusiastic about NAFTA throughout these years (58% in 2000 saying NAFTA benefited their country a lot or quite a bit), and even the typically less popular policy arena of privatization was at its peak popularity during this time (e.g., 56% agreed that privatization had helped the country in 1998).

This liberal ascendancy started to unravel after 2000 during President Vicente Fox's *sexenio* (2000–2006). Mexicans' mood shifted in a more statist direction. By 2002, just 30% of Mexicans were expressing favorable attitudes toward privatization, and support for NAFTA had fallen by twenty-seven percentage points by 2003. President Felipe Calderón's *sexenio* (2006–12) subsequently featured Mexicans at their most fickle. For the first three years, Mexicans trended back toward the liberal pole, as exemplified by a fifteen-percentage-point surge in their support for privatization. Yet the rebound was short lived. By the end of Calderón's term, Mexicans' mood was nearly back where it was at its least liberal point in 2005. All told, the 1990s saw Mexicans at their most liberal, while the 2000s have seen them much less so, save an ephemeral move liberalward as the millennium's first decade closed.

What caused these shifts? In other words, what moves Mexican mood? A full analysis is beyond the scope of this chapter, but it is worth pointing out that Mexicans' mood on economic policy is not simply a product of macroeconomic health, meaning it is not just a proxy for retrospective economic evaluations. The correlation between the mood estimate and annual gross domestic product growth is virtually zero, and it is clear from figure 5.2 that Mexico's years of economic contraction (1995, 2001, 2009) were no more likely to trigger a more statist mood than were years of rapid economic growth (1997, 2000, 2010). Rather, previous research on the sources of public opinion toward market reforms suggests that mass attitudes are caused by rather focused and well-reasoned evaluations by citizens of Washington Consensus policies themselves (Baker

2009). Concrete experiences with and (to a lesser extent) knowledge gleaned from elites and the mass media about privatization, free trade, and foreign investment have been the primary drivers of citizen support and opposition to the market-friendly shift. Consumer-oriented considerations have been of particular importance, such as the impact of trade liberalization and utility privatization on prices and the quality of goods and services.

In Mexico, for example, the years following the implementation of trade liberalization measures, including NAFTA in 1994, were associated with massive gains in consumer welfare. Citizens, who before 1985 had been captive audiences in many product markets during Mexico's decades-long experiment with import substitution and foreign capital restrictions, suddenly had access to higher-quality and less expensive foreign products. This consumer euphoria even outlived the 1995 peso crisis, as Mexican mood remained near its liberal peak through 2000. After that year, the prevailing sentiment shifted precipitously in a statist direction. The novelty of the consumer gains from trade and foreign investment faded as these gains became normalized. Moreover, by the 2000s, consumer-oriented doubts about the Washington Consensus arose on the basis of what could be called the "Carlos Slim effect." The privatization of Mexico's primary telecommunications firm Telmex in the 1990s had turned a state-owned near-monopoly into a private one, owned mostly by business magnate Carlos Slim. Because the firm faced minimal competition, Mexicans paid some of the world's highest fees for fixed-line and mobile phone services as well as for broadband. Proposed reforms to de-monopolize the sector became increasingly politicized (and resisted by Slim) during the 2000s.

Individual-Level Tests of Positional Issues Voting

Can these moods and shifts in moods explain anything? Do they correspond to aggregate changes in voters' ideological preferences at the ballot box, and thus to shifts in the relative Election Day success of competing parties? Before answering these questions, I take a brief foray into individual-level survey data to determine whether Mexicans are positional issue voters. If the answers to these questions are to be "yes," then a necessary condition that one must obtain is that Mexicans are positional issue voters in national elections: statist citizens are more likely to vote for the more statist PRD, liberal citizens are more likely to vote for the more liberal PAN, and citizens with relatively moderate views on economic policy are more likely to vote for the centrist PRI. Similarly, a move by a citizen in the issue space toward the liberal pole will increase her likelihood of voting for the most liberal candidate. Given the presence of some scholarly skepticism of positional issue voting in Mexico, the burden is surely on me to give some evidence that these economic policy issues constituting the statist–liberal mood meta-dimension matter in Mexican voting behavior.

I run tests using the 2006 panel data to determine whether individual-level attitudes on economic policy debates help to predict vote choice. Panel data are valuable because they can address some of the endogeneity problems posed by cross-sectional analyses. A partial correlation between issue positions and vote choice in a cross section could be due to positional issue voting, but it could also be due to citizens simply learning their issue preferences from their long-preferred party (Zaller 1992). A panel can control for past issue positions and political predispositions, and thus narrow in on whether short-term changes in issue positions are causing short-term changes in vote intention. Panel data also mimic the temporal patterns underlying the expected impacts of changes in policy mood: changes in policy attitudes yield subsequent changes in vote choice.

The three-wave panel contains repeated questions on four economic policy issues, each of which can be characterized as part of a statist–liberal divide: privatization of the electricity sector, the scope of commercial relations with the United States, government versus individual responsibility for well-being, and redistribution through higher taxation on the rich. (Wordings are in an ancillary appendix; see www.press.jhu.edu.) Any single item is rife with measurement error, especially because each is measured solely as a dichotomy or trichotomy. Use of these items in their unaltered forms would increase the chances of Type II error (Achen 1975; Ansolabehere, Rodden, and Snyder 2008). To partially address this problem, I create an index constructed from the shared variation across the four variables. All four variables scaled onto a single dimension in a principal components analysis. The index is called Economic Liberalism, and it is coded so that higher values mean more liberal sentiments on the part of the respondent.

All four items were repeated in the three survey waves, as were vote intention, presidential approval, and partisan identification. As a result, I construct a multinomial logit panel model of vote choice that controls for past vote intentions (i.e., the lagged dependent variable), past and present issue preferences, past and present presidential approval, and past and present partisan identification. Given this full set of lags and contemporaneous values, the model allows me to isolate the effect of changing issue preferences on changes in vote choice.

This structure automatically controls for the potential effects of omitted variables that do not vary between panel waves, such as union membership or crucial demographic variables (De Boef and Keele 2008). One drawback is that, given the inclusion of lagged values, the model estimates vote choice/intention only for waves two and three because there are no lagged values for wave one ($n = 2,824$). The full list of coefficients and standard errors is reported in an ancillary appendix available at www.press.jhu.edu. Here I simply describe patterns of statistical significance and the weight of substantive effects.

The model results reveal that voters' shifting preferences on economic policy issues during the 2006 campaign had a notable impact on their vote choices. (Recall that the three major candidates were Calderón of the PAN, AMLO of the PRD, and Madrazo of the PRI.) The model was set up with an AMLO vote as the base category in a series of pairwise comparisons. The coefficient on the contemporaneous value of economic liberalism is statistically significant for the PRI versus PRD pairwise comparison, and that for the PAN versus PRD comparison is also statistically significant. (Interestingly, the impact of economic liberalism in the Calderón versus Madrazo pairwise comparison falls just below conventional statistical significant levels, a point upon which I elaborate below.) Among voters who were leaning toward a López Obrador vote in wave two, a shift toward the liberal end of the economic liberalism variable from the 25th to the 75th percentile lowered their probability of voting for him (as reported in wave three) by eight percentage points and raised their probability of voting for Calderón by nearly an equivalent amount, a net change in the probability gap between the two candidates of sixteen percentage points.[6] Madrazo also benefited with this shift, relative to AMLO, by closing the probability gap with him by nine percentage points. Among Calderón leaners, this shift in issue attitudes from the 25th to 75th percentile raised their chances of voting for Calderón also by .08 while lowering the probability of an AMLO vote by .05, for a net shift of thirteen percentage points. Among these voters, Madrazo gained ground with this shift on AMLO (closing the gap by five percentage points) while losing ground to Calderón (eight percentage points). All told, the microfoundations of the argument that changes in policy mood yield shifts in aggregate election outcomes are confirmed.

Explaining Election Outcomes with Mood

What, then, about the central macroquestion? Can mood explain election outcomes? Figure 5.3 reports the outcome to be explained, a numerical way of conveying the ideological propensity of the Mexican electorate as expressed through its voting behavior in each presidential election since 1994. This measure is called vote-revealed rightism (VRR) and, for any given election, it can be thought of as the sum of all parties' ideological scores after weighting each party by its vote share. More precisely, I first assign each candidate i in election s an ideology score that has a theoretical range from 1 (furthest left) to 20 (furthest right). The ideology scores come from those assigned to (nearly) all Latin American parties in Baker and Greene (2011), which relied heavily on the expert surveys conducted by Wiesehomeier and Benoit (2009).[7] I then multiplied each candidate's ideology score by his proportion of the vote received in election s and then summed these products for all candidates to produce the VRR of election s. More formally, for candidates $i = [1 \ldots n]$, VRR for election s is given by

$$\text{VRR}_s = \sum_{i=1}^{n} \text{Ideology}_{is} \times \text{VoteShare}_{is}$$

Figure 5.3 plots each presidential election's VRR as a black diamond. This axis is shown across its entire theoretical range, from 1 to 20. To give readers a substantive sense of what these ideology numbers mean, the figure places

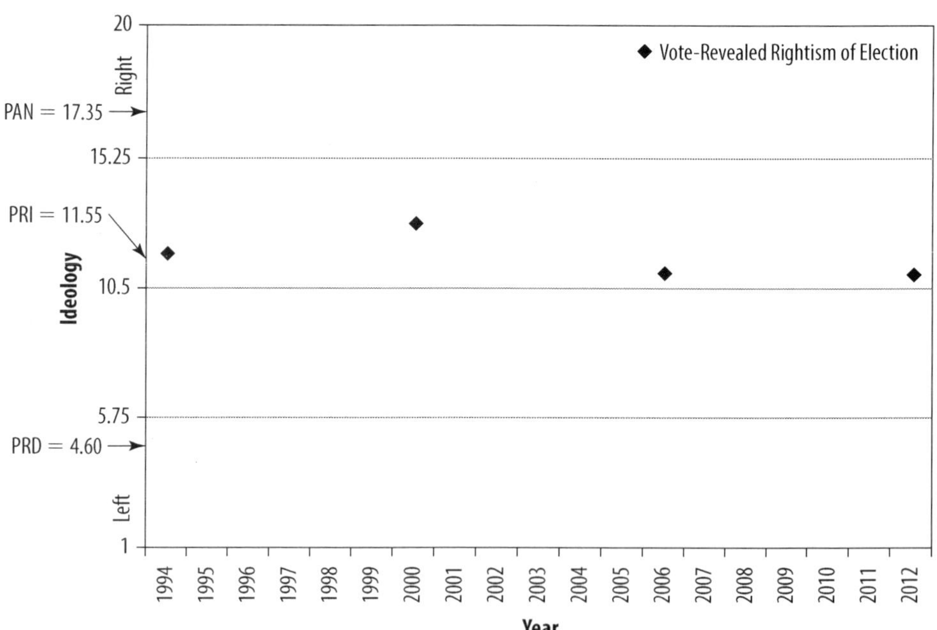

Figure 5.3. Vote-revealed rightism in four presidential elections

Mexico's three major parties—the PRD (4.60), the PRI (11.55), and the PAN (17.35)—at their positions on the scale. VRR was at its peak in 2000 (12.83) for Fox's historic victory, also a year in which the PRD fared poorly. It was at its lowest point (furthest left) in 2012 (10.89) when the PAN fared poorly and the PRD came in a close second, although it was virtually the same (10.96) in 2006 for the PRD's best-ever showing.

Figure 5.4 zooms in to the middle portion of figure 5.3 to more clearly depict the nature of the ideological movements taking place in these four elections. In most party systems, highly meaningful ideological swings occur between elections on a scale of one- or two-point shifts, not ten- to twenty-point shifts, so the wide range of figure 5.3 downplays the importance of meaningful change. The figure also superimposes the mood estimates themselves, although readers should keep in mind that the mood line is not scaled to the ideology scores of the *y* axis.

Can mood explain these ideological differences across elections? All told, it does so fairly well, with only some minor deviations from expectations. (Although the number of cases is only four, it is worth reporting that the

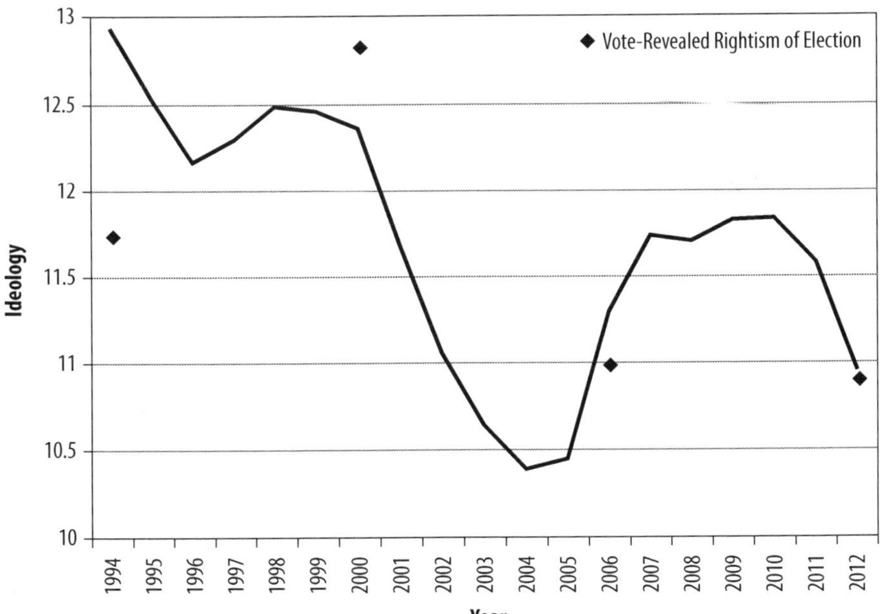

Figure 5.4. Mexican policy mood and vote-revealed rightism in four presidential elections: A closer look

correlation between mood and VRR is +.70.) During the era of liberal ascendancy from 1994 to 2000, VRR was at its highest for the two presidential elections that bookended it. The leftist PRD finished third in both elections because of, according to the mood model, voters' relatively high level of enthusiasm for the Washington Consensus. Most importantly, the liberal era culminated in the victory of the PAN, one of Latin America's more unabashedly pro-business and pro-market political parties.

By contrast, the era broke soon after Fox's victory, giving way to a more statist mood. Correspondingly, Mexican elections saw the rise of the PRD as the strongest challenger. The PRD finished a close second not once but twice. To be sure, the conservative PAN won the 2006 election, but it was a virtual tie with the newly surging PRD.[8] This election actually occurred on the cusp of two eras, near the trough of liberal mood in 2005 and around the beginning of a short-lived liberal surge. Regardless of its precise timing, Mexican voters were clearly in a much more statist mood in 2006 than they were in 2000. (It is tempting to take the mood model to its logical conclusion and assert that, had the election occurred in 2005 and not 2006, López Obrador would have won. Indeed, López Obrador was ahead in the polls throughout late 2005 and early 2006, only to be squeaked out by Calderón's late surge.)

Mexican mood went on a roller coaster ride during the Calderón *sexenio*, but it ended in 2012 virtually in the same place it began in 2006: a low point for economic liberalism. Of course, on standard measures the presidential election outcome in 2006 was dramatically different from that in 2012, as the PRI and the PAN swapped places. But in terms of the ideological balance of the electorate, at least as expressed through its collective choice at the polling booths, the outcomes in the two were virtually equivalent. The dramatic fall of the rightist PAN and slight fall of the leftist PRD were counterbalanced by the rise of the centrist PRI. The mood model thus explains the 2012 election's center of ideological gravity quite well. In sum, the mood model is largely successful. It explains the leftward shift in the Mexican electorate's voting behavior after 2000 extremely well. It also explains the stability in the electorate's ideological propensity between 2006 and 2012.

But two failings of the model must be mentioned. First, it cannot explain the swap in the order of finish that occurred between the PRI and the PAN between 2006 and 2012. To be sure, this occurrence goes a bit beyond the intended purpose of the mood model. The goal is to explain the ideological center of gravity of an election result, and in a three-party (or more) system there are an infinite number of election results that are compatible with each VRR value. Still, this weakness in explaining the allocation of votes among competing parties is evident in the 2006 versus 2012 contrast and needs to be stated. Second, the mood model cannot explain the noticeable shift in the ideological center of gravity between 1994 and 2000 that led to the historic victory of the PAN. In 2000, Mexicans were no more liberal in mood than they were in 1994, yet their VRR shifted an entire point rightward, enough to secure Fox's easy victory.

One piece of speculation that can be drawn from both the successes and failures of the model is that voters see the PRI and the PAN as close substitutes on the economic policy dimension, such that mood swings affect the balance of support for the PRD versus the PAN/PRI tandem, but they do not affect the balance of support between the PRI and the PAN. Stated differently, liberal issue voters are more likely to be indifferent in making the pairwise comparison between the PAN and PRI than they are in deciding between the PRD and these two competitors. After all, it was PRI presidents Miguel de la Madrid (1982–88) and Carlos Salinas de Gortari (1988–94) who initiated and accomplished the most in moving Mexico toward the dictates of the Washington Consensus, effectively adopting in the 1980s a major piece of the PAN's platform.[9]

Two sets of findings support this claim. First, the PRD's electoral success has far greater elasticity with mood than does the electoral success of the PRI and the PAN. The correlation between mood and the PRD's vote share in the four presidential elections (−.92) is greater in magnitude than that between mood and the PRI's vote share (+.65) and that between mood and the PAN's vote share (+.11). In other words, mood swings in the statist direction help the PRD more than they hurt the PRI, but they also hurt the (supposedly centrist) PRI more than they do the PAN. (For example, the PRI lost more ground than the PAN during the precipitous fall in liberal sentiment between 2000 and 2006.) Second, in the multinomial logit model estimated and described above, the coefficient on the economic liberalism variable is statistically significant for the PRI versus PRD pairwise comparison and for the PAN versus PRD comparison. It is not statistically significant for the PRI versus PAN pairwise comparison, however. In other words, changes in individual-level policy attitudes did not have a statistically discernible effect on the probability of shifting one's vote choice between the PAN and the PRI. All told, the leftist PRD is the most sensitive to shifts in mood, while the impact of mood swings on the PAN and PRI are slightly more ambiguous given their closer proximity to one another in the statist–liberal issue space. This fact helps to explain some of the mood model's shortcomings.

Conclusion

This chapter is an attempt to revive the aggregate analysis of Mexican—and for that matter Latin American—elections. Scholars have focused most of their efforts on individual-level analyses, perhaps because of well-founded warnings against committing errors of ecological inference. But in doing so, they risk missing the forest for the trees. Being able to explain and predict the ideological center of gravity, and thus perhaps the winner, of an election is fundamentally an aggregate question, even if grounded in microlevel decisions.

This chapter is also a vote for the explanatory power of positional issue voting models. Retrospective economic evaluations are not—and cannot be—the sole determinant of aggregate election outcomes in multiparty systems. When times are bad, voters have a choice of which candidate they reward with their anti-incumbent sentiment. The near-victory of AMLO in 2006 and the actual victories of leftists throughout Latin America during the 2000s, for example, were not mere accidents of retrospective voting (Arnold and Samuels 2011). Rather, voters' decisions had policy content and positional issue intentions. In Mexico, the shift leftward in election outcomes after 2000 was due to a souring of enthusiasm for the Washington Consensus. A similar correlational pattern emerged elsewhere in the region during the same decade, ushering in a number of leftist governments throughout the hemisphere (Baker and Greene 2011). Overall, mood and positional issues hold great potential for supplementing the predominant retrospective voting model of Mexican and Latin American voting behavior.

ACKNOWLEDGMENTS

The author is extremely grateful to Alejandro Moreno and Jennifer Wolak for their assistance with data collection and analysis. He also thanks the editors of this volume for their valuable constructive criticisms.

NOTES

1. Some dissenting voices that successfully employ models of Mexican voting behavior using a positional issue space do exist (Greene 2007, chap. 7; Magaloni 2006, chap. 6; Zechmeister 2008).

2. The eleven dimensions were (in descending order of average importance to the three major parties) privatization, religiosity, regional economic integration, globalization, crime, fiscal policy, social/moral issues, decentralization, indigenous peoples' rights, regulation of party financial and campaigning activities, and environmental regulation.

3. That said, a social/moral dimension about abortion, homosexuality, divorce, and euthanasia ranked only seventh.

4. Do not knows, nonresponses, and ambivalent responses were dropped. In the end, the percentages were calculated as follows:

$$\frac{\text{\# supporting liberal position}}{\text{\# supporting liberal position} + \text{\# supporting statist position}}.$$

5. Because of this problem, I ran the Stimson mood estimates through a time series (double exponential) smoother before finalizing them.

6. These probabilities are derived from model predictions.

7. The Wiesehomeier and Benoit data were supplemented by Coppedge (1998), Lodola and Queirolo (n.d.), and Pop-Eleches (2009) to create the data set used by Baker and Greene (2011).

8. Domínguez (2009) argues that the PRD performed well in 2006 (and thus perhaps again in 2012) because of the charisma of its candidate, López Obrador. The mood series suggests that the party's performance was in line with the country's statist mood shift, however, a shift that had occurred throughout much of Latin America and ushered in various leftist governments in the region (Baker and Greene 2011).

9. Evidence from party manifestoes (in some contrast to the Wiesehomeier-Benoit scorings) shows the PRI and PAN to be virtually indistinguishable in ideology after 1988 (Bruhn and Greene 2009, 113).

REFERENCES

Achen, Christopher. 1975. "Mass Political Attitudes and the Survey Response." *American Political Science Review* 69, no. 4: 1218–31.

Ansolabehere, Stephen, Jonathan Rodden, and James M. Snyder Jr. 2008. "The Strength of Issues: Using Multiple Measures to Gauge Preference Stability, Ideological Constraint, and Issue Voting." *American Political Science Review* 102, no. 2: 215–32.

Arnold, Jason Ross, and David J. Samuels. 2011. "Evidence from Public Opinion." In *The Resurgence of the Latin American Left*, ed. Steven Levitsky and Kenneth M. Roberts, 31–51. Baltimore: Johns Hopkins University Press.

Baker, Andy. 2003. "Why Is Trade Reform So Popular in Latin America? A Consumption-Based Theory of Trade Policy Preferences." *World Politics* 55, no. 3: 423–55.

———. 2009. *The Market and the Masses in Latin America: Policy Reform and Consumption in Liberalizing Economies.* New York: Cambridge University Press.

Baker, Andy, and Kenneth F. Greene. 2011. "The Latin American Left's Mandate: Free-Market Politics and Issue Voting in New Democracies." *World Politics* 63, no. 1: 43–77.

Bruhn, Kathleen, and Kenneth F. Greene. 2009. "The Absence of Common Ground between Candidates and Voters." In *Consolidating Mexico's Democracy: The 2006 Presidential Campaign in Comparative Perspective*, ed. Jorge I. Domínguez, Chappell Lawson, and Alejandro Moreno, 109–28. Baltimore: Johns Hopkins University Press.

Buendía, Jorge. 1996. "Economic Reform, Public Opinion, and Presidential Approval in Mexico, 1988–1993." *Comparative Political Studies* 29, no. 5: 566–91.

Buendía Laredo, Jorge. 2001. "Economic Reforms and Political Support in Mexico, 1988–1997." In *Public Support for Market Reforms in New Democracies*, ed. Susan C. Stokes, 131–59. New York: Cambridge University Press.

Campbell, James E. 2012. "Forecasting the 2012 American National Elections." *PS: Political Science and Politics* 45, no. 4: 610–13.

Converse, Philip E. 1964. "The Nature of Belief Systems in Mass Publics." In *Ideology and Discontent*, ed. David E. Apter, 206–61. London: Free Press of Glencoe.

Coppedge, Michael. 1998. "The Dynamic Diversity of Latin American Party Systems." *Party Politics* 4, no. 4: 547–68.

De Boef, Suzanna, and Luke Keele. 2008. "Taking Time Seriously." *American Journal of Political Science* 52, no. 1: 184–200.

Domínguez, Jorge I. 2009. "Conclusion: The Choices of Voters during the 2006 Presidential Election in Mexico." In *Consolidating Mexico's Democracy: The 2006 Presidential Campaign in Comparative Perspective*, ed. Jorge I. Domínguez, Chappell Lawson, and Alejandro Moreno, 285–303. Baltimore: Johns Hopkins University Press.

Domínguez, Jorge I., and Chappell H. Lawson, eds. 2004. *Mexico's Pivotal Democratic Election: Candidates, Voters, and the Presidential Campaign of 2000*. Stanford, CA: Stanford University Press.

Domínguez, Jorge I., and James A. McCann. 1995. "Shaping Mexico's Electoral Arena: The Construction of Partisan Cleavages in the 1988 and 1991 National Elections." *American Political Science Review* 89, no. 1: 34–48.

———. 1996. *Democratizing Mexico: Public Opinion and Electoral Choices*. Baltimore: Johns Hopkins University Press.

Greene, Kenneth F. 2007. *Why Dominant Parties Lose: Mexico's Democratization in Comparative Perspective*. New York: Cambridge University Press.

———. 2009. "Images and Issues in Mexico's 2006 Presidential Election." In *Consolidating Mexico's Democracy: The 2006 Presidential Campaign in Comparative Perspective*, ed. Jorge I. Domínguez, Chappell Lawson, and Alejandro Moreno, 246–67. Baltimore: Johns Hopkins University Press.

———. 2011. "Campaign Persuasion and Nascent Partisanship in Mexico's New Democracy." *American Journal of Political Science* 55, no. 2: 398–416.

Gunther, Richard, and Kuan Hsin-chi. 2007. "Value Cleavages and Partisan Conflict." In *Democracy, Intermediation, and Voting on Four Continents*, ed. Richard Gunther, José Ramón Montero, and Hans-Jürgen Puhle, 255–320. New York: Oxford University Press.

Hershberg, Eric, and Fred Rosen. 2006. "Turning the Tide?" In *Latin America after Neoliberalism: Turning the Tide in the 21st Century?*, ed. Eric Hershberg and Fred Rosen, 1–25. New York: New Press.

Kitschelt, Herbert, Kirk A. Hawkins, Juan Pablo Luna, Guillermo Rosas, and Elizabeth J. Zechmeister. 2010. *Latin American Party Systems*. New York: Cambridge University Press.

Kramer, Gerald. 1983. "The Ecological Fallacy Revisited: Aggregate versus Individual-Level Findings on Economics and Elections, and Sociotropic Voting." *American Political Science Review* 77, no. 1: 92–111.

Lane, Robert Edwards. 1962. *Political Ideology: Why the American Common Man Believes What He Does*. New York: Free Press of Glencoe.

Lawson, Chappell H. 2002. *Building the Fourth Estate: Democratization and the Rise of a Free Press in Mexico*. Berkeley: University of California Press.

Lewis-Beck, Michael S., and Tom W. Rice. 1992. *Forecasting Elections*. Washington, DC: CQ Press.

Lodola, German, and Rosario Queirolo. n.d. "Ideological Classification of Latin American Political Parties." Pittsburgh, PA: University of Pittsburgh.

Lora, Eduardo, Ugo Panizza, and Myriam Quispe-Agnoli. 2004. "Reform Fatigue: Symptoms, Reasons and Implications." *Economic Review* 9, no. 2: 1–28.

Magaloni, Beatriz. 2006. *Voting for Autocracy: Hegemonic Party Survival and Its Demise in Mexico*. New York: Cambridge University Press.

Magaloni, Beatriz, and Alejandro Moreno 2003. "Catching All Souls: The PAN and the Politics of Catholicism in Mexico." In *Christian Democracy in Latin America: Electoral Competition and Regime Conflicts*, ed. Scott Mainwaring and Timothy R. Scully, 247–74. Stanford: Stanford University Press.

McCann, James A., and Chappell H. Lawson. 2003. "An Electorate Adrift: Public Opinion and the Quality of Democracy in Mexico." *Latin American Research Review* 38, no. 3: 60–81.

Moreno, Alejandro. 2009. "The Activation of Economic Voting in the 2006 Campaign." In *Consolidating Mexico's Democracy: The 2006 Presidential Campaign in Comparative Perspective*, ed. Jorge I. Domínguez, Chappell Lawson, and Alejandro Moreno, 209–28. Baltimore: Johns Hopkins University Press.

Pop-Eleches, Grigore. 2009. *From Economic Crisis to Reform: IMF Programs in Latin America and Eastern Europe*. Princeton, NJ: Princeton University Press.

Remmer, Karen L. 1991. "The Political Impact of Economic Crisis in Latin America in the 1980s." *American Political Science Review* 85, no. 3: 777–800.

Rieff, David. 2006. "The Populist at the Border." *New York Times*, June 4. http://www.nytimes.com/2006/06/04/magazine/04mexico.html?pagewanted=print&_r=0.

Roberts, Kenneth. 2008. "The Mobilization of Opposition to Economic Liberalization." *Annual Review of Political Science* 11: 327–49.

Samuelson, Robert. 2002. "Global Economics under Siege." *Washington Post*, October 16, A25.

Singer, Mathew M., and Ryan E. Carlin. 2013. "Context Counts: The Election Cycle, Development, and the Nature of Economic Voting." *Journal of Politics* 75, no. 3: 730–42.

Stimson, James A. 1991. *Public Opinion in America: Moods, Cycles, and Swings*. Boulder, CO: Westview Press.

Wiesehomeier, Nina, and Kenneth Benoit. 2009. "Presidents, Parties, and Policy Competition." *Journal of Politics* 71, no. 4: 1435–47.

Zaller, John R. 1992. *The Nature and Origins of Mass Opinion*. New York: Cambridge University Press.

Zechmeister, Elizabeth J. 2008. "Policy-Based Voting, Perceptions of Feasible Issue Space, and the 2000 Mexican Elections." *Electoral Studies* 27, no. 4: 649–60.

6

Campaign Effects in Mexico since Democratization

KENNETH F. GREENE

Many elements of Mexico's political system would make it seem like a paragon of stability, especially among new democracies. It features three main political parties that have endured over time with histories that predate the transition to fully open partisan competition; the major issues in electoral contests have remained fairly stable since the mid-1980s; and the country has avoided the rise of maverick and antisystem candidates who have emerged in other countries in Latin America.

Yet despite this stability at the elite level, voting behavior is rife with preelectoral volatility, and voters are surprisingly susceptible to persuasive campaign messages. Two of Mexico's three fully democratic presidential elections since 2000 featured come-from-behind victories by candidates who would have lost without the effects of the campaigns. In 2000, Vicente Fox, candidate of the Partido Acción Nacional (PAN), polled as much as seven percentage points behind Francisco Labastida, candidate of the Partido Revolucionario Institucional (PRI), but bested the dominant party's standard-bearer by more than six points on Election Day. In 2006, Andrés Manuel López Obrador, candidate of the Partido de la Revolución Democrática (PRD), seemed certain to win after leading by as many as fifteen percentage points, but he eventually lost the razor-close election to the PAN's Felipe Calderón. Although Enrique Peña Nieto led throughout the brief three-month campaigns in 2012, he would not have won had another candidate claimed the votes that were swayed by the campaigns.[1]

Such large and persistent campaign effects are surprising for two reasons. First, most research in comparative politics focuses on incentives for voters to align themselves with partisan options over time on the basis of class identity, employment profile, ethnicity, or association with other social cleavages such as religion or localism (Bartolini 2000; Chandra 2004; Evans 2000; Horowitz 1987; Kitschelt 1994; Lipset and Rokkan 1967). If these identities drive voting, then the campaigns should just help voters learn how to line up their preexisting and unchanging preferences with the most suitable partisan option (Gelman and King 1993). We might see some volatility in vote intentions during campaigns, but in a stable party system, voters' preferences should settle over time as citizens learn about the platforms and governing styles of the continuing parties. Second, stable party systems should also promote partisan identification that scholars of American politics have treated as an "unmoved mover" of vote choices (Johnston 2006). Although we would not necessarily expect a new democracy to rapidly instill partisan identification in its voters (McCann and Lawson 2003), Converse (1969) argued that electorates in such countries experience "a kind of 'settling down' or habituation to a competitive party system, which occurs at a mass level as a secular trend over time" (141). He argued that this should yield a "'binding in' of popular loyalties to one or another of the traditionally competing political parties" (141). Thus the major statements about voting behavior applicable to new democracies strike an optimistic note when it comes to preelectoral instability: whether due to the projection of social identities onto vote choices or the creation of partisan sympathies, volatility should be low and should diminish as new democracies age. This should especially occur in new democracies with stable party systems like Mexico, where elites offer voters nearly the same set of partisan options over time.

As I show below, not only are campaign effects large in Mexico, but they also have increased in magnitude since democratization. In prior work, I show why many more voters are vulnerable to the persuasive power of campaigns in Mexico than in the United States or other long-established democracies (Greene 2011). Here I describe and explain the surprising trend of increasing campaign effects over time. Unlike in transitions to democracy from fully closed authoritarian regimes that experience stark discontinuities between the authoritarian and democratic eras, I argue that Mexico's protracted transition from authoritarian single-party dominance was marked by progressive partisan dealignment that has endured well into the democratic period. Weak and weakening partisan identities among many voters leave increasing portions of the electorate vulnerable to the persuasive effects of political campaigns. Mexico actually presents a hard test of this "authoritarian legacies" argument because its highly stable elite politics should provide fertile ground for growing stability in mass voting behavior, and because the radical limitations on campaigns imposed on the 2012 contest should have decreased campaign effects in the most recent election.

This chapter also serves as a justification for a key aspect of the Mexico Panel Studies that began in 2000. One of the inspirations behind these projects has been to collect data appropriate for analyzing campaign effects.[2] Analysts have examined the effects of mass media advertising (Greene 2011; Lawson and McCann 2005), candidate rhetoric and advertising (Moreno 2004, 2009), debates (Lawson 2004), issues (Magaloni and Poiré 2004), candidate images (Greene 2009), voter ideology (McCann 2009), partisanship (Greene 2011; McCann and Lawson 2003), and other campaign events on voters' final choices at the polls. These works highlight important aspects of the campaigns, but they do not test explicitly for campaign effects and cannot distinguish among effects of different strength. For instance, the campaigns would weakly influence vote choice if a PRI partisan in the 2000 elections considered supporting challenger Vicente Fox for the presidency but, after hearing the campaigns, came home to support standard-bearer Francisco Labastida. The campaigns would have had a much stronger influence if that same partisan intended to vote for Labastida months before the election but after receiving the content of the campaigns defected to support Fox. Whereas the first voter wavers momentarily but ultimately supports the continuation of Mexico's authoritarian dominant-party system, the second voter is persuaded to help oust the PRI and usher in an unprecedented era of fully competitive democracy in 2000. Most prior studies of voting behavior in Mexico cannot distinguish between these types of campaign effects.

In the next section of this chapter, I develop the theoretical argument in more detail. The second section documents the aggregate incidence of changes in vote intentions during presidential campaigns since 2000. Doing so helps orient readers to the dynamics of vote intentions during the campaigns, but it is insufficient for understanding campaign effects. In the third and fourth sections, I introduce a statistical procedure for uncovering campaign effects and show both the aggregate vote swing and the type of campaign effects among individual voters during the three presidential elections. I use the fifth section to demonstrate that the large and increasing group of independent voters in Mexico is particularly susceptible to campaign effects. In the final section before the conclusion, I show that the campaigns were important in producing Peña Nieto's victory, even though his was not a dramatic come-from-behind win like those of his predecessors. Throughout I limit my analysis to documenting the degree of campaign effects. I do not analyze the content or strategies of the campaigns that gave rise to these effects, which other chapters in this volume address, although I briefly discuss the menu of possible types of campaigns effects in the conclusion.

The Power of Campaigns in Mexico's New Democracy

Whether due to the influence of social identities on vote choices or as the result of partisan identities that solidify over time, existing research predicts that new democracies should experience decreasing voter volatility during campaigns as democracy ages. Why, then, has Mexico experienced large and increasing campaign effects that convince many voters to abandon their initial vote intentions as well as the candidate most closely associated with their precampaign dispositions, which are typically rooted in social and partisan identities?

In prior work, I showed why many voters are susceptible to campaign effects in new democracies, including Mexico (Greene 2011). I demonstrated that partisanship operates as a perceptual bias that leads partisans to discount negative information about their most preferred candidate as well as positive information about their less preferred candidate or candidates (see also Bartels 2002; Zaller 1992). Thus weaker partisan identities make voters more susceptible to the influence of persuasive campaign communications. These effects are heightened when there are imbalances in the flow of information about the candidates. Empirically, I showed that weak partisan identities and an advertising advantage for Calderón in 2006 led large portions of the electorate to vote against their precampaign dispositions and early vote intentions, accounting for most of Calderón's come-from-behind victory.

If many voters were persuadable in 2006, why would the campaigns still have the power to sway so many voters in 2012? In addition to the strong theoretical reasons, detailed above, that lead us to expect that campaign effects should reduce as Mexico's democracy ages, new elections legislation in force for the 2012 contest meant that the campaign period was reduced from more than a year to just three months. As a result, candidates had much less time to change voters' minds than in the past.

I argue that the type of prior authoritarian regime and the legacies it bequeaths condition both the magnitude of campaign effects in early democratic elections and the direction of change in campaign effects as democracies age. Where partisanship solidifies, campaign effects will diminish and new democracies will experience substantially more stability in voting patterns. Where partisanship instead remains weak, campaign effects will induce substantial volatility in vote intentions. In these latter cases, candidates can rise and fall during the campaign season like a series of swells on the sea.

Most fully authoritarian regimes experience sharp political discontinuities in their transitions to democracy. Elite pacts or regime breakdown lead to founding elections that feature if not entirely new parties then a preponderance of new actors. The absence of electoral competition during the authoritarian era means that voters lack partisan identities during founding elections. In this context, early campaigns should have the largest and strongest effects on voters; however, as partisanship develops from near zero, campaign effects should decline over time, relative to their zenith. Converse (1969) may have been thinking about this stylized version of democratization—the type of transitions that occurred with the collapse of the Soviet Union or the end of military dictatorships in Argentina and Chile—when he argued that the passage of time generates increasing partisan stability in new democracies.

Competitive authoritarian regimes, and in particular dominant-party authoritarian regimes such as Mexico, experience much greater political continuity during their transitions to democracy. Formerly authoritarian parties typically survive, and many of the major (formerly opposition) parties are founded before democratization. As a result, protracted transitions to democracy depend on opposition parties gaining strength in the electorate relative to the incumbent through a process of partisan dealignment (Greene 2007).

The key question is whether voters that dealign from the former incumbent party then identify with the rising opposition parties or become independent voters. If they become partisans of the former opposition or if the former dominant party staunches its hemorrhage of voters, then elite–mass relations will settle more quickly and campaigns will have smaller effects, much as they do in the United States and other established democracies (Bartels 1993, 266; Berelson, Lazarsfeld, and McPhee 1954, 16; Campbell 2000; Finkel 1993, 14; Holbrook 1996; Kaufmann, Petrocik, and Shaw 2008, 167–68; Markus 1988, 150; Shaw 1999, 2006). If, instead, dealigning voters become independents—as they have in Mexico since 2000—then a larger portion of the electorate will be more susceptible to persuasive campaign messages, and we should expect greater pre-election volatility in vote intentions as clever campaigns draw voters away from the candidate associated with their precampaign dispositions. In systems like

Mexico's, Converse's (1969) optimistic predictions are turned on their head: the passage of time can yield less stable patterns of mass partisanship.

Changes in Vote Intentions during Mexico's Presidential Election Campaigns

If campaigns shift voters' intentions and choices among the competing candidates, then those changes should be observable in the weeks and months leading up to Election Day. Such changes cannot be observed in cross-sectional data that are readily available through numerous preelection polls. Even though such polls show volatility across the entire electorate, they hide the individual-level changes in vote intentions and choices that result from campaign effects. Panel studies are uniquely suited to show these individual-level effects.

Data from the Mexico 2000, 2006, and 2012 Panel Studies help characterize the degree of volatility among individual voters leading up to Election Day. The three studies differ in important ways, but each one straddles the relevant campaign period. Because Vicente Fox started his 2000 campaign far ahead of his party's nomination battle in the attempt to claim advantage over his internal rivals (Bruhn 2004; Greene 2007; Shirk 2005), the 2000 presidential campaigns lasted about eighteen months. The Mexico 2000 Panel Study includes four waves, beginning in February 2000. For the 2006 presidential election, Andrés Manuel López Obrador began to campaign more than a year ahead of time, touring the country in an attempt to build a grassroots movement (Bruhn 2009; Langston and Benton 2007). The Mexico 2006 Panel Study includes three waves, beginning in October 2005. The 2012 presidential campaigns were restricted by law to the three months before the election. Thus the Mexico 2012 Panel Study included just two waves, beginning in April. Importantly, each panel study includes waves that are well timed to capture shifts in vote choices from the start of the campaigns to Election Day.

In all three elections, a large proportion of the electorate shifted its support among the contenders from the three main parties. Naturally, panel studies that interview voters more often will register more shifts in vote intentions. I am interested in the analytically equivalent time periods across election years, whether the campaigns lasted eighteen months or just three. So I use Wave 1, which was timed to correspond to the beginning of the campaigns, and the postelection wave in each panel study. These results show remarkable similarity in the degree of volatility in voter intentions over time: 33.0% of voters that ultimately voted for one of the major candidates changed their vote intentions in 2000, 33.8% in 2006, and 34.2% in 2012.[3]

Lurking behind these figures are hints about the effectiveness of the campaigns themselves. In 2000, the PRI's candidate, Francisco Labastida, had a retention rate among initially aligned voters that was higher than that of the other candidates, but among voters who changed their minds and initially undecided voters, most flowed to Fox. In 2006, it was the PRD's candidate, Andrés Manuel López Obrador, who claimed the most loyalists, but most changers and initially undecided votes flowed to the PAN's candidate, Felipe Calderón. In 2012, Enrique Peña Nieto of the PRI not only maintained by far the most loyalists but also attracted more voters during the campaign season. Rather than the come-from-behind victories produced by the campaigns in 2000 and 2006, the 2012 campaigns featured notable movement toward the early front-runner.

These large vote swings show us that the campaigns deeply affected voters, but they do not show us what effects the campaigns had. It is possible that changes in vote intentions amounted to nothing more than flirtation with one candidate and voters later "came home" to their "natural" candidate by Election Day (Gelman and King 1993). If this process underlies vote swings, then the campaigns would have minor effects, simply helping voters align their personal preferences with those of their "natural" candidate. If voters instead shifted from an intention to vote for their natural candidate at the outset of the campaigns to a vote for another candidate in July, then the campaigns would have had a much more dramatic effect. In order to figure the impact of the campaigns, we need to know not only voters' intentions compared to their final choices, but also how those intentions and choices compare to their precampaign dispositions. The next section presents a statistical procedure for untangling these elements and allows us to estimate the net effects of the campaigns on electoral outcomes.

Campaign Effects in Mexico's Presidential Elections, 2000–2012

A voter's precampaign disposition tells us which candidate that voter would have chosen absent the campaigns. Unfortunately, we cannot discern this natural candidate from vote intentions at the start of a campaign because intentions may be at odds with dispositions. Imagine an election between a leftist candidate from a well-known party who wants to defend public enterprises and a rightist candidate, also from a well-known party, who wants to privatize them.

A public sector employee who votes mainly on economic issues would be naturally disposed to vote for the leftist candidate. However, for whatever set of reasons, when asked at the beginning of the campaign season, she might say she intends to vote for the rightist candidate (perhaps she does not yet know that the candidate wants to privatize the company for which she works). If this voter ultimately chooses the leftist candidate, we would not want to conclude that she voted against her precampaign disposition simply because she changed her vote choice during the campaign season. "Coming home" to a candidate associated with one's dispositions is clearly a less powerful campaign effect than being "converted away" from one's natural candidate.

In order to understand not just the amount of campaign effects but also their power, we need to uncover voters' precampaign dispositions and then compare these dispositions to their vote intentions before the campaign and vote choices on Election Day. Uncovering such dispositions requires the use of somewhat involved statistical methods. I present models of vote choices, one for each election, that contain two types of variables: voters' attitudes and preferences at the outset of the campaigns, as measured by the first wave of each panel study, and variables that represent changes in those attitudes and preferences from Wave 1 to July (hereafter referred to as "change scores"). The variables measured in Wave 1 represent precampaign dispositions, and the change scores represent the effects of the campaign. The advantage of this type of model is that we can simulate erasing the campaign by removing the effects of the change scores. Then we can predict which candidate each voter would have supported had she not experienced the campaign at all. That is, we can figure out likely vote choice solely on the basis of precampaign dispositions. In addition, by examining the partial effect of the change scores, we can also isolate the effect of the campaigns, controlling for precampaign dispositions.

The statistical models appear in an ancillary appendix (available at www .press.jhu.edu) and include the standard variables typically used to study vote choice in Mexico and elsewhere: party identification, retrospective evaluations of the outgoing administration, preferences over economic policy, and ratings of each candidate's competence. The model for 2000 also includes assessments of the state of democracy in Mexico as a proxy for more complex preferences over the maintenance of authoritarian single-party dominance under the PRI or transition to fully competitive democracy (Domínguez and McCann 1996). The model for 2012 includes preferences over how to prosecute the war against illegal drugs. Finally, all models include assessments of the trailing candidate's chances of winning.[4] I include this last variable because, in multiparty elections, voters may abandon the trailing candidate in order to support a less preferred candidate who has a better chance of winning (Cox 1997; Duverger 1954). For all variables, I also include change scores between Wave 1 and July.

Unlike the analysis for the 2000 and 2006 elections, the models for 2012 employ a postsample weighting scheme. I used this approach for three reasons. First, postelection polls often register a bandwagon effect where voters report choosing the winner even when they did not. We would expect this effect to be large in 2012, when the winning margin was much bigger than in the prior election. Second, panel studies, especially those with complex logistics such as our nationwide in-person poll, fail to reinterview all respondents after the initial survey wave, and this attrition can affect vote choice analyses.

Finally, polling during the 2012 election season faced several heightened challenges compared to the two prior presidential elections. Certain areas of the country were plagued with sufficient violence that polling firms sometimes replaced sampled locales with others that were demographically similar but safer for their pollsters. Because living under the threat of violence may influence political attitudes and preferences, such replacement could have affected findings from survey research. In addition, the lackluster and sometimes embarrassing campaign ran by Vázquez Mota may have discouraged her supporters from revealing their preferences. Finally, some natural supporters of López Obrador may have been uneasy about declaring their support for him early in the campaign season. This candidate's rhetorical attack against democratic institutions and his leadership of protests that snarled traffic in Mexico City for months following his narrow defeat in 2006 raised questions that López Obrador struggled to answer during the early days of the short campaign season in 2012. For these reasons, and perhaps others, virtually all publicly available preelection surveys in 2012 "seemed" to provide vote share estimates that were off the mark. We do not know for sure, of course, because preelection estimates of vote intentions cannot be validated or invalidated with election results owing to the effects of the intervening campaigns. Nevertheless, the distance between preelection findings and the balloting were notably larger in 2012 than in the two prior presidential elections. The fact that the most reputable exit polls came close to the election result implies that measurement error or sampling challenges likely contributed to difficulties with preelection polls.

To address these three issues, the 2012 models presented here are based on postsample weights that adjust gender to the proportions found in the voter registration rolls, adjust for attrition with a basic model of demographic variables, and compensate for bandwagoning by constructing a vote choice variable on the basis of respondents' feeling thermometer ratings of the candidates (see ancillary appendix for details; www.press.jhu.edu).

To determine how much the campaigns affected vote choices above and beyond voters' precampaigns dispositions, we can conduct two analyses. First, we can use the model referenced above to calculate the proportion of the vote that each candidate would have won had there been no campaign and compare it to the predicted vote when voters experience the entire campaign (Finkel 1993). The latter prediction includes the effects of the campaigns and should therefore mirror the election results. But note that this prediction may be at odds with vote intentions as measured in cross-sectional surveys. In other words, these "no campaign" predictions are not the same as asking voters who they would support if the election were today. Those "in-the-moment" answers may be affected by considerations that are at odds with voters' precampaign dispositions owing to any number of forces, such as the administration of the survey itself, voters' lack of information about the candidates—information that they would gather before Election Day regardless of campaign content—or simply an answer given on a whim as voters flirt with supporting various candidates. Instead, the "no campaign" estimates given in table 6.1 are based on voters' measured dispositions, and I believe that they better represent precampaign levels of support for the candidates than can be gleaned from standard campaign season polling.

The net vote swing due to the campaigns shows that Fox may have won the 2000 elections because of the effects of the campaigns. At the time of the first wave of the panel survey in late February, Fox held a tenuous lead (according to the vote choice models presented in an ancillary appendix; see www.press.jhu .edu) that was certainly within the margin of error. Having heard the campaigns, 5% of voters abandoned Labastida and nearly the same proportion voted for Fox, putting Fox well over the top. It would not be an exaggeration to argue that without Fox's deft campaign, and Labastida's bad one, single-party rule would not have ended in 2000 (Greene 2007). In even more dramatic fashion, Calderón won the 2006 elections because of the campaigns. Had the election been held in October 2005 at the time of the first wave of the panel survey, López Obrador would have won handily. Instead, almost 7% of voters changed to Calderón and more than 5% abandoned López Obrador after hearing the content of the campaigns.

Table 6.1.   Effect of the campaigns on candidate vote shares
(in percentages), 2000–2012

Election	Predicted vote without campaign	Predicted vote with campaign	Net campaign "effect"
2000			
Fox (PAN)	43.6	48.5	4.9
Labastida (PRI)	42.6	37.6	−5.0
Cárdenas (PRD)	13.8	13.9	0.1
Total net vote share moved			10.0
2006			
Calderón (PAN)	36.9	43.8	6.9
Madrazo (PRI)	21.4	19.7	−1.7
López Obrador (PRD)	41.7	36.6	−5.1
Total net vote share moved			13.7
2012			
Vázquez Mota (PAN)	31.6	26.2	−5.4
Peña Nieto (PRI)	33.2	37.1	3.9
López Obrador (PRD)	35.2	36.7	1.5
Total net vote share moved			10.8

Table 6.1 also shows that the 2012 campaigns moved 10.8% of the vote, slightly more than was moved in the historic 2000 elections. During the 2012 campaign season, Vásquez Mota lost 5.6 percentage points, while Peña Nieto gained 3.9 and López Obrador gained 1.5. This finding differs a bit from the early standard narrative about 2012. In that story, López Obrador closed in on a flagging Peña Nieto as the campaign season wore on. Although it is clearly true that the leftist candidate did win supporters as Election Day neared, the PRI's candidate also benefited from Vázquez Mota's decline. A close inspection of results from preelection cross-sectional polls corroborates this version of events, showing an upswing in Peña Nieto's vote share from the start of the campaigns in April to Election Day in July.[5] Table 6.1 thus shows that although Peña Nieto did not come from behind to win in 2012, as did Fox in 2000 and Calderón in 2006, the campaigns still moved a large proportion of the vote. In fact, in all three presidential elections in Mexico since 2000, campaign effects dwarfed those in the United States where 4% of the vote was moved, on average, in presidential elections between 1940 and 1994 (Bartels 1993, 266; Berelson et al. 1954, 16; Campbell 2000; Finkel 1993, 14; Holbrook 1996; Kaufmann et al. 2008, 167–68; Markus 1988, 150; Shaw 1999, 2006).[6]

Clearly, there has not been a decline in campaign effects at the aggregate level. Yet to fully appreciate the type and amount of campaign effects, we need to move from the aggregate vote swing shown here to an individual-level analysis. The aggregate data might hide substantial movement because the net result may include shifts in vote choices that cancel each other out. For instance, if the campaigns encourage one voter to abandon Fox and another to choose him, Fox nets zero votes.

The second main analysis we can do using the models above focuses on the vote choices of individuals. In prior work, I describe the various possible influences that campaigns can have on voters (Greene 2011), listed here from strongest to weakest:

1. *Conversion away* from a vote intention that is consistent with precampaign dispositions to a vote choice that is inconsistent.
2. *Partial conversion* of an initially undecided voter to vote against her precampaign dispositions.
3. *Conversion home* from an intention that is inconsistent with precampaign dispositions to a vote choice that is consistent.
4. *Activation* of an initially undecided voter to come home to the candidate associated with her precampaign dispositions.
5. *Reinforcement* of initial dispositions.

Campaigns that reinforce and activate, as they do in long-established democracies such as the United States (Berelson et al. 1954; Finkel 1993; Lazarsfeld, Berelson, and Gaudet 1948), have small effects. Campaigns that convert do more. Campaigns that convert away can truly transform elections.

To assess the type of campaign effects present in Mexico's presidential elections, I compare each voter's predicted choice based on her precampaign dispositions using the vote choice models above to her self-reported vote intention from Wave 1 and final vote choice in July (Finkel 1993; Lazarsfeld et al. 1948).[7] I represent the various types of campaign effects in figure 6.1 (see ancillary appendix to view the same data in table format; www.press.jhu.edu). For ease of interpretation, the bottom three areas represent campaign effects that yield a final vote choice for the voter's "natural" candidate, whereas the top three areas represent effects that cause voters to choose another candidate.

In all three elections, the dominant campaign effect was to reinforce voters' intention to choose the candidate most closely associated with their precampaign dispositions, referred to in figure 6.1 as "reinforcement (home)." As

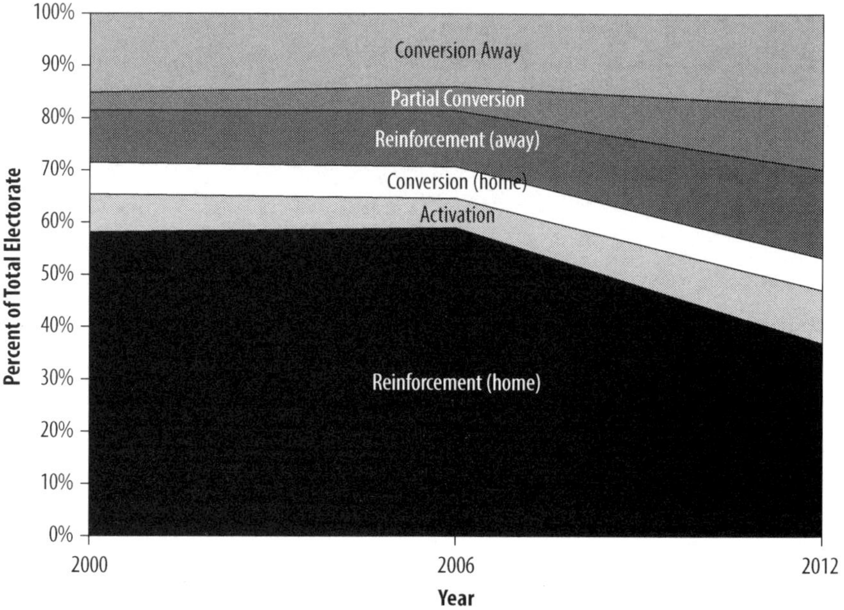

Figure 6.1. Campaign effects in Mexico's presidential elections, 2000–2012

expected, most voters make final decisions that square with their initial preferences on the major issues, socioeconomic status, and other dispositions. But figure 6.1 also shows that the campaigns do not reinforce the vote intentions of all voters. Rather, the campaigns "do something." They convince about 15% of voters to abandon the candidate most closely associated with their dispositions and for whom they intended to vote at the beginning of the campaign season. The campaigns exert such a powerful influence on these voters that they are swayed to vote for another candidate. To add some context, one example would be an upper-class practicing Catholic with free market economic policy preferences initially deciding to vote for the PAN's candidate, Josefina Vázquez Mota, at the outset of the 2012 campaign season; however, after listening to the content of the campaigns, deciding to abandon the conservative choice for either the PRI's Enrique Peña Nieto or leftist Andrés Manuel López Obrador of the PRD. Such "conversion away" is so powerful that it only moved about 2% of voters in the 1940 US presidential election and 2.6% in 1980 (Finkel 1993, 15; Lazarsfeld et al. 1948, 102). Many more of Mexico's voters have been moveable during its first three fully democratic presidential elections. In 2012, this proportion rose to 17% of the electorate.

Even more impressive is the overall size of the electorate that was convinced to support a candidate who was not in line with their precampaign dispositions. This sum is represented by adding the areas in figure 6.1 associated with conversion away, partial conversion, and reinforcement away. These processes together affected nearly 29% of the electorate in 2000 and 2006, and more than 46% in 2012.

Finally, figure 6.1 shows that, far from diminishing over time, campaign effects that move voters away from (or keep them away from) the candidate most closely associated with their precampaign dispositions are on the rise. For reasons detailed below, including the short campaign period, the strict limits on mass media advertising, and the limits on campaign content, 2012 should have witnessed fewer campaign effects than the previous elections. Instead, it shows more.

Dealignment without Realignment and Rising Campaign Effects

To this point, the analysis has shown that campaigns sway large portions of the electorate in Mexico and such effects have increased over time. Here I show that a principal reason for this increase concerns the rise in the proportion of independent voters since the transition to fully competitive democracy in 2000.

Mexico is a clear case of voter dealignment without realignment. Some voters that stuck with the PRI even after it lost the presidency continued to peel away in the years after 2000 as its prospects for a quick return to the federal executive appeared bleak and its ability to deliver patronage jobs and other selective benefits diminished. Access to patronage certainly varied across the national territory and was higher in the ten states where the PRI never lost access to public resources than in the remaining twenty-one states and the Federal District, where turnover limited the formerly dominant party's access, at least when it was out of power.

While the PRI lost partisans, the former opposition parties did not invest significantly in building their organizations. They have remained geographically regionalized, with the PAN maintaining most of the non-PRI support in northern and Bajío (Mexico's central "Bible belt") states and the PRD accounting for most non-PRI support in southern states and in Mexico City. Despite some recent reforms, both parties have maintained high barriers to activist recruitment and advancement that tend to open the party mainly to the type of citizens already represented in their structures rather than recruiting from wider groups in society. And although their presidential candidates have sometimes made broader appeals, the leaders of the party apparatuses themselves have continued to make niche-oriented appeals designed to attract traditional core constituencies (Greene 2007, 2012). As a result, the former opposition parties have brought few new partisans on board and have instead allowed the ranks of independent voters to swell.

At the onset of Mexico's fully competitive democracy in 2000, the PRI still retained the plurality of voters' sympathies, accounting for about 38% of the electorate. Over the following six years, voters continued to abandon the PRI, much as they had been doing, bit by bit, since the mid-1980s (Greene 2007; Moreno 2003). As voters deserted the formerly dominant party, they began to self-identify as independents without a partisan affiliation. Amazingly, even the ruling PAN lost partisan sympathizers. The PRD experienced a small bump in 2006—likely associated with the first-time presidential candidacy of the charismatic López Obrador—and then a return to its prior level of partisan identification. By 2012, both the PAN and PRD held below 20% of the electorate's sympathies, and independent voters had soared to more than 40% of the electorate. Even as Mexico passed over the threshold of democratization in 2000, the voter dealignment process that helped transform its regime continued to advance.

Independent voters are much more susceptible to persuasive campaign messages than are partisans (Bartels 2002; Greene 2011). As a result, the rise of independents helps account for the increase in campaign effects over time that I documented above. To determine the degree of citizens' susceptibility to persuasive campaign messages, I examine the proportion of each partisan group that experienced the strongest campaign effects: "partial conversion" and "conversion away." Both of these campaign effects bring a voter from a vote intention at the beginning of the campaigns that is in line with her predispositions (e.g., a dyed-in-the-wool leftist intending to vote for the leftist candidate) to a vote choice that is at odds with her dispositions (e.g., that same leftist voting for the rightist candidate). In all three general elections since 2000, independents experienced partial conversion and conversion away at the highest rates. These rates have increased over time, topping out at 39.2% in 2012 (compared to 25.3% for partisans in that year). In other words, not only are independents the largest group in the electorate and not only are they most susceptible to campaign influence, they are becoming more susceptible over time. This is, of course, exactly the opposite of Converse's (1969) prediction that

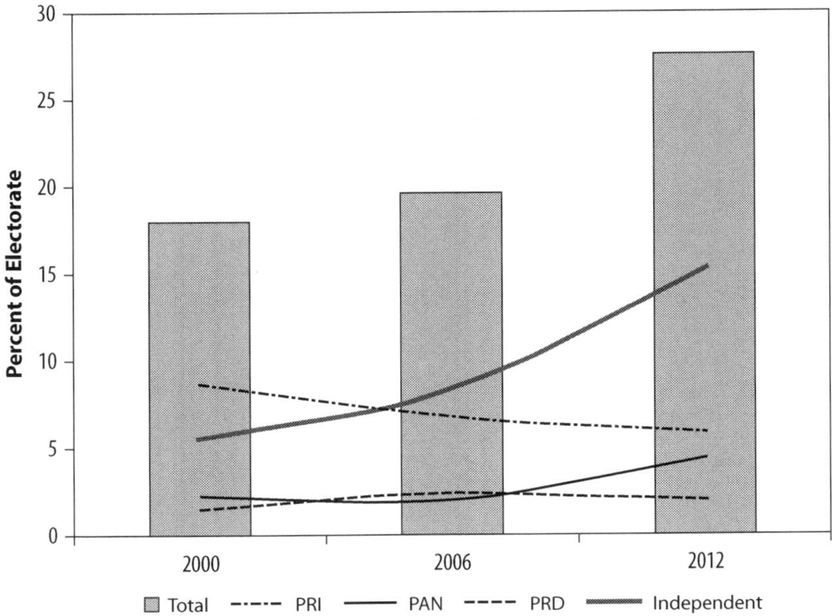

Figure 6.2. The strongest campaign effects by partisan group and total (as a percentage of the electorate), 2000–2012

partisanship would increasingly take root in new democracies and campaign effects would fade.

Figure 6.2 combines information on the size of each partisan group in the electorate with information about each group's likelihood of experiencing the strongest campaign effects. It thus shows the electoral relevance of campaign effects by group. With continued partisan dealignment, the proportion of PRI identifiers has continued to fall over time. As more voters become independents, and when paired with independents' greater susceptibility to campaign effects, these nonpartisans have come to represent the largest proportion of swayable votes. From a candidate's perspective, this group is the most important to attract during the campaign season. As can be appreciated in figure 6.2, the rise in vulnerability to the strongest campaign effects over time is driven by an increase in susceptible independents. If the PRI had staunched its hemorrhage of partisans or the formerly opposition parties had managed to realign voters, much less of the electorate would be swayable, and we would observe a decline in campaign effects over time rather than an increase.

Campaign Effects and the Return of the PRI

The trend since Mexico's transition to fully competitive democracy is clear: voter dealignment continues to swell the ranks of nonpartisans, and this mass of voters allows persuasive campaign content to sway large portions of the electorate during campaign seasons. In this section, I argue that Peña Nieto's victory and the return of the PRI—an event that was nearly unthinkable just a few years ago—was strongly influenced by the 2012 campaigns.

As shown above, Peña Nieto began the campaign season with such a large following that he would have won the 2012 election even if the subsequent campaigns had not existed; however, enough voters abandoned their initial choice during the three-month campaigns that Peña Nieto would have lost had another candidate attracted the voters that ended up switching. The centrality of the campaigns in 2012 is especially surprising, not only because it defies existing theory but also because of the electoral rules that governed the contest. The 2012 presidential election was the first held under the dramatic 2007 election reform (see Eric Magar, chap. 3, this volume). The reform shortened the official campaign season from what had been about one year to just three months (April to July) and put strict limits on negative advertising. The attenuated campaign period and restrictions on ad content meant that voters were exposed to less persuasive campaigns than in 2000 and 2006.[8]

In addition, the candidates emphasized issues in their campaigns that should have been less effective in changing voters' preferences. To be sure, the consequences of electing one or another of the candidates were substantial. Vázquez Mota pledged to continue Calderón's economic policies that had garnered mixed success during his term. There were also indications that she would continue Calderón's war on drugs with little change. López Obrador ran a notably more centrist campaign than he had as the left's candidate in 2006 but still pledged to revisit important details of the North American Free Trade Agreement and the trade relationship with the United States more generally, as well as to challenge the oligopolistic or monopolistic control of key industries. He also spoke of combatting violence through "love not war," which implied the possibility that he would remove the army from its policing duties. Peña Nieto staked out a vague middle ground, suggesting his interest in moving toward greater private investment in the oil and gas sector and challenging selected oligopolies while pledging to maintain the status quo when it came to commercial relations with the United States. He also hinted at redeploying drug war resources in a manner that would reduce violence without turning a blind eye to trafficking. (See Kathleen Bruhn, chap. 2, this volume, for more detail on the campaigns.)

Yet voters listening to the content of the campaigns would have been hard pressed to identify these plans. The candidates made only vague references to reducing the drug violence that had claimed 50,000 lives since 2006, and their economic policy alternatives focused more on the consensus issue of growing the economy rather than making the tough policy choices designed to actually do it.

The lack of strong policy differentiation among the candidates during the campaigns meant that voters would have learned little more than they already knew at the start of the campaign season. Polling data show that voters easily identified the state of the economy and public security as the country's two main problems, and there was a general understanding of where the candidates stood on these issues. Further, López Obrador's 2006 campaign meant that voters were already well informed about his perspective when the 2012 campaigns began. Vázquez Mota's association with President Calderón meant that there were few surprises in the content of her campaign message. In addition, all of the main candidates come from long-established parties with well-known profiles. These were not temporary campaign vehicles created for a single election that one finds in other new democracies with more fragile party systems. Rather, these were stable parties that had endured for decades with fairly consistent policy positions on key issues (Greene 2007). Voters arguably knew the least about Peña Nieto. Outside of his home state of Mexico, voters may have been less certain about his policy stands, and his purposefully vague campaign gave them little to go on. As a result, we might expect fewer campaign effects in this election than others in Mexico or in other new democracies.

Nevertheless, the campaigns moved a large proportion of the vote between April and July. Although Peña Nieto did well among all groups of voters discussed here, he won more votes than his challengers among those who were converted away from a vote intention that was in line with their natural candidate and from those for whom the campaign reinforced an intention to support someone other than their natural candidate.

These two groups accounted for a large proportion of the electorate in 2012. More than 17% of voters intended to vote for a candidate who was not associated with their dispositions when interviewed in April and reported voting for that candidate on Election Day. This level of reinforcement away dwarfs that of prior election years. Peña Nieto not only won the plurality of this large group (45.5%), his share was twice as large as López Obrador's. Peña Nieto similarly dominated his opponents among voters who were converted away from a vote intention in April that was consistent with their dispositions to a vote choice in July that was inconsistent. In fact, Peña Nieto's share of this bloc (46%) was almost as large as the sum of his two major rivals' shares. These two campaign effects together netted Peña Nieto 15.6% of the entire electorate in his bid for the presidency. Perhaps unsurprisingly, these groups contained more independent voters than the others.

The fact that so many voters were convinced to vote for Peña Nieto even though their dispositions pushed them toward a different candidate implies two other interesting findings. First, the PRI's comeback was likely not due to its residual hold over the Mexican psyche (but for a contrasting argument, see James A. McCann, chap. 4, this volume). The PRI entered the 2012 race with only a few more percentage points of identified voters than the PAN. Had voters remained deeply attached to the PRI despite its twelve years out of power, they would have supported the PRI at the outset of the campaigns in April rather than been convinced to support it after hearing three months of campaign messages. Second, Peña Nieto's win was probably not due to the performance or policy failures of the outgoing PAN administration of President Felipe Calderón either. Had Calderón's tenure been viewed as such a failure, then voters would have supported Peña Nieto or López Obrador at the outset. But in fact many voters initially supported Vázquez Mota, only to switch their choice (mainly to Peña Nieto) by Election Day. It was the content of the campaigns that voters heard, not the influence of precampaign dispositions that propelled voters toward the eventual winner.

The extent and depth of the campaigns' influence on vote choices in 2012, despite good reasons for them to diminish compared to prior presidential elections, highlights voters' amazing susceptibility to advertising in the mass media. Although I do not draw this link causally here (but see Greene 2011), there is circumstantial evidence to suggest that voters were swayed by Peña Nieto's advantages in mass media advertising. Interestingly, part of the inspiration behind the new election law in effect for 2012 was to reduce advertising inequality across the candidates; in practice, however, it did not happen. The formula in use distributed 70% of radio and television advertising time to each party proportional to its vote share in the 2009 midterm elections and 30% equally to each registered party. The PRI's strong performance in the 2009 elections coupled with a technical decision by the PRD to form its multiparty coalition in a particular way that diminished its access to the mass media meant that the PRI-led coalition came away with nearly half of all media time, whereas the PAN and the PRD-led coalition split the other half. This asymmetry was even greater than the imbalance during the 2006 presidential elections, then favoring the PAN (Greene 2011). On the face of it, such a sizeable difference should have advantaged the Peña Nieto campaign much as Calderón's advertising fueled his come-from-behind victory six years earlier.

Conclusion

Mexico's voters are not only strikingly susceptible to campaign effects compared to their counterparts in the United States, their susceptibility has increased since the onset of fully free and fair party competition for high office. Existing theory about the ineluctable advance of partisan identification in new democracies as well as the legal context and candidate strategies surrounding the 2012 elections suggest that campaign effects should have decreased. The fact that they have not implies two avenues of inquiry.

First, the rising proportion of independent voters is evidence of a representational chasm between parties and voters. Kathleen Bruhn and I have documented this chasm using evidence on voters' and congressional candidates' issue preferences (Bruhn and Greene 2009), and other scholars have discussed various concerns about the quality of political representation in Mexico since democratization (Crow 2010). At present, Mexico stands out among Latin American countries for its high level of stability among political elites. The same parties have competed in elections since 1991, and the three major players account for more than 90% of the vote. Yet as more voters become nonpartisan, the party system may lose structure. Nonpartisan voters are probably also more susceptible to vote-buying attempts (Stokes 2005). Might Mexico increasingly come to look like many other countries in the region where new parties emerge and disappear regularly? The legal barriers to party registration and current party finance regulations may forestall such an outcome for the time being, but representational problems have a way of eventually projecting themselves into the party system.

Second, although this chapter has documented the existence of campaign effects and their surprising increase over time since the historic 2000 elections, it has been almost silent on key aspects of how the campaigns sway voters. The preceding analysis makes it clear that the campaigns do more than provide useful information; rather, they actively sway voters. But the analysis does not tell us more about what the campaigns "do."

One possibility is that the campaigns prime voters to weigh certain elements more heavily in their choices. For instance, when Peña Nieto campaigned on keeping his promises, voters may have come to decide that trustworthiness was more important to them than they previously thought. Another possibility is that the campaigns persuade voters to change their minds on issues that help inform their vote choices. Peña Nieto's focus on competence, for instance, may have changed voters' perceptions of his trustworthiness. Or perhaps some voters experienced a deeper level of persuasion on the issues. When López Obrador campaigned on the theme of change, citing the importance of deepening Mexico's democracy to increase participation and spread the fruits of economic growth more broadly, some voters who had previously thought that Mexico had become a fully functioning democracy after the PRI lost in 2000 might have been persuaded that the country needed a new and deeper level of political change. A third possibility is that the legitimate campaigns waged in the mass media and through stump speeches across the country were not responsible for voters' shifting preferences, but rather clientelist payoffs overrode these more subtle psychological effects.

Whether voters were primed, persuaded, or paid off, what are the mechanisms that generated these processes? Do voters receive partisan information from paid or earned mass media coverage, or are social networks increasingly playing the role that was previously reserved for radio and television? To what extent did the campaigns use each of these communication technologies as part of their strategic plan to sway voters? If payoffs were key, are they used to sway all voters or just selected groups that may not respond as strongly to mass media advertising and word-of-mouth campaigns? These and other themes are taken up in other chapters in this volume.

The number of competitive democracies in the world has doubled since 1974. As a result, a great many countries, including Mexico, now feature intensely fought campaigns for high office. If we move away from the notion that citizens' social identities determine their vote choices, then the dynamics and effects of partisan campaigns become more than an object of fascination for strategists and consultants. Instead, they become central in our understanding of vote choice, electoral mandates, and, by extension, policy outcomes in new democracies.

NOTES

1. Preelection volatility is not limited to presidential elections in Mexico. Lawson (1999) shows a twenty-point swing in favor of Cárdenas during his victorious 1997 campaign for mayor of Mexico City. Other countries in Latin America also feature massive swings in voters' preferences during campaigns (Baker, Ames, and Renno 2006).

2. Unlike cross-sectional surveys that provide snapshots and help characterize the state of public opinion at any given time, panel surveys interview the same citizens at multiple points during the campaigns and can thus help characterize how and why voters' preferences and vote intentions change.

3. Using all available panel waves shows that an amazing 86.2% of voters changed vote intention at least once in the four-wave 2000 study and 45.2% changed at least once in the three-wave 2006 study.

4. I estimate the models using multinomial logit. See Dow and Endersby (2004) for a justification of this model when estimating vote choice. Retrospective evaluations is an additive index that combines presidential approval as well as both pocketbook and sociotropic measures of economic well-being. Economic policy preferences is an additive index that combines preferences over privatizing Pemex and raising taxes to fund antipoverty programs. Candidate competence is an additive index that combines ability to manage the economy, tackle corruption, enhance public security, and reduce poverty. Drug war policy is an additive index that combines using the army to combat trafficking organizations, negotiating with traffickers, and legalizing drugs.

5. See the poll of polls at http://www.adnpolitico.com/encuestas#tabla. Examine the "brute" values and remove the daily tracking poll from Grupo de Economistas y Asociados-Indagaciones y Soluciones Avazadas, which used an alternative sampling approach. For a poll of polls that supports the "standard" narrative and contradicts the one presented here, see the model that includes "house" effects to adjust for potential biases at each polling firm at http://blog.diegovalle.net/2012/06/final-poll-of-polls .html.

6. This is the median effect across studies with each study cited counted as one estimate. Using the mean yields a 3.4% margin shift on average. A large number of studies on the United States examine the effects of specific elements of campaigns, including television advertising, radio advertising, direct mail, telephone calls, canvassing, debates, nominating conventions, and candidate appearances. Some but not all of these studies report aggregate effects on vote choices. For excellent summaries, see Kaufmann et al. (2008, 167–68) and Vavreck (2009).

7. A voter is predicted to vote for a particular candidate when the probability of voting for that candidate (generated from the model in an ancillary appendix; see www.press .jhu.edu) is higher than for any other candidate.

8. The Federal Electoral Institute's monitoring program in 2006 shows a total of 1,391,166 hours of campaign-related advertising on radio and television from January to July (Federal Electoral Institute 2006). This figure is more than tenfold higher than the 107,851 hours of broadcasting in 2012 from April to July (Federal Electoral Institute 2012), despite the fact that the 2012 data offer a census of broadcasts whereas the 2006 data exclude a large number of smaller broadcasters. Even if we include the 2012 precampaigns (i.e., before the candidates were chosen) and the so-called intercampaign period before April, the 2012 total rises to just 364,637 hours of advertising.

REFERENCES

Baker, Andy, Barry Ames, and Lucio Renno. 2006. "Social Context and Campaign Volatility in New Democracies: Networks and Neighborhoods in Brazil's 2002 Elections." *American Journal of Political Science* 50, no. 2: 382–99.

Bartels, Larry. 1993. "The Impact of Electioneering in the United States." In *Electioneering: A Comparative Study of Continuity and Change*, ed. D. Butler and A. Ranney, 244–86. Oxford: Clarendon.

———. 2002. "Beyond the Running Tally: Partisan Bias in Political Perceptions." *Political Behavior* 24, no. 2: 117–50.

Bartolini, Stefano. 2000. *The Class Cleavage: The Electoral Mobilization of the European Left 1880–1980*. Cambridge: Cambridge University Press.

Berelson, Bernard, Paul Lazarsfeld, and William McPhee. 1954. *Voting: A Study of Opinion Formation in a Presidential Campaign*. Chicago: University of Chicago Press.

Bruhn, Kathleen. 2004. "The Making of the Mexican President, 2000: Parties, Candidates, and Campaign Strategy." In *Mexico's Pivotal Democratic Election: Candidates, Voters, and the Presidential Campaign of 2000*, ed. Jorge I. Domínguez and Chappell Lawson. Stanford and La Jolla, CA: Stanford University Press and Center for US–Mexican Studies.

———. 2009. "López Obrador, Calderón, and the 2006 Presidential Campaign." In *Consolidating Mexico's Democracy: The 2006 Presidential Campaign in Comparative Perspective*, ed. Jorge I. Domínguez, Chappell Lawson, and Alejandro Moreno, 169–90. Baltimore: Johns Hopkins University Press.

Bruhn, Kathleen, and Kenneth F. Greene. 2009. "The Absence of Common Ground between Candidates and Voters." In *Consolidating Mexico's Democracy: The 2006 Presidential Campaign in Comparative Perspective*, ed. Jorge I. Domínguez, Chappell Lawson, and Alejandro Moreno, 109–28. Baltimore: Johns Hopkins University Press.

Campbell, James. 2000. *The American Campaign*. College Station: Texas A&M University Press.

Chandra, Kanchan. 2004. *Why Ethnic Parties Succeed: Patronage and Ethnic Headcounts in India*. Cambridge: Cambridge University Press.

Converse, Phillip. 1969. "Of Time and Partisan Stability." *Comparative Political Studies* 2, no. 2: 139–71.

Cox, Gary. 1997. *Making Votes Count: Strategic Coordination in the World's Electoral Systems*. New York: Cambridge University Press.

Crow, David. 2010. "The Party's Over: Citizen Conceptions of Democracy and Political Dissatisfaction in Mexico." *Comparative Politics* 43, no. 1: 41–61.

Domínguez, Jorge I., and James McCann. 1996. *Democratizing Mexico: Public Opinion and Electoral Choices*. Baltimore: Johns Hopkins University Press.

Dow, Jay, and James Endersby. 2004. "Multinomial Probit and Multinomial Logit: A Comparison of Choice Models for Voting Research." *Electoral Studies* 23: 107–22.

Duverger, Maurice. 1954. *Political Parties: Their Organization and Activity in the Modern State*. New York: Taylor and Francis.

Evans, Geoffrey. 2000. "The Continued Significance of Class Voting." *Annual Review of Political Science* 3: 401–17.

Federal Electoral Institute. 2006. "Reporte final de los monitoreos de promicionales." Mexico City: Federal Electoral Institute. http://www.ife.org.mx/documentos/proceso_2005-2006/docs/rep_final_monitoreos.pdf.

———. 2012. "Reporte cumplimiento nacional acumulado." Mexico City: Federal Electoral Institute.

Finkel, Steven. 1993. "Reexamining the 'Minimal Effects' Model in Recent Presidential Campaigns." *Journal of Politics* 55: 1–21.

Gelman, Andrew, and Gary King. 1993. "Why Are American Presidential Election Campaign Polls so Variable When Votes Are so Predictable?" *British Journal of Political Science* 23: 409–51.

Greene, Kenneth F. 2007. *Why Dominant Parties Lose: Mexico's Democratization in Comparative Perspective*. New York: Cambridge University Press.

———. 2009. "Images and Issues in Mexico's 2006 Presidential Election." In *Consolidating Mexico's Democracy: The 2006 Presidential Campaign in Comparative Perspective*, ed. Jorge I. Domínguez, Chappell Lawson, and Alejandro Moreno, 246–67. Baltimore: Johns Hopkins University Press.

———. 2011. "Campaign Persuasion and Nascent Partisanship in Mexico's New Democracy." *American Journal of Political Science* 55, no. 2: 398–416.

———. 2012. "The Niche Party: Regime Legacies and Party-Building in New Democracies." Unpublished manuscript.

Holbrook, Thomas. 1996. *Do Campaigns Matter?* Thousand Oaks, CA: SAGE.

Horowitz, Donald. 1987. *Ethnic Groups in Conflict*. Berkeley: University of California Press.

Johnston, Richard. 2006. "Party Identification: Unmoved Mover or Sum of Preferences?" *Annual Review of Political Science* 9: 329–51.

Kaufmann, Karen, John Petrocik, and Daron Shaw. 2008. *Unconventional Wisdom: Facts and Myths about American Voters*. Oxford: Oxford University Press.

Kitschelt, Herbert. 1994. *The Transformation of European Social Democracy*. New York: Cambridge University Press.

Langston, Joy, and Allyson Benton. 2007. "'A Ras de Suelo': Candidate Appearances and Events in Mexico's Presidential Campaign." Working Paper, Centro de Investigación y Docencia Económicas, Mexico City.

Lawson, Chappell. 1999. "Why Cárdenas Won: The 1997 Elections in Mexico City." In *Toward Mexico's Democratization: Parties, Campaigns, Elections and Public Opinion*, ed. Jorge I. Domínguez and Alejandro Poiré, 147–73. New York: Routledge.

———. 2004. "Mexico's Great Debates: The Televised Campaign Encounters of 2000 and Their Electoral Consequences." In *Mexico's Pivotal Democratic Election: Candidates, Voters, and the Presidential Campaign of 2000*, ed. Jorge I. Domínguez and Chappell Lawson, 211–42. Stanford and La Jolla, CA: Stanford University Press and Center for US–Mexican Studies.

Lawson, Chappell, and James McCann. 2005. "Television Coverage, Media Effects, and Mexico's 2000 Elections." *British Journal of Political Science* 35, no. 1: 1–30.

Lazarsfeld, Paul, Bernard Berelson, and Henri Gaudet. 1948. *The People's Choice: How the Voter Makes Up His Mind in a Presidential Campaign*. New York: Columbia University Press.

Lipset, Seymour Martin, and Stein Rokkan. 1967. "Party Systems and Voter Alignments." In *Party Systems and Voter Alignments*, ed. Seymour Martin Lipset and Stein Rokkan, 1–64. New York: Free Press.

Magaloni, Beatriz. 2006. *Voting for Autocracy: Hegemonic Party Survival and Its Demise in Mexico*. New York: Cambridge University Press.

Magaloni, Beatriz, and Alejandro Poiré. 2004. "The Issues, the Vote, and the Mandate for Change." In *Mexico's Pivotal Democratic Election: Candidates, Voters, and the Presidential*

Campaign of 2000, ed. Jorge I. Domínguez and Chappell Lawson, 269–92. Stanford and La Jolla, CA: Stanford University Press and Center for US–Mexican Studies.

Markus, Gregory. 1988. "The Impact of Personal and National Economic Conditions on the Presidential Vote." *American Journal of Political Science* 32, no. 1: 137–54.

McCann, James. 2009. "Ideology in the 2006 Campaigns." In *Consolidating Mexico's Democracy: The 2006 Presidential Campaign in Comparative Perspective*, ed. Jorge I. Domínguez, Chappell Lawson, and Alejandro Moreno, 268–84. Baltimore: Johns Hopkins University Press.

McCann, James, and Chappell Lawson. 2003. "An Electorate Adrift? Public Opinion and the Quality of Democracy in Mexico." *Latin American Research Review* 38, no. 3: 60–81.

Moreno, Alejandro. 2003. *El votante mexicano*. Mexico City: Fondo de Cultura Económica.

———. 2004. "The Effects of Negative Campaigns on Mexican Voters." In *Mexico's Pivotal Democratic Election: Candidates, Voters, and the Presidential Campaign of 2000*, ed. Jorge I. Domínguez and Chappell Lawson, 243–68. Stanford and La Jolla, CA: Stanford University Press and Center for US–Mexican Studies.

———. 2009. "The Activation of Economic Voting in the 2006 Campaign." In *Consolidating Mexico's Democracy: The 2006 Presidential Campaign in Comparative Perspective*, ed. Jorge I. Domínguez, Chappell Lawson, and Alejandro Moreno, 209–28. Baltimore: Johns Hopkins University Press.

Shaw, Daron. 1999. "The Effect of TV Ads and Candidate Appearances on Statewide Presidential Votes, 1988–1996." *American Political Science Review* 93: 345–61.

———. 2006. *The Race to 270: The Electoral College and the Campaign Strategies of 2000 and 2004*. Chicago: University of Chicago Press.

Shirk, David. 2005. *Mexico's New Politics: The PAN and Democratic Change*. Boulder, CO: Lynne Rienner.

Stokes, Susan. 2005. "Perverse Accountability: A Formal Model of Machine Politics with Evidence from Argentina." *American Political Science Review* 99, no. 3: 315–25.

Vavreck, Lynn. 2009. *The Message Matters: The Economy and Presidential Campaigns*. Princeton, NJ: Princeton University Press.

Zaller, John. 1992. *The Nature and Origins of Mass Opinion*. New York: Cambridge University Press.

7

Drugs, Bullets, and Ballots

The Impact of Violence on the 2012 Presidential Election

EDGAR FRANCO VIVANCO, JORGE OLARTE,
ALBERTO DÍAZ-CAYEROS, AND BEATRIZ MAGALONI

This chapter studies the impact of violence on voting behavior in the presidential election of 2012.[1] During the administration of President Felipe Calderón, Mexico experienced a significant escalation of violence as a result of the domestic drug war and government confrontations with various criminal organizations.[2] The war against drug traffic organizations (DTOs) claimed more than 50,000 lives over the six-year term of President Calderón. In several cities the violence reached fatality levels on par with some of the bloodiest civil wars around the world.[3] Using precinct-level electoral returns, we estimate the degree to which violence affected voting decisions across Mexico, controlling for a host of structural sociodemographic and political conditions.

Drug-related violence could have influenced voting behavior through two channels. The first channel would be through a change in the decision to participate in the election, thereby shifting turnout patterns. From a theoretical perspective, it is not evident whether violence should decrease or increase turnout because the effects of violence leading citizens to stay at home on Election Day might be offset by greater civic engagement as an affirmation of the democratic process as the appropriate response to the challenges of organized crime and violence. In terms of the classic calculus of voting equation, it is possible that the benefit of citizen duty may increase even as the costs of the voting act itself become significantly higher.

The second channel involves vote choices. If they turn out, voters must decide how to cast their vote. The patterns of voting observed at the regional, state, electoral district, or municipal levels are the consequence of aggregating those vote choices. Violence may elicit a backlash against incumbents, or a specific party that can credibly offer to restore order and peace could garner greater support in places experiencing violence. The effects of violence on electoral preferences might be determined by how citizens perceive who is to blame for the violent state of affairs, what strategy voters believe the various challengers would follow if they were elected, and whether the incumbent party can succeed in claiming credit for its performance vis-à-vis violence. Risk-averse voters may decide to support the incumbent, even when they deem his performance wanting, so it is not necessarily the case that voters will radically shift their voting behavior in order to curb the power of criminal organizations.

The rhetoric and campaign statements of the electoral process itself did not provide a firm expectation as to what the effect of violence on the election could be. Some expected the elections to be disrupted by violence, which never materialized. Others feared that candidates for federal office would be assassinated as the election months advanced, as has happened in mayoral races; again, a fear that did not pan out. The incumbent party candidate (Josefina Vázquez Mota, or JVM) was not running on a hawkish platform of *mano dura* or law and order as would be typical of a rightwing party under conditions of violence. The leftist candidate (Andrés Manuel López Obrador, or AMLO) was running mostly on a platform of social issues that tended to deemphasize the war on drugs as a major campaign theme. And the Institutional Revolutionary Party (PRI) comeback was couched on its appeal to rural, less educated, and traditional voters whose affinity for the PRI did not privilege a particular grievance.

The party platforms of the three candidates were ideologically convergent, particularly in their economic proposals, and a left-right division of voters into a profile mirroring the ideological party spectrum was not present. What was somewhat remarkable about the campaign process itself is how little the question of violence and the appropriate state response to organized crime figured in the presidential race or the televised candidate debates. Hence the potential issues of violence for the campaign were either minimized or ignored by the candidates. But this does not mean that, in making their voting calculations, citizens did not have some expectations regarding what each candidate would do (or was capable of doing) regarding drug violence.

We explore the impact of violence on the 2012 election from an electoral geography perspective.[4] In order to assess the effect of violence on turnout and voting patterns, we take a territorial approach, using the actual electoral outcomes. Using the official vote tallies at the electoral precinct (*sección electoral*) level, we estimate the likely effect of the differential geographic patterns of violence throughout Mexico.[5] We are well aware of some of the dangers of drawing inferences from aggregate electoral data. But dangers of ecological inference are muted because our units of analysis are extremely small and internally homogenous. We model vote patterns at the precinct level as differences in vote results in order to mitigate problems of omitted variable bias. Those patterns represent an aggregation of individual-level choices. We provide a large set of control variables, both for the sociodemographic characteristics (at the precinct level) and the geographic context (with an explicit modeling of spillover effects through spatial lags), that allow us to isolate the independent effect of violence. Thus our empirical strategy (detailed in an ancillary appendix; see www.press.jhu.edu) allows us to isolate and identify the effect of violence on turnout and vote choices.

Our results paint a varied picture with regard to the effects of violence on voting behavior in the 2012 election. Drug-related violence lowered turnout by around three percentage points in the country's most violent localities. Many citizens did not go to the polls on Election Day. Whether this was due to psychological mechanisms of fear or a relatively objective assessment of the real risks of going out to the street, our data analysis cannot gauge, although we speculate that fear of some disruption of the electoral process probably played a key role. Regarding the violence effect on voting outcomes, we observed two complementary patterns. First, López Obrador firmly captured a larger share of votes in the violent areas. Second, Peña Nieto was the candidate most adversely affected by violence. In this sense, his victory cannot be interpreted as a reaction against the government of Felipe Calderón and its presumed relationship with escalating violence in Mexico. In fact, in violent zones of states led by National Action Party (PAN) or Party of the Democratic Revolution (PRD) governors prior to the elections, citizens voted in favor of Josefina Vázquez Mota, the PAN candidate. And in violent zones led by PRI governors, they voted against the incumbent governor's candidate, Enrique Peña Nieto. Future research should explore further the meaning of this behavior, but it suggests that while violence depressed electoral participation, it did not boost the fortunes of the formerly hegemonic party candidate; on the contrary, it points to a voter's reaction against this party in violent places.

Violence and Voting Behavior

The relationship between violence and voting behavior has been analyzed more widely in international case studies, most of which focus on terrorism and civil war conflicts. One consistent finding is that the electorate reacts to violent acts by supporting parties that give fewer concessions and are more intransigent toward the organizations behind the attacks. In a study of the impact of terrorist acts on political preferences within the context of Israeli–Palestinian conflict, Berrebi and Klor (2008) find that fatal terrorist acts cause an increase in the relative support for rightwing parties. Additionally, they find that the total number of fatalities has no significant effect on the turnout rates. In a similar study on Turkey, Kibris (2011) finds that the electorate punishes the incumbent for terrorist attacks. In addition, casualties have a significant positive effect on voting for opposition rightwing parties, suggesting that Turkish voters also align their preferences with parties less willing to tolerate violence, as in the Israeli case.

In the Mexican context, however, challenger parties may be rewarded with greater electoral support in places where violence is out of control, given that security—namely, the capacity of governments to deal with criminal behavior—has become a valence issue. Voters seem to judge the performance of parties according to their capacity to curb crime as it affects them directly in their everyday life. Consonant with the terrorism literature, however, we expect the incumbent candidate to be rewarded for fighting criminal groups with more support in places with the highest conditions of violence.

Comparative research on the effects of violence on electoral participation exhibits mixed findings. Surveys show a positive effect in voting participation and civil engagement for violence victims of civil wars in Africa (Bellows and Miguel 2009; Blattman 2009). Experiments in Nigeria show that intimidation and violence by politicians are effective in reducing voter turnout (Collier and Vicente 2014). In a comparative study of criminal violence across five continents, Bateson (2013) finds greater political engagement among crime victims (e.g., participating in community meetings and political protests). In the Colombian case, however, Gallego (2011) finds that increasing guerrilla violence decreases voter turnout, while paramilitary violence has no significant effect. Moreover, in municipalities affected by paramilitary violence, electoral competition has had a tendency to be lower. Additionally, guerrilla violence is significantly higher during election years, while paramilitary violence is lower. This is consistent with the hypothesis that the guerrilla's strategy is to sabotage elections, while paramilitaries establish alliances with certain candidates.

Studying the effect of reducing violence on electoral outcomes, Ferraz and Vaz (2012) examine the Unidad de Policia Pacificadora (UPP), a pacification strategy implemented in highly violent areas of Rio de Janeiro. These authors find that support for incumbent governor, Sergio Cabral (who took credit for the UPP), increased by almost 20% in those places where the pacification strategy was implemented. While this intervention involved many aspects related to embedding the police in the communities, one of the most dramatic and visible effects of the intervention was a reduction in homicide rates.

Other studies confirm how elections can also play a significant role in the dynamics of violence; in particular, violence can be used to influence the results of elections. For example, Wilkinson (2004) finds that town-level electoral incentives in India predict where electoral violence will break out. He argues that violence is used as a political tool during competitive elections to mobilize one's group against an opponent. In addition, state-level incentives also determine where the state government mobilizes the police to prevent violence outbreaks. While the evidence from these studies may be contextually limited, their conclusions are persuasive and provide a solid background to study the effects of violence in other cases.

Little is known about the effect of violence on electoral outcomes in Mexico. Trelles and Carreras (2012) provide the first thorough study of the effects of criminal violence on electoral participation in Mexico. Using municipal-level data for four federal elections (1997–2009), they find that electoral turnout is lower in the most violent regions of Mexico. Specifically, they identify a direct negative effect of violence on turnout in a municipality of around 0.66% for each additional death per 1,000. In addition, they find that deaths in neighboring municipalities produce a 2.8% decrease in turnout from each additional death per 1,000.[6] In that study the effect of violence on turnout is far stronger when violence occurs in neighboring municipalities than in one's own municipality. Trelles and Carreras (2012) interpret these findings as suggesting that "this effect is probably related to the mediatic framing of violence and how citizens perceive crime in their surroundings. In other words, urban areas where most of the municipalities are affected by high crime rates are more likely to generate negative and fearful voters than large urban areas where violence is concentrated in a few specific neighborhoods" (107).

While this interpretation may be reasonable, it does not emerge from the statistical analysis. Most of the variation in municipal-level data sets in Mexico comes from rural, rather than urban, units (the poor rural state of Oaxaca alone contributes 570 of the 2,454 municipalities in the study; more than half of the municipalities in Mexico are in the poor indigenous southern states).

With the surge in violence in the period of study, homicide rates per 1,000 have exhibited dramatic increases in rural places with small populations.

While the interpretation provided in the study seems to make sense of how one may conceive of the behavior of voters confronted with violence in large metropolitan urban areas like Ciudad Juárez, in fact this particular city is only one point in the data set because it comprises a single municipality. Most of the variation in the data set does not come from what is happening in urban settings, but from rural ones.

We provide a better unit of analysis than the municipality, namely, the electoral precinct. Trelles and Carreras (2012) are primarily concerned with taking advantage of the temporal dimension of their panel data, producing estimators that control for time-invariant cross-sectional variation (coming from census variables). In our estimation, we exploit instead the variation of electoral behavior within a municipality, accounting for the sociodemographic characteristics of electoral precincts. The units of our analysis include both rural and urban precincts with widely differing voting patterns, weighting urban units more heavily. Given that we do not have homicide rates at the precinct level, we capture spillover effects of violence in the context of the whole municipality.

The advantage of using a strategy of precinct-level data coupled with municipal violence indicators is that we can be relatively confident that we are controlling for a host of sociodemographic variables that influence vote patterns and turnout at the lowest level of aggregation possible, while taking the municipality as the relevant jurisdiction where voters assess the violence that surrounds them. In order to account for spillovers in voting patterns, we estimate the effects of violence on the dependent variable, including spatial lags.[7] We thus explicitly model spatial correlations among territorially contiguous precincts, providing confidence that the patterns of electoral behavior reflect local dynamics at the neighborhood and village levels.

We explicitly model a point made by the comparative literature, namely, the suggestion that high levels of violence may produce effects on voting behavior that may be quite distinctive from a simple increase in homicides rates. In particular, we test whether, beyond homicide rates, the presence of DTOs or thresholds of civil war–type violence produces differential effects on turnout. We specifically test the hypothesis that violence will decrease turnout in proportion to its intensity, as measured by homicide rates (per 1,000 people). We also assess whether the presence of DTOs, as reflected in the occurrence of homicides from executions or confrontations between criminal organizations, will decrease turnout. And we analyze whether extreme levels of violence akin to those observed in civil wars (which are operationalized as more than twenty-five drug rivalry–related deaths per year) decrease turnout even further, as in the literature on civil wars.

The Electoral Geography of 2012

Electoral geography can be used to visualize some of the overarching factors that divide Mexican society and motivate citizens to express distinct electoral preferences across the national territory.[8] Regional patterns of voting and turnout reflect not only variations across space in socioeconomic characteristics but also distinct local experiences. In the same way that unemployment, inflation, or other economic shocks or events that may affect retrospective or prospective voting affect local economies, the experience of violence and the associated fear among the population may lurk behind some of the differences in regional electoral behavior.[9]

Using a statistical analysis that encompasses the more than 66,000 electoral units based on the 2010 census cartography (created through a joint effort by the Federal Electoral Institute, or IFE, and the National Statistical Office, or INEGI), it is possible to isolate various factors that are correlated with voting behavior from the impacts of drug-related violence. One of the great advantages of working with "electoral section" data is that they reflect the actual voting decisions of millions of voters. The risk of inference is that electoral precincts represent aggregated rather than individual data. Owing to ballot secrecy, we do not know how each individual behaved. With aggregated data we cannot be absolutely certain that what happens in the aggregate also applies to individuals. It is well known that a correlation in the aggregate could be exactly the opposite with individual data; this is usually referred to as the ecological fallacy.[10] But this problem is diminished to the extent that the disaggregated units are internally homogenous. If within any electoral section most members share some attributes (similar levels of schooling, ethnicity, or income), we can be relatively confident that the differences in voting patterns between precincts are attributable to factors that vary across units of analysis rather than within them.

In order to provide a single visualization of the electoral geography of the 2012 federal election, figure 7.1 provides a depiction of the territorial distribution of party strength at the precinct level. The size of precincts varies in Mexico owing to demographic trends that are regionally diverse. While some rural areas have lost population, some urban locations have witnessed explosive growth, which is reflected in larger precinct sizes. The average number of voters registered in each electoral section is 1,194. The median size is smaller, at 1,007 voters, and 90% of the precincts have fewer than 1,325 registered voters.[11] Although there are differences in precinct sizes, they are the most homogenous political partition of Mexico's geography, far more tightly distributed around the mean than municipalities or electoral districts.

Figure 7.1 shows the party that gained the plurality of votes in each precinct.[12] Given that the precinct is not an electoral district or a political jurisdiction, it is not strictly correct to call these pluralities victories. Electoral rules and the drawing of political units generate an aggregation that determines what those pluralities mean in terms of political victory. But the map provides a summary of the combined votes of the three main candidates. Figure 7.1 obscures the fact that a plurality might represent different vote shares depending on the particular configuration of political competition in each district. In a precinct where only two parties concentrate the votes, for example, the plurality will represent more than 50% of the precinct support. But with a three-way split in the vote share, it may be enough for one candidate to have slightly more than one-third of the votes to be shaded for that party in the map.

A choropleth map always shades precincts according to the land area, not the population involved. In Mexico, this means that precincts in the north will be more visible than those in the metropolitan areas and the central highlands.[13] However, the shading reflects a more nuanced perspective than what emerges from a municipal- or state-level mapping of electoral victories. Clearly some densely populated areas in the center and east of the country represent a large number of votes for the PAN and the PRD. But the density of precincts in the map gives a sense of how important different regions are for the overall support of each party, somehow hiding the patterns within cities. Because those cities are spread throughout the country, however, the map gives a good sense of the regional partisan support.

Peña Nieto's electoral support was more widely distributed throughout the country because in almost every precinct the winning candidate obtained at least 25% of total votes.[14] The territorial distribution of vote shares for AMLO and Vázquez Mota are quite different. Whereas AMLO's electoral support is concentrated in southern states and the nation's capital, Josefina Vázquez Mota had relative strength in many of the northern states, as well as Campeche, Jalisco, Veracruz, and Yucatán. Figure 7.1 illustrates how, even if PAN and

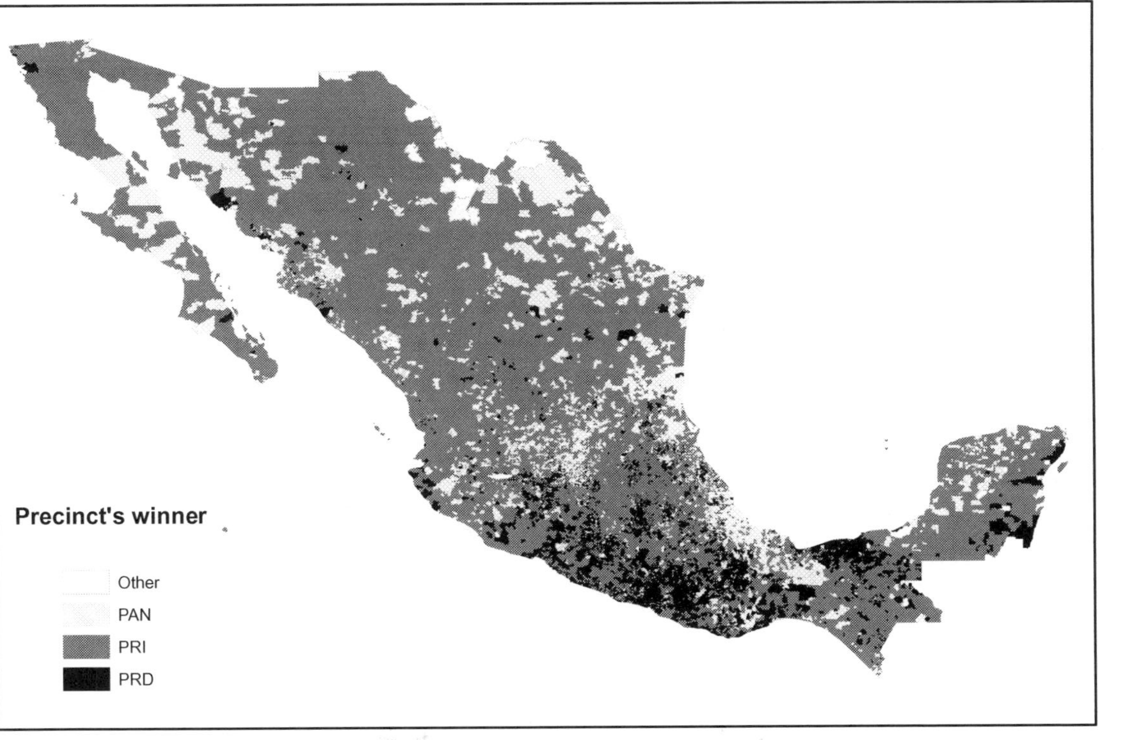

Figure 7.1. Territorial distribution of party strength. *Note*: Precincts in white represent missing data, ties, and places with no polling stations installed.
Source: Authors' calculations based on the Instituto Federal Electoral Conteo Distrital data set (http://computos2012.ife.org.mx/)

PRD had comparable levels of support at the national level, their regional bases are quite different.

The regional specialization of party support is relatively well known among observers of Mexican politics.[15] In the visualization of precinct-level data, however, we see islands of support for every party even amidst strongholds of the other parties. PAN support, in fact, is spread throughout the country—although not as evenly distributed as PRI, with the exception of those states where the PRD has the strongest support. That is, in towns and cities or precincts within metropolitan areas, the PAN performs relatively well, even if the region or the state is dominated by the PRI or the PRD. The PRD has some of those islands of support in PRI territory, but they are sparse and relatively less common.

These patterns of territorial electoral strength help us understand why the Mexican left struggles every election in reaching a large enough share of the national votes: even with its overwhelming dominance in Mexico City, the party does not have a large enough base of unconditional supporters, so-called core voters, in most of the country. In contrast, the PRI remained a viable party to a large extent because it never lost its territorial reach even as it lost many state governorships or local elections. And the PAN appears less weak than its overall performance in the general election results because it has a relatively good combination of regional strongholds and places with support scattered throughout the country.[16]

The complexity of the electoral geography described above requires some care when measuring the dependent variables of interest. In particular, a three-way contest like the presidential race in Mexico means that the vote share of a candidate depends on the dynamics of competition between the remainder two candidates. This dependence could be modeled as a multivariate distribution.[17]

We chose in our analysis of voting patterns to express vote distributions as differences (measured in total number of votes) between candidates in each precinct. By including as an independent variable the precinct size in all the estimations, we can standardize the effects, making the transformation into vote shares unnecessary. The difference in vote tallies is close to a normal distribution. In all the precincts of the country, the average difference of votes between Enrique Peña Nieto (EPN) and AMLO is fifty-nine; the difference between AMLO and JVM is thirty-eight; and the difference between EPN and JVM is the sum of both differences, ninety-seven. Every precinct can hence be characterized by the combination of two vote differences between any two candidates.

There are several advantages of using vote differences as a dependent variable. First, it is easy to interpret the estimated coefficients because they simply reflect the effect of an independent variable on additional vote differences between candidate pairs.[18] Second, by expressing vote tallies as differences between candidates, we control for any omitted variable that may have affected both candidates equally. Third, in contrast to the nonlinear character of a log transformation, the estimations provide predicted values that are invariant to calibrations at various places in the range of the dependent variable.

The Geography of Violence

The Felipe Calderón presidency (2006–12) was characterized by an escalation of violence as a result of Mexico's war on drugs and the bloody conflicts against criminal organizations. During those years, television news and newspapers were inundated with chilling images. Estimates put the death toll from the war at over 50,000, at least 10,000 missing, and an unknown number of displaced persons in just six years. For many people, especially in the states of Baja California, Chihuahua, Durango, Guerrero, Jalisco, Michoacán, Nuevo León, Sinaloa, Tamaulipas, and Veracruz, the war is a daily threat that leaves irreparable traces in its wake. Beginning with his home state, Michoacán, Calderón decided to deploy the army in nine joint operations aimed at containing criminal organizations.[19] While violence was contained in some of these states, in others it continued to escalate as criminal organizations diversified their portfolio of illegal activities and competed for territorial control, plazas, and strategic routes.

The effectiveness of federal government interventions in the war, as well as assessments of the military action, varies widely depending on the region; some regions are in a constant state of warfare, while the situations in other regions may be sensationalized and exaggerated by the media. In many states, the attorney general and the state police are viewed as accomplices of the criminal organizations, protectors of their turf,[20] and responsible for the bloody crimes that go unpunished. It is not surprising that in many places the army has a more credible reputation in opinion polls, despite allegations of violations of human rights in reports from national and international watchdog organizations.[21] In other states, the public has feared the army for decades. In Guerrero, for example, the dirty war of the 1970s and the repression of the peasant population contributed to entrenched and legitimate fears in the population, while in the poorest mountain regions they gave way to a community police force whose principal objective was, since its beginning, to defend its forces against allegations of police and authority abuse over targeting criminal organizations.[22]

We utilize a database of deaths resulting from criminal rivalries as presented in *Fallecimientos por presunta rivalidad delincuencial* by the Mexican government. In the analysis we use the number of homicides that occurred between December 2006 and December 2010. The majority of the homicides were concentrated in northern Mexico and in the states of Guerrero and Michoacán. Many of the states with more drug-related deaths have been governed by the PRI, such as Chihuahua, Coahuila, Durango, Michoacán, Nuevo León, San Luis Potosí, Tamaulipas, Veracruz, and Zacatecas.

Violence affects voting patterns in a heterogeneous manner. Electoral results at the state level suggest that the PAN lost in the north except in two states, Tamaulipas and Nuevo León, which have suffered from high levels of violence and are hosts to joint operation forces. In both states, the PAN won the majority of the vote in the presidential elections. Veracruz is another state where the PAN was strongly supported, and it has also experienced an escalation of violence and daily clashes between criminal organizations. The aggregate data at the state level are crude, however, and can certainly mask important patterns in voting behavior.

Precinct-Level Analysis

Individual decisions regarding electoral choices and turnout have been linked in the voting literature to many variables related to individual-level traits: gender, schooling, income, place of residence, partisan identification, and so on. From an electoral geography perspective, however, a large host of contextual local factors are often neglected in survey-based individual-level studies. Survey instruments cannot ask every conceivable contextual question, such as the role of the terrain, weather conditions, electoral machinery, or many other local social or political dynamics. In electoral geography, such local context is captured by territorial proximity and the characterization of the locations where electoral behavior occurs. Contiguous places are likely to share similar conditions, and therefore electoral dynamics will be similar. Voters living in the same places might share similar political attitudes because they also happen to share similar life experiences or sociodemographic characteristics. Even if we might not be able to directly measure all those local variables, the geographic approach can control for them.

We seek to isolate the effect of the dynamics of violence in Mexico on electoral behavior in the 2012 election. In order to isolate these effects, our empirical strategy involves estimating models of turnout and electoral preferences that control for a large host of geographic conditions and local characteristics at the precinct level. The models we estimate include variables that may be of great interest in their own right for many researchers.[23] But in the current setup they are simply control variables that enable us to separate the independent effects of drug-related violence on turnout and electoral choices. In particular, our models include control variables for the following local-level features:

1. *Spillovers and precinct size.* Voting choices in an electoral precinct are not independent from the political behavior of neighboring areas. Given the small size of precincts in Mexico (around 1,200 voters), we expect that campaign events in territorially contiguous places will generate a diffusion of political attitudes across space. To control for such spillover effects (and to provide a correction for spatial autocorrelation), we include two spatial lags of the dependent variable, captured by the first- (next closest) and second-order neighboring electoral precincts. Although all precincts are initially drawn to have the same size, demographic processes lead to a differential loss or gain of population in precincts through time.[24] The Federal Electoral Institute periodically updates the drawing of the *secciones electorales*, but we also include a variable to correct for potential effects of demographic heterogeneity by including a variable for the precinct size, represented by the number of registered voters in each precinct in 2012.

2. *Socioeconomic correlates of voting.* Turnout and voting choices are affected by social, economic, and demographic conditions that reflect differences in income and social status. In order to control for the heterogeneity in voting patterns that arises from social difference, we have included a poverty index calculated according to the methodology of El Consejo Nacional de Evaluación de la Política de Desarrollo Social (CONEVAL) for measuring locality-level social deprivation,[25] the unemployment rate, whether the precinct is in a rural locality with fewer than 5,000 inhabitants, the share of population speaking an indigenous language, and migration flows reflected in the share of population in the precinct that is living in a different state or abroad. We calculate these variables using information from the 2010 census, regrouped by IFE-INEGI (2012) to the precinct level.

3. *Access to media and social services.* We separate from the social correlate control variables some other indicators that are related to access to media and social services. Although intrinsically related to sociodemographic patterns, they are distinct because they involve local dynamics of social networks and particular state interventions that make some services more or less available. In particular, we control for the coverage of Internet access and availability of media through the percentage of the precinct-level population with Internet and television; we include a control for the percentage of youth in the precinct (18- to 35-year-olds) and the percentage of population with access to medical services (through the Instituto Mexicano del Seguro Social, or IMSS; Instituto de Seguridad y Servicios Sociales de los Trabajadores del Estado, or ISSSTE; or Seguro Popular systems). All these variables were calculated on the basis of data from IFE-INEGI (2012).

4. *Local partisanship.* We include dummy variables for the partisanship of the mayor in each municipality, as well as estimations controlling for the partisanship of the governor. The combination of these variables can be thought of as a fixed effect over those characteristics that are shared among precincts owing to their executives belonging to the same political organization. The variable is coded on the basis of the Base de Datos Electorales of the Centro de Investigación para el Desarrollo A.C. (CIDAC).

In measuring violence, we estimate the effect of three independent variables that seek to capture three different dynamics affecting citizens in different ways. These variables reflect measures of violence standardized by population (rates) and as discrete events. The first is a measure of violence as indicated by municipal murders, expressed as homicide rates (per 100,000) by Sistema Nacional de Información en Salud (SINAIS). The mortality information of this variable is generated by the Mexican health system, and it reflects the death certificates listing homicide as the cause of death for the years between 2006 and 2011.

The second variable is a dichotomous indicator of whether a municipality exhibits DTO presence, as measured by the existence of at least one drug-related homicide. Drug-related homicides are determined on the basis of the federal government's database of fatalities presumably related to rivalry between criminal groups from Presidencia de la República. An important point to clarify is that a municipality can have murders unrelated to DTO presence.

We include a third variable related to extreme violence experienced in a municipality, which we establish through a threshold of more than twenty-five drug-related homicides per year. This measure is equivalent to the commonly used criteria of absolute numbers of battle deaths as a way to classify a conflict.[26] In the comparative literature, a civil conflict emerges with more than twenty-five battle deaths per year, and a civil war is in place with more than 1,000.

Using these three measures of violence, table 7.1 provides an ordinary least squares (OLS) estimation of the effects of violence on turnout. Electoral participation is measured as the share of votes cast by registered voters at the precinct level in 2012. The effects are calculated controlling for any district-level differences in voting patterns, as the estimation includes 300 electoral district fixed effects. Hence we control for individual single-member district victories or events peculiar to specific races for congressional candidates. Given that violence is measured at the municipal level, standard errors are clustered at that level. Column (1) presents a model estimating the effects only controlling for spatial autocorrelation (i.e., the electoral patterns of neighboring precincts) and the size of the precinct. Column (2) includes social correlates, column (3) adds precinct-level media and social service access variables, and column (4) includes municipal partisanship dummy variables.

The effects are consistent and only become stronger as we add more controls. Violence indeed depresses political participation. All the coefficients exhibit negative signs. We do not find statistically significant evidence, however, suggesting that the overall levels of violence, as reflected by murder rates, produce an effect on voter turnout. The statistically significant coefficients are the ones related to the specific violence related to drugs, either in the form of the presence of DTO activity or in the escalation of violence to what we label as civil war levels. Both effects of the dummy variables have a remarkably similar magnitude. They constitute two thresholds of shifts in social life and local interaction.

The estimates suggest that, without controlling for any sociodemographic features, there is a depression of around one percentage point in turnout when a drug-related murder occurs in a municipality; put another way, places with no drug violence have more political participation. An additional percentage point of participation is lost when violence escalates to the levels of civil war. When including those categorical variables, there is no independent effect of murders on turnout. After all, homicide rates in Mexico, if we discount drug-related violence, have been decreasing steadily for almost two decades. There is no reason to expect that turnout will be affected by common criminal

Table 7.1. Estimated effects of violence on turnout in the 2012 election

	(1)	(2)	(3)	(4)
Homicide rates 2006–11	−0.00000985	−0.000000654	−0.00000415	−0.00000457
	(0.00000619)	(0.00000679)	(0.00000738)	(0.00000743)
DTO presence	−0.00908***	−0.0117***	−0.0160***	−0.0172***
	(0.00142)	(0.00154)	(0.00181)	(0.00182)
Civil war murder levels	−0.00886***	−0.0137***	−0.0172***	−0.0174***
	(0.00268)	(0.00290)	(0.00317)	(0.00314)
		Controls		
Spatial correlation and precinct size	Y	Y	Y	Y
Social correlates		Y	Y	Y
Media, occupation, and access to social services			Y	Y
Municipal co-partisanship				Y
R^2 adjusted	0.337	0.344	0.367	0.367
N	66,338	66,254	66,254	66,254

Note: Spatial correlation with two lags. Social correlates controls include unemployment, marginality index, rural condition, percentage of indigenous population, and migration levels. Media, occupation, and access to social services controls include percentage of population with Internet/TV; percentage of population with IMSS, ISSSTE, or Seguro popular ascription; and percentage of young population at precinct level. Municipal co-partisanship controls are a series of dummies determining the party of the municipal president. Standard errors clustered at municipal level.

$^*p < 0.05$, $^{**}p < 0.01$, $^{***}p < 0.001$.

behavior and other homicides, because those will not create a generalized fear among the population. When sociodemographic and media and social service controls are included, the effects almost double. Municipal partisan controls leave the magnitude of turnout effects virtually unaffected, suggesting that the partisan affiliation of the mayor is not an important conditioning variable for the effects of violence on turnout.

Table 7.2 turns to the patterns of voting choice. Recall that the metric of these estimations is the vote difference between two candidates. The first panel shows the difference between Peña Nieto and López Obrador. The second panel shows differences between López Obrador and Vázquez Mota. And the third panel shows, for the sake of completeness, the estimates for the differences between Peña Nieto and Vázquez Mota. Note that the coefficients of the third panel can always be replicated by adding the coefficients of the first and second panels:

$$[EPN - JVM] = [EPN - AMLO] + [AMLO - JVM].$$

The estimations (1)–(4) are ordered according to the same principle of table 7.1, incorporating increasingly more control variables. In addition, we included the three estimates (5)–(7) that separate the effects according to the partisanship of the governor. Our analysis generates results that point to a complex relationship between voting and violence. PRI candidate Enrique Peña Nieto, and not the incumbent PAN, clearly suffered the most electorally from the presence of violence. This is exhibited by the coefficients of the DTO presence variable, which is always negative and statistically significant for the comparison of EPN versus AMLO. Estimations (1)–(4) suggest that López Obrador got a marginal advantage of around eight votes per precinct over Peña Nieto in the places that had experienced drug-related violence. Perhaps even more surprisingly, the same disadvantage was observed for Peña Nieto in the comparison with Josefina Vázquez Mota. In places with DTO presence, the PRI candidate gets around nine fewer votes than the incumbent PAN candidate. Civil war–level violence exhibits the same pattern, although the coefficients, depending on the control variables, do not always reach statistical significance. Concentrating on estimation (4), the effect of extreme violence is of around seven fewer votes for Peña Nieto compared to AMLO. In that specification, we do not find an effect statistically distinguishable from zero for the comparison of the PRI candidate to Vázquez Mota. The estimations of the second panel of table 7.2, for the comparison between Vázquez Mota and AMLO, do not show any statistically significant effect of violence on partisan preferences.

Table 7.2.   Estimated effects of violence on vote choices in the 2012 election

	(1)	(2)	(3)	(4)	(5)	(6)	(7)
EPN versus AMLO							
Homicide rates 2006–11	0.0204**	0.00800	0.0172*	0.0159*	0.0177*	0.0588	0.0357
	(0.00702)	(0.00616)	(0.00671)	(0.00668)	(0.00757)	(0.0406)	(0.0288)
DTO presence	−10.94***	−8.303***	−8.299***	−8.525***	−5.926*	−17.39*	−5.678
	(2.344)	(2.204)	(2.198)	(2.215)	(2.510)	(7.148)	(12.01)
Civil war murder levels	−11.09***	−4.946	−6.684*	−7.251*	−5.132	−29.79	16.82*
	(2.891)	(3.000)	(3.021)	(2.951)	(4.092)	(18.97)	(6.708)
R^2 adjusted	0.645	0.647	0.649	0.649	0.609	0.666	0.703
AMLO versus JVM							
Homicide rates 2006–11	−0.00475	0.00546	0.00521	0.00592	0.00729	−0.0231	−0.0254
	(0.00756)	(0.00669)	(0.00660)	(0.00669)	(0.00667)	(0.0309)	(0.0381)
DTO presence	0.157	−2.063	−0.605	−0.422	2.357	11.81	−28.41*
	(2.461)	(2.331)	(2.437)	(2.453)	(2.655)	(8.912)	(14.07)
Civil war murder levels	3.870	−2.408	2.717	3.321	0.417	12.76	−28.31***
	(3.046)	(2.964)	(3.065)	(2.931)	(3.617)	(18.57)	(8.158)
R^2 adjusted	0.658	0.660	0.657	0.667	0.647	0.624	0.763

EPN versus JVM

Homicide rates 2006–11	0.0165**	0.0138**	0.0244***	0.0234***	0.0286***	0.0322	0.0183
	(0.00530)	(0.00524)	(0.00607)	(0.00601)	(0.00737)	(0.0184)	(0.0249)
DTO presence	−11.02***	−10.35***	−9.438***	−9.549***	−2.723	−1.900	−32.88*
	(2.179)	(2.123)	(2.415)	(2.441)	(2.622)	(6.257)	(13.55)
Civil war murder levels	−7.274**	−7.263*	−3.421	−3.387	−5.652	−15.92	−9.219
	(2.803)	(2.850)	(2.828)	(2.891)	(3.881)	(8.662)	(7.098)
R^2 adjusted	0.569	0.571	0.591	0.591	0.604	0.493	0.719
Controls							
Spatial correlation and precinct size	Y	Y	Y	Y	Y	Y	Y
Social correlates		Y	Y	Y	Y	Y	Y
Media, occupation, and access to social services			Y	Y	Y	Y	Y
Municipal co-partisanship				Y	Y	Y	Y
Restricted by state incumbent governor					PRI	PAN	PRD
N	66,338	66,254	66,254	66,254	36,355	10,866	10,259

Note: Spatial correlation lagged at two levels. Social correlates controls include unemployment, marginality index, rural condition, percentage of indigenous population, and migration levels. Media, occupation, and access to social services controls include percentage of population with Internet/TV; percentage of population with IMSS, ISSSTE, or Seguro popular ascription; and percentage of young population at precinct level. Municipal co-partisanship controls are a series of dummies determining the party of municipal president. Columns 5, 6, and 7 are restricted data sets by partisanship of the state's incumbent governor. Standard errors are clustered at the municipal level.

$^*p < 0.05$, $^{**}p < 0.01$, $^{***}p < 0.001$.

In contrast to the turnout estimations, the coefficients for the homicide rate are now statistically significant, exhibiting the opposite effects as drug-related violence. Peña Nieto seems to benefit from higher murder rates, but the effects are relatively small.

Estimation (5) probes deeper into the question of why Peña Nieto seems to lose votes from the presence of drug-related violence. The estimation only includes the precincts in which the governor in the state is a member of the PRI. These are the majority of the precincts but they have a specific territorial distribution, which is correlated with some locations with the most drug-related violence. In PRI-governed states, EPN does not lose votes to JVM, which may reflect a predisposition of voters in favor of the governor's co-partisan candidate. But in these states voters take away votes from EPN in favor of AMLO when there is DTO presence. The result is striking when compared with column (6), which shows the effect of violence in places governed by the PAN. The estimated effect of rejecting the PRI candidate in places with drug-related violence is more pronounced when a state was governed by the PAN, when comparing Peña Nieto to AMLO, and when a state was governed by the PRD, when comparing Peña Nieto to Vázquez Mota, as though voters believed that the alternative non-PRI candidate would be the best one to curb violence. Neither the incumbent governor party candidate nor the PRI's gained an advantage in places with DTO presence in the states governed by the PAN or the PRD. This is reflected by the nonsignificant coefficients of EPN versus JVM in specification (6) and EPN versus AMLO in specification (7).

The OLS estimations describe systematic patterns that allow us to identify correlates but do not reveal a causal relationship. The correlations show that people living in violent regions tended to vote against the PRI, but we cannot be sure that violence, and not some other omitted variable, was the reason for this behavior. We are not particularly worried about reverse causation because we do not believe that expressing a partisan preference or failing to participate in the 2012 federal elections could have produced the drug-related violence of the previous years. A partisan story suggesting that the relative strength of the parties before the election caused the violence is perhaps plausible, but would involve many assumptions about the social processes that generate violence.[27] It could be that there are factors not included in the model—such as the specific interventions made by the federal government or the concrete activities of DTOs that are correlated with violence—and that they independently impact the vote.[28] That is, it is possible that citizens do not react to homicides per se but that drug-related violence is a proxy for some other phenomena that affect the perceptions and assessments of citizens, which in turn influenced their vote choice.

Further research should explore the complex problems of causal inference involved in the interpretation of our findings. From a descriptive perspective, however, citizens in the municipalities with DTO presence did vote for López Obrador over Peña Nieto, even though the aggregate data show little presence of the PRD in those areas of the country. The violent areas tended to punish the PRI probably because the party controls a large number of local governments in these states, suggesting that voters attribute more of the violence to the corruption and possible complicity of the local authorities than it would seem at first glance, and more than they attributed to the national government.

The research agenda also includes the exploration of the robustness of our results. In this regard, the inclusion of plausible omitted variables such as previous electoral results, or the use of placebo tests and instrumental variables, could determine whether the estimates are biased. Because electoral results are correlated from election to election, for example, we might be overestimating the effect of drug-related violence. But this electoral persistence might not be distributed homogeneously among the country; specific violent regions could have higher fluctuations from election to election.

Conclusion

There are two main findings in our analysis of the effects of violence on the 2012 election in Mexico. The first is that turnout was depressed as a direct consequence of the presence of DTOs and the escalation of violence to levels similar to those observed in civil wars. The second is that the candidate who suffered at the polls from violence-related voter defections was not the PAN's Josefina Vázquez Mota but rather the PRI's Enrique Peña Nieto. In the states governed by the PRI, violence likely affected the electoral fortunes of the candidate of the incumbent governors because voters held the party accountable for the violence they were experiencing.

We estimate that violence kept 3% of potential voters from participating. We do not know what the electoral behavior of those abstention votes would have been had they voted. But this effect is large when contrasted with empirical studies of turnout elsewhere. For example, in a widely admired study of get-out-the-vote efforts in the United States, Gerber, Green, and Larimer (2008) find effects on turnout of between 1.8% (owing to civic duty) and 8.1% (owing to social pressure). The setting in that study is an experimental one, in which voters were treated with mail messages saying they would be exposed publicly for not having voted. In a different experiment studying Facebook contagion effects in US elections (Bond et al. 2012), the authors estimate 60,000 direct and 280,000 indirect (out of 90,000,000 voters) additional voters were mobilized owing to social networks. A different perspective of how large a 3% depression in turnout is may be gained from comparing with studies that have looked into the effect of weather on turnout. Estimates suggest that there is a 1% increase in turnout for each additional inch of precipitation (Hansford and Gomez 2010). Hence the estimated effects are quite large.[29]

Nonetheless, the 2012 election was won by EPN for reasons not related to violence or the war on drugs. This correct interpretation of the election results in relation to violence is essential because it affects how Peña Nieto and his team should interpret their mandate. The message for Enrique Peña Nieto is that citizens most affected by violence seem to attribute the serious problems of violence and organized crime to state governors from his party. The president's party will have to begin at home by consoling voters with deep reforms to institutions and practices at the state level by preventing impunity, punishing corruption, and providing security to citizens. Because the federal government has no legal jurisdiction over matters of law enforcement in the states, this reform is not possible without a political compromise between the president and the governors of his own party.

APPENDIX: METHODOLOGY

To test the effects of violence and DTO presence in the federal election, we specify the following model:

$$
\begin{aligned}
y_{p,m,d} = \beta_0 &+ \beta_1 Murder_{m,d} + \beta_2 DTO_{m,d} + \beta_3 WAR_{m,d} \\
&+ \rho w_{p,m,d} y_{p,m,d} + \lambda X_{p,m,d} + \theta_d + \varepsilon_{p,m},
\end{aligned}
\tag{1}
$$

where the dependent variable $y_{p,m,d}$ is the difference in number of votes between two given candidates in a precinct p in a municipality m in a district d. This dependent variable determines vote choices of the electorate and provides a more straightforward interpretation of the coefficients. Here we have three variables of interest. The coefficient β_1 describes the effect of murder rates in a given municipality between 2006 and 2012. The coefficient β_2 describes the effect of DTO presence in a given municipality; the associated variable is a dummy that turns on if the municipality had at least one murder associated with organized crime during this period. The coefficient β_2 explains the effects of violence levels associated with civil war in a given municipality; to specify these levels, we considered conflicts with at least twenty-five casualties per year (one hundred over the four-year period) as civil wars.

Additionally, we included spatial lags of order one and two defined by $w_p y_p$, where w_p is the row p for the connectivity matrix W. Here the connectivity vector w_p acquires nonzero values for all $j \neq p$ precincts adjacent to p. Controlling for spatial lag is necessary given the high correlation between each precinct voting outcomes, so including these variables helps to reduce biased estimators and avoids inflating the R^2 artificially.

The vector $\mathbf{X}$ includes precincts' population and socioeconomic covariates at the precinct level, such as unemployment rate, marginality index, rural/urban characterization, percentage of indigenous population, and migration rates. Another set of covariates controls for development-related and state capacity variables such as Internet coverage, percentage of households with a television, percentage of youth population, percentage of population with an IMSS or ISSSTE affiliation (an indicator of employment in the formal and public sectors), and percentage of population with Seguro Popular, the public health insurance for people with no affiliation to IMSS or ISSSTE. Finally, we include a set of dummies controlling for party affiliation of the incumbent municipal president.

In order to control for particular characteristics of a given district related to electoral campaign such as parties' internal organization or strategic alliances, we included fixed effects at the district level (θ_d). Because our violence variables are coded at the municipal level, standard errors are clustered at that level in order to avoid artificially deflating their standard errors. Additionally, we censored the data separating states by each governor's party in order to observe heterogeneous effects.

The model for turnout at the precinct level was also computed with essentially the same characteristics of model 1:

$$turnout_{p,m,d} = \beta_0 + \beta_1 Murder_{m,d} + \beta_2 DTO_{m,d} + \beta_3 WAR_{m,d}$$
$$+ \rho w_{p,m,d} y_{p,m,d} + \lambda X_{p,m,d} + \theta_d + \varepsilon_{p,m}. \tag{2}$$

The models are estimated using the rich data on electoral outcomes and census variables available at the precinct level (IFE-INEGI). By using the more than 66,000 precincts, we are able to control for several factors and observe actual rather than reported data from exit polls.

ACKNOWLEDGMENTS

An early version of this chapter was presented at the Mexico 2012 Public Opinion and Election Conference: The 2012 Public Opinion Panel Project at Harvard University, January 24–25, 2013. Preliminary analysis was reported by Díaz-Cayeros, Magaloni, Olarte, and Franco (2012). The authors thank participants in the workshop as well as Edna Jaime and the staff of Mexico Evalúa for helpful suggestions and comments. Díaz-Cayeros received support from the Center for US–Mexican Studies of the University of California, San Diego. Olarte and Franco acknowledge support from the Poverty and Governance Program at the Center for Democracy, Development, and Rule of Law at Stanford University.

NOTES

1. For analysis of the election, see Díaz-Cayeros et al. (2012), Flores Macías (2013), Schedler (2013), and the contributions in this volume. The literature on elections during the era of PRI hegemony is vast, but a good place to start is Magaloni (2006). On the democratization process, see Domínguez and McCann (1996); on the dynamics of local elections, see Hiskey and Canache (2005); and on party organization, see Greene (2007).

2. On the drug war in Mexico, see Dell (2012), Grillo (2011), and Molzahn, Rios, and Shirk (2012).

3. The Uppsala Conflict Data Program (2013) places Afghanistan, Pakistan, Somalia, Sudan, and Yemen as the locations of the conflicts that reached the "war" category (more than 1,000 battle-related deaths) in 2012. In that study, Mexico is placed in a different category (a nonstate conflict) given that the state is not considered one of the warring parties. See the worldwide locations of armed conflicts in 2012 at: http://www.pcr.uu.se /digitalAssets/196/196101_armedconflicts_2012jpg.jpg.

4. For a discussion of the renewed interest in electoral geography, see Rodden (2010).

5. We do not use pre- or postelectoral survey data because turnout models would be unreliable and reported voting intentions were too volatile, shifting during the campaign and in the aftermath of the election (voter rationalization of the winner's reported vote is exaggerated). Exit poll data could solve the problems of voter rationalization, but they cannot assess effects on participation. Furthermore, the sample size of exit polls does not provide enough coverage in areas of the most intense violence.

6. Their study supplements these findings with survey data that seem to confirm that citizens exposed to high levels of criminal violence are less likely to report an intention to vote. They find a decrease of around seven percentage points in the reported intention to vote (typically high at around 81% in the overall sample) in places of high violence. Note, however, that the levels of reported intention to vote are typically much higher than the actual turnout.

7. Similar to time series analysis, we are modeling the spatial dependence in the dependent variable (Anselin 1988).

8. Contributions studying Mexican elections from a geographic perspective include Fernández-Durán, Poiré, and Rojas-Nandayapa (2004) and Vilalta y Perdomo (2004).

9. On prospective and retrospective assessments in Mexican elections, see Domínguez and McCann (1996), Klesner and Lawson (2004), Magaloni (2006), Moreno (2009), and Poiré (1999).

10. See King, Rosen, and Tanner (2004).

11. Precinct size is negatively correlated with poverty, emigration, and rurality, but positively correlated with the share of population speaking an indigenous language.

12. The white precincts in the map are accounted as follows: four where the plurality corresponds to the fourth candidate, Gabriel Quadri; 290 ties; eleven with no reported votes; and 217 with missing data. The IFE does not provide an explanation for the missing data, notwithstanding that its official report indicates that only four polling booths failed to be installed on Election Day.

13. An ancillary figure (available at www.press.jhu.edu) presents a cartogram of electoral precincts (constructed with turnout data), which shows the precincts according to their location and true electoral size rather than their land area. This cartogram shows that the biggest drawback of the choropleth map is not the north versus south comparison, but rather the relative importance of *secciones electorales* in cities throughout the country.

14. This can be seen in the baryocentric graph in an ancillary figure available at www .press.jhu.edu.

15. See Klesner (2005).

16. Although the map does not show the turnout rates, these are also geographically heterogeneous.

17. In multiparty settings, the established methodology to do this would express vote shares as log odd ratios, turning one of the party vote shares into a base category. Such transformation ensures that the distribution of the dependent variable approximates a normal (Gaussian) curve, and that the values recovered from the econometric estimation are always between 0 and 1. It would then be possible to estimate simultaneously all the log odds ratios (one fewer equation than the number of parties involved).

18. The alternative would have been a logarithmic transformation that would complicate the interpretation at different points in the vote distribution (because logarithms are not linear, a well-known feature of such models is that an estimated coefficient at one level of aggregation will always be different from the one that would be obtained from a different level of aggregation).

19. Joint operations are a federal force that constitutes a collaborative effort between parts of the Mexican Army, Navy, and Federal Police. Up to now, they have launched operations in Baja California (Tijuana), Chihuahua (Ciudad Juárez), the "Golden Triangle" (at the intersection of the states of Chihuahua, Durango, and Sinaloa), Guerrero, Michoacán, Nuevo León, Oaxaca (the southern border isthmus region), Tamaulipas, and Veracruz.

20. Commonly referred to as "plazas" in the Mexican drug war context.

21. On human rights violations, see Human Rights Watch (2012).

22. On community policing, see Sierra (2012).

23. The literature exploring the sociodemographic correlates of voting in Mexico is vast. See Moreno (2003).

24. An ancillary figure (available at www.press.jhu.edu) shows the importance of correcting for spatial lags by displaying graphs of the spatial lags and Moran I spatial correlations of all the dependent variables.

25. The poverty index is constructed with census variables that indicate social deprivation and can be measured at disaggregated levels when income data are unavailable. In

the current methodology (CONEVAL 2007), the *índice de rezago* includes the illiteracy rate; the share of school-age children with no schooling; the share of children not completing primary school; the population with no access to health services; and the number of dwellings with dirt floors and without toilet, sewerage, drinking water connected to the public network, electricity, washing machine, or refrigerator. The index was calculated with precinct-level data through a principal components method by a research team at the Center for US–Mexican Studies, led by Alberto Díaz-Cayeros.

26. The Correlates of War Project establishes a threshold of 1,000 battle deaths to declare a civil war. We are using municipalities with a threshold of one hundred drug-related deaths in the four-year period between 2008 and 2011 to declare them DTO conflict zones, which in fact is already a large threshold. The conflicts in the world that include more than twenty-five battle deaths are accounted for at the level of a full country.

27. While there is important research by Villarreal (2002, 2004) showing a correlation between murder rates and PRI dominance, the findings correspond mostly to phenomena of rural violence that have changed a lot since the transition to democracy. Murder rates in Mexico are now primarily an urban phenomenon, with levels of non-drug-related crimes being much lower than what prevailed at the time of his study.

28. Even with such caveats, the analysis does control for electoral district fixed effects, which is equivalent to having a dummy variable for idiosyncratic vote patterns that may have been produced by interventions targeting particular districts. If the mobilization of troops and police forces in joint operations were circumscribed to areas that correspond with districts, for example, it constitutes a control for such confounding variables.

29. Our results are somewhat at odds with Trelles and Carreras (2012), who find a 0.66 (municipal violence) | 2.77 (for spatial lag) percentage decrease in turnout for each additional death per 1,000 inhabitants, a much stronger effect. We believe the difference lies mostly in that our estimation controls for the spatial lags in turnout and is less affected by large spikes in murder rates in small municipalities.

REFERENCES

Anselin, Luc. 1988. *Spatial Econometrics: Methods and Models.* Dordrecht: Kluwer Academic.

Bateson, Regina. 2013. "Crime Victimization and Political Participation." *American Political Science Review* 106, no. 3: 570–87.

Bellows, J., and E. Miguel. 2009. "War and Local Collective Action in Sierra Leone." *Journal of Public Economics* 93, no. 11–12: 1144–57.

Berrebi, C., and E. Klor. 2008. "Are Voters Sensitive to Terrorism? Direct Evidence from the Israeli Electorate." *American Political Science Review* 102, no. 3: 279–81.

Blattman, C. 2009. "From Violence to Voting: War and Political Participation in Uganda." *American Political Science Review* 103, no. 2: 231–47.

Bond, R., C. Fariss, J. Jones, A. Kramer, C. Marlow, J. Settle, and J. Fowler. 2012. "A 61-Million-Person Experiment in Social Influence and Political Mobilization." *Nature* 489, no. 7415: 295–98.

Collier, P., and P. Vicente. 2014. "Votes and Violence: Evidence from a Field Experiment in Nigeria." *Economic Journal* 124, no. 574: F327–55.

CONEVAL. El Consejo Nacional de Evaluación de la Política de Desarrollo Social. 2007. "Los Mapas de Pobreza en México: Anexo Técnico Metodológico." Mexico City: CONEVAL. http://www.coneval.gob.mx/rw/resource/coneval/med_pobreza/1024.pdf.

Dell, Melissa. 2012. "Trafficking Networks and the Mexican Drug War." Cambridge, MA: Harvard University.

Díaz-Cayeros, Alberto, Beatríz Magaloni, Jorge Olarte, and Edgar Franco. 2012. *La geografía electoral de 2012*. Mexico City: México Evalúa.

Domínguez, Jorge I., and James McCann. 1996. *Democratizing Mexico: Public Opinion and Electoral Choices*. Baltimore: Johns Hopkins University Press.

Fernández-Durán, J. J., A. Poiré, and L. Rojas-Nandayapa. 2004. "Spatial and Temporal Effects in Mexican Direct Elections for the Chamber of Deputies." *Political Geography* 23, no. 5: 529–54.

Ferraz, C., and B. Vaz. 2012. "The Effects of the Pacification Police on Crime and Violence." Paper presented at the Annual Lemann Dialogue: Brazil and the Future of the Global City, Harvard University, Cambridge, MA.

Flores Macías, Gustavo. 2013. "Mexico's 2012 Elections: The Return of the PRI." *Journal of Democracy* 24, no. 1: 128–41.

Gallego, J. 2011. "Civil Conflict and Voting Behavior: Evidence from Colombia." New York: New York University. http://papers.ssrn.com/sol3/papers.cfm?abstract_id=1911983.

Gerber, A., D. Green, and C. Larimer. 2008. "Social Pressure and Voter Turnout: Evidence from a Large-Scale Field Experiment." *American Political Science Review* 102, no. 1: 33–48.

Greene, Kenneth F. 2007. *Why Dominant Parties Lose: Mexico's Democratization in Comparative Perspective*. New York: Cambridge University Press.

Grillo, Ioan. 2011. *El Narco: Inside Mexico's Criminal Insurgency*. New York: Bloomsbury Press.

Hansford, T., and B. Gomez. 2010. "Estimating the Electoral Effects of Voter Turnout." *American Political Science Review* 104, no. 2: 268–88.

Hiskey, Jonathan, and Damarys Canache. 2005. "The Demise of One-Party Politics in Mexican Municipal Elections." *British Journal of Political Science* 35, no. 2: 257–84.

Human Rights Watch. 2012. "World Report." New York: Human Rights Watch.

IFE-INEGI. 2012. *Estadísticas Censales a Escalas Geoelectorales: Censo de Poblacion y Vivienda 2010*. Mexico: INEGI. http://gaia.inegi.org.mx/geoelectoral/viewer.html.

Kibris, A. 2011. "Funerals and Elections: The Effects of Terrorism on Voting Behavior in Turkey." *Journal of Conflict Resolution* 55, no. 2: 220–47.

King, Gary, Ori Rosen, and Martin Tanner. 2004. *Ecological Inference: New Methodological Strategies*. Cambridge: Cambridge University Press.

Klesner, Joseph. 2005. "Electoral Competition and the New Party System in Mexico." *Latin American Politics and Society*, 47, no. 2: 103–42.

Klesner, Joseph, and Chapell Lawson. 2004. "Political Reform, Electoral Participation, and the Campaign of 2000." In *Mexico's Pivotal Democracy Election: Candidates, Voters, Campaign Effects, and the Presidential Race of 2000*, ed. Jorge I. Domínguez and Chapell Lawson Stanford, CA: Stanford University Press.

Magaloni, Beatriz. 2006. *Voting for Autocracy*. Cambridge: Cambridge University Press.

Molzahn, Cory, Viridiana Rios, and David Shirk. 2012. *Drug Violence in Mexico*. San Diego: Trans-Border Institute, University of San Diego.

Moreno, Alejandro. 2003. *El votante mexicano: Democracia, actitudes políticas y conducta electoral*. Mexico City: Fondo De Cultura Economica.

———. 2009. *La Decisión Electoral: Votantes, Partidos Y Democracia, México*. Mexico City: Estados Unidos Mexicanos, Cámara de Diputados, LX Legislatura, Consejo Editorial.

Poiré, Alejandro. 1999. "Retrospective Voting, Partisanship and Loyalty in Presidential Elections: 1994." In *Toward Mexico's Democratization: Parties, Campaigns, Elections, and Public Opinion*, ed. Jorge I. Domínguez and Alejandro Poiré. New York: Routledge.

Rodden, Jonathan. 2010. "The Geographic Distribution of Political Preferences." *Annual Review of Political Science* 13: 321–40.

Schedler, Andreas. 2013. "The Societal Subversion of Electoral Integrity: Mexico's Civil War Democracy." Paper presented at the Concepts and Indices of Electoral Integrity workshop, Harvard University, Cambridge, MA, June 3–4.

Sierra, María Teresa. 2012. "Indigenous Women Fight for Justice: Gender Rights and Legal Pluralism in Mexico." In *Gender Justice and Legal Pluralities*, ed. Rachel Sieder and John Andrew McNeish. New York: Routledge.

Trelles, A., and M. Carreras. 2012. "Bullets and Votes: Violence and Electoral Participation in Mexico." *Journal of Politics in Latin America* 4, no. 2: 89–123.

Uppsala Conflict Data Program. 2013. *UCDP Conflict Encyclopedia*. Uppsala: Uppsala University. www.ucdp.uu.se/database.

Vilalta y Perdomo, Carlos. 2004. "The Local Context and the Spatial Diffusion of Multiparty Competition in Urban Mexico, 1994–2000." *Political Geography* 23, no. 4: 403–23.

Villarreal, Andrés. 2002. "Political Competition and Violence in Mexico: Hierarchical Social Control in Local Patronage Structures." *American Sociological Review* 67: 477–98.

———. 2004. "The Social Ecology of Rural Violence: Land Scarcity, the Organization of Agricultural Production and the Presence of the State." *American Journal of Sociology* 110: 313–48.

Wilkinson, S. 2004. *Votes and Violence: Electoral Competition and Ethnic Riots in India*. New York: Cambridge University Press.

8

How Governmental Corruption Breeds Clientelism

ANA DE LA O

It has long been recognized that clientelism and the misuse of public office for private gain feed upon each other.[1] When politicians design and implement policies with the aim of generating income and political support for themselves, a vicious circle consolidates in which public services become an instrument "to generate revenue which can then be appropriated by politicians through various means such as bribes and kickbacks, or left to clients as remuneration for political support" (Kurer 1993, 262). The assumption that clientelism is strongly associated with governmental corruption is so widespread that in some studies the two phenomena are used interchangeably.[2]

A few recent studies have begun to explore the relationship between corruption and clientelism (Kawata 2006). Szeftel (2000), for example, argues that patron–client relations in Africa are for the most part responsible for the corruption that affects the region. Singer (2009) further argues that because clientelism undermines the ability of citizens to hold public officials accountable, it fosters corruption. In these accounts, corruption is an outcome of clientelism. Yet this direction of causation is unlikely to tell the complete story. Despite the centrality of corruption and clientelism to the governance deficit afflicting many countries in the developing world, how public corruption affects citizens' willingness to engage in patron–client relations remains largely unexplored.

In this chapter, I show that citizens' perceptions of corruption among public officials make them more likely to believe that their communities are rife with vote selling and more willing to sell their own votes. The misconduct of public officials is thus pernicious to democracy not only because corrupt politicians can use misappropriated resources to strengthen their clientelist networks (Della Porta and Vannucci 1997), but also because corruption can lead to citizens' dissatisfaction with the political system (Anderson and Tverdova 2003; Mishler and Rose 2001; Morris and Klesner 2010; Pharr 2000), as well as make citizens skeptical of their political institutions (Clausen, Kraay, and Nyiri 2011), driving them to find clientelism more appealing (Cleary and Stokes 2006).

It is perhaps no surprise that the relationship between corruption—understood as the misuse of public office for private benefit—and clientelism—"the direct exchange of a citizen's vote in return for direct payment or continuing access to employment, goods, and services" (Kitschelt and Wilkinson 2007)—is a social trap. To date, scholars have suggested that when public officials perceive that others in the public sector are engaged in corrupt behavior, they find fewer reasons not to engage in corruption themselves (Rothstein 2005). Similarly, however, if citizens perceive that politicians are corrupt, they may find less reason to value programmatic politics over clientelist appeals. Therefore understanding how corruption leads to clientelism is particularly relevant to getting a fix on the governance problem posed by machine politics.

The context of this chapter is Mexico's 2012 presidential election, which marked the return of the Institutional Revolutionary Party (PRI) to the presidency after twelve years of National Action Party (PAN) administrations. President Enrique Peña Nieto garnered 38% of the vote. The runner up, leftist politician Andrés Manuel López Obrador, garnered 31% of the vote. Despite a margin of victory of seven percentage points, allegations that the PRI bought five million votes tainted the election. To date, the extent to which clientelism influenced election results remains a controversial issue (see the introduction to this volume for more details on the election).

This chapter contributes to two strands of literature that have developed separately. One is the literature that shows that the misconduct of public officials has a negative effect on democracy. Scholarship over the last decade provides ample evidence that corruption leads citizens to question the legitimacy of their political system (Seligson 2002), erodes citizens' confidence in government and trust in political institutions (Anderson and Tverdova 2003; Mishler and Rose 2001; Morris and Klesner 2010; Pharr 2000), and casts doubts about the effective enjoyment of legally sanctioned rights (Della Porta and Vannucci 1997). Maladministration also has behavioral consequences. Corruption drives voters away from the voting booth (Chong, De La O, Karlan, and Wantchekon 2011; McCann and Domínguez 1998) but induces a greater inclination to participate in antigovernment protests (Gingerich 2009). The other strand of literature is the vast scholarship on clientelism, where various determinants of vote buying have been studied, including poverty, partisanship (Díaz-Cayeros,

Estévez, and Magaloni 2007, 2009; Kitschelt and Wilkinson 2007; Magaloni, Díaz-Cayeros, and Estévez 2007; Nazareno, Stokes, and Brusco 2006; Nichter 2008; Stokes 2005; Stokes, Dunning, Nazareno, and Brusco 2013), institutions like the secret ballot (Balan and Robinson 2012), the size of the electorate (Seymour 1915), and voter's perceptions about the role of partisan networks in access to publicly funded goods (Calvo and Murillo 2013), among others. The findings in this chapter connect these two strands of literature and suggests that, under circumstances similar to those in Mexico in 2012, high levels of corruption breed forms of political behavior that are detrimental to a well-functioning democracy, such as the persistence of patron–client relations.

Clientelism and Corruption in Mexico

Latin America is widely seen as fertile ground for corruption (Morris 2006) and clientelism (Mainwaring 1995). Despite democratization, the spread and tenacity of the misconduct of public officials have not subsided (Robinson 1998, 2). On the contrary, it seems that the level of corruption increased as democracy made its way through the region (Geddes and Ribeiro Neto 1992; Weyland 2008). Clientelism seems to be subsiding in some countries; however, machine politics continues to exist throughout the region (Stokes et al. 2013. Mexico is no exception to this trend. Mexico's one-party dominant political system slowly eroded throughout the 1980s and 90s, with isolated opposition party victories at the local level coming first, and national-level victories second. Heightened electoral competition culminated in the defeat of the PRI in the 2000 presidential elections. By then, a large share of the population lived in a competitive electoral system.[3] Throughout the democratization process, Mexicans became increasingly committed to democratic values (Domínguez and McCann 1996), and the government began to undertake administrative reforms to curb corruption (Morris 2008). Notwithstanding these trends, generalized corruption in the Mexican government, both local and national, remains an obstacle to good governance.

The Mexican Chapter of Transparency International reports 200 million incidences of corruption, specifically of bribery, in 2011. The average price of a bribe, or *mordida*, as it is commonly referred to in Mexico, was 165 pesos. Bribes to access public services amounted to approximately 32 million pesos. On average, Mexican households spend 14% of their income in bribes. Furthermore, corruption is regressive because low-income households spend 33% of their income in bribes (Transparencia Mexicana 2011).

Democracy did not eradicate clientelism, either. Throughout its long rule, the PRI created an efficient and highly adaptable political machine for distributing selective benefits in exchange for political support (Bruhn 1996; Camp 2003; Cornelius and Craig 1991; Díaz-Cayeros et al. 2007, 2009; Eckstein 1988; Magaloni 2006). There are signs that electoral competition has eroded machine politics in Mexico (De La O 2013; Dion 2010). Also, the country has developed autonomous institutions to administer elections, and a series of electoral reforms have curbed electoral fraud. Although clientelism appears to be diminishing (Cornelius 2004; Domínguez, Lawson, and Moreno 2009; Moreno 2003), it has not disappeared from politics. Clientelist practices have spread to parties other than the PRI (Greene 2012), and in the 2012 presidential election, the leftwing candidate accused the PRI of buying five million votes. The extent to which machine politics still influence electoral results remains an open question, however. Perhaps surprisingly, corruption and clientelism survived the transition to multiparty democracy in Mexico.

Examining the Relationship between Corruption and Clientelism

Citizens in Mexico vary considerably in terms of whether they are willing to sell their votes to a political party's broker in exchange for money, a gift, a favor, or access to a public service. Whereas most people would not consider selling their vote, some do so routinely. Still others opt to accept gifts and money from multiple parties. What motivates people to engage in patron–client relations?

Scholars have postulated two factors as critical to explain these divergent positions. First, poverty is associated with clientelism (Bruhn and Greene 2007; Díaz-Cayeros et al. 2007, 2009; Domínguez et al. 2009; Greene 2011; Klesner 2009; McCann and Lawson 2003). Political brokers buy the votes of poor voters because for them the value of the gift, favor, or access to a public service is greater than the value of casting a ballot for a political party ideologically close to them (Stokes 2005). Second, the strength of partisanship determines whether people engage in clientelism. Stokes (2005) argues that if a clientelist machine has the option of targeting loyal, weakly opposed, or opposition voters, it targets the weakly opposed. A vast research program has developed to explore this issue, with some evidence pointing in the direction of Stokes's seminal article, and some evidence suggesting that a clientelist machine would first and foremost target its loyal supporters, especially when it is in need of mobilizing them (Nichter 2008). But poverty and the strength of partisanship do not exhaust the variation in people's willingness to sell their votes (see, e.g., Simeon Nichter and Brian Palmer-Rubin, chap. 9, this volume).

A third factor that explains why some but not other people are willing to sell their vote relates to citizen's perceptions of—and experiences with—corruption among public officials. When politicians are exposed as corrupt, citizens' trust in the political class and their perceptions of the legitimacy of the system erode (Anderson and Tverdova 2003; Mishler and Rose 2001; Morris and Klesner 2010; Pharr 2000; Seligson 2002).[4] Distrust may lead citizens to be skeptical of campaign promises and to find clientelism more appealing (Cleary and Stokes 2006). A citizen in a context of high levels of public corruption has good reasons to believe that the spoils from public office are large. As a consequence, she may prefer to receive a share from such spoils over being excluded from them. Selling her vote may be one way to participate in the spoils.

Next, I discusses how clientelism, corruption, poverty, and the strength of partisanship can be operationalized using the Mexico 2012 Panel Study, and I use these concepts in a statistical analysis of clientelism. The empirical strategy in this chapter proceeds as follows. First, I examine how perceptions of corruption correlate with clientelism (measured in various ways). Then I examine the same correlation in a multivariate regression that controls for observable personal characteristics like age, gender, religion, education, poverty, and partisanship, as well as locality-fixed effects to take into account factors that are unobserved and time invariant in respondents' localities. From this analysis, a question that remains is whether corruption perceptions lead people to think that their communities are rife with clientelism and therefore are more willing to sell their vote, or the other way around. To get a better sense of the direction of causation, I combine the Mexico 2012 Panel Study with data from Transparencia Mexicana, which contain information on the extent of bribery in a respondent's state the year before the data collection of the Mexico 2012 Panel Study. Because the extent of bribery is measured before (and independently of) the Mexico 2012 Panel Study, this analysis captures the effect of the extent of bribery on clientelism, and not the other way around.

The empirical strategy therefore allows us to see whether corruption perceptions relate to clientelism, whether this correlation persists even after taking into account individual-level observed characteristics as well as locality-level unobserved and constant characteristics, and, finally, whether corruption leads to clientelism.

If corruption perceptions make people more likely to think that their communities are rife with vote selling, respondents who report that corruption is widespread should also report that clientelism abounds in their neighborhoods. Two survey items in the Mexico 2012 Panel Study ask respondents whether they agree with statements about the engagement of others in their community in clientelism. The first statement refers to the behavior of politicians in the respondent's community, and the second statement refers to the behavior of people in the respondent's community.

Respondents were asked whether they totally agreed, somewhat agreed, somewhat disagreed, or totally disagreed with the following statements:

1. In my community, politicians frequently try to buy votes with gifts, favors, or access to public services.
2. In my community, many sell their votes in exchange of gifts, favors, or access to public services.

Perceptions about politicians making clientelist offers and people accepting them abound in Mexico. Of all respondents, 22% report totally agreeing that politicians frequently try to buy votes in their community, and 21% agree that many in their community sell their votes in exchange for gifts, favors, or access to a service. I create two binary variables; each takes the value of one if the respondent says he totally agrees with each statement and takes the value of zero otherwise.

Like perceptions about clientelism, perceptions about corruption are overwhelming. To measure them, the panel includes a widely used question that asks respondents whether they totally agree, somewhat agree, somewhat disagree, or totally disagree with the following statement: "Public employees can take advantage of their jobs for personal benefit without any legal consequence." In the first wave of the panel, 46% of respondents report totally agreeing with this statement, 30% said they somewhat agree, 12% said they somewhat disagree, and 11% said they totally disagree. I create binary variables for each of the possible responses to the corruption survey question.

Perceptions about corruption and clientelism go hand in hand. People who totally agree that governmental corruption is widespread are thirty-five percentage points more likely to say that parties frequently try to buy votes in their community, compared to respondents who totally disagree that corruption is widespread; see column (1) in table 8.1.[5] This result is statistically significant at the 1% level. People who agree or somewhat disagree that governmental corruption is widespread are indistinguishable from people who disagree with the statement in terms of the probability of seeing parties trying to buy votes in their communities. Only people who strongly perceive corruption as widespread report more attempts of vote buying by parties.

Similarly, people who totally agree that corruption is widespread are thirty percentage points more likely to report that other people in their community sell their votes in exchange for favors, gifts, or access to public services. This result is statistically significant at the 1% level; see column (3) in table 8.1. People who agree and somewhat agree with the statement about corruption are not statistically different from people who disagree with the statement. Corruption, then, makes people more likely to think that their communities are rife with clientelism.

The advantage of measuring clientelism with indirect survey items, like asking about politicians' or other people's participation in clientelism, is that their answers may be more truthful than their answers to a direct question because respondents do not need to reveal their personal involvement in a patron–client relation. The disadvantage, however, is that answers to indirect items measure respondents' perceptions about the behavior of others. Presumably, people are likely to report that their community acts in a similar fashion as them. Yet it is also possible that those people behave differently from others in their community. Indirect survey items thus capture perceptions about the extent of vote buying and vote selling in communities, but to measure personal involvement in clientelist exchanges, we need a different survey item.[6]

The Mexico 2012 Panel Study directly asks respondents whether a political party offered a favor, gift, or access to public services in exchange for their vote. The direct question of vote buying is widely used in the literature. The extent of clientelism measured this way can be compared to the extent of clientelism in other elections in Mexico and in other countries. The exact wording of the question is: "In the last weeks, has anyone made you a favor, offered you a gift or access to a public service in exchange for your vote?" Out of all respondents, 2.7% admit that they received a gift, favor, or access to a service in exchange for their vote. Of those who report receiving a gift or favor in exchange for their vote, 31% report that it came from the PRI, 18% from the PRD, and 9% from the PAN.

While corruption perceptions make people believe that their communities are rife with vote buying and vote selling, it does not lead people to sell their

Table 8.1. Effects of perceptions of corruption, poverty, and the strength of partisanship on clientelism: Evidence from the Mexico 2012 Panel Study

| | Linear probability models | | | | | | Ordinary least squares regressions | |
| | Parties always buy votes | | Neighbors always sell votes | | Received gift or favor | | List experiment | |
	(1)	(2)	(3)	(4)	(5)	(6)	(7)	(8)
Corruption								
Totally agree	0.347***	0.357***	0.305***	0.319***	−0.005	−0.004	0.413***	0.394***
	(0.040)	(0.039)	(0.041)	(0.041)	(0.020)	(0.020)	(0.147)	(0.150)
Agree	0.023	0.034	−0.028	−0.019	−0.009	−0.011	0.129	0.127
	(0.037)	(0.037)	(0.038)	(0.038)	(0.019)	(0.020)	(0.155)	(0.155)
Somewhat disagree	−0.001	0.008	−0.043	−0.029	−0.026	−0.026	0.302*	0.296
	(0.042)	(0.042)	(0.041)	(0.041)	(0.021)	(0.021)	(0.175)	(0.183)
Poverty index		−0.005		0.013		−0.006		−0.086**
		(0.014)		(0.013)		(0.006)		(0.042)
Party identification								
Weak		0.039		0.078**		0.003		0.299**
		(0.031)		(0.030)		(0.012)		(0.123)
Strong		0.025		0.055*		0.024*		0.125
		(0.030)		(0.029)		(0.014)		(0.118)
Constant	0.116***	−0.091	0.135***	0.052	0.038**	0.017	1.526***	1.105***
	(0.032)	(0.079)	(0.034)	(0.086)	(0.017)	(0.036)	(0.100)	(0.206)
Observations	1,224	1,224	1,224	1,224	1,224	1,224	1,196	1,196
R^2	0.249	0.278	0.255	0.278	0.044	0.090	0.171	0.212
Controls	no	yes	no	yes	no	yes	no	yes

Note: Robust standard errors in parentheses. All models include locality fixed effects.

***$p<0.01$, **$p<0.05$, *$p<0.1$.

own votes. As indicated in column (5) of table 8.1, perceptions of corruption have no statistically nor substantive effect on the direct question of vote buying. Before concluding that corruption perceptions do not matter in the personal decision to sell one's vote, however, we need to consider that, because clientelism is an illicit activity, people may be unwilling to report to surveyors that they participated in such an exchange. This measurement problem could explain why perceptions of corruption are not associated with decisions to sell votes. The Mexico 2012 Panel Study included a nonintrusive survey item to measure vote buying that helps circumvent this problem.

List experiments are a useful tool to study social phenomena where people are reluctant to offer truthful answers to surveyors. In political science, this measurement technique has been used to study racial prejudice, corruption, and religious attendance, and more recently Gonzalez-Ocantos, de Jonge, Meléndez, Osorio, and Nickerson (2012) conducted a list experiment to study vote buying. The attractiveness of list experiments is that they grant respondents a certain degree of anonymity when answering sensitive questions. The list experiment in the Mexico 2012 Panel Study poses the following question: "I will read a list of activities, and I would like you to tell me how many of these activities you have done during the last weeks. Please, do not tell me which activities you have done, just tell me how many." The sample of respondents is split in halves. Half of the respondents, the control group, are given the following list of activities.

1. Watch news mentioning a political candidate on television.
2. Attend a campaign event.
3. Talk to other people about politics.

The other half of respondents receives the same list of activities, but vote buying is added in the middle.

1. Watch news mentioning a political candidate on television.
2. Attend a campaign event.
3. Receive a gift, favor, or access to a public service in exchange for your vote.
4. Talk to other people about politics.

The difference between the average number of activities reported in the treatment and control groups is a measure of the extent of clientelism. Compared to Gonzalez-Ocantos et al.'s (2012) experiment, the list experiment in the Mexico 2012 Panel Study includes activities that respondents could have done, instead of activities that parties could have done. Thus the focus is on respondents' behavior, not parties. Respondents in the treatment group are similar to respondents in the control group in terms of baseline covariates (please see the online appendix, www.press.jhu.edu). We can therefore be sure that the difference in average number of activities between the treatment and control groups is due to the list experiment, and not to any other differences between the experimental groups.

The list experiment detects almost three times more clientelism than the direct survey question. In the first wave of the panel, respondents in the control group report an average of 1.3 activities, and respondents in the treatment group report in average 1.37 activities; in wave 1, the extent of vote buying was 7% ($[1.37 - 1.3] \times 100 = 7$). As a reminder, the direct question detected almost 3% of vote buying.

When using the list experiment, the relationship between corruption and clientelism reappears. In this analysis, the outcome of interest is a count variable that captures the number of items from the list that respondents reported. The independent variables are a dummy variable indicating whether the respondent was part of the treatment or control group; dummy variables for totally agree, agree, and somewhat disagree with the statement about corruption; and interaction terms between treatment and each of the dummies for perceptions about corruption. I report the coefficients corresponding to the interaction terms.[7] Table 8.1, column (7), shows that people who strongly agree that corruption is widespread are forty-one percentage points more likely to sell their vote compared to respondents who totally disagree with the statement that corruption is widespread. This result is also statistically significant at the 1% level.

Corruption perceptions and clientelism are related in the Mexico 2012 data. Yet a comparison between people who have perceptions of high levels of corruption and people with perceptions of low levels of corruption may conflate the effect corruption with that of preexisting differences, if they exist. Thus it is useful to determine whether the correlation between the two phenomena is robust by controlling for various factors such as gender, age, religion, poverty, and education. The even-numbered columns in table 8.1 show that corruption perceptions are still related to clientelism outcomes even after sociodemographic controls are included in the multivariate regression, in addition to the locality fixed effects. Corruption perceptions are therefore an important correlate of clientelism.

To get a sense of how important corruption perceptions are, it is useful to compare the magnitude of the effect of corruption perceptions to the magnitude of other factors, such as poverty and the partisanship strength. In the statistical models, I include a poverty index that summarizes household characteristics such as not having access to tubed water, electricity, and a gas stove, among others.[8] Partisanship strength is measured as two dummy variables. One takes the value of 1 for respondents who are weakly identified with a party, and 0 otherwise. The other takes the value of 1 for respondents who are strongly identified with a party. The reference group is respondents without partisan identification.[9]

Comparing the magnitude of the effects of corruption perceptions and poverty, the former has a more systematic and substantive effect than the latter. Table 8.1 shows that the poverty index has a statistically significant effect only when measuring vote buying with the list experiment. A standard deviation of 1 in the poverty index leads to nine-percentage-point decrease in vote buying. This result is significant at the 5% level. Considering the estimates in column (8) with the list experiment, strong perceptions that governmental corruption is widespread have a 4.8 times larger effect on vote buying compared to poverty.

To compare the effects of perceptions of corruption and the effects of the strength of partisanship, consider again the estimates when using the list experiment reported in column (8). Strong perceptions that corruption is widespread have an effect similar in magnitude to weak partisan identification (39% vs. 30%, respectively). A strong party identification, however, has a three times smaller effect compared to strong perceptions of corruption and it is not statistically significant. Compared to alternative explanations of clientelism, the magnitude of the effect of corruption is as important as the strength of partisanship and is substantively more important than poverty.

The analysis so far has shown that corruption and clientelism are strongly associated. Yet the question remaining is whether corruption makes people more likely to think their communities are rife with vote selling and more willing to sell their own votes, or the other way around. To get a better sense of whether it is corruption that makes people more likely to engage in vote selling, I merged with the Mexico 2012 Panel Study an aggregate measure of bribery in respondents' states on the basis citizen surveys from Transparencia Mexicana. Because this measure was taken before the Mexico 2012 Panel Study and is an average of bribery in respondents' states—not of respondents' own experience with bribery—we can be confident that the analysis is capturing how bribery makes respondents more likely to sell their votes and not the other way around.

Transparencia Mexicana has collected, every two years since 2001, the National Survey on Corruption and Good Governance (NSCG). The NSCG records the frequency with which households face governmental corruption in the provision of thirty-five public services over the course of a year.[10] Specifically, the surveys record the payment of a bribe in order to speed up, modify the result of, or hinder the provision of a public service of the three levels of government: federal, state, and municipal. The NSCG samples are representative at the national and state level. Each survey has a sample size of approximately 15,000 observations and has the same urban-rural structure as the most updated census.[11]

On the basis of the NSCG surveys, Transparencia Mexicana produces an index of corruption by federal entity called the National Index of Corruption and Good Governance (INCBG). The formula to calculate the index is as follows.

INCBG = (number of times a bribe was paid in the thirty-five services /
total number of times that the thirty-five services were used) × 100

The index takes values between 0 and 100, with higher numbers indicating higher corruption. At the national level the frequency of corruption was 10.6 in 2001, 8.5 in 2003, 10.1 in 2005, 10.0 in 2007, and 10.3 in 2007.[12]

To estimate the effects of exposure to corruption, I include the change in the corruption index from 2001 to 2010, and I control for the initial value of the index in 2001. This combination of aggregate corruption measures captures that the level and the trend in corruption matter to explain clientelism. A respondent living in a state where corruption is initially high and continues to increase (e.g., Guerrero) may have a different disposition toward clientelism compared with a respondent living in a state where corruption was initially high but over time has decreased (e.g., Durango). Because aggregate measures of exposure to corruption in the past (2001, and the change between 2001 and 2010) are not determined by respondents' answers to the clientelism survey items in 2012, estimates from these regressions surmount, at least partially, the challenge of simultaneity.

Table 8.2 presents results of the analysis combining the Mexico 2012 Panel Study with Transparencia Mexicana data. Odd-numbered columns present the results without control variables, and even-numbered columns with control variables. Columns (1)–(6) present the estimates on the basis of linear probability models, and the last two columns present ordinary least squares regressions. All models include robust standard errors. Because the independent

Table 8.2. Effects of state-level corruption on individual reports of clientelism: Evidence from the Mexico 2012 Panel Study and Transparency International data

| | Linear probability models | | | | | | Ordinary least squares regressions | |
| | Parties always buy votes | | Neighbors always sell votes | | Received gift or favor | | List experiment | |
	(1)	(2)	(3)	(4)	(5)	(6)	(7)	(8)
INCBG change	0.065***	0.057***	0.059***	0.044***	−0.005**	0.003	0.138***	0.125***
	(0.006)	(0.006)	(0.006)	(0.006)	(0.002)	(0.002)	(0.022)	(0.023)
INCBG 2001	0.003***	0.002***	0.001**	0.001***	−0.000***	−0.000	0.016***	0.012***
	(0.000)	(0.000)	(0.000)	(0.000)	(0.000)	(0.000)	(0.001)	(0.001)
Constant	0.233***	0.123***	0.234***	0.244***	0.037***	0.052***	1.097***	0.616***
	(0.004)	(0.009)	(0.004)	(0.010)	(0.001)	(0.004)	(0.008)	(0.020)
Observations	1,328	1,328	1,328	1,328	1,328	1,328	1,299	1,299
R^2	0.001	0.045	0.001	0.045	0.000	0.055	0.010	0.074
Controls	no	yes	no	yes	no	yes	no	yes

Note: Robust standard errors in parentheses. Observations are weighted by frequencies per state.

***$p < 0.01$, **$p < 0.05$, *$p < 0$.

variables of interest in these specifications are aggregated at the state level, and some states have more observations than others in the Mexico 2012 Panel Study, I weighted the data by the number of observations by state.[13]

Column (1) in table 8.2 shows that a standard deviation increase of one in the change of INCBG from 2001 to 2010 leads to a six-percentage-point increase in the probability that respondents totally agree that parties frequently try to buy votes in their communities. This result is statistically significant at the 1% level, and it is robust to the inclusion of control variables; see columns (1) and (2). Similarly, a standard deviation increase of one in the change of INCBG increases the probability that respondents totally agree that others in their communities sell their votes in exchange for a gift, favor, or access to a public service by six percentage points. This result is also significant at the 1% level, and robust to including controls in the specification.

When measuring vote buying with the direct question, the magnitude of the effect of changes in the corruption index is substantively smaller than when measuring clientelism with indirect questions. Compare, for example, the estimates in column (6) to the estimates in column (1): the effect of changes in INCBG is six times higher when using the indirect question compared to the direct question. As mentioned above, however, the difference in magnitudes could be attributable in part to social desirability bias when using the direct survey item. With the list experiment, the effect of changes in INCBG is again substantively important. A standard deviation increase of one in changes in the corruption index leads to a thirteen-percentage-point increase in vote buying. This result is statistically significant at the 1% level. Once controls are included, the effect of changes in corruption lead still to a substantively important effect of a twelve-percentage-point increase in vote buying, significant at the 1% level.

Compared to the effect of changes in corruption, the effect of baseline corruption as measured by INCBG in 2001 has a substantively small effect (close to zero in most models). Although the magnitude of the effect is small, it is positive and statistically different from zero in most models. Overall, table 8.2 shows that aggregate changes in corruption are important determinants of vote buying. Moreover, these results lend more suggestive evidence that corruption is indeed a determinant of clientelism.

Conclusion

Corruption and clientelism are widely perceived as interrelated phenomena. Yet the ways in which corruption shape clientelist exchanges have been elusive to scholars. This chapter provides evidence of a strong relationship between public corruption and clientelism in the context of presidential elections in Mexico. The findings in this chapter speak to the empirical regularity that "on average citizens in low- [and middle-] income countries are relatively more willing to condone corruption and less likely to want to use their electoral power to vote out the corrupt" (Pande 2008, 3157). Such empirical regularity is puzzling from the perspective of democratic accountability. This study suggests that, to fully understand why citizens tolerate corruption, we need to further explore how governmental corruption breeds forms of political behavior that are detrimental to a well-functioning democracy.

NOTES

1. See, for example, Scott (1969). Also, see more recent studies: Della Porta (2000), Heywood (1997), Hutchcroft (1997), Keefer (2007), and Kitschelt and Wilkinson (2007).

2. Hicken (2011), for example, notes that Persson, Tabellini, and Trebbi (2003) and Keefer (2007) use corruption as a proxy for the level of clientelism.

3. The emergence of competitive elections at the subnational level was highly uneven, however, with the acceptance of multiparty electoral competition in some areas by the mid-1990s and the continued electoral dominance of the PRI into the twenty-first century in other parts of the country (Fox 1994; Hiskey and Bowler 2005; Lawson 2000).

4. Public corruption can also cast doubts about the effective enjoyment of legally sanctioned rights (Della Porta and Vannucci 1997).

5. Nonlinear models, such as probit or logit, are widely used to model dichotomous outcome variables, such as the outcomes in columns (1)–(6) in table 8.1. Yet nonlinear models are cumbersome when specifications include fixed effects or when using panel data. As an alternative, linear probability models (LPMs) work well with fixed effects and panel data. LPMs present some challenges, too: their estimates are not constrained to the unit interval, and their standard errors may be heteroskedastic. However, both concerns can be easily addressed. First, given that the main purpose of the analysis is to estimate marginal effects—and not to make predictions—then the possibility that some predicted values are outside the unit interval is not relevant (Wooldridge 2002). Second, it is straightforward to estimate heteroskedasticity-consistent robust standard errors (Angrist and Pischke 2008).

6. It could also be that respondents interpret the indirect questions as a measure of trust in politicians or their neighbors, in which case the survey items are not capturing clientelism in a meaningful way.

7. The full set of coefficients is available upon request.

8. The index is the standardized sum of eight survey questions that relate to households traits. Compared to separately including household traits as independent variables, the index has the advantage of reducing measurement error. Ansolabehere, Rodden, and Snyder (2008) show that averaging survey items on the same broadly defined issue area eliminates a large amount of measurement error.

9. The exact question in the panel study is: "Generally, do you consider yourself *panista*, *priísta*, or *perredista*?"

10. The services include, from the least frequent to the most frequent: pay property taxes (*predial*); request a scholarship; receive mail; receive military service certificate (or exemption); enroll in social programs; install a telephone line; enroll in a public school; install or regularize services (water, sewage, public electricity, roads, parks); obtain or expedite a passport; obtain a credit from a public institution; connect or reconnect water or sewage; connect or reconnect household electricity; obtain an academic degree or access to exams; obtain or expedite birth, marriage, divorce, or death certificates; visit a patient in a hospital out of visiting hours; get a governmental job; access a public hospital or expedite medical attention; obtain a driver's license; request a permit for a commerce; regularize vehicle papers; request a certificate from Registro Público de la Propiedad; obtain a license or permit of *uso de suelo*; approve vehicle pollution verification; obtain a license to build or demolish; present a case to a jury; obtain water from the municipality reserve; collect trash; permit to work or sell in the street; prevent an arrest; denounce a crime; follow up on a case; recover a stolen car; perform border-related transactions; park on the street; and prevent an infraction.

11. The interviews were based on a strictly random national sample. Each Mexican household had exactly the same chance of being selected for the study (Transparencia Mexicana 2011).

12. Among the least corrupt states are Aguascalientes, Baja California Sur, Durango, Nayarit, and Yucatán. Among the most corrupt states, as indicated by the 2010 NSCG, are Distrito Federal, Estado de Mexico, Guerrero, Hidalgo, and Oaxaca. States where corruption has decreased are Baja California Sur, Durango, Morelos, and Yucatán. States where corruption has increased are Colima, Guerrero, Hidalgo, and Oaxaca.

13. A regression gives equal weight to each observation. In this case, some states have more observations than others; therefore for some states there is more information to estimate the effects than for others. To take this into account, I weighted the data by the frequency by state.

REFERENCES

Anderson, Christopher J., and Yuliya V. Tverdova. 2003. "Corruption, Political Allegiances, and Attitudes toward Government in Contemporary Democracies." *American Journal of Political Science* 47, no. 1: 91–109.

Angrist, Joshua D., and Jörn-Steffen Pischke. 2008. *Mostly Harmless Econometrics: An Empiricist's Companion*. Princeton, NJ: Princeton University Press.

Ansolabehere, Stephen, Jonathan Rodden, and James M. Snyder. 2008. "The Strength of Issues: Using Multiple Measures to Gauge Preference Stability, Ideological Constraint, and Issue Voting." *American Political Science Review* 102: 215–32.

Balan, Jean-Marie, and James A. Robinson. 2012. "The Political Value of Land: Political Reform and Land Prices in Chile." *American Journal of Political Science* 56, no. 3: 601–19.

Bruhn, Kathleen. 1996. "Social Spending and Political Support: The Lessons of the National Solidarity Program in Mexico." *Comparative Politics* 28, no. 2: 151–77.

Bruhn, Kathleen, and Kenneth F. Greene. 2007. "The Absence of Common Ground between Candidates and Voters." In *Consolidating Mexico's Democracy: The 2006 Presidential Campaign in Comparative Perspective*, ed. Jorge I. Domínguez, Chappell Lawson, and Alejandro Moreno, 109–28. Baltimore: Johns Hopkins University Press.

Calvo, Ernesto, and Victoria Murillo. 2013. "When Parties Meet Voters: Partisan Networks and Distributive Expectations in Argentina and Chile." *Comparative Political Studies* 46, no. 7: 851–82.

Camp, Roderic Ai. 2003. *Politics in Mexico: The Democratic Transformation.* 4th ed. New York: Oxford University Press.

Chong, Alberto, Ana L. De La O, Dean Karlan, and Leonard Wantchekon. 2011. "Looking beyond the Incumbent: The Effects of Exposing Corruption on Electoral Outcomes." Working Paper 17679. Cambridge, MA: National Bureau of Economic Research.

Clausen, Bianca, Aart Kraay, and Zsolt Nyiri. 2011. "Corruption and Confidence in Public Institutions: Evidence from a Global Survey." *World Bank Economic Review* 25, no. 2: 212–49.

Cleary, Matthew R., and Susan C. Stokes. 2006. "Democracy and the Culture of Skepticism: Political Trust in Argentina and Mexico." New York: Russell Sage Foundation.

Cornelius, Wayne A. 2004. "Mobilized Voting in the 2000 Elections: The Changing Efficacy of Vote Buying and Coercion in Mexican Electoral Politics." In *Mexico's Pivotal Democratic Election*, ed. Jorge I. Domínguez and Chappell Lawson, 47–65. Stanford, CA: Stanford University Press.

Cornelius, Wayne A., and Ann Craig. 1991. *The Mexican Political System in Transition.* Monograph Series 35. La Jolla: Center for US–Mexican Studies, University of California, San Diego.

De La O, Ana L. 2013. "Do Conditional Cash Transfers Affect Electoral Behavior? Evidence from a Randomized Experiment." *American Journal of Political Science* 57, no. 1: 1–14.

Della Porta, Donatella. 2000. "Social Capital, Beliefs in Government, and Political Corruption." In *Disaffected Democracies: What's Troubling the Trilateral Countries?*, ed. Susan J. Pharr and Robert D. Putnam, 202–28. Princeton, NJ: Princeton University Press.

Della Porta, Donatella, and Alberto Vannucci. 1997. "The Perverse Effects of Political Corruption." *Political Studies* 45: 516–38.

Díaz-Cayeros, Alberto, Federico Estévez, and Beatriz Magaloni. 2007. "Strategies of Vote Buying: Social Transfers, Democracy and Welfare in Mexico." Unpublished manuscript.

———. 2009. "Welfare Benefits, Canvassing and Campaign Handouts." In *Consolidating Mexico's Democracy: The 2006 Presidential Campaign in Comparative Perspective*, ed. Jorge I. Domínguez, Chappell Lawson, and Alejandro Moreno. Baltimore: Johns Hopkins University Press.

Dion, Michelle. 2010. *Workers and Welfare: Comparative Institutional Change in Twentieth-Century Mexico.* Pittsburgh: University of Pittsburgh Press.

Domínguez, Jorge I., Chappell Lawson, and Alejandro Moreno, eds. 2009. *Consolidating Mexico's Democracy: The 2006 Presidential Campaign in Comparative Perspective.* Baltimore: Johns Hopkins University Press.

Domínguez, Jorge I., and James A. McCann. 1996. *Democratizing Mexico: Public Opinion and Electoral Choices.* Baltimore: Johns Hopkins University Press.

Eckstein, Susan. 1988. *The Poverty of Revolution: The State and Urban Poor in Mexico.* Princeton, NJ: Princeton University Press.

Fox, Jonathan. 1994. "The Difficult Transition from Clientelism to Citizenship: Lessons from Mexico." *World Politics* 46, no. 2: 151–84.

Geddes, Barbara, and Artur Ribeiro Neto. 1992. "Institutional Sources of Corruption in Brazil." *Third World Quarterly* 13, no. 4: 641–61.

Gingerich, Daniel W. 2009. "Corruption and Political Decay: Evidence from Bolivia." *Quarterly Journal of Political Science* 4: 1–34.

Gonzalez-Ocantos, Ezequiel, Chad Kiewiet de Jonge, Carlos Meléndez, Javier Osorio, and David Nickerson. 2012. "Vote Buying and Social Desirability Bias: Experimental Evidence from Nicaragua." *American Journal of Political Science* 56, no. 1: 202–17.

Greene, Kenneth. F. 2011. "Campaign Persuasion and Nascent Partisanship in Mexico's New Democracy." *American Journal of Political Science* 55, no. 2: 398–416.

———. 2012. "The Mexico 2012 Panel Study: Clientelism and Campaigns in a New Democracy." Unpublished manuscript.

Heywood, Paul. 1997. "Political Corruption: Problems and Perspectives." *Political Studies* 45: 417–35.

Hicken, Allen. 2011. "Clientelism." *Annual Review of Political Science* 14: 289–310.

Hiskey, Jonathan T., and Shaun Bowler. 2005. "Local Context and Democratization in Mexico." *American Journal of Political Science* 49, no. 1: 57–71.

Hutchcroft, Paul D. 1997. "The Politics of Privilege: Assessing the Impact of Rents, Corruption, and Clientelism on Third World Development." Special issue, *Political Studies* 45, no. 3: 639–58.

Kawata, Junichi, ed. 2006. *Comparing Political Corruption and Clientelism*. Burlington, VT: Ashgate.

Keefer, Philip. 2007. "Clientelism, Credibility, and the Policy Choices of Young Democracies." *American Journal of Political Science* 51, no. 4: 804–21.

Kitschelt, Herbert, and Steven Wilkinson, eds. 2007. *Patrons, Clients, and Policies*. New York: Cambridge University Press.

Klesner, Joseph L. 2009. "A Sociological Analysis of the 2006 Elections." In *Consolidating Mexico's Democracy: The 2006 Presidential Campaign in Comparative Perspective*, ed. Jorge I. Domínguez, Chappell Lawson, and Alejandro Moreno, 50–70. Baltimore: Johns Hopkins University Press.

Kurer, Oskar. 1993. "Clientelism, Corruption, and the Allocation of Resources." *Public Choice* 77: 259–73.

Lawson, Chappell. 2000. "Mexico's Unfinished Transition: Democratization and Authoritarian Enclaves." *Mexican Studies* 16, no. 2: 267–87.

Magaloni, Beatriz. 2006. *Voting for Autocracy: Hegemonic Party Survival and Its Demise in Mexico*. New York: Cambridge University Press.

Magaloni, Beatriz, Alberto Díaz-Cayeros, and Federico Estévez. 2007. "Clientelism and Portfolio Diversification: A Model of Electoral Investment with Applications to Mexico." in *Patrons, Clients, and Policies*, ed. Herbert Kitschelt and Steven I. Wilkinson, 182–205. New York: Cambridge University Press.

Mainwaring, Scott. 1995. *Building Democratic Institutions: Party Systems in Latin America*. Stanford, CA: Stanford University Press.

McCann, James A., and Jorge I. Domínguez. 1998. "Mexicans React to Electoral Fraud and Political Corruption: An Assessment of Public Opinion and Voting Behavior." *Electoral Studies* 17, no. 4: 483–503.

McCann, James A., and Chappell Lawson. 2003. "An Electorate Adrift? Public Opinion and the Quality of Democracy in Mexico." *Latin American Research Review* 38, no. 3: 60–81.

Mishler, William, and Richard Rose. 2001. "What Are the Origins of Political Trust? Testing Institutional and Cultural Theories in Post-Communist Societies." *Comparative Political Studies* 34, no. 1: 30–62.

Moreno, Alejandro. 2003. *El Votante Mexicano: Democracia, Actitudes Políticas y Conducta Electoral*. Mexico City: Fondo de Cultura Económica.

Morris, Stephen D. 2006. "Corruption in Latin America." *Latin Americanist* 49, no. 2: 5–16.

———. 2008. "Disaggregating Corruption: A Comparison of Participation and Perceptions in Latin America with a Focus on Mexico." *Bulletin of Latin American Research* 27, no. 3: 388–409.

Morris, Stephen D., and Joseph L. Klesner. 2010. "Corruption and Trust: Theoretical Considerations and Evidence from Mexico." *Comparative Political Studies* 43, no. 10: 1258–85.

Nazareno, Marcelo, Susan Stokes, and Valeria Brusco. 2006. "Réditos y Peligros Electorales del Gasto Público en la Argentina." *Desarrollo Economico* 46, no. 181: 63–88.

Nichter, Simeon. 2008. "Vote Buying or Turnout Buying? Machine Politics and the Secret Ballot." *American Political Science Review* 102, no. 1: 19–31.

Pande, Rohini. 2008. "Understanding Political Corruption in Low Income Countries." In *Handbook of Development Economics*, vol. 4, ed. T. Paul Schultz and John Strauss, 3155–84. Amsterdam: Elsevier.

Persson, Torsten, Guido Tabellini, and Franceso Trebbi. 2003. "Electoral Rules and Corruption." *Journal of the European Economic Association* 1, no. 4: 958–89.

Pharr, S. J. 2000. "Corruption and Public Trust: Perspectives on Japan and East Asia." *Harvard Asia Pacific Review* 4, no. 2: 1–40.

Robinson, Mark. 1998. "Corruption and Development: An Introduction." In *Corruption and Development*, 1–14. London: Frank Cass.

Rothstein, Bo. 2005. *Social Traps and the Problem of Trust*. New York: Cambridge University Press.

Scott, James C. 1969. "Corruption, Machine Politics, and Political Change." *American Political Science Review* 63: 1142–58.

Seligson, Mitchell A. 2002. "The Impact of Corruption on Regime Legitimacy: A Comparative Study of Four Latin American Countries." *Journal of Politics* 64, no. 2: 408–33.

Seymour C. 1915. *Electoral Reform in England and Wales: The Development and Operation of the Parliamentary Franchise, 1832–1885*. New Haven, CT: Yale University Press.

Singer, Matthew. 2009. "Buying Voters with Dirty Money: The Relationship between Clientelism and Corruption." Paper presented at the annual meeting of the American Political Science Association Meeting, Toronto.

Stokes, Susan C. 2005. "Perverse Accountability: A Formal Model of Machine Politics with Evidence from Argentina." *American Political Science Review* 99, no. 3: 315–25.

Stokes, Susan C., Thad Dunning, Marcelo Nazareno, and Valeria Brusco. 2013. *Brokers, Voters, and Clientelism*. New York: Cambridge University Press.

Szeftel, Morris. 2000. "Clientelism, Corruption and Catastrophe." *Review of African Political Economy* 27, no. 85: 427–41.

Transparencia Mexicana. 2011. "Indice Nacional de Corrupcion y Buen Gobierno: Informe Ejecutivo." Mexico City: Transparencia Mexicana.

Weyland, Kurt. 2008. "Neoliberalism and Democracy in Latin America: A Mixed Record." *Latin American Politics and Society* 46, no. 1: 135–57.

Wooldridge, Jeffrey. 2002. *Econometric Analysis of Cross Section and Panel Data*. Cambridge, MA: MIT Press.

9

Clientelism, Declared Support, and Mexico's 2012 Campaign

SIMEON NICHTER AND BRIAN PALMER-RUBIN

Vote buying and other forms of clientelism, which may be generally defined as the provision of material benefits in contingent exchange for political support, have long marked Mexican elections. After Mexico's pivotal democratic election in 2000, Wayne Cornelius cogently argued that the diminished efficacy of vote buying contributed to the defeat of the Institutional Revolutionary Party (PRI). Electoral reforms during the 1990s had undermined numerous fraudulent tactics such as stuffing ballot boxes and altering returns, which left the PRI increasingly reliant on vote buying (Cornelius 2004, 48–49). During the 2000 campaign, opposition parties undermined such clientelist tactics as well, urging voters "to take the gift, but vote as you please."

Now, over ten years later, many Mexicans accuse the PRI of reverting to their same old tricks. Accusations of clientelism commanded substantial attention during the 2012 campaign, and some partisans even contend that handouts helped clinch the presidential victory of Enrique Peña Nieto. Indeed, while contesting the election outcome, second-place finisher Andrés Manuel López Obrador named vote buying as one of the key crimes allegedly committed by Peña Nieto's campaign. As we explore below, electoral officials deemed these allegations to be unfounded, and scholars argue that the many clientelist goods distributed were far from sufficient to turn the election in Peña Nieto's favor (Greene 2012; Simpser 2012). Nevertheless, the sheer magnitude of attention paid to clientelism during recent Mexican campaigns suggests that the phenomenon—which has serious consequences for democratic accountability and responsiveness (Kitschelt and Wilkinson 2007; Stokes 2005)—deserves careful investigation.

We explore clientelism during the 2012 campaign, using evidence from qualitative sources as well as from the Mexico 2012 Panel Study.[1] First, we provide an overview that examines how parties reportedly distributed benefits and estimates the prevalence of handouts during the campaign. Second, we examine which types of citizens were most likely to experience clientelism. Then we investigate an intriguing relationship that the literature on machine politics rarely considers: the relationship between "declared support" (Nichter 2009) and clientelist rewards. Statistical evidence suggests that citizens who publicly declare support (by placing political advertisements on their homes) are disproportionately more likely to receive gifts during the campaign. Overall, the evidence presented in this chapter suggests that machine politics is alive and well in Mexico.

Overview of Clientelism in the 2012 Campaign

Political parties distributed a wide range of clientelist benefits during the 2012 Mexican elections. In a national survey conducted on Election Day by the nongovernmental organization Alianza Cívica, 28% of voters reported that they or somebody they knew was exposed to vote buying or pressured to vote in a certain way.[2] Newspapers point to a broad array of handouts, including money, food, clothing, gift cards, and even sheep. Although Mexico's electoral governance body (the Instituto Federal Electoral, or IFE) has made impressive strides in reducing many forms of electoral malfeasance, such as stuffed ballot boxes and rigged vote-counting machines, the perceived validity of elections continues to be threatened by widespread reports of clientelism. A 2010 AmericasBarometer survey found that 7.5% of Mexicans reported "frequently" receiving offers to exchange votes for benefits in recent elections, while an additional 9.2% reported receiving offers "sometimes" ($N = 1,541$).

The Mexico 2012 Panel Study provides evidence about the prevalence of clientelism during the most recent presidential election. As shown in table 9.1, 7.7% of survey respondents reported receiving offers of gifts during either of the survey waves. Experiences with clientelism were far more prevalent later in the campaign: while 2.8% of respondents reported offers during the first wave, 5.7% did so during the second wave. While the overall incidence of clientelist offers may appear rather low, these aggregate figures belie substantial geographic heterogeneity. Consider that the survey included over 1,300 respondents from sixty-five localities across the country. In 38% of localities, not a single respondent reported receiving a gift offer during either wave of the panel survey. By contrast, in 20% of localities, at least 15% of respondents reported receiving such offers. The reported prevalence of clientelism is much greater when asking questions about respondents' communities instead of about their personal experiences. Across all respondents in the second wave, 63% believe that politicians frequently try to buy votes in their respective communities, while 62% believe that many citizens in their communities sell their votes.[3]

The figures in table 9.1 most likely underestimate the true prevalence of clientelist handouts in Mexico. Although only 7.7% of respondents reported receiving an offer during the overall campaign when asked directly, Gonzalez-Ocantos, de Jonge, Meléndez, Osorio, and Nickerson (2012) show that such "obtrusive" questions often dramatically underestimate the actual prevalence of the phenomenon (see also Corstange 2010). Given that exchanging votes for benefits is illegal, social desirability bias leads citizens to underreport receiving handouts during campaigns. One sign that such bias might exist in the Mexican context is the fact that there is over an order of magnitude difference between the proportion of citizens who report in the second wave that they were offered a gift (5.7%) and the proportion who say vote buying happens in their community (63%).

One way of circumventing the social desirability problem is through the use of a list experiment (also known as the item count technique), which can be

Table 9.1.   Gifts and declared support (in percentages), 2012

	First Wave	Second Wave	Either Wave
Any gift	2.8 (37)	5.7 (53)	7.7 (71)
Gift from PRI	0.8 (10)	2.6 (24)	2.9 (27)
Gift from PAN	0.2 (3)	0.9 (8)	1.1 (10)
Gift from PRD	0.5 (6)	0.4 (4)	1.0 (9)
Any declaration	5.9 (79)	9.6 (89)	16.7 (154)
Declared for PRI	2.6 (35)	5.0 (46)	8.2 (76)
Declared for PAN	0.7 (9)	2.6 (24)	3.3 (30)
Declared for PRD	1.1 (15)	2.2 (20)	2.8 (26)

Note: Data from the Mexico 2012 Panel Study. Figures for gifts reflect the percentage (and number, in parentheses) of respondents who indicated in a direct closed-ended question that they had been offered a gift. Gifts from the PAN, PRD, and PRI reflect respondents identifying the respective party (or its candidates or operatives) when asked an open-ended follow-up question about who offered the gift. Figures for declarations reflect whether the enumerator observed any political advertisement on respondents' homes ("any declaration") or for any of the denoted parties (subsequent rows). According to the procedure by which enumerators coded advertisements, "declared for PRD" includes advertisements for PRD or the other two parties that joined López Obrador's coalition (the Workers' Party and Movimiento Ciudadano). The universe for "either wave" includes only respondents who participated in both waves of the panel survey. For gifts, $N = 1{,}318$ (Wave 1) and $N = 923$ (Wave 2 and Either Wave). For declared support, $N = 1{,}328$ (Wave 1) and 923 (Wave 2 and Either Wave).

used to provide an indirect measure of clientelism. This method provides a list of statements and only asks respondents how many statements apply to them, not which particular statements. By comparing the mean count from the treatment group (given a list of vote buying and three innocuous statements) and the control group (given only the list of three innocuous statements), the analyst is able to derive an unobtrusive estimate of the prevalence of clientelist rewards. As Ana De La O also examines in chapter 8 in this volume, the list experiment provides a much higher estimate of clientelism: 6.9% received gifts in the first wave, and 22.1% received gifts in the second wave.[4] In other words, the prevalence of clientelism is two to four times as high when using an indirect measure that addresses the sensitive nature of the topic instead of the direct question. But the two measures examine quite different aspects of vote buying. Whereas the list experiment examines *receiving* a gift, the direct question examines *being offered* a gift. Most likely, the list experiment would have reported an even greater incidence of clientelism if it had examined gift offers. In that case, the gap between the two measures would have been even larger.

Even if the direct question about rewards is interpreted as a lower bound on the prevalence of clientelism, it has the added advantage of shedding light on who provided the benefits. Respondents who reported receiving a gift offer were asked an open-ended follow-up question about who offered the gift. While political operatives from all three major parties almost certainly engaged in some modicum of clientelist tactics, the vast majority of allegations across Mexico have been levied against the PRI and its victorious candidate, Peña Nieto. As shown in table 9.1, the panel study similarly suggests that the PRI most frequently engaged in clientelism. Across both waves, the proportion of citizens who named the PRI (2.9%) is more than the corresponding figures for the National Action Party (PAN) and Party of the Democratic Revolution (PRD) combined (1.1% and 1.0%, respectively). And while one party by no means has a monopoly on clientelist tactics in Mexico, the identical pattern of PRI predominance was also observed in the 2000 and 2006 panel studies. Indeed, in both sets of surveys, the PRI also reportedly bought more votes than the PAN and PRD combined (Cornelius 2004, 53; Díaz-Cayeros, Estévez, and Magaloni 2009, 241).

This survey evidence about the PRI's disproportionate (though by no means exclusive) use of clientelism dovetails with a broader scholarly consensus about patterns of machine politics in Mexico. Various scholars, such as Kenneth Greene (2007) and Beatriz Magaloni (2006), argue that clientelism and patronage played crucial roles in sustaining the PRI's dominance during most of the twentieth century. Over a decade since the PRI's 2000 electoral defeat, the party continues to have the most extensive patronage network across Mexico; it has developed and maintained deep ties among poor communities in many urban and rural areas since the Mexican Revolution. Clientelism is typically more successful when a party has extensive partisan infrastructure and social networks in poor communities (Kitschelt and Wilkinson 2007; Stokes 2005). Insight can be gleaned from a woeful (and certainly not disinterested) campaign manager we interviewed after the 2012 gubernatorial election in Jalisco. His candidate had lost to the PRI in the governor race by just four percentage points, and he passionately lamented about the role of the PRI's extensive patronage network: "I imagine that inside the PRI's campaign structure there is a department that's called 'vote buying.' And there you have an army of staff that are able to identify people that have needs and are willing to sell their votes."[5] In addition to extensive party infrastructure, the PRI's control over many state and municipal governments was also likely to facilitate clientelism in some contexts. At the time of the 2012 election, the PRI held the governorship in twenty out of thirty-one states. Given the common practice of diverting discretionary spending, social programs, and subsidies for electoral purposes, the PRI may have enjoyed a clientelist advantage because it had more funds at its disposal than the PAN or PRD.

Without a doubt, the PRI was not the only party to engage in clientelism during the 2012 campaign. But, given the findings of the panel survey and the broader scholarly consensus, it seems safe to assume that the López Obrador and Vázquez Mota campaigns engaged in relatively less clientelism than the Peña Nieto campaign. A key question that emerges is why they distributed fewer handouts. One possibility is that the PAN and PRD preferred not to deliver contingent benefits owing to fear that it would turn off middle-class voters who are less amenable to clientelist strategies (see Weitz-Shapiro 2012 in the case of Argentina). This explanation would be more applicable to the PAN, whose base of support is predominantly the urban middle class. In the case of the PRD, which similar to the PRI has a predominant base of poor voters, a lack of machine infrastructure across Mexico is a relatively more plausible explanation. In most areas, the PRD lacks the deep penetration of partisan operatives and dense social networks needed to distribute rewards as effectively as the PRI. The strength of the PRD in Mexico City may well be the exception that proves the rule. Hilgers (2008) argues that the PRD engages in substantial clientelism in Mexico City because it has been able to establish dense patronage networks there through the cooptation of neighborhood associations and urban popular movements. Overall, while such explanations about the PAN and PRD remain tentative (and undoubtedly serve as partial explanations at best), the bottom line is that evidence suggests the PRI was the predominant distributor of hand-outs during the most recent presidential campaign.

Competitors cast vitriolic aspersions about the PRI's use of clientelism during the 2012 campaign. As mentioned briefly above, complaints about the PRI's alleged vote buying played a key role in PRD candidate Andrés Manuel López Obrador's contestation of the election. López Obrador, along with his political movement MORENA, or Movimiento de Regeneración Nacional, presented a list of ten electoral crimes allegedly committed by Peña Nieto's campaign to the national electoral tribunal (Tribunal Electoral del Poder Judicial de la Federación, or TEPJF).[6] Several of these accusations centered on vote buying. Most prominently, the Peña Nieto campaign was accused of distributing gift cards that could be used at Soriana, a national supermarket chain, after the election. Anti-PRI activists claimed that Peña Nieto's campaign had distributed cards worth between 100 and 1,000 pesos (roughly $8 to $80) in the days leading up to the election. López Obrador's representatives submitted to the TEPJF 3,500 such cards with logos connected to the PRI and charged that Peña Nieto's campaign had distributed 1.8 million cards to voters in Mexico State (Peña Nieto's home state) alone. Other vote-buying accusations levied by the López Obrador campaign against the PRI pertained to the distribution of debit cards operated by Monex, a financial services company, and cellular phone credit in exchange for votes.[7]

The PRI's purported Soriana and Monex schemes offered particularly effective modalities of clientelism because their gift cards would only be redeemable after the election. In general, a major challenge to politicians offering clientelist benefits is the threat of opportunistic defection by citizens. Once citizens receive benefits, they can often simply vote for their preferred candidate anyway. After all, nearly 87% of panel survey respondents believe that their vote choices remain secret unless they explicitly tell others for whom they voted (from Wave 2). By employing the strategy of "deferred delivery" (Schaffer and Schedler 2007, 24), the PRI could allegedly make the validity of gift cards contingent on a favorable election outcome. Interestingly, despite the favorable election outcome, one reason the Soriana scandal became so public following the election was that many card recipients complained their cards turned out to be worth less than promised, or nothing at all. As one might expect, Peña Nieto's campaign vigorously disputed charges by López Obrador (and others) that it had used such programs to buy votes. PRI and Soriana representatives argued that the cards were not used to buy votes, but rather comprised payments to campaign staff and state social program benefits.[8]

After considering López Obrador's claims against Peña Nieto, which in addition to vote buying also included exceeding campaign spending limits, money laundering, and misappropriating public funds in PRI-governed states, the national electoral tribunal (TEPJF) unanimously declined to annul the 2012 election. The tribunal concluded that López Obrador failed to provide conclusive evidence that clientelism or other serious electoral violations had taken place.[9] Note, however, that even if the tribunal had found evidence of clientelism, it is highly improbable that it would have been enough to annul the election, as it was extremely unlikely that the PRI bought off enough citizens to secure their margin of victory of 3.2 million votes (Greene 2012; Simpser 2012). Given the failure of the claimants to provide sufficient evidence of the alleged infractions, the tribunal was not obligated to judge whether sufficient clientelism had taken place to cast doubt on the election's result.

Beyond López Obrador's formal appeal to the TEPJF, public protests also fanned the nation in the weeks following the election, and demonstrators frequently complained about clientelism. Thousands of López Obrador supporters, as well as leaders of the anti–Peña Nieto student movement #YoSoy132, thronged the streets protesting the election. #YoSoy132, whose name refers to its Twitter handle, was born out of protests led by students of the Mexico City Ibero-American University when Peña Nieto visited the campus. As Alejandro Díaz-Domínguez and Alejandro Moreno examine thoroughly (chap. 10, this volume), the movement centrally objected that electoral coverage on Televisa, a major television network, was unduly favorable to Peña Nieto. Many Mexicans groaned "there he goes again" as López Obrador led protestors down Avenida Reforma, a major artery of Mexico City where he had initiated his famous protest to demand a recount following the 2006 presidential election. While these public protestations cast aspersions on a wide array of purported electoral crimes—not just clientelism—demonstrators frequently cited vote buying as one of their chief concerns. For example, citizens from all thirty-one Mexican states displayed goods that were allegedly handed out by PRI campaign staff in exchange for votes during a widely publicized event called ExpoFraude. This multiday gathering, sponsored by MORENA, was held a month after the election in the Zócalo, the central plaza in Mexico City's *centro histórico*.[10]

Targeting of Clientelist Handouts

Thus far, evidence suggests that clientelism played a substantial (though not decisive) role in Mexico's 2012 campaign, and that the PRI was arguably the primary distributor of rewards. We now turn to another important question: which types of citizens were most likely to receive handouts during the campaign? A burgeoning literature on clientelism, employing both formal and empirical methods, suggests that political machines often target citizens with specific characteristics. In this section, we investigate whether such patterns of targeting are evident in the panel study, employing both the direct question and list experiment.

Many studies on clientelism suggest that citizens with particular socioeconomic characteristics are targeted with rewards. Income is the most frequently cited factor: the poor are targeted because the declining marginal utility of income suggests that they place greater value on a given reward size (e.g., Dixit and Londregan 1996; Stokes 2005). But gathering even more attention than such socioeconomic factors in the clientelism literature are political characteristics. Clientelist handouts are frequently targeted on the basis of two key political characteristics of individuals: partisan preferences and likelihood of turning out on Election Day. Investigating whether gifts in Mexico are targeted using such political criteria is important because it can help identify whether handouts actually represent vote buying or another form of clientelism altogether. Distinct strategies of clientelism target citizens using different political criteria. Vote buying, the focus of most studies, targets opposing or indifferent voters in an effort to influence their vote choices. By contrast, turnout buying targets nonvoting supporters in order to induce them to go to the polls (Cox 2009; Nichter 2008). Other strategies include abstention buying (paying opposing voters to stay home), double persuasion (inducing votes from citizens who neither vote nor prefer the machine), and rewarding loyalists (providing rewards to supporters who would vote anyway). Another important possibility is that distributed benefits involve a broader set of strategies than just elite payoffs to citizens during campaigns. Auyero (2000), Lawson (2009), and Scott (1969), for example, discuss patterns of relational clientelism that involve ongoing relationships of mutual support and dependence.[11]

In order to explore whether such clientelist targeting on the basis of political and socioeconomic characteristics is observable in the Mexico 2012 Panel Study, we now turn to table 9.2, which presents regression analyses examining how each listed characteristic is associated with clientelism. The first four columns employ logistic regressions, in which the dependent variable is whether a respondent reported receiving a gift offer (in a direct question asked just after the election). More specifically, columns (1) and (2) reflect gift offers from any political party, while columns (3) and (4) focus exclusively on direct reports of gift offers from the PRI. The coefficients reflect marginal effects, and robust standard errors clustered at the district level are shown. Column (5), which we discuss more extensively below, reports results from the list experiment about clientelist benefits actually received.

We provide a brief description of each covariate shown in table 9.2; the same variables are also included in later tables. Each variable is from the first wave of the survey in order to reduce potential endogeneity from gift offers (which are measured in Wave 2). All specifications include seven political covariates, six of which are dummy variables scoring whether the respondent strongly or weakly identifies with each of three major parties in Mexico (PAN, PRD, PRI). Strong partisans are those who reported feeling very *panista*, *perredista*, or *priísta* when first asked. Weak partisans are those who responded feeling somewhat *panista*, *perredista*, or *priísta*, or reported no partisan preference at first but admitted sympathizing with the party when asked a second time. We also include a dichotomous variable reflecting whether the respondent predicted in Wave 1 that she was "very likely" to vote. Socioeconomic variables include age, gender, and education (ordinal levels of educational attainment). The survey did not ask how much respondents earn owing to potential response bias and measurement error, so we include a "poverty" variable, which reflects the respondent's self-placement on a five-point scale of how much difficulty she has making ends meet (higher values indicate more economic difficulties). Additionally, regressions control for a housing variable, which measures the interviewer's appraisal of the socioeconomic level of the respondent's house on a four-point scale.

We first turn to column (1) in table 9.2, which examines gift offers from any political party. What is perhaps most notable about this specification is that only one variable is significantly associated with reported gift offers. Weak PRD supporters are 3.7 percentage points more likely to report a gift offer than nonpartisans, a finding that is only significant at the 10% level. Column (2)

Table 9.2.   Correlates of clientelism

	Direct question: Gifts from any source		Direct question: Gifts from PRI		List experiment
	(1)	(2)	(3)	(4)	(5)
Strong PAN supporter	0.026	−0.022	0.039**	0.091+	0.239
	(0.03)	(0.06)	(0.01)	(0.05)	(0.25)
Weak PAN supporter	0.011	−0.031	0.022	0.047	0.318
	(0.02)	(0.05)	(0.02)	(0.05)	(0.20)
Strong PRI supporter	−0.005	−0.056	−0.013	−0.042	0.184
	(0.03)	(0.05)	(0.03)	(0.08)	(0.19)
Weak PRI supporter	−0.046	−0.127*	0.002	0.002	0.461*
	(0.04)	(0.06)	(0.02)	(0.06)	(0.20)
Strong PRD supporter	−0.001	−0.019	−0.329**	−0.827**	0.131
	(0.04)	(0.07)	(0.06)	(0.07)	(0.27)
Weak PRD supporter	0.037+	0.033	0.039*	0.096+	−0.048
	(0.02)	(0.04)	(0.02)	(0.06)	(0.22)
Likely voter	−0.007	−0.012	−0.016	−0.028	−0.084
	(0.02)	(0.03)	(0.01)	(0.03)	(0.14)
Income	0.007	0.010	−0.013+	−0.044*	0.150+
	(0.01)	(0.02)	(0.01)	(0.02)	(0.09)
Education	0.005	0.021*	0.000	0.013	−0.004
	(0.00)	(0.01)	(0.00)	(0.01)	(0.03)
Housing	0.001	0.020	−0.009	−0.012	−0.077
	(0.01)	(0.02)	(0.01)	(0.02)	(0.08)
Age	−0.000	−0.000	−0.000	0.001	−0.003
	(0.00)	(0.00)	(0.00)	(0.00)	(0.00)
Female	0.024	0.046	0.010	0.024	0.034
	(0.01)	(0.03)	(0.01)	(0.03)	(0.13)
Fixed effects	no	municipal	no	municipal	no
Pseudo-R^2	0.033	0.141	0.115	0.176	
Observations	900	490	900	317	879

Note: Data from the Mexico 2012 Panel Study. Columns 1–4 are logit regressions: coefficients are marginal effects; robust standard errors are clustered at district level. For columns (1) and (2), binary dependent variables are coded as 1 if the respondent reported an offer of gift in Wave 2; they are coded 0 otherwise. For columns (3) and (4), dependent variables are only coded 1 if the respondent identified the PRI as offering a gift. Estimates in column (5) represent all gifts, derived using the item count technique regression function of Blair and Imai's (2012) List package in R. Constants are included but not shown. See the text for descriptions of independent variables.

$+p < 0.10$, $^*p < 0.05$, $^{**}p < 0.01$

then adds municipal fixed effects, a step that controls for omitted variables that do not vary across individuals in a given municipality. This relatively more rigorous specification suggests that weak PRI supporters are 12.7 percentage points less likely to report gift offers than nonpartisans, controlling for other included variables (at the 5% significance level). In addition, respondents with greater education are significantly more likely to report gift offers (2.1 percentage points for each point increase on a nine-point ordinal scale). One reason the findings in columns (1) and (2) are so different is that nearly half of the survey observations are dropped with fixed effects, and the underlying selection process is unlikely to be random. Many municipalities have no variation in the dependent variable; in 48% of localities surveyed, not a single respondent reported a gift offer in the second wave. All in all, these two specifications, which examine reported gift offers from any political party, do not provide robust evidence of reward targeting.

By contrast, examining PRI gift offers reveals evidence that is relatively more consistent with political targeting. Column (3) suggests that strong PAN supporters, as well as weak PRD supporters, are 3.9 percentage points more likely to report PRI gift offers than nonpartisans (at the 1% and 5% levels of significance, respectively). By contrast, strong PRD supporters are significantly less likely to report PRI gift offers—in fact, none of the sixty-five respondents in the second wave who identified as strong PRD supporters reported gift offers from the PRI. Income is the only socioeconomic factor that is statistically significant, but its sign is the opposite of theoretical predictions: poorer respondents are less likely to report PRI gift offers (at the 10% significance level). Column (4) reveals findings that are similar when including municipal fixed effects even though the number of observations falls by almost two-thirds for the reason mentioned above. Looking at variation within a given municipality, strong PAN supporters are 9.1 percentage points more likely—and weak PRD supporters are 9.6 percentage points more likely—to report gift offers from the PRI (both at the 10% significance level). Moreover, the coefficients for strong PRD support and poverty continue to be significant. Taken together, such evidence could be interpreted as relatively more consistent (albeit weakly so) with a PRI vote-buying explanation, rather than a turnout-buying or other explanation discussed above. But another plausible explanation, which affects many studies of clientelism, cannot be ignored. When opposing voters are asked specifically about who offered them gifts, they may be pointing accusatory fingers at the winner of the election (PRI), even if not true.

Finally, we examine the correlates of rewards using the list experiment measure. This measure addresses the sensitive nature of electoral gifts but does not provide evidence about who offered rewards. Column (5) in table 9.2 employs Blair and Imai's (2012) item count regression technique, which predicts each covariate's effect on the likelihood of responding affirmatively to the sensitive item of the list experiment, as if this quantity were measured independently for each respondent. Findings diverge sharply from results using the direct question. With the list experiment, weak PRI supporters are 46.1 percentage points more likely to report that they received a gift than nonpartisans (significant at the 5% level), while no other political variables are significant. This finding contrasts with estimates from the direct question: recall that columns (3) and (4) indicate the targeting of PAN/PRD rather than PRI supporters, and column (2) suggests weak PRI supporters are actually significantly less likely to experience clientelism. One possible interpretation of such differences is that, when asked directly, weak PRI supporters refrained from reporting offers of handouts, which were predominantly undertaken by their favored party. They may well underreport gifts because they are relatively invested in the perceived legitimacy of the election, given that their favored candidate, Peña Nieto, won. Separately, another contrast is that, unlike the direct measure, the list experiment suggests poorer respondents are 15.0 percentage points more likely to receive gifts. This finding for poverty is consistent with theoretical predictions. When interpreting the different findings for both the weak PRI supporter and poverty variables, two points should be kept in mind. First, as noted above, while the list experiment examines receiving a gift, the direct question examines being offered a gift. And second, unlike the direct question, the list experiment does not inquire about which party provided clientelist handouts. Owing to both points, different estimates across specifications may well reflect true differences across related but distinct aspects of clientelism.

Summing up, these analyses provide important insights about the types of citizens who experienced clientelism. While some specifications point to targeting based on political and socioeconomic criteria, they do not unambiguously suggest a uniform pattern. One possible explanation is that measurement error, often a problematic issue in the study of clientelism, undermines our ability to identify the true patterns of clientelism used in Mexico. Another potential explanation is that political operatives actually mix several strategies of electoral clientelism, such as both vote buying and turnout buying, which is why they do not exclusively target citizens on the basis of political preferences or turnout propensity. As Gans-Morse, Mazzuca, and Nichter (2014) show formally, combining several strategies is the most effective way to maximize votes with a given clientelist budget (see also related work by Magaloni, Díaz-Cayeros, and Estévez 2007). We now turn to another strategy of clientelism that is relatively understudied in the existing literature—declared support. As we show, the Mexico 2012 Panel Study reveals robust findings about this strategy.

Declared Support in Mexico

Whereas the distribution of clientelist rewards in Mexico remained surreptitious and mostly hidden from view, another use of campaign dollars exploded in plain sight during the 2012 election. Mexican journalists widely reported a dramatic surge in the use of political posters, banners, and other printed advertisements. As explored below, political campaigns increasingly relied on printed materials in part because of heightened restrictions on electoral advertising in mass media. Printed advertisements not only became ubiquitous in the public arena but, as is often the case across the world, were also visible on the homes of many citizens. The remainder of this chapter explores the relationship between such public declarations of support and clientelism.

Recent research suggests that political propaganda can play a key role in clientelist linkages between citizens and elites. The link between declared support and clientelism can be demand driven or supply driven. The demand-driven logic of declared support involves efforts of citizens to obtain clientelist benefits by placing political advertisements on their homes. In the context of Brazil, Nichter (2009, 2012) argues that many citizens engage in "declared support"—for example, placing banners on their homes, wearing party T-shirts, and attending rallies—in an effort to obtain future benefits. His analysis focuses primarily on postelection benefits and explores how declaring support can be risky in contexts with clientelism. If a voter declares support for a candidate who wins the election, she may be rewarded with greater access to handouts and social services. But if a voter declares support for a candidate who loses the election, she may be penalized with reduced access to such benefits. Given the risks involved, many voters choose to remain undeclared, which foregoes favorable treatment but also avoids the risk of unfavorable treatment. Overall, the demand-driven logic of declared support suggests that citizens may place ads on their homes in an effort to obtain clientelist benefits either before or after the election.

Declared support may also involve a supply-driven logic. Parties may require citizens to place political advertisements on their homes as a condition of delivering current or future clientelist benefits. In environments with information asymmetries, declared support can help sort a party's supporters from its opposers because citizens may find it costly (from an expressive utility standpoint) to declare for parties they dislike. Declared support can also limit opportunistic defection by reward recipients for two reasons. First, the visible declaration would make two-timing more difficult: citizens would be less credible when trying to engage in additional clientelist transactions with other parties. Second, citizens' future consumption may depend on the electoral fortunes of the party for whom they declared. As Kitschelt and Wilkinson (2007) explain, "By forcing members of a group to publicly pledge support to the incumbent party rather than the opposition, for example, group members are effectively then cut off from any expectation of rewards should the opposition win" (15). In addition, politicians can obtain increased advertising exposure in a community by inducing citizens to declare support. But persuasive benefits may be limited if clientelist reasons for declaring support are common knowledge. Overall, the supply-driven logic of declared support suggests that parties may induce citizens to place ads on their homes using clientelist benefits before or after the election.

In order to investigate declared support, below we examine whether citizens with political advertisements on their homes are more likely to receive gifts during the campaign. We find a robust relationship between declared support and clientelism, but at the outset we emphasize that we cannot adjudicate whether this pattern reflects the demand-driven or the supply-driven logic described above, or whether it reflects a combination of these two explanations. Nevertheless, we offer robust quantitative evidence of the link between declared support and clientelism, which is a substantial contribution to the literature on machine politics in Mexico. Before presenting such evidence, we first explain why print advertising surged during the 2012 campaign, and show how often citizens declared support by placing such ads on their homes.

The surge in printed advertisements observed during the 2012 campaign was in large part an unintended consequence of a reform in campaign funding regulations. Political parties and campaigns in Mexico are publicly funded, and candidates are not legally allowed to supplement public funds with outside resources. Candidates do not all receive the same amount; a formula that takes into account the party's vote share in the previous election determines the funding for each party. Mexico's electoral governance body, IFE, reformed advertising rules after the 2006 election such that it would contract and pay for television and radio spots (see the broader discussion by Eric Magar, chap. 3, this volume). This reform intended to create a more equal playing field for campaign advertisements; many observers complained that when parties directly procured ads under the previous arrangement, certain television channels had given favorable treatment to candidates by charging less money for airtime or by providing exclusive access to advertising during periods of high-volume viewership. Although IFE's centralization of television and radio ads left parties in control of smaller campaign budgets—public campaign funds declined by one-third from 2.5 billion pesos in 2006 to 1.7 billion pesos in 2012—the reform freed remaining campaign funds for alternative activities. Thus the unintended consequence of the reform was that it left more funds available for old-fashioned types of campaigning such as rallies, canvassing, and, most notably, printed advertisements.

In response to IFE's electoral reform, political parties devoted far greater funds to printed advertisements. As the campaign director for Aristóteles Sandoval, the PRI's victorious nominee for governor of Jalisco, explains, "To the extent that there have been attempts to regulate, to establish campaign spending limits and to have an authority watching that they control expenditures, together with the fact that campaigns can no longer directly contract the mass media as they did in the past . . . without a doubt campaign strategies have changed. Candidates have to look for alternative outlets, and that explains why signs and stickers have become crucial tools for all of the candidates."[12] Independent analysis confirms what was obvious to any Mexican commuting to work or school: the 2012 election involved a tremendous amount of printed political advertising, including banners, bumper stickers, and signs on homes and businesses. An association of plastic producers reported that 30% more plastic was used in campaign advertisements than in 2006.[13] *Reforma*, a national newspaper, tallied the number of printed advertisements on main thoroughfares and public spaces in Mexico's three largest metropolitan areas (Guadalajara, Mexico City, and Monterrey) about three months prior to the election. It found 3,625 advertisements, 60% of which were for Peña Nieto.[14] The newspaper calculated that maintaining the same level of advertisements in the observed areas of these three cities alone throughout the campaign would cost Peña Nieto 95 million pesos, or roughly 28% of his limit for all spending during the three-month campaign.

Amidst this bewildering array of political propaganda visible across the public sphere during the 2012 campaign, many citizens placed such materials on their homes. Survey enumerators in the Mexico 2012 Panel Study were instructed to observe the outside of each respondent's residence and to report if it displayed an advertisement for any political party or organization. As shown in table 9.1, 16.7% of respondents had an advertisement visible on their home at the time that either of the waves of the survey was administered. Over the course of the campaign, the most frequent type of political advertisement observed on homes was for the PRI (8.2% of surveyed households), followed by the PAN (3.3%) and the PRD (2.8%). Declared support increased over time: 5.9% of respondents had political advertisements on their homes at the time of the Wave 1 interview, while 9.6% had advertisements during the Wave 2 interview.

Although many Mexico 2012 Panel Study respondents placed advertisements on their homes, the prevalence of this behavior was by no means uniform across the country. Much to the contrary, substantial geographic concentration of declarations is observed. Recall that the survey included over 1,300 respondents from sixty-five localities across the country. In a significant number of these localities, not a single respondent placed an advertisement on his home: 58% of localities in Wave 1, and 43% in Wave 2. In fact, over one-quarter of localities had no survey respondents declaring in either wave. Yet while some localities had little in the way of political advertisements, others had many. In a quarter of localities visited, for example, at least 25% of respondents declared during one of our survey waves. And, remarkably, in two localities surveyed in southern Mexico—Villa Corzo, Chiapas, and Dzemul, Yucatán—at least 90% of respondents had a political advertisement on their homes during the campaign.

The reader might wonder whether this marked heterogeneity of declarations across Mexico is just an artifact of the particular houses randomly chosen to participate in the panel study. Evidence points away from this possibility. To obtain a broader perspective, enumerators were also asked to stand with their backs to the doors of respondents' homes and to observe whether any political advertising was visible in the immediate surrounding neighborhood. In a quarter of localities, our enumerators observed that less than 10% of respondents had any political advertisements in the vicinity. At the other extreme, in over a quarter of localities, our enumerators reported that over 60% of respondents had such advertising visible in the surrounding neighborhood.

All in all, evidence suggests that while political advertisements on homes are relatively commonplace in some localities, in other areas such activity is rare or nonexistent.

What types of citizens were most likely to publicly declare support for a candidate during the campaign? And what geographical characteristics are associated with greater concentrations of declared support? Logistic regressions in table 9.3 examine these questions. First, we consider individual-level factors. One might expect that partisans would be more likely to place political propaganda on their homes. This expected relationship is indeed observed, and is most robust for PRI supporters. Strong PRI supporters are significantly more likely to declare across all specifications in table 9.3 (at the 1% level). In fact, holding other included covariates at their average values, a strong PRI supporter is fifteen to seventeen percentage points more likely to have a political advertisement on his home than a nonpartisan. The magnitude of this association is particularly striking given that the baseline probability that a citizen declares is just 17%. Weak PRI supporters also have a significantly greater probability of declaring, though the relationship is relatively less robust than observed for strong PRI partisans. Across most specifications, weak PRI supporters are ten to eleven percentage points more likely to declare than nonpartisans (at the 5% level of significance). However, column (2) shows that this association is not statistically significant when including municipal fixed effects. This lack of statistical significance can be partially explained by the fact that including municipal fixed effects drops a quarter of observations (those in municipalities with no declared support). Looking beyond the PRI, specifications in table 9.3 also suggest that strong PRD supporters are ten to fifteen percentage points more likely to declare support than nonpartisans, ceteris paribus. Depending on the specification, this association is significant at the 5–10% level. But weak PRD supporters—as well as strong or weak PAN supporters—are not significantly more or less likely to place political advertisements on their homes. Moreover, across all specifications, individual-level socioeconomic factors (such as poverty, gender, age, and education) are not significantly associated with higher or lower levels of declared support.

Declared support is associated not just with respondents' political preferences, but also with the political characteristics of places where respondents reside. In table 9.3, column (3) includes municipal characteristics, whereas column (4) includes both municipal and state characteristics. Individuals who live in municipalities where the PRI is relatively more powerful are more likely to

Table 9.3. Correlates of declared support

	(1)	(2)	(3)	(4)
Strong PAN supporter	0.101	0.050	0.043	0.072
	(0.08)	(0.07)	(0.06)	(0.05)
Weak PAN supporter	0.029	−0.012	0.013	0.023
	(0.05)	(0.05)	(0.04)	(0.05)
Strong PRI supporter	0.170**	0.147**	0.149**	0.153**
	(0.04)	(0.05)	(0.04)	(0.04)
Weak PRI supporter	0.112*	0.083	0.097*	0.110**
	(0.04)	(0.05)	(0.04)	(0.04)
Strong PRD supporter	0.096+	0.146+	0.140*	0.100+
	(0.06)	(0.08)	(0.06)	(0.05)
Weak PRD supporter	0.048	0.048	0.082	0.051
	(0.05)	(0.07)	(0.06)	(0.05)
Likely voter	0.019	0.046	0.027	0.031
	(0.03)	(0.04)	(0.03)	(0.03)
Income	0.017	0.002	0.010	0.017
	(0.02)	(0.02)	(0.02)	(0.02)
Education	0.006	0.003	−0.001	0.004
	(0.01)	(0.01)	(0.01)	(0.01)
Housing	0.029	−0.004	0.025	0.021
	(0.02)	(0.03)	(0.02)	(0.02)
Age	−0.000	−0.001	−0.001	−0.000
	(0.00)	(0.00)	(0.00)	(0.00)
Female	0.012	0.007	−0.001	0.012
	(0.03)	(0.03)	(0.02)	(0.02)
PRI mayor share			0.423*	0.346**
			(0.21)	(0.13)
Mayor vote margin			0.569**	−0.122
			(0.20)	(0.13)
Log municipal GDP			0.042	0.036
			(0.05)	(0.05)
Log municipal population			−0.083	−0.069
			(0.06)	(0.07)
PRI governor share				−0.009
				(0.21)
Governor vote margin				−0.451*
				(0.19)
Log state GDP				0.052
				(0.04)
Log state population				−0.014
				(0.04)
Fixed effects	no	municipal	state	no
Pseudo-R^2	0.042	0.172	0.162	0.097
Observations	926	715	851	926

Note: Binary dependent variables are coded 1 if the enumerator observed a political advertisement on a respondent's home during Wave 1 or 2; they are coded 0 otherwise. Coefficients are marginal effects; robust standard errors are clustered at district level. Constants are included but not shown. See the text for descriptions of independent variables.

+$p < 0.10$, *$p < 0.05$, **$p < 0.01$.

declare support; see columns (3) and (4). In particular, for each additional ten percentage points of vote share that the PRI received in the previous mayoral election, an individual is 3.5 to 4.2 percentage points more likely to declare support. This association is significant at the 1–5% level, depending on the specification employed. Column (3) in table 9.3 shows that the degree of political competitiveness in a municipality is also associated with declared support. But this relationship is only significant when explaining variation in declared support within a given state; across Mexico, individuals in highly competitive municipalities are no more or less likely to declare support; see column (4). In addition, controlling for other included covariates, individuals in smaller or poorer municipalities do not have a higher or lower probability of placing political advertisements on their homes. Turning to state-level characteristics, as shown in column (4), we observe that respondents in states where the PRI is relatively more powerful (as measured by PRI governor vote share) are no more or less likely to declare support. By contrast, individuals who live in states with greater political competition (i.e., smaller governor vote margins) have a significantly greater probability of declaring support (at the 5% level). Just as with the municipal regressions, respondents residing in less populous or poorer states are not more or less likely to place political advertisements on their homes. Overall, specifications in table 9.3 point to important political characteristics at the individual, municipal, and state level that are associated with declared support. Future work will employ hierarchical linear modeling to explore such relationships further.

Declared Support and Clientelism

Thus far, we have observed that partisans—especially supporters of the PRI—are disproportionately likely to place political advertisements on their homes. Given that declared support has been linked to clientelism in other contexts such as Brazil, a crucial question that emerges is whether respondents with political signs, posters, or paintings on their homes are more likely to receive handouts during campaigns.

In order to investigate this relationship, we first examine how experiences with clientelism differ between citizens with political advertisements on their homes (declarers) versus citizens without such advertisements (nondeclarers). While such analysis does not control for other important factors, it provides important motivation for later analyses employing both logistic and item count regressions. Declarers are substantially more likely to receive rewards than nondeclarers, using both the direct vote-buying question and the list experiment. For the direct question, 9.4% of declarers received offers of gifts, versus only 5.2% of nondeclarers. This difference is statistically significant at the 10% level, and nearly at the 5% level ($p=0.057$). Results are even more striking when using the list experiment, which provides an unobtrusive measure of whether respondents actually received gifts. Among respondents with political advertisements on their homes during Wave 1, nearly 57% reported receiving gifts during the campaign when asked in Wave 2. By contrast, only 16% of nondeclarers reported receiving gifts. This difference is statistically significant at the 5% level. In short, descriptive evidence suggests that Mexicans who placed political advertisements on their homes experienced clientelism significantly more than those who did not.

While such evidence suggests that declarers are far more likely to experience clientelism, it does not control for important factors that could potentially affect results. Declarers would likely be highly partisan, for example, and analyses in table 9.2 suggested that some partisans might be more likely to receive rewards. In order to address such concerns, table 9.4 presents logistic regressions examining the relationship between declared support and reporting a vote-buying offer during the second wave of the Mexico 2012 Panel Survey. Column (1) suggests that respondents with political advertisements on their homes during either wave are four percentage points more likely to report gift offers than those without such ads (significant at the 5% level). This specification includes individual-level political and socioeconomic controls, none of which are statistically significant. Column (2) introduces municipal fixed effects, a step that controls for any omitted variables that do not vary across individuals in a given municipality. In this specification, the association between declarations and clientelism more than doubles in magnitude—citizens who declare support are 8.3 percentage points more likely to report gift offers than citizens who do not declare support (significant at the 5% level). As discussed above, one explanation for this difference is that including municipal fixed effects drops nearly half of the observations because many municipalities have no variation on the dependent variable. The next specification in column (3) introduces several municipal variables, as well as state fixed effects. Declared support remains a significant correlate of clientelism: placing a political advertisement on one's home is associated with a 5.2-percentage-point increase in gift offers (significant at the 5% level). Although we showed above that municipal political characteristics are significantly associated with declared support, factors such

 Correlates of clientelism with declared support

	Direct question				List experiment
	(1)	(2)	(3)	(4)	(5)
Declared support	0.040*	0.083*	0.052*	0.044*	0.358+
	(0.02)	(0.04)	(0.03)	(0.02)	(0.19)
Strong PAN supporter	0.021	−0.021	0.000	0.022	0.141
	(0.02)	(0.06)	(0.04)	(0.02)	(0.25)
Weak PAN supporter	0.009	−0.028	0.003	0.009	0.319
	(0.02)	(0.05)	(0.03)	(0.02)	(0.20)
Strong PRI supporter	−0.013	−0.066	−0.036	−0.016	0.108
	(0.03)	(0.05)	(0.04)	(0.03)	(0.19)
Weak PRI supporter	−0.050	−0.135*	−0.063+	−0.052	0.432*
	(0.04)	(0.06)	(0.04)	(0.03)	(0.20)
Strong PRD supporter	−0.004	−0.028	−0.009	−0.000	0.046
	(0.04)	(0.06)	(0.04)	(0.04)	(0.27)
Weak PRD supporter	0.036	0.034	0.049+	0.040+	−0.021
	(0.02)	(0.04)	(0.03)	(0.02)	(0.22)
Likely voter	−0.008	−0.016	−0.008	−0.007	−0.055
	(0.02)	(0.03)	(0.02)	(0.02)	(0.14)
Income	0.006	0.008	0.007	0.006	0.137
	(0.01)	(0.02)	(0.01)	(0.01)	(0.09)
Education	0.005	0.020*	0.010+	0.006	−0.008
	(0.00)	(0.01)	(0.01)	(0.00)	(0.03)
Housing	0.000	0.016	0.012	0.004	−0.089
	(0.01)	(0.02)	(0.02)	(0.01)	(0.08)
Age	0.000	0.000	−0.000	−0.000	−0.004
	(0.00)	(0.00)	(0.00)	(0.00)	(0.00)
Female	0.023	0.043	0.021	0.023	0.041
	(0.01)	(0.03)	(0.02)	(0.01)	(0.13)
PRI mayor share			0.089	0.036	
			(0.17)	(0.07)	
Mayor vote margin			0.133	−0.056	
			(0.11)	(0.06)	
Log municipal GDP			0.035	0.015	
			(0.05)	(0.03)	
Log municipal population			−0.036	−0.013	
			(0.06)	(0.03)	
PRI governor share				0.002	
				(0.09)	
Governor vote margin				−0.006	
				(0.08)	
Log state GDP				−0.046*	
				(0.02)	
Log state population				0.059*	
				(0.02)	
Fixed effects	no	municipal	state	no	no
Pseudo-R^2	0.043	0.154	0.141	0.063	
Observations	900	490	710	900	879

Note: Binary dependent variables are coded 1 if the respondent reported an offer of a gift from any source in Wave 2; they are coded 0 otherwise. Columns (1)–(4) are logit regressions: coefficients are marginal effects; robust standard errors are clustered at district level. Estimates in column (5) are derived using the item count technique regression function of Blair and Imai's (2012) List package in R. Constants are included but not shown. See the text for descriptions of independent variables.

+$p < 0.10$, *$p < 0.05$, **$p < 0.01$.

as PRI vote share and vote margin in municipal elections are not statistically linked to clientelism. With the inclusion of state political variables in column (4), declared support is significantly associated with a 4.4-percentage-point increase in gift offers (at the 5% level). While neither PRI vote share nor political competition is significant at the state level, results suggest that individuals in poorer and larger states tend to have a greater probability of experiencing gift offers (both at the 5% level). Across specifications in table 9.4, other socioeconomic and political correlates shown do not have robust significant associations with gift offers.

In column (5) of table 9.4, we also examine the relationship between declared support and clientelism using the list experiment. More specifically, we rerun the earlier specification in column (5) of table 9.2 employing Blair and Imai's (2012) method and now include a variable for declared support. Results suggest that respondents with political advertisements on their homes are 35.8 percentage points more likely to receive benefits in exchange for their votes than those without such ads (significant at the 10% level, with a p value of 0.065). Given that the share of respondents receiving gifts is just 22.1% in the overall sample with the list experiment, this effect is striking in magnitude. Parallel to findings in table 9.2, weak PRI supporters are significantly more likely to receive gifts when asked indirectly through the list experiment (at the 5% level). Most important, analyses using both the direct question and the list experiment in table 9.4 suggest that respondents who placed political advertisements on their homes disproportionately experienced clientelism.

These analyses provide considerable evidence of a significant association between declared support and clientelism. As usual with observational studies, selection bias remains an important concern. In order to test the robustness of this relationship, we also conducted matching using a genetic search algorithm (Sekhon 2011). Similar to propensity score matching and other related methods, genetic matching pairs treatment units (in this case declarers) with control units (nondeclarers) that are similar on a set of observable characteristics. As with other forms of matching, the procedure seeks to improve inference in the absence of a true counterfactual by constructing an artificial comparison group. Genetic matching suggests that the difference in gift offers between declarers and matched nondeclarers is significant at the 5% level (not shown). This robustness test of genetic matching is additional evidence of a link between declared support and clientelism, though it should be emphasized that the technique still does not provide a rigorous test of causality.

Conclusion

During the 2012 campaign, allegations of clientelism proliferated across Mexico. Although it is unlikely that Peña Nieto's victory hinged on the provision of contingent benefits—despite such claims by the opposition—both qualitative and quantitative evidence suggest that this electoral tactic remained in the playbooks of many political operatives. The Mexico 2012 Panel Study reveals that 7.7% of citizens reported receiving clientelist offers at some point during the campaign. The prevalence of handouts is far higher, over 22% in the postelection wave, when using an unobtrusive list experiment instead of a direct question prone to social desirability bias. Although citizens report all major parties as buying votes, the PRI continues to be identified as the most frequent transgressor, in line with Díaz-Cayeros et al.'s (2009) finding during the 2006 campaign that the "PRI was more prone to resort to these clientelist practices than its rivals" (241). Analyses in this chapter provide important insights about the types of citizens who experienced clientelism. While some findings point to targeting based on political and socioeconomic criteria, they do not unambiguously suggest a uniform pattern.

Allegations of clientelism during the 2012 campaign raise an important question regarding democratic processes in Mexico. Are electoral officials paying sufficient attention to clientelism? On the heels of the election, Leonardo Valdés, the president of IFE's General Council, proclaimed that "this election is the fairest in [Mexico's] democratic lifetime, and the cleanest and most impartial that we have organized. In this election, we advanced in the consolidation of a democracy that is more transparent and also more equal." To be sure, IFE has made remarkable progress in fighting fraud in recent years and has greatly improved the mechanics of recording and counting votes. But the 2012 election revealed a troubling shortcoming in Mexico's electoral institutions: a high degree of ambiguity regarding electoral authorities' responsibility to even investigate claims of clientelism. Following the election, the onus fell on the aggrieved candidate, López Obrador, to provide conclusive evidence of the PRI's alleged vote buying and to show it was widespread enough to justify annulment. Many of López Obrador's supporters contend that the IFE itself should have assumed the responsibility to collect such evidence and to take corresponding legal action. In some countries such as Brazil, electoral authorities take a relatively more proactive role in investigating and ousting candidates who buy votes. The extent to which the IFE should similarly take a more aggressive stance against clientelism is a pressing question for Mexico, as the decision has fundamental consequences for democracy.

Our findings also shed light on an important relationship rarely considered in the literature on machine politics: the link between publicly declaring one's support and clientelist rewards. The 2012 campaign witnessed a surge in printed advertisements, in large part owing to newly introduced electoral regulations. As political campaigns increasingly relied on print advertising, many citizens placed banners and posters on their own homes. We present robust quantitative evidence of the link between declared support and clientelism. Statistical findings suggest that citizens who publicly declare support with political posters on their homes are significantly more likely to receive offers of electoral rewards. Our future work will continue to investigate the link between declared support and clientelist handouts in Mexico, building on additional quantitative specifications as well as interviews with politicians. A key question is whether declared support in Mexico tends to be demand driven (citizens placing ads to attract benefits) or supply driven (politicians requiring recipients to place ads). Ethnographic research on the distribution and use of printed materials can address related questions, such as: How many voters declare out of allegiance to a party on programmatic grounds versus the prospect of obtaining clientelist rewards? Do clientelist brokers demand that reward recipients declare support, and if so, what mechanisms do operatives use to enforce such agreements? Understanding the answers to such questions is important in part because demand- and supply-driven patterns of declared support may have different implications for the quality of democratic representation in Mexico.

More broadly, the evidence presented in this chapter suggests that machine politics is alive and well in Mexico. One important direction for scholarly research is understanding more deeply the strategies of clientelism employed not just by the PRI—which frequently bought votes during its dominance of Mexican politics during the twentieth century—but also by opposition parties. Another key question to investigate: Do recent PRI victories signal the rebirth of its twentieth-century machine, or rather the innovation of clientelist tactics in a multiparty environment, perhaps with an increased reliance on declared support?

NOTES

1. The Mexico 2012 Panel Study was a nationally representative, face-to-face survey consisting of two waves in sixty-five localities. The first wave had 1,328 participants (in late April and early May), and 952 of these individuals participated in the second wave (in July after the election).

2. Alianza Cívica, *Boletín de Prensa*, Mexico City, July 3, 2012. This survey was carried out by Alianza Cívica's 500 election observers, who conducted the survey with 3,158 voters at polling locations in twenty-one states.

3. Figures are based on Wave 2 data for citizens who entirely or somewhat agreed with corresponding statements about these phenomena. For Wave 1 data regarding these two questions, see De La O, chapter 8, this volume.

4. These figures are based on respondents who participated in both waves of the survey and whose treatment assignment passed consistency checks.

5. Clemente Castañeda, interview with Brian Palmer-Rubin, February 22, 2013.

6. In early 2014, MORENA formally applied to IFE for registration as a political party.

7. José David Estrada, "Reparte el PRI tarjetas 'compravotos', acusan," *Reforma*, June 29, 2012; Leslie Gómez y Claudia Salazar, "Acumula IFE quejas por compra de votos," *Reforma*, July 11, 2012; Rosalía Vergara, "Enviará AMLO al TEPJF decálogo para invalidar la elección," *Proceso*, August 7, 2012; Jenaro Villamil, "El 'Sorianagate', fraude al voto," *Proceso*, July 3, 2012.

8. "Niega cadena uso de tarjetas para depósitos," *Reforma*, July 4, 2012; Armando Guzmán, "El PRI pagó con tarjetas de Monex a sus operadores políticos en Tabasco," *Proceso*, July 18, 2012; Josefina Quintero, "Compras de pánico en Soriana ante el temor de que el PRI cancelara tarjetas," *La Jornada*, July 3, 2012.

9. See "Monreal entrega pruebas de presunto desvío de recursos de Edomex a EPN," *Proceso*, August 12, 2012; "Las tarjetas de Monex y Soriana no comprueban nada: IFE," *Proceso*, July 19, 2012; "Desestima TEPJF invalidez de elección," *Reforma*, August 30, 2012; Jesusa Cervantes y José Gil Olmos, "Compra masiva de votos, una operación transatlantica," *Proceso*, July 28, 2012; Érika Hernández, "Acusan que PRI gastó 1,817 mdp," *Reforma*, July 9, 2012.

10. "#YoSoy132 presenta al TEPJF segundo informe de irregularidades electorales," *Noticias MVS*, August 2, 2012; Antonio Baranda, "Exhiben 'fraude' hasta con borrego," *Reforma*, August 13, 2012; Rosalía Vergara, "Lo hacen otra vez: Miles contra EPN, el IFE, la compra de votos y Televisa," *Proceso*, July 22, 2012; Rosalía Vergara, "Exhiben en el Zócalo evidencias del supuesto fraude," *Proceso*, August 12, 2012.

11. An important distinction should be made between "electoral" clientelism that delivers all benefits during electoral campaigns, and "relational" clientelism that provides ongoing benefits (Nichter 2010). A broader literature on distributive politics examines parties' distribution of targetable goods (such as infrastructure projects). Two major formal studies provide contrasting predictions: Cox and McCubbins (1986) contend that parties distribute targetable goods to core supporters, while Lindbeck and Weibull (1987) find that they target swing voters.

12. Ricardo Villanueva, interview with Brian Palmer-Rubin, January 8, 2013.

13. "Más de 2 mil toneladas de propaganda electoral invadirán a México," *Vanguardia*, March 6, 2012.

14. "La pelea por la calle," *Reforma*, April 24, 2012. See interactive map at: http://www.reforma.com/libre/offlines/cazaEspectacular/. The count included thirty-eight streets in Monterrey, fifteen streets in Guadalajara, and 2,500 public spaces in Mexico City.

REFERENCES

Auyero, Javier. 2000. *Poor People's Politics: Peronist Survival Networks and the Legacy of Evita.* Durham, NC: Duke University Press.

Blair, Graeme, and Kosuke Imai. 2012. "Statistical Analysis of List Experiments." *Political Analysis* 20, no. 1: 47–77.

Cornelius, Wayne. 2004. "Mobilized Voting in the 2000 Elections: The Changing Efficacy of Vote Buying and Coercion in Mexican Electoral Politics." In *Mexico's Pivotal Democratic Elections: Candidates, Voters, and the Presidential Campaign of 2000,* ed. Jorge I. Domínguez and Chappell Lawson, 47–65. Stanford, CA: Stanford University Press.

Corstange, Daniel. 2010. "Vote Buying under Competition and Monopsony: Evidence from a List Experiment in Lebanon." Paper presented at the annual meeting of the American Political Science Association, Washington, DC.

Cox, Gary W. 2009. "Swing Voters, Core Voters and Distributive Politics." In *Political Representation,* ed. Ian Shapiro, Susan Stokes, Elisabeth Wood, and Alexander Kirshner, 342–57. New York: Cambridge University Press.

Cox, Gary W., and Mathew D. McCubbins. 1986. "Electoral Politics as a Redistributive Game." *Journal of Politics* 48, no. 2: 370–89.

Díaz-Cayeros, Alberto, Federico Estévez, and Beatriz Magaloni. 2009. "Welfare Benefits, Canvassing and Campaign Handouts." In *Consolidating Mexico's Democracy,* ed. Jorge I. Domínguez, Chappell Lawson, and Alejandro Moreno, 229–45. Baltimore: Johns Hopkins University Press.

Dixit, Avinash, and John Londregan. 1996. "The Determinants of Success of Special Interests in Redistributive Politics." *Journal of Politics* 58, no. 4: 1132–55.

Gans-Morse, Jordan, Sebastian Mazzuca, and Simeon Nichter. 2014. "Varieties of Clientelism: Machine Politics during Elections." *American Journal of Political Science* 58, no. 2: 415–32.

Gonzalez-Ocantos, Ezequiel, Chad Kiewiet de Jonge, Carlos Meléndez, Javier Osorio, and David W. Nickerson. 2012. "Vote Buying and Social Desirability Bias: Experimental Evidence from Nicaragua." *American Journal of Political Science* 56, no. 1: 202–17.

Greene, Kenneth. 2007. *Why Dominant Parties Lose: Mexico's Democratization in Comparative Perspective.* Cambridge: Cambridge University Press.

———. 2012. "Se compró la elección presidencial?" Paper presented at the Seminario Proceso Electoral 2012, TEPJF, Mexico City.

Hilgers, Tina. 2008. "Causes and Consequences of Political Clientelism: Mexico's PRD in Comparative Perspective." *Latin American Politics and Society* 50, no. 4: 123–53.

Kitschelt, Herbert, and Steven Wilkinson. 2007. *Patrons, Clients, and Policies: Patterns of Democratic Accountability and Political Competition.* Cambridge: Cambridge University Press.

Lawson, Chappell. 2009. "The Politics of Reciprocity: Trading Selective Benefits for Popular Support." Unpublished manuscript, Massachusetts Institute of Technology.

Lindbeck, Assar, and Jorgen W. Weibull. 1987. "Balanced-Budget Redistribution as the Outcome of Political Competition." *Public Choice* 52, no. 3: 273–97.

Magaloni, Beatriz. 2006. *Voting for Autocracy: Hegemonic Party Survival and Its Demise in Mexico.* Cambridge: Cambridge University Press.

Magaloni, Beatriz, Alberto Díaz-Cayeros, and Federico Estévez. 2007. "Clientelism and Portfolio Diversification: A Model of Electoral Investment with Applications to Mexico." In *Patrons, Clients, and Policies: Patterns of Democratic Accountability and*

Political Competition, ed. Herbert Kitschelt and Steven Wilkinson, 182–205. Cambridge: Cambridge University Press.

Nichter, Simeon. 2008. "Vote Buying or Turnout Buying? Machine Politics and the Secret Ballot." *American Political Science Review* 102, no. 1: 19–31.

———. 2009. "Declared Choice: Citizen Strategies and Dual Commitment Problems in Clientelism." Paper presented at the annual meeting of the American Political Science Association, Toronto.

———. 2010. "Politics and Poverty: Electoral Clientelism in Latin America." PhD diss., Department of Political Science, University of California, Berkeley.

———. 2012. "Political Clientelism and Social Policy: The Case of Brazil." In *Political Clientelism, Social Policy, and the Quality of Democracy: Evidence from Latin America, Lessons from Other Regions,* ed. Diego Abente and Larry Diamond, 130–51. Baltimore: Johns Hopkins University Press.

Schaffer, Frederic C., and Andreas Schedler. 2007. "What Is Vote Buying?" In *Elections for Sale: The Causes and Consequences of Vote Buying,* ed. Frederic C. Schaffer, 17–30. Boulder, CO: Lynne Rienner.

Scott, James C. 1969. "Corruption, Machine Politics, and Political Change." *American Political Science Review* 63, no. 4: 1142–58.

Sekhon, Jasjeet S. 2011. "Multivariate and Propensity Score Matching Software with Automated Balance Optimization: The Matching package for R." *Journal of Statistical Software* 42, no. 7: 1–52.

Simpser, Alberto. 2012. "Could the PRI Have Bought Its Electoral Result in the 2012 Mexican Election? Probably Not." *The Monkey Cage* (blog), July 10. http://themonkeycage .org/2012/07/10/could-the-pri-have-bought-its-electoral-result-in-the-2012-mexican -election-probably-not/.

Stokes, Susan C. 2005. "Perverse Accountability: A Formal Model of Machine Politics with Evidence from Argentina." *American Political Science Review* 99, no. 3: 315–25.

Weitz-Shapiro, Rebecca. 2012. "What Wins Votes: Why Some Politicians Opt Out of Clientelism." *American Journal of Political Science* 56, no. 3: 568–83.

10

Effects of #YoSoy132 and Social Media in Mexico's 2012 Presidential Campaigns

ALEJANDRO DÍAZ-DOMÍNGUEZ AND ALEJANDRO MORENO

One unique feature of the 2012 Mexican presidential election process was the emergence of a politicized student movement. Known as #YoSoy132, it combined ideologically diverse students from private and public universities who united against biased media coverage of the election campaigns. The movement initially took a stance against the Institutional Revolutionary Party (PRI) and protested against its presidential candidate, Enrique Peña Nieto, but it had no clear leanings toward any of the other candidates. Nevertheless, the student movement gradually became more identified as supportive of the leftist candidate, Andrés Manuel López Obrador. The student movement ran a campaign of its own, relying heavily on Internet and social media, but also holding public meetings and organizing street protests that were attended mainly by young people. It organized a live, Internet-based presidential debate, attended by all presidential candidates except Peña Nieto (who declined to participate).

Our purpose in this chapter is to analyze the effects of #YoSoy132 in the 2012 presidential election. We rely on the Mexico 2012 Panel Study to analyze whether voters changed their political views over the course of the presidential campaign. As past panel studies in Mexico show, changes can be linked to campaign events (Flores-Macías 2009; Lawson 1999, 2004), as well as to campaign strategies and messages (Moreno 2004, 2009a). We focus on the dynamic effects that can be observed in the two-wave panel data, particularly on changes in candidate images and vote choices.

The student movement in 2012 can be analyzed from various perspectives, but our objective is not to document the movement's characteristics or to understand its motives and causes, but to assess its possible effects on voters. The student movement relied heavily on the Internet and social media, and it aimed at the mobilization of young voters. For these reasons we test the role of new information technologies in the campaigns, and we focus on voters under age 30 to assess whether they "behaved" differently than older voters. Because the role of the Internet and social media in politics and elections is of increasing theoretical and comparative interest (Coleman and Blumler 2009; Norris 2000; Semetko 2007), we include analysis of media use, considering both traditional (television, radio, print) and new media (Internet and social media). In this portion of the chapter, we aim to contribute to an emerging literature on the Internet and social media in campaigns and elections in Latin America (Iasulaitis 2013; Moreno and Mendizábal 2013; Telles, Santos Mundim, and Lopes 2013) as well as their impact on political participation in other regions of the world (Howard 2010; Vergeer, Hermans, Sams 2013). To model changes in attitudes toward #YoSoy132, we employ the technique used to analyze student protests in France in May 1968, which also relied on panel data.

First we offer a brief context of the 2012 presidential campaigns and the emergence of the student movement. We move on to an analysis of how opinions about #YoSoy132 influenced vote choices and candidate images. We then report how the #YoSoy132 feeling thermometer stands out as one of the main predictor of changes in candidate image during the campaigns. We also explain feelings toward the student movement and the role that social media plays; we comment on the effects of both factors in explaining perceptions of biased media coverage during the campaigns, one of the movement's central reasons for protest. Finally, we offer a brief analysis of media use in the 2012 election that can be put in comparative perspective. Our main argument is that the emergence of #YoSoy132 helped crystallize two political camps that are ideologically distinct and supportive of the PRI and the left—a conflict dimension that shares some features of the old PRI/anti-PRI in Mexico but is also distinctive. We conclude that the student movement exerted significant campaign effects that form an important part of the story behind the 2012 campaign.

The Emergence of #YoSoy132

On May 11, 2012, a group of students protested during the PRI presidential candidate's visit to Ibero-American University, a private college in western Mexico City known for many things but not for political activism. Banners scattered among the crowd ranged from relatively soft messages of rejection— "Get out, get out" and "Peña Nieto: Ibero does not like you"—to tougher messages and accusations directed at the PRI candidate—"I hate you," "Murderer,"

"No more feminicide." The situation was tense. The students' shouting competed with cheering from Peña Nieto supporters in campus. The candidate had to cancel an interview with Radio Ibero and left the university while being chased by several people. The press dubbed this event "Black Friday" for Enrique Peña Nieto's campaign, and the event soon became a trending topic on social media. At the time, no one knew that the protest of anti–Peña Nieto students at Ibero would be only the beginning of massive student mobilization from both private and public universities against the PRI candidate and against the major television networks, which, as the students claimed, were overtly and unfairly supportive of Peña Nieto.

The PRI's response was to dismiss the importance of the event while attempting to discredit its participants. PRI leaders claimed that protesters consisted of 131 agitators who were not students. In response, Ibero students used social media to demonstrate that they were legitimately registered at the university, and students from other private and public universities joined the protests in solidarity, expressing themselves through social media. The #YoSoy132 hashtag recognized the original group of Ibero students and invited participation in a growing movement in which every new protester, generally a young university student, was participant number 132.

The emergence of anti-PRI protests and manifestations in social media shook the notion that the PRI's return to the presidency was inevitable, or at least uncontested. Most polls showed Peña Nieto with a double-digit advantage over the other candidates. Political commentaries in the traditional media had created a climate of opinion where no significant opposition to Peña Nieto was felt.

At the time the protests began, the governing National Action Party (PAN), whose candidate ranked second in the polls during the early campaign period, well behind Peña Nieto, faced internal divisions. Many voters were dissatisfied with the economic situation and had major concerns about public safety and the war on drugs. Although President Calderón enjoyed broad public support (a 66% approval rating in March 2012, prior to the beginning of the campaigns, according to *Reforma*), his popularity did not translate into enough support for his party to challenge Peña Nieto. The PAN candidate, Josefina Vázquez Mota, ran a campaign emphasizing her "difference" (as a woman and as political leader) that could be interpreted if not as an overt rejection of Calderón's government at least as a sign that she took some distance from it. López Obrador, meanwhile, began his campaign in third place in the polls, suffering from public reactions to his decision to contest the outcome of the 2006 elections and overt dismissal of the country's institutions. Political commentators took for granted that Peña Nieto faced no real challenge and would win the election handily.

Events in May combined to change that narrative. Peña Nieto would face a real challenge after all. A first televised debate in May would possibly contribute to raise López Obrador as a serious contender. But the first weeks of May also witnessed the emergence of #YoSoy132, the anti–Peña Nieto student movement that took to the streets and dominated the political space of new information technologies, particularly social media. Opinion polls published that month showed a slight decrease in support for Peña Nieto, a substantial decrease for Vázquez Mota, and a solid increase for López Obrador. Peña Nieto's advantage was significantly reduced. *Reforma* national polls showed a twenty-three-point difference between Peña Nieto and López Obrador in March (with the latter in third place), a fifteen-point difference an April, and only a four-point difference in late May, with López Obrador in second place. Other polls showed a wider gap between Peña Nieto and López Obrador but similar trends.

Much of this change was due to independent voters, who significantly switched preferences in favor of López Obrador in May. As shown in table 10.1, Peña Nieto lost twenty points among independents from November 2011 to May 2012, as his support among this group decreased from 46% to 26% (eight points from April to May). In contrast, support for López Obrador grew fifteen points in the same period, increasing from 28% to 43% (twelve points from April to May). Independents are an important segment that ranges from 35%

Table 10.1.   Voting preferences among independent voters (in percentages)

	November 27, 2011	March 28, 2012	April 25, 2012	May 31, 2012	June 19, 2012	June 27, 2012
Andrés M. López Obrador	28	26	31	43	41	37
Enrique Peña Nieto	46	42	34	26	26	28
Josefina Vázquez Mota	25	29	29	21	23	25
Gabriel Quadri	1	3	6	10	10	10
Difference (Peña Nieto minus López Obrador)	18	16	3	−17	−15	−9

Source: Reforma national polls ($n = 1{,}515$ each month)

to 45% of the whole electorate, and they represent about a third of the vote on Election Day according to exit polls. Independents are expected to have more volatile political preferences than partisan voters during election campaigns, and campaigns effects may be more clearly observed among them. Besides a significant shift in preferences for López Obrador among independents until May, the data shown in table 10.1 also suggest a smaller shift away from him in June (a point to which we return below).

The first televised debate in May might have helped boost López Obrador's standing as a serious contender. But the emergence of #YoSoy132 was undoubtedly an important factor. The student movement launched protests and contributed to the flow of political information every day, remaining a trending topic on social media almost by the minute. We find that the student movement exerted a significant influence on voters in 2012, not only by connecting opinions about the movement to vote choices but also by driving opinion change about the main presidential candidates. The effects of #YoSoy132 were most likely two sided. By taking an anti–Peña Nieto stand, the student movement may have gained votes for the leftist candidate at first, but its continued activities may have also activated an anti-leftist attitude that favored Peña Nieto. These polarizing effects are observable in the panel study and they show that, once again, campaign events matter in Mexican presidential elections. But unlike the previous presidential campaigns of 2000 and 2006, this time new information technologies, particularly social media, were the driver.

Voting Preferences

Data from the panel study show a strong relationship between opinions about the student movement and support for the two leading presidential candidates. Support for López Obrador increased as opinions about the student movement became more favorable. In contrast, support for Peña Nieto was higher among voters who had more negative opinions about the movement. The data show no relationship between opinions of the movement (on an eleven-point "feeling thermometer") and support for the PAN candidate, Josefina Vázquez Mota, which leads to the conclusion that views about the student movement were linked to opinions of the PRI and the leftist candidates only. There is a strong and positive Pearson correlation between the student movement opinion thermometer and López Obrador's (0.52), and a more modest but still statistically significant negative correlation between the former and Peña Nieto's opinion thermometer (−0.20). #YoSoy132 was a conflict dimension that divided voters' views about the two candidates who ended up finishing at the top of the polls, Peña Nieto and López Obrador.

Besides being differentiated by views about the student movement, preferences for the PRI and the leftist candidates also reflect a strong left-right ideological divide. Correlations between candidate feeling thermometers and the left-right self-placement scale are in all cases statistically significant in the expected directions: there is a positive correlation between ideological orientations and opinions about Peña Nieto and Vázquez Mota (both candidates being more popular among center-right and rightwing voters), and a negative correlation with opinions about López Obrador, a more popular candidate among center-left and leftwing voters. Leftwing voters were also more supportive of the movement; rightwing voters were more hostile. These correlations suggest the presence of two contrasting political camps: a leftist, pro-student, pro–López Obrador side, and a rightwing, antimovement, pro–Peña Nieto side. The fact that opinions about the student movement do not correlate with views about the PAN's candidate suggests that Vázquez Mota was not part of this conflict dimension.

Analysis of the panel data indicates that opinions about the student movement had an impact on vote choice, even when controlling for other factors that normally influence voting behavior.[1] These factors include: sex, age,[2] education, and rural residence as structural factors; left-right self-placement, party identification, and religiosity (as measured by self-reported church attendance) as long-term political predispositions; and presidential approval, retrospective economic evaluations, and opinions about the student movement as short-term campaign effects. (We leave candidate image out of the model for now, returning to it not as an explanatory factor of the vote choice per se but as a dynamic dependent variable through which the effects of the student movement can be observed.) Because we are also interested in the role of the Internet and social media, below we include indicators of news exposure through both traditional and new media: television, radio, newspapers, and Internet and social media such as Facebook and Twitter.

Figure 10.1 shows the results of multinomial logistic regression model, including all four presidential candidates, using the vote for López Obrador as reference category. (Results for Gabriel Quadri, who got less than 3% of the national vote, are not shown.) Among the structural factors group, only gender had a statistically significant independent influence on the vote: women were significantly more likely to vote for Peña Nieto and Vázquez Mota than

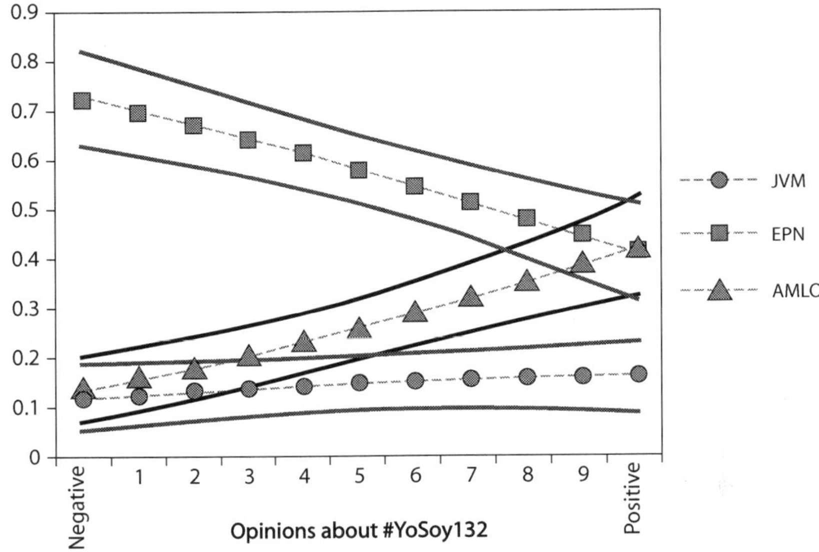

Figure 10.1. Vote choice for president: A multinomial logistic regression model. AMLO, López Obrador; EPN, Peña Nieto; JVM, Vázquez Mota.

for López Obrador. The gender effect on the vote is stronger in the case of the PAN candidate, which means that the only female candidate in the race really attracted more votes among women. Perhaps surprisingly, age (under 30), education, and rural residence are not significant.

The variables intended to measure political predisposition show results that are consistent with theoretical expectations. Ideology and party identification are important influences on the vote, in all cases showing a statistically significant relationship with candidate support in expected ways. The short-term factors show modest results. Presidential approval and retrospective economic evaluations were important factors in favor of the PAN vote, but their influence is clearly more modest than that of the long-term political predispositions.

The last variable shown in this analysis is the #YoSoy132 opinion thermometer (MOV132). The panel study shows that this is an important influence on the vote choice between Peña Nieto and López Obrador: opinions about the student movement are the third most important predictor of the choice between those two candidates, after party identification and ideology. #YoSoy132 was a salient feature of the 2012 campaign. Opinions about the movement helped to shape the vote choice between Peña Nieto and López Obrador.

Candidate Images

Here we analyze candidate images using a slightly modified explanatory model, retaining the structural variables, long-term political predispositions, and short-term factors in preparation for a more dynamic analysis. We include a category for the ideological center, a group of voters who may be most likely to change their minds about candidates, and replace the partisan groups with independent voters, who also more likely to change their political views or to be influenced by campaign information and events. We also add a measure of political interest (and retain religiosity). Among the short-term factors, we keep presidential approval and our main variable of interest (opinions about the student movement). Finally, we include measures of news exposure through television, radio, newspapers, Internet, and social media. We run this model of candidate image on the basis of the panel study's second (postelection) wave, which included the feeling thermometer for #YoSoy132.

The results of the analysis of candidate opinion thermometers are shown in table 10.2. This is a static analysis, as we focus only on Wave 2 of the panel survey. We will later change to a more dynamic analysis that considers opinion change from Wave 1 to Wave 2. These results confirm that gender was a significant factor behind political support, as men were more likely to think favorably about the leftist candidate than women. However, the analysis does not show any particular advantage of Vázquez Mota over Peña Nieto among women. As shown, age and education lacked any significant relationship with candidate images; so did political interest, which does not have any significant coefficients. The link between ideology and political support is confirmed in this analysis, as the coefficient for the leftwing ideological category is statistically significant in all cases. Ideological centrism had no significant effect on the candidates' feeling thermometers, but independents were (as expected) less likely to support the PRI candidate.

From a separate analysis that we conducted using Wave 1 of the panel study (not shown), we observed that the coefficient for independents was not statistically significant at that time, which led us to interpret this as a change that took place over the campaigns, when independent voters were mobilized against the PRI candidate, and in favor of the leftist candidate. This determination suggests that independent voters leaned toward the López Obrador camp and took an anti-PRI position during the campaigns, as shown above (table 10.1). Previous research has shown that independent voters are likely to have anti-PRI views,

Table 10.2.   Static analysis of opinion thermometers for the presidential candidates: A linear regression model using the panel survey's Wave 2

	Beta		
	López Obrador	Peña Nieto	Vázquez Mota
Female	−0.10**	−0.01	0.05
Age under 30	0.00	−0.03	0.07
Education	−0.04	0.00	−0.02
Political interest	−0.03	0.05	0.05
Left	0.22***	−0.26***	−0.08*
Center	0.01	0.01	0.00
Independent	0.04	−0.14***	0.02
Church attendance	0.00	0.03	−0.01
Presidential approval	−0.03	0.01	0.43***
MOV132	0.48***	−0.14***	0.19***
News			
Television (frequency)	−0.05	0.00	0.01
Radio	−0.02	−0.03	0.03
Newspaper	−0.02	−0.03	0.06
Internet	0.04	−0.05	0.02
Social media	−0.02	0.07	−0.13*
Adjusted R^2	0.33	0.10	0.23
n	735	734	734

Source: Mexico 2012 Panel Study (Wave 2), authors' calculations
Note: Standardized coefficients shown.
p < 0.05, **p* < 0.01, ***p* < 0.001.

as evidence from the 2000 and 2006 presidential elections shows (Moreno 2009b). But the panel data in 2012 indicate that they may have been also mobilized around that view.

To what extent #YoSoy132 was a likely cause of that mobilization is a question that we address with more detail in the dynamic model, but the results of this static analysis indicate that opinions of the movement produced statistically significant results for all three major candidates, and even more strongly for López Obrador and Peña Nieto: favorable opinions about the student movement related positively with López Obrador's feeling thermometer and negatively with Peña Nieto's. In fact, the feeling thermometer for #YoSoy132 is the strongest predictor of opinions about López Obrador, suggesting that the campaign did mobilize the movement's sympathizers for the leftist cause. The analysis for Vázquez Mota also shows a significant effect of the movement's feeling thermometer, but more modestly: the effect is not nearly as strong as the negative impact on Peña Nieto or the positive impact on López Obrador. As we show above, this effect did not translate into votes for her. But the fact that the #YoSoy132 feeling thermometer is modestly yet positively related to Vázquez Mota's image confirms that opinions about the student movement were strongly charged by an anti-PRI sentiment.

This analysis confirms that the PAN candidate benefited from presidential approval. Interestingly, only social media use exerted a significant influence on the PAN candidate's feeling thermometer. Social media users were more likely to think negatively about the PAN candidate, but there is no significant effect on opinions about the other two main candidates. We find somewhat different results, suggesting that media use can be better understood taking into consideration the dynamics of a campaign.

So far we have discussed the influence of several factors in the candidates' feeling thermometers. But the panel study also allows us to analyze them in a more dynamic fashion, focusing on opinion change from the preelection Wave 1 to the postelection Wave 2. In the dynamic analysis we keep the same explanatory variables from the last model, but in this case the dependent variable is the differential in feeling thermometers for each candidate (taking the score in Wave 2 and subtracting the score in Wave 1). The resulting variable ranges from −10 to +10, with negative scores representing unfavorable changes in opinions and positive signs indicating favorable changes. As the feeling thermometer differentials are distributed roughly normally for each candidate, we use linear regression for this analysis.

The results of the multivariate analysis are shown in table 10.3. There are two model specifications for each candidate, one with the student movement's feeling thermometer and the other without it, to show the contribution of that variable to opinion change. The results show that none of the structural factors (sex, age, or education) is significantly linked with opinion change for any of the three candidates; neither is political interest nor church attendance. Leftism does have a significant effect on opinion change for López Obrador and Peña Nieto, in the expected direction, but (also as expected) not for Vázquez Mota. Centrist voters improved their opinions of the PRI candidate, and the independents expressed increasingly negative opinions of him, neither of which is particularly surprising given past behavior of voters in Mexico. The main determinant of opinion change for Vázquez Mota was presidential approval, which means that despite her efforts to "differentiate" herself, the PAN candidate

Table 10.3. Dynamic analysis of opinion thermometers for the presidential candidates: Opinion change from Wave 1 to Wave 2 of the panel study

	Beta					
	López Obrador		Peña Nieto		Vázquez Mota	
	Wave 1	Wave 2	Wave 1	Wave 2	Wave 1	Wave 2
Female	−0.01	0.01	−0.02	−0.02	0.00	−0.03
Age under 30	−0.04	−0.05	0.02	0.02	0.00	−0.03
Education	−0.02	−0.06	0.02	0.03	−0.01	0.02
Political interest	−0.06	−0.08	−0.02	0.01	0.00	0.01
Left	0.14***	0.12**	−0.10**	−0.13**	−0.01	−0.01
Center	0.04	0.04	0.09**	0.09*	0.02	0.02
Independent	0.06	0.01	−0.07*	−0.07	−0.01	0.00
Church attendance	−0.02	−0.05	0.03	0.03	0.00	0.02
Presidential approval	0.04	0.02	0.02	−0.01	0.16***	0.16***
MOV132		0.25***		−0.03		0.09*
News						
Television (frequency)	0.01	0.00	0.06	0.07[a]	0.05	0.04
Radio	−0.02	0.00	0.00	−0.02	0.01	0.01
Newspaper	0.01	−0.03	−0.04	−0.03	0.02	0.00
Internet	0.11	0.17*	−0.07	−0.07	−0.01	0.00
Social media	−0.11	−0.17*	0.08	0.07	−0.05	−0.07
n	884	712	894	717	868	698

benefited from the outgoing president's popularity (or, put another way, that she lost support among those who were not already strong supporters of the president). Meanwhile, television users grew modestly more favorable toward the PRI candidate—not surprising given allegations of media bias on television.

Opinions of #YoSoy132 translated into somewhat more positive views of Vázquez Mota and much more positive views of López Obrador, meaning that both gained in standing relative to Peña Nieto. Indeed, opinions about the student movement are the single strongest predictor of opinion change about the leftist candidate during the campaigns. The data also show statistically significant associations between the use of the Internet and social media and changes in López Obrador's image, but the effects are differentiated. Internet users became more favorably disposed toward the leftist candidate, whereas social media users became more opposed. This latter result was not expected, but it is statistically significant with the inclusion of the student movement feeling thermometer into the equation. All told, these changes in candidate image reveal differentiated media effects on voters. The analysis of opinion change confirms the role played by the student movement in mobilizing or influencing feelings toward the candidates. News exposure through social media helps to explain change in political opinion.

Predictors of #YoSoy132 Feeling Thermometer: The Role of Social Media

With these differentiated effects in mind, we model opinions about the student movement by employing explanatory variables from the first wave of the panel study, when the student movement had not yet emerged in the campaigns. This design follows research on the May 1968 student movement in France, in which scholars analyzed a panel survey conducted the during the 1967 legislative elections, with a second round of interviews after the 1968 spring protests (Pierce and Converse 1989). They used the 1967 responses as explanatory variables and the 1968 self-reported participation in demonstrations and strikes as dependent variables. The resemblance of our approach to the French design is not only methodological; both aimed at an understanding of public opinion involving a politically significant student movement that opened or reinforced an existing but latent political divide.

Predicting attitudes in Wave 2 with citizens' characteristics and attitudes collected in Wave 1 of the panel study differs from other models using panel data about social movements and protests, which attempt to predict past behavior on the basis of information collected more recently (Green and Shapiro 1994). Our model design is appropriate because the student movement did not exist during the first wave of interviews and because predicting opinions about it with variables from the same wave may ignore past participation and attitudinal changes owing to the success or failure of the movement (Finkel and Muller 1998). In order to deal with causal inference problems, we also perform a preprocessing technique using the panel's first wave, matching two groups to avoid model dependence problems (Ho, Imai, King, and Stuart 2007).[3]

One of the most important demands of #YoSoy132 was fairness in media coverage of the campaigns, particularly by television networks. The student movement contended that major television networks favored the PRI candidate. Calls for the "democratization of mass media" were a recurrent theme in the 2012 campaign, suggesting that demands for unbiased coverage of the campaign helped fuel the movement among students from different and ideologically diverse universities in the country, as well as expressions of solidarity from students abroad. The students' demands for the democratization of mass media used a Web-based platform rather than channel demands through traditional media, which further justifies our interest in the role of new information technologies during the 2012 presidential campaigns.

Blogging as a particular feature of political campaigns started to become relevant outside of the candidates' campaign teams in the 2006 presidential election. Blogs such as *Sendero del Peje* in favor of López Obrador, and *México en peligro* in favor of Calderón, had 1.4 and 1.2 million unique site visits during 2006, respectively. After a blogging boom well known from the 2008 US presidential campaign, Facebook and Twitter became key tools for campaign strategists, especially when appealing to young, educated, and connected segments of the electorate who tend to be politically more independent and therefore more potentially volatile. The Twitter experience has been analyzed for the 2009 European Union legislative elections (Vergeer et al. 2013), and examples of Web and social media campaigns in Latin America include Antanas Mockus's presidential campaign in Colombia in 2010, as well as Marina Silva's presidential campaign in Brazil's 2010 presidential election (Telles et al. 2013). In 2012, political campaigns also emphasized the importance of social media (Moreno and Mendizábal 2013).

One important aspect of Internet-based campaigns and the political use of social media is a top-down information flow, for example, from candidates and activists to citizens and followers through so-called Web 1.0 and 2.0 features

(Lilleker and Jackson 2010). The new information technologies also allow a bottom-up information flow, however, which is what happened with student movements in South Asia and during the Arab Spring (Lee 2010). In sum, although social media may exhibit both types of directionality, top-down and bottom-up, variation in how information circulates among specific segments of the electorate reveals how salient independent social media might be among young and interconnected voters (Moreno and Mendizábal 2013).

Social media are a crucial tool for new social movements, such as #YoSoy132 in Mexico's 2012 campaign. And, as we show, being a user of Twitter, Facebook, or other social media predicts the extent to which a voter supports the student movement or not. When estimating statistical models, we also include different covariates from our previous models.

In order to empirically overcome potential problems regarding an endogenous model, and additional cross-terms relationships among different variables, we estimated a simple matching technique using the nearest-neighbor method and calculating a propensity score, in which the preprocessing data follow an experimental design in order to reduce model dependence and make valid causal inferences (Ho et al. 2007). The treatment that we estimated is whether a respondent uses social media in both waves of the panel survey. We thus created two groups in each wave that were as similar as possible except in one characteristic—those who use social media belong to one group, and those who do not use social media belong to the second group. The estimation of the matched groups included gender, age by cohort, education, social class, rural or urban residence, cell phone use, and exposure to news through television, radio, Internet, and newspapers. The matching technique considerably reduces sample size, allowing controlled comparisons between two fairly similar groups. In this case, the nearest-neighbor method only included 197 respondents by group, leaving 558 respondents unmatched for the first wave, and 183 respondents by group, leaving 572 respondents unmatched for the second wave.

We ran linear regression models of the #YoSoy132 feeling thermometer using a preprocessing data technique and then matching and producing similar results by wave. The results are shown in table 10.4. In terms of structural variables, neither gender nor rural residence is significantly related to opinions about the student movement, but education and age are. Education is negatively and significantly related to the movement's feeling thermometer using independent variables from the first wave, when the movement did not exist: less educated and older voters were apparently more open to receive the movement

Table 10.4. #YoSoy132 opinion thermometer models

	Beta					
	Wave 1			Wave 2		
Female	−0.03	−0.03	−0.02	0.10	0.01	0.09
Age under 30	−0.12*	−0.12*	−0.12*	0.14*	0.08	0.13*
Education	−0.25***	−0.25***	−0.25***	0.10*	0.11*	0.10*
Rural	0.03	0.03	0.03	0.07	0.06	0.07
Left	0.17***	0.17***	0.17***	−0.08	−0.05	−0.08
Center	0.09	0.09	0.09	0.05	0.03	0.05
Priísta	−0.06	−0.06	−0.07	−0.39***	−0.39***	−0.39***
Panista	−0.06	−0.06	−0.06	−0.26***	−0.24***	−0.26***
Independent	0.03	0.04	0.03	−0.29***	−0.28***	−0.29***
Church attendance	−0.11**	−0.11**	−0.11**	−0.02	0.02	−0.01
Presidential approval	0.15***	0.15***	0.15***	0.02	0.00	0.02
National economy	0.04	0.04	0.04	0.05	0.06	0.05
Political interest	−0.15***	−0.15***	−0.15***	−0.08	−0.09	−0.08
Television	−0.13**	−0.13**	−0.13**	0.04	0.04	0.04
Radio	−0.05	−0.05	−0.05	0.04	0.01	0.04
Newspaper	0.08	0.08	0.08	0.02	−0.01	0.02
Internet	0.01	—	0.08*	0.65	—	0.60
Social media	0.08	0.09*	—	0.08	0.07	—
Propensity score	0.32***	0.32***	0.32***	−0.74	−0.13	−0.64
n	394	394	394	366	366	366
R^2	0.13	0.13	0.13	0.11	0.10	0.10
F test	3.25	3.43	3.32	2.07	2.13	2.13

Source: The Mexico 2012 Panel Study; multiple imputation technique only including panelists using EMI algorithm via library (Amelia) in R.2.14

Note: Robust corrected standard errors. The dependent variable is the #YoSoy132 feeling thermometer in Wave 2.

*p < 0.05, **p < 0.01, ***p < 0.001.

favorably. In the second wave, however, the, young and educated voters defined more clearly who supports the student movement. Both variables show a positive and significant coefficient, which means that #YoSoy132 enjoyed broader support among young and more educated Mexicans. Other demographics such as class did not exert any influence on opinions about the movement.

Partisan and ideological variables in Wave 1 relate differently to the movement's feeling thermometer than they do in Wave 2: partisanship was not important, but the left ideological category was. Also, partisan identifications in Wave 2 were strong predictors of opinions about #YoSoy132, but the effect of ideology faded. Identification with the left was a significant factor behind support for the movement, and identification with the PRI was the main factor against it. Among the other variables, TV news consumption, political interest, church attendance, and presidential approval in Wave 1 all decreased support for the movement. Nonetheless, by Wave 2, their effects were gone. The same happened with Internet and social media use. Interestingly, 77% of those with Internet access also have access to social media, such as a Twitter account or Facebook profile when considering the first wave. We therefore estimated two models including either Internet or social media, and we found modest statistical evidence of the impact of Web-based channels in favor of the #YoSoy132 movement.

In sum, results from the second wave in this analysis suggest a relative polarization of citizens' attitudes toward student movement, in which all the statistical power went from cognitive variables to partisan views. PRI supporters developed more unfavorable opinions about a student movement that protested against and rejected the PRI presidential candidate. PAN identifiers and independents also showed their dissatisfaction with the movement in the results from the second wave, suggesting a backlash against the movement and especially the leftist candidate. As shown in table 10.1 above, both Vázquez Mota and Peña Nieto regained a few points of support among independent voters, which may well reflect an increasing dissatisfaction with the student movement. One interpretation of these findings is that the movement's positive effects on López Obrador's support among some voters compensated for negative attitudes toward him among others.

It is worth noting that #YoSoy132 brought a sense of political cohesion among some segments of the electorate, similar to French protesters in May 1968. Anti-Gaullist leftists were supportive of the student protests because their demands appealed to public goods such as quality education, and these demands agreed with those of other social and political groups (Pierce and Converse 1989, 236). In Mexico's case, demands focused on unbiased political information, fair election coverage by traditional mass media, and truth telling about the events at the Ibero. The movement evoked an anti-PRI sentiment that might reflect the old PRI/anti-PRI political divide that was salient in Mexican politics prior to democratization (Domínguez and McCann 1996; Molinar 1991). In our view, the political conflict in 2012 was not exactly a revival of the old regime dimension, as young voters did not experience and may not necessarily remember the old politics, but it certainly activated some of its features among the electorate.

One of the differences from the old regime cleavage is shown in the regression analysis of the #YoSoy132 feeling thermometer: the role of social media. There is a connection between social media and Internet users and opinions about the student movement. The effect of social media users on feelings toward the student movement is statistically significant across all types of regression models used (poisson, negative binomial, and ordered logit, which are not shown here). When incorporating uncertainty in the estimation through 1,000 simulations, this effect, although fairly modest, remains significant. For the sake of simplicity, on the basis of the linear regression model, the effect of using social media translates into about a half point on a ten-point scale. In contrast, the impact of PRI identifiers on #YoSoy132 in the second wave is 4.7, whereas being a PRD supporter is 5.6 on an eleven-point scale. In summary, opinions about the student movement are mainly explained by long-term political predispositions such as identification with the PRI, left-right ideological orientations, and interest in politics, but also by social media use and exposure to TV news.

We now add an element to our previous depiction of two contrasting political camps in the 2012 presidential race: a leftist, pro-student movement, and pro–López Obrador side that relied heavily on information from social media versus a rightwing, anti–student movement, and pro–Peña Nieto side that relied on more traditional media outlets, particularly television. Although this resembles the old PRI/anti-PRI divide, there are some important differences: the old anti-PRI camp included young, educated, and urban voters, mirrored by a pro-PRI camp of older, less educated, and rural voters (Moreno 2003). In 2012, age did not have a direct effect on political preferences but education did, showing that highly educated voters disliked both front-runners. Additionally, exposure to TV news seems to have played against the PRI in the 2000 election, when that party lost the presidency (Lawson 2004), but in 2012, as our analysis documents, exposure to news on television had a positive influence in voting for Enrique Peña Nieto. We may argue that the 2012 political divide between pro–Peña Nieto right and center-right voters relying on traditional media, versus a pro–López Obrador left and center-left camp relying more heavily on new information technologies, resembles but is not the same as the old regime cleavage in Mexican politics. Age, education, and rural residency, central components of the old cleavage, were not present in this new political divide.

A significant proportion of the Mexican electorate split their preferences in 2012 between Peña Nieto and López Obrador (who got about 71% of the national vote combined). The choice between them was based significantly on partisanship as well as on a strong ideological component (left versus right), with clear policy contents and different patterns of information (television versus Internet and social media). The latter is a new feature of Mexican campaigns, as no other presidential election had such a significant number of users of new information technologies.

Predictors of Media Use

Given the role of social media in the 2012 election, here we show that different types of voters in Mexico use different media outlets. We employed a logistic regression model with dichotomous dependent variables: frequent exposure to television and radio news, newspapers, the Internet, and social media use. We compare results from Waves 1 and 2 of the panel study to determine whether there were differences in patterns of media consumption during the campaigns. Our independent variables resemble the model used throughout this chapter, including in this case only structural factors and long-term political predispositions.

Results of the analyses are shown table 10.5. They indicate that gender is only associated with newspaper readership (women are less likely to follow news in print newspapers than men), and this relationship is stronger in Wave 2 than in Wave 1 of the panel survey. Wave 2 also shows a modest relationship of gender with Internet use, with women being less likely than men to get information through that medium. In Wave 1, age exerts a modest influence on exposure to news through television and newspapers (with younger voters being less likely to follow news in those traditional media), a modest influence on Internet use, and a strong influence on social media use, with younger voters being more likely to follow news through these new information technologies.

In Wave 2, the effects of age on traditional media use disappear, but the effects of age on Internet and social media use are actually stronger, which suggests that young voters may have increasingly turned to those new media for information over the course of campaigns.

Education is a significant predictor of newspaper readership as well as Internet and social media use, but it makes little difference in exposure to radio (in Wave 1) and no difference in exposure to television news. This is a consistent finding with global patterns of political news exposure based on comparative election surveys and with the argument that some media, such as newspaper readership, require higher levels of education than television exposure (Beck and Gunther 2014). In Wave 2, education had a stronger effect on radio exposure and continued to have a significant effect on newspaper readership as well as Internet and social media use, but it had no effect on television exposure whatsoever. Rural voters are less likely to follow news in print newspapers (an urban medium in Mexico) and they are also less likely to use the Internet and social media, which are more likely to be found in urban and middle-class environments of Mexico and, to some extent, Latin America (Moreno and Mendizábal 2013). An indicator of subjective social class included in this analysis confirms a positive though modest association between not only class and Internet and social media use, but also television, at least in the first round of the panel study, which shows that class is negatively related to radio exposure.

In the political predispositions group of variables, political interest is positively related to exposure to all media in different degrees, also consistent with observed global patterns of political information (Beck and Gunther 2014). Ideology is a less consistent predictor of media use, but leftist voters seem clearly linked to the use of new technologies such as the Internet and social media. By contrast, centrist voters do not show any clear association with use of any media, something that independent voters do: they are less likely to follow news through the traditional media. This finding has obvious implications for campaign strategists because independents are, in theory, more open to campaign stimuli and more likely to change their political views. Finally, church attendance shows a modest relationship with exposure to radio and social media in the panel's first wave, but the effects disappear in the second wave.

In sum, there are significant differences in the use of traditional media as opposed to new technologies for political information. The latter are more common among younger, highly educated, and more politically leftist voters.

Table 10.5.   Media use: A logistic regression model

	Television (49%)		Radio (52%)		Newspapers (44%)		Internet (23%)		Social Media (18%)	
	B	Wald	B	Wald	B	Wald	B	Wald	B	Wald
Wave 1										
Female	−0.05	0.2	−0.21	3.0	−0.30	6.5*	−0.04	0.1	−0.05	0.1
Age under 30	−0.26	4.1*	−0.17	1.7	−0.25	3.5[a]	0.26	3.3[a]	0.47	9.7**
Education	0.05	3.0	0.06	3.7[a]	0.22	50.2***	0.30	72.1***	0.26	48.0***
Rural	0.19	1.9	−0.13	0.8	−0.31	4.6*	−0.48	6.3*	−0.29	2.1
Subjective class	0.14	4.9*	−0.12	3.3[a]	0.11	2.9[a]	0.17	5.0*	0.18	4.8*
Political interest	0.26	18.7***	0.30	23.0***	0.20	10.7**	0.24	11.2**	0.13	2.8[a]
Left	0.08	0.3	0.38	5.9*	0.16	1.1	0.45	6.8**	0.38	4.4*
Center	0.11	0.6	0.09	0.4	0.01	0.0	0.17	1.0	0.27	2.4
Independent	−0.32	7.1**	−0.28	5.3*	−0.27	4.6*	0.13	0.8	0.15	1.0
Church attendance	0.02	0.2	0.11	4.7*	−0.02	0.2	0.08	2.3	0.15	6.4*
R^2 (Cox and Snell)	0.04		0.05		0.10		0.15		0.11	

	Television (45%)		Radio (45%)		Newspapers (39%)		Internet (17%)		Social Media (15%)	
	B	Wald	B	Wald	B	Wald	B	Wald	B	Wald
Wave 2										
Female	−0.06	0.2	−0.02	0.0	−0.62	22.9***	−0.28	3.2[a]	−0.07	0.2
Age under 30	0.05	0.1	−0.12	0.7	−0.15	1.1	0.80	25.8***	0.77	22.6***
Education	0.02	0.3	0.11	13.0***	0.18	28.6***	0.30	55.8***	0.26	40.8***
Rural	0.05	0.1	−0.12	0.7	−0.60	15.7***	−0.31	2.4	−0.37	3.1[a]
Subjective class	−0.09	1.6	−0.17	5.9*	−0.03	0.2	0.14	2.7	0.14	2.3
Political interest	0.54	48.1***	0.13	3.2[a]	0.36	22.3***	0.39	18.1***	0.35	13.6***
Left	0.02	0.0	0.13	0.7	0.03	0.0	0.41	4.9*	0.36	3.5[a]
Center	0.06	0.1	0.09	0.3	−0.27	2.4	0.12	0.4	0.18	0.7
Independent	−0.36	6.9**	−0.29	4.5*	−0.29	4.3*	0.10	0.4	0.08	0.2
Church attendance	0.01	0.1	−0.08	2.5	0.01	0.0	0.03	0.2	−0.01	0.0
Constant	−0.56	2.9	0.36	1.3	−0.81	6.2*	−4.43	105.4***	−4.27	93.7***
R^2 (Cox and Snell)	0.06		0.03		0.11		0.15		0.12	

Source: The Mexico 2012 Panel Study (Waves 1 and 2)
Note: Wave 1, $n = 1,313$; Wave 2, $n = 1,135$.
*$p < 0.05$, **$p < 0.01$, ***$p < 0.001$, [a]$p < 0.1$.

Political interest remains a crucial predictor of news exposure across all media while education has differentiating effects, contributing to more exposure to news in print newspapers and new technologies but less in television and radio. These findings are generally consistent with comparative surveys on media use and political behavior.

Conclusion

In this chapter, we explored several possible effects of the student movement #YoSoy132 on voters during the 2012 election campaigns. The student movement emerged as an anti–Peña Nieto movement, and it protested against television networks demanding unbiased election coverage. Our analysis, based on panel survey data, shows a strong relationship between opinions about the movement and support for the presidential candidates: voters with a favorable opinion about the movement were significantly more likely to vote for López Obrador. The #YoSoy132 feeling thermometer stands out as the main predictor of opinion change in the opinion thermometers for the two main presidential candidates, Peña Nieto and López Obrador.

Our various analyses also suggest that the 2012 campaign crystallized two political camps in a conflict dimension that left out the PAN's candidate. On one side, we observe a leftist, pro-student movement, and pro–López Obrador camp that relied on information through new technologies. On the other side, we observe a center-right, antistudent, and pro–Peña Nieto camp that relied on more traditional media outlets, particularly television, for political information. Policy and attitude differences helped each camp to cohere.

The student movement #YoSoy132 changed the campaign dynamics in 2012, challenging the view that Peña Nieto would not find significant opposition and that he would win the election easily. Our analyses show that views about the student movement reflect possible campaign effects that helped López Obrador gain votes among some segments of the electorate, but it also created an antistudent reaction among PRI loyalists, who closed lines behind the PRI candidate and rejected #YoSoy132 claims and activities. It is also likely that some PAN identifiers, who could have voted for López Obrador, ultimately decided to choose Peña Nieto, given that their candidate was trailing in third place in the polls. As in past presidential elections, campaigns mattered, and this time the student movement was a key stimulus in a campaign that initially seemed to point to Peña Nieto's inevitable victory.

NOTES

1. The choice of these control variables broadly reflects a "funnel of causality" model, which has been used in established and new democracies (Campbell et al. 1960; Evans 2004; Gunther, Montero, and Puhle 2007; Lobo, Bellucci, Gunther, and Lisi, 2014; Thomassen 2005). The funnel of causality differentiates at least three types of determinants of the vote: structural factors, long-term political predispositions, and short-term and campaign-related factors. These determinants include gender (Finkel and Muller 1998; Lee 1997), age by cohort (Finkel and Muller 1998; Jian-Hua and Rosen 1993; Lee 1997), education (Jian-Hua and Rosen 1993; Lee 2010; Lipset 1967; Pierce and Converse 1989; Vergeer et al. 2013), social class (Finkel and Muller 1998; Jian-Hua and Rosen 1993), political ideology (Domínguez and McCann 1996; Lee 1997; Pierce and Converse 1989), partisanship (Jian-Hua and Rosen 1993; Pierce and Converse 1989), interest in politics (Lee 1997), and access to other mass media, such as television, radio, and newspaper as traditional channels of information, when compared to online channels as social media (Rojas 2010).

2. We use a simple dichotomous measure: older or younger than age 30.

3. There are several explanations about citizens' attitudes toward social movements, in which how and why people protest are tangentially discussed. Literature about citizens' attitudes toward social movements explains the importance of microscopic incentives on the effectiveness of public rallies and demonstrations, in which scholars usually highlight a relevant dilemma: individual-level versus collective-level incentives. In this way, some scholars advocate the relevance of "public goods" among individuals, such as quality of education (Pierce and Converse 1989), or collective interests after controlling for selective payoffs (Finkel and Muller 1998; Tarrow 1996). The notion of this combination among collective good and incentives at the individual level illustrates how collective efficacy informs participation decisions over time (Lee 2010). The public good perspective, commonly shared by activists, sustains that individual willingness to participate in a social movement can be explained by attitudes and demographic measures at the individual level when the goals of participation are shared.

REFERENCES

Beck, Paul, and Richard Gunther. 2014. "Global Patterns of Political Intermediation." Paper presented at the meeting of the Comparative National Elections Project, Marrakech, Morocco.

Campbell, Angus, Philip E. Converse, Warren E. Miller, and Donald E. Stokes. 1960. *The American Voter*. New York: John Wiley & Sons.

Coleman, Stephen, and Jay G. Blumler. 2009. *The Internet and Democratic Citizenship: Theory, Practice, and Policy*. Cambridge: Cambridge University Press.

Domínguez, Jorge I., and James A. McCann. 1996. *Democratizing Mexico: Public Opinion and Electoral Choices*. Baltimore. Johns Hopkins University Press.

Evans, Jocelyn A. 2004. *Voters and Voting: An Introduction*. London: SAGE.

Finkel, Steven E., and Edward N. Muller. 1998. "Rational Choice and the Dynamics of Collective Political Action: Evaluating Alternative Models with Panel Data." *American Political Science Review* 92, no. 1: 37–50.

Flores-Macías, Francisco. 2009. "Electoral Volatility in 2006." In *Consolidating Mexico's Democracy: The 2006 Presidential Campaign in Comparative Perspective*, ed.

Jorge I. Domínguez, Chappell Lawson, and Alejandro Moreno, 191–208. Baltimore: Johns Hopkins University Press.

Green, Donald P., and Ian Shapiro. 1994. *Pathologies of Rational Choice Theory*. New Haven, CT: Yale University Press.

Gunther, Richard, José Ramón Montero, and Hans-Jürgen Puhle. 2007. *Democracy, Intermediation, and Voting on Four Continents*. Oxford: Oxford University Press.

Ho, Daniel, Kosuke Imai, Gary King, and Elizabeth Stuart. 2007. "Matching as Nonparametric Preprocessing for Reducing Model Dependence in Parametric Causal Inference." *Political Analysis* 15: 199–236.

Howard, Philip N. 2010. *The Digital Origins of Dictatorship and Democracy*. Oxford: Oxford University Press.

Iasulaitis, Sylvia. 2013. "Experiencias interativas em websites de campanhas eleitorais." In *Comunicação Política e Comportamento Eleitoral América Latina*, ed. Helcimara Telles and Alejandro Moreno, 397–435. Belo Horizonte: Universidade Federal de Minas Gerais.

Jian-Hua, Zhu, and Stanley Rosen. 1993. "From Discontent to Protest: Individual-Level Causes of the 1989 Pro-Democracy Movement in China." *International Journal of Public Opinion Research* 5, no. 3: 234–49.

Lawson, Chappell. 1999. "Why Cárdenas Won: The 1997 Elections in Mexico City." In *Toward Mexico's Democratization: Parties, Campaigns, Elections, and Public Opinion*, ed. Jorge I. Domínguez and Alejandro Poiré, 147–73. New York: Routledge.

———. 2004. "Mexico's Great Debates: The Televised Candidates Encounters of 2000 and Their Electoral Consequences." In *Mexico's Pivotal Democratic Election: Candidates, Voters, and the Presidential Campaign of 2000*, ed. Jorge I. Domínguez and Chappell Lawson, 211–42. Baltimore: Johns Hopkins University Press.

Lee, Aie-Rie. 1997. "Exploration of the Sources of Student Activism: The Case of South Korea." *International Journal of Public Opinion Research* 9, no. 1: 48–65.

Lee, Francis, L. F. 2010. "The Perceptual Bases of Collective Efficacy and Protest Participation: The Case of Pro-Democracy Protests in Hong Kong." *International Journal of Public Opinion Research* 22, no. 3: 392–411.

Lilleker, Darren G., and Nigel A. Jackson. 2010. "Towards a More Participatory Style of Election Campaigning: The Impact of Web 2.0 on the UK 2010 General Election." *Policy and Internet* 2, no. 3: article 4, doi:10.2202/1944-2866.1064.

Lipset, Seymour M. 1967. "University Politics in Underdeveloped Countries." In *Student Politics*, ed. Seymour M. Lipset, 3–53. New York: Basic Books.

Lobo, Marina Costa, Paolo Bellucci, Richard Gunther, and Marco Lisi. 2014. "The Changing Determinants of the Vote." Paper presented at the meeting of the Comparative National Election Project, Marrakech, Morocco.

Molinar, Juan. 1991. *El tiempo de la legitimidad*. Mexico City: Cal y Arena.

Moreno, Alejandro. 2003. *El votante mexicano*. Mexico City: Fondo de Cultura Económica.

———. 2004. "The Effects of Negative Campaigns on Mexican Voters." In *Mexico's Pivotal Democratic Election: Candidates, Voters, and the Presidential Campaign of 2000*, ed. Jorge I. Domínguez and Chappell Lawson, 243–68. Baltimore: Johns Hopkins University Press.

———. 2009a. "The Activation of Economic Voting in the 2006 Campaign." In *Consolidating Mexico's Democracy: The 2006 Presidential Campaign in Comparative Perspective*, ed. Jorge I. Domínguez, Chappell Lawson, and Alejandro Moreno, 209–28. Baltimore: Johns Hopkins University Press.

———. 2009b. *La decisión electoral: Votantes, partidos y democracia en México*. México City: Miguel Ángel Porrúa.

Moreno, Alejandro, and Yuritzi Mendizábal. 2013. "El uso de las redes sociales en México." In *Comunicação Política e Comportamento Eleitoral América Latina*, ed. Helcimara Telles and Alejandro Moreno, 397–435. Belo Horizonte: Universidade Federal de Minas Gerais.

Norris, Pippa. 2000. *A Virtuous Circle: Political Communication in Postindustrial Societies.* Cambridge: Cambridge University Press.

Pierce, Roy, and Philip E. Converse. 1989. "Attitudinal Roots of Popular Protest: The French Upheaval of May 1968." *International Journal of Public Opinion Research* 1, no. 3: 221–41.

Rojas, Hernando. 2010. " 'Corrective' Actions in the Public Sphere: How Perceptions of Media and Media Effects Shape Political Behaviors." *International Journal of Public Opinion Research* 22, no. 3: 343–63.

Semetko, Holli A. 2007. "Political Communication." In *Oxford Handbook of Political Behavior*, ed. Russell J. Dalton and Hans-Dieter Klingemann, 123–43. New York: Oxford University Press.

Tarrow, Sidney. 1996. "Social Movements in Contentious Politics: A Review Article." *American Political Science Review* 90, no. 4: 874–83.

Telles, Helcimara, Pedro Santos Mundim, and Nayla Lopes. 2013. "Internautas, verdes e pentecostais: Emergencia de novo comportamiento politico no Brasil?" In *Comunicação Política e Comportamento Eleitoral América Latina*, ed. Helcimara Telles and Alejandro Moreno, 152–220. Belo Horizonte: Universidade Federal de Minas Gerais.

Thomassen, Jacques, ed. 2005. *The European Voter.* Oxford: Oxford University Press.

Vergeer, Maurice, Liesbeth Hermans, and Steven Sams. 2013. "Online Social Networks and Micro-Blogging in Political Campaigning: The Exploration of a New Campaign Tool and a New Campaign Style." *Party Politics* 19, no. 3: 477–501.

11

Mexico's 2012 Presidential Election

Conclusions

JORGE I. DOMÍNGUEZ

Guadalupe Loaeza (1994) asked, "What could be worse, that there be fraud or that millions of Mexicans would vote for the PRI?" The Mexican public intellectual penned that devilish sentence in the immediate aftermath of Ernesto Zedillo's election to the presidency in 1994, the first Mexican presidential election ever that even opposition analysts believed that the PRI (Partido Revolucionario Institucional, or Institutional Revolutionary Party) presidential candidate won. Critics in 1994 still believed that there were pockets of fraud committed during the election, but Mexico had already changed a great deal, enabling Zedillo to claim a more democratic mandate. Yet Loaeza gave voice to the disgust of many at the spectacle that so many Mexicans would vote for a party that, some changes notwithstanding, had governed Mexico in authoritarian fashion since 1929.

In 2012, Enrique Peña Nieto led the PRI, after twelve years in the opposition, to win back the presidency and a plurality in both chambers of congress. Fraud had been remaindered as an issue of the past, thanks in particular to the establishment of the IFE (Instituto Federal Electoral, or Federal Electoral Institute), which had toiled extensively and effectively to eliminate it starting in the 1997 midterm national legislative election (Eric Magar, chap. 3). Yet, as table 11.1 shows, in the 2012 presidential election, over eight million more voters cast their ballots for the PAN (Partido Acción Nacional, or National Action Party) candidate, Josefina Vázquez Mota, plus for the candidate of the PRD (Partido de la Revolución Democrática, or Party of the Democratic Revolution) and its coalition, Andrés Manuel López Obrador, than they did for Peña Nieto, the candidate of the PRI. For these PAN and PRD supporters, echoes of Loaeza's (1994) lament lingered. The 2012 supporters and participants of the social media movement #YoSoy132 voiced some of this anger during the 2012 presidential campaign (Alejandro Díaz-Domínguez and Alejandro Moreno, chap. 10). Across the decades, a cultural—not just a political—rejection of the PRI was a key to some Mexicans' civic self-identity.

"And, upon waking up, the dinosaur was still there," Lorenzo Meyer (1994), one of Mexico's leading historians, commented on the 1994 presidential election, quoting from a micronovel by Augusto Monterroso, as Kathleen Bruhn opens chapter 2. Meyer voiced amazement at the sheer endurance of the PRI's machine and its relentless capacity to win and win yet again, notwithstanding Mexico's transformation over the previous six decades from a rural to an urban country and from a producer of primary products to an exporter of manufactures. The Soviet Union had collapsed. Mexico's PRI had survived. But it survived just one more six-year presidential term. Vicente Fox in 2000 and Felipe Calderón in 2006, both heading the PAN, defeated the respective PRI presidential candidates Francisco Labastida and Roberto Madrazo.

Disgusting to some, antediluvian to others, Mexico's PRI had remained a successful and popular party even when its candidates lost presidential elections. As the electoral data in table 11.1 show, PRI candidates for the chamber of deputies outperformed the losing PRI presidential candidates in the 2000 and, markedly, 2006 presidential elections. In the elections for the chamber of deputies in 1997, 2000, 2003 (in alliance with the Green Ecologist Party, or

Table 11.1.   Votes cast in presidential and deputy elections for PAN, PRD, and PRI candidates (in millions of votes), 2000–2012

Election	Party	2000	2003	2006	2009	2012	2012
Presidency	PRI	13.58		9.30		19.16	16.35
Deputy	PRI	13.80	9.28	11.68	12.81		15.96
Presidency	PAN	15.99		15.00		12.73	12.73
Deputy	PAN	14.32	8.22	13.85	9.71		12.96
Presidency	PRD	6.26		14.76		15.85	11.12
Deputy	PRD	6.98	4.71	12.01	4.23		9.19

Source: http://siceef.ife.org.mx/pef2012/SICEEF2012.html#app=ff36&88fe-selected Index=0&bd55-s

Note: For deputy elections, the reported votes are for the proportional-representation party lists. For 2003, 2009, and the second column of 2012, the votes are for each party standing alone. In the second column for 2012, coalition votes are allocated to parties according to Mexican federal electoral law. For 2000, 2006, and the first column of 2012, the votes are for the coalition for both presidential and deputy elections, attributing the votes to the lead party in each coalition, although the reported votes are for the respective entire coalitions. In 2000 the PRI (and in 2006 the PAN) ran without a coalition partner.

PVEM), and 2009, the PRI won between 42% and 47% of the seats, in each instance the largest plurality in the chamber (in the 2006 deputy elections, with the ballot headed by a disastrous presidential candidacy, the PRI's share of the chamber's seats fell to 21%). Moreover, out of the thirty-two units in the Mexican federation, between 2000 and 2012 the PRI won between seventeen and twenty elections for state governor per election cycle (Hernández Rodríguez and Pansters 2012). In many of these elections—including in emblematic states where the PAN had strong and deep roots, such as Chihuahua and Nuevo León—the PRI had lost the governorship to the PAN but would regain it from the opposition in a subsequent election.

In this chapter, I compare aspects of the 2012 presidential election to those of 2000 and 2006 and highlight some of this book's key findings. I review and revise some of my own findings in previous studies of earlier elections. But first I situate the 2012 Mexican presidential election in comparative context in order to understand how the former ruling party came back to again elect Mexico's president.

The PRI's Regeneration in Comparative Perspective

"We cannot continue as we have. A radical transformation of the party is not a tactical concession, but a question of political survival" (Grzymała-Busse 2002, 1). In January 1989, Jacek Zdrojewski, a member of the Polish United Workers' Party, summarized the predicament of the Polish Communist Party as it faced the onslaught of the democratic wave that washed away the Communist authoritarian regimes in east central Europe. Grzymała-Busse (2002) analyzed the response of the Polish Communists, comparing it with the Czech, Hungarian, and Slovak Communist parties. All four parties were forced from power in 1989, and each faced a capable opposition that contested the elections and further discredited them.

Grzymała-Busse (2002) formulated a set of explanations to shed light on the regeneration of some former ruling parties in east central Europe; her framework can be applied to explain the return of the PRI to the presidency. She first identified a set of ruling Communist Party practices that predispose a party to adapt and survive or to fossilize and fail. Communist parties were more likely to regenerate if their past practices had emphasized the recruitment of pragmatists over ideologues, the significance of political negotiations as a key party tool, and past experience with some significant policy reform. Pragmatism, negotiation, and experience with reform gave Communist parties a usable past as well as resources that its elites could deploy in new democratic settings. Second, Grzymała-Busse argues that, upon democratization, the old parties had to convince voters and other parties of their democratic intentions and capabilities. To do so, she argued, Communist parties had to be centralized in order to respond readily to voter preferences, impose flexibility on party organization in the face of new challenges, and sustain parliamentary discipline. The Polish and Hungarian parties would obtain the largest pluralities of the votes cast in elections in the mid and late 1990s, returning to national power at the head of respective coalitions. In contrast, the Czech and Slovak parties did not fare as well.

Between its first presidential defeat in 2000 and its victory in the 2012 election, the PRI followed a more elongated and complex trajectory than what is indicated for the more successful cases of formerly authoritarian party regeneration in east central Europe. The PRI survived as a large and influential party for gubernatorial and parliamentary elections but would go on to lose the presidency even more badly in 2006.

The PRI had not been an ideological party since the 1940s. It exemplified what Juan Linz (1975) called the "mentalities" of authoritarian regimes. The PRI sought to promote economic growth and the widest possible inclusion of organized economic and social groups under the ruling party and its president, and to sustain nationalism featuring a modicum of sovereign autonomy in the face of US power. It had chosen pragmatic leaders, especially between 1982 and 2000, skilled in negotiations with friend and foe, who implemented dramatic market-conforming economic and social policy changes in those years. The PRI benefited from this inherited tool kit of skills and cadres that was portable from the authoritarian to the democratic regime. Taking serious note of a rising opposition electoral challenge in 1988 and increased public contestation, the PRI in the early 1990s under Presidents Carlos Salinas de Gortari (1988–94) and Ernesto Zedillo (1994–2000) attempted to position itself to host and run a democratic election, what Slater and Wong (2013) call "conceding to thrive," or making concessions as an authoritarian ruling party in order to increase the likelihood of remaining a ruling party (albeit no longer authoritarian). But the PRI had depended on the country's president as its internal coordinating mechanism; having lost the presidency, the PRI responded to this breakdown of its coordination mechanism in three ways.

One response was entirely expected. Having lost the presidency, the PRI decentralized instantly to the units of the federation. PRI state governors became the new PRI coordinators within their respective territories. The PRI could not construct the party centralization that Grzymała-Busse (2002) had found was a key to Communist Party regeneration in east central Europe. The outcome for the PRI resembled the response of Argentina's Partido Justicialista (Peronists) after it lost the 1983 presidential election. Peronist governors sustained the party in the provinces by means fair and foul. So, too, would PRI state governors after 2000. The empirical details differed but the outcomes— subnational autonomy and party survival—were comparable (Gibson 2012; Giraudy 2013). This organizational outcome—devolution of PRI coordination to PRI state governors—could only happen because most Mexican gubernatorial elections are not held at the same time as national elections for president or congress. PRI governors elected before the 2000 election thus remained in office, and new PRI candidates would subsequently run for governorships in their respective states on days of local electoral salience, far removed from the democratic wave that had swept their party from the presidency. As noted above, after 2000 the PRI consistently held more than half of the state governorships, and it remained the only party with a sufficient nationwide state partisan organization to contest effectively every gubernatorial election save the Mexico City Federal District. PRI governors oversaw and shepherded the election of PRI municipal, state, and federal officials, thereby saving the party albeit in decentralized fashion.

The second, perhaps unexpected, response was to maintain extraordinary party discipline in congress. Consider the chamber of deputies, where the challenging task of keeping 211 PRI deputies in line, with a PAN president and multiple governors jockeying for influence, could have led to the party's early parliamentary splintering. During the 1997–2000 sessions, with PRI President Ernesto Zedillo in office, the PRI's party discipline in the chamber of deputies, as measured by the Rice Index, was 99%. PRI deputies disobeyed the party whips in only 1.4% of the bills that came before the chamber. Matters changed, as would be expected after the loss of the presidency in 2000, for the 2000– 2003 parliamentary sessions, but the change was barely perceptible. PRI party discipline fell only to 92%, and the proportion of bills on which deputies disobeyed the party whips rose just to 5.9%. The PRI sustained comparable levels of party discipline in the years that followed (Casar 2008, 241, 247).

With the advantage of hindsight, two explanations for this amazing feat of parliamentary centralization are worth noting. The first is structural. The Mexican Constitution barred reelection for all executive posts and immediately consecutive reelection for legislative posts; it mandated the circulation of elites in the authoritarian period and carried over to the democratic period. Mexican deputies serve three-year terms. Their political careers necessarily required partisan loyalty to secure support for their next post, whether city council, mayor, governor, state legislator, or federal senator. Incumbent deputies depended on the PRI floor leader and on PRI governors to help them win their next posts to sustain a political career. This constitutional rule also automatically made all candidates for the legislature nonincumbents who depended disproportionately on party resources to get elected. Although Mexico elected 300 of its 500 federal deputies through single-member districts (the remaining 200 were elected from party lists through proportional representation), constitutionally mandated nonincumbency tilted even single-member district deputies toward high partisan loyalty.

The second possible explanation, therefore, is the first PRI floor leader after the 2000 election defeat: Beatriz Paredes Rangel. She was only the second woman in Mexican history to become a state governor (of Tlaxcala). Within the PRI, she rose through the party-led National Peasant Confederation. Before returning to the chamber of deputies in 2000, she had twice served as federal deputy and once as federal senator, providing her with significant legislative, executive, and partisan experience. She knew how to make use of the institutional resources that enhanced the likelihood of party loyalty in her chamber. And she kept together her PRI by the sheer force of smarts, energy, and commitment of time.

Subnational gubernatorial coordination and parliamentary discipline did not suffice, however, to make the PRI happy. Deep interpersonal and factional battles broke out as politicians struggled for control of the national party organization. Their fierce jockeying for power at least conveyed their belief that the PRI was worth fighting for. Roberto Madrazo, former governor of the State of Tabasco—who had lost the PRI primary to Francisco Labastida, the defeated PRI presidential candidate in 2000—ran for the party presidency, outpolling Paredes for the latter post. Madrazo went on to win the PRI's presidential nomination for the 2006 election, but in the process he provoked an alliance of PRI governors who had nothing in common except their opposition to him. Madrazo himself was smart and charming but bedeviled by allegations of abuse of power and corruption as Tabasco governor. Fragmented, factionalized, and thus enfeebled, the PRI in 2006 suffered its worst national election defeat ever (Hernández Rodríguez 2009; Pacheco Méndez 2009; Prud'homme 2010, 151–53).

To explain how the PRI responded to its 2006 election defeat, we examine the experience of Taiwan's Kuomintang Party. The Kuomintang and the PRI were for decades the two principal examples of long-ruling noncommunist parties in political regimes founded by military leaders who had devolved power over time to civilian leaders. The Kuomintang and the PRI were both defeated in presidential elections held in 2000, each for the first time ever. Antiauthoritarian themes combined with a strong critique of prevalent corruption to help defeat both. In each case, significant splits had weakened the ruling party. In Mexico, the principal breakaway dated from the late 1980s, but even through the 1990s significant PRI politicians defected time and again to the PRD or to minor parties. In Taiwan, the Kuomintang's centralized top-down approach to candidate nominations led to a proliferation of rebel candidacies. Yet the most lethal rebellion occurred during the 2000 election itself when a former Kuomintang politician, who had lost the party's presidential nomination, formed his own party, divided the formerly united Kuomintang electorate, and opened the doors for the victory of the Democratic Progressive Party (DPP; see Fell 2013, 157; Solinger 2001).

The Kuomintang, as had been the case with the PRI, retained significant strengths even after its 2000 presidential election defeat. It remained the majority party in the Legislative Yuan. It retained impressive organizational strength. As with the PRI, the Kuomintang had edged over time from ideology toward "mentalities," of which the most salient were its commitment to ensure high rates of economic growth and its affirmation of its nationalist identity as "China." Pragmatism, negotiating skills, and experience with successful market-conforming growth policies were part of the Kuomintang's tool kit, as they were of the PRI's. The Kuomintang had also depended on the country's president to enforce coordination. Yet Taiwan's president had been unable to ward off the party split that led to defeat in 2000. Early centralization of coordination did not serve the Kuomintang well because it fostered a counterproductive rigidity (Hsieh 2002).

The key to the Kuomintang's comeback was to establish a reliable alliance with those who had left it for other parties in the 2000 presidential election. In the 2004 presidential election, the Kuomintang and its ally together won fewer votes than they had won separately in 2000, but they set the bases for future victory. In the 2008 legislative election, a now-unified party under the Kuomintang banner, which won an outright majority of the vote, replaced this alliance (Tan 2009; Tan and Wu 2005). By the 2008 presidential election, the Kuomintang was a united party, running against the two terms of DPP presidential administrations, now vulnerable to corruption charges and facing the early stages of a significant economic slowdown. The Kuomintang ran on a classic platform that emphasized party identification—the clearest and strongest divisor between it and the DPP (Lacy and Niou 2012, 131)—and proven competence—a key valence issue—to manage the country's salient worry, the economy, against a DPP that had underperformed (Ho, Clarke, Chen, and Weng 2013). The Kuomintang's presidential candidate, Ma Ying-jeou, ran an effective and disciplined campaign.

The PRI's comeback strategy would feature similar elements: minimize new internal splits, forge alliances with other parties, avoid positional issues (the presidential candidate should say as little as possible on the issues of the day), emphasize the valence issue of competence as a critique of the governing party (no incumbent president ran for reelection in Taiwan in 2008 or in Mexico in 2012), and build on the party's remarkable organizational strengths. Recall the good aspects of the past as a reliable upholder of public order, pragmatic and good at negotiating skills, and the architect of Mexico's market-economy transition.

The Road Back to the Presidency

The PRI built the road back to Los Pinos, the presidential compound, starting from its base as a strong, powerful, and popular party. Consider the nadir of the PRI's national electoral performance, namely, coming in third for the presidential race in the 2006 presidential election. At that time, 2.3 million more Mexicans voted for PRI deputy candidates than they did for the PRI presidential candidate; core PRI supporters were prepared to dump Roberto Madrazo but not the PRI. In the midterm 2009 election with no presidential candidates running, PRI deputy candidates ranked first by a wide margin in the aggregate national vote (table 11.1). The PRI began the 2012 campaign with a clear advantage among core partisans.

After its 2000 election defeat, the PRI discovered the utility of alliances with minor parties, albeit never with the PAN or the PRD, in order to win state elections. The PRI entered no such alliances during the 1988–94 presidential term and only one during the 1994–2000 presidential term. But the PRI made an alliance in seventeen out of the thirty-three state elections during the 2000–2006 presidential term, principally with two small parties: in all seventeen elections with the PVEM and in six elections with the PT, or Workers' Party (Reynoso 2011, 23–25, 27). As shown in table 11.1, the PVEM added

2.8 million votes for Enrique Peña Nieto in 2012. Alliances have worked for the PRI. It garners votes for its candidates without requiring a direct vote for the PRI, which many voters still hold in disdain.

The PRI displayed its coalescent tendencies at the national level as well. Nearly half of the prominent national officeholders in Vicente Fox's presidency, and over a third of those in Felipe Calderón's, were PRI affiliates (Camp 2010, 63). After 2000, tactical coalescent behavior characterized all Mexican parties, including the PRI. During the six years of Vicente Fox's administration, a majority of the bills approved by congress were enacted with the unanimous support of all political parties (Casar 2008, 241).

Humiliated by the 2006 defeat, PRI governors and parliamentarians also rallied. In 2007, Beatriz Paredes was elected party president; she would serve until 2011 and, in the interim, became a key architect of the PRI's highly successful midterm national parliamentary election in 2009 (table 11.1). Paredes's election came about after a change in the party's internal procedures required various party conferences to choose her, thereby generating an ambience for consensus as well as the basis for renewed cooperation between PRI state governors, PRI congressional leaders, and the party's national organization (Prud'homme 2010, 152). The PRI rebuilt its cohesion thanks to its already noted skills in pragmatic negotiation. Principles need not matter. Victory does.

Enrique Peña Nieto, governor of the State of Mexico (2005–11)—Mexico's most populous state located in the nation's heartland with ready access to nationwide television and radio broadcasting—was the PRI's candidate from a film's central casting. As Bruhn notes in chapter 2, he was young and handsome. He and his family were well connected to the world of politics, business, and the media, with his wife a glamorous television star. He seemed to have no interest in, and no talent for, policy positioning or analysis. He said as little as possible about his views regarding policy issues during the entire campaign, but he did promise again and again that he would be supremely competent to govern Mexico—the classic valence issue. The claim to competence was in part comparative, namely, "I can do better than the outgoing government," which had presided over a time with high criminal violence, and "I am better than my opponents," one of whom had been a minister in the outgoing government and the other had already lost one presidential election and thrown a prolonged temper-tantrum thereafter, which would cost him votes in 2012. Taiwan's Ma had campaigned in the same way for his first election.

Peña Nieto was able at long last to implement Grzymała-Busse's recommendation to centralize power inside the party. As Bruhn argues in chapter 2, he plotted to win Mexico's presidency during his six-year term as governor of the State of Mexico. He emphasized promises rather than views on positional issues. This strategy served him well not just during the general election campaign but also much earlier to unite the PRI behind his candidacy in advance of the campaign. The PRI had been internally divided on economic and social policies; it was quite heterogeneous across Mexico's regions. Thus it was good to say little about the issues that would split the party (Paolino 2009). Instead, Peña Nieto would get a pothole fixed and call it a campaign promise fulfilled to the cheers of PRI identifiers. Early on, he mobilized his connections to get Mexico's television networks to portray him as Mexico's inevitable next president, as Chappell Lawson indicates in chapter 1. Inevitability helped to build PRI cohesion and to impose his central will on the PRI organization throughout the country. The imagined certainty of a Peña Nieto presidency, overflowing from television coverage, explains the fury of the response of devotees of social media, active in the #YoSoy132 movement (see Díaz-Domínguez and Moreno, chap. 10). The use of social media was of course hip and modern, but, for Peña Nieto's opponents, it was also a political necessity given television network broadcasts oozing with pro–Peña Nieto messaging. Peña Nieto's disciplined and centralized approach to his campaign, mum on the issues other than his competence, worked to elect him president of Mexico.

This miracle of PRI regeneration shines brightly in James A. McCann's chapter 4. Three considerations explain the vote for Peña Nieto. Two have been explanatory workhorses of Mexican elections since political democratization began, namely, assessments of the presidential candidates and party identification. The novelty was the positive assessment of the PRI's past governance—conditions were better, the economy was better managed, and the government was more representative. This variable—the views of the old regime—remained statistically significant even after applying controls for partisanship, candidate traits, and a host of other factors. Crucially, as McCann also shows, the vote for the PRI did not result from an authoritarian mind-set among voters. Mexicans did not want to elect a tyrant. They wanted to democratically elect someone to competently govern them. Voters did not support the PRI to return to the authoritarian past. Voters trusted the PRI's brand and its aura of reliable governance (regarding party brands, see Lupu 2013). Mexicans had nostalgia for the future.

The desire for competence, not for tyranny, surfaces also in Kenneth F. Greene's chapter 6. The PRI had been losing supporters for decades, and on the eve of the 2012 campaign its core backing was a minority of the electorate. Peña Nieto had to work hard to persuade those who did not identify with the PRI to vote for him. Television did a lot of the work; he had to smile handsomely and exude executive decisiveness. His victory did not result from resurfaced authoritarian values but rather from persuading voters to back a candidate toward whom they had not been predisposed.

Peña Nieto won the presidency in 2012 on the backs of the four variables that have best explained the vote in the three presidential elections (2000, 2006, and 2012) during the democratic regime: partisanship, candidate traits, assessments of the outgoing administration, and economic policy preferences. Bruhn's chapter 2 shows the intertwining of these elements during the unfolding campaign. The 2012 election was not, however, merely a rerun.

The 2012 Presidential Election: Discontinuities and Continuities

For the first time in Mexico's democratic political regime, in 2012 the early front-runner in the end won the presidency. Peña Nieto began the campaign ahead of the competition, and he won. In 2000 and 2006, the PRI's Labastida and the PRD's López Obrador were the respective early front-runners, but both lost.[1] Common across all three elections, however, was the impact of the campaign in shifting votes toward the eventual winner, as Greene shows in chapter 6. Peña Nieto's personal and political traits no doubt helped him in this campaign success, but being the candidate of Mexico's largest party, a factor that preceded the campaign, was surely enormously helpful. Parties matter.

For the first time also in a fully democratic Mexican presidential election, negative advertising mattered much less. As Magar shows in chapter 3, the change in the electoral rules that followed the 2006 election prohibited the private sale or purchase of electoral advertisements on radio and television as well as all negative advertisements. Lawson (chap. 1) thus explains the kind of messaging that remained lawful and possible, while Díaz-Domínguez and Moreno (chap. 10) highlight the turn of activist opponents of Peña Nieto to social media. On social media, these activists could denigrate Peña Nieto in ways expressly forbidden by the new mass media laws.

For the first time in Mexican elections, social media had a significant impact on voting behavior and public opinion. Díaz-Domínguez and Moreno (chap. 10) demonstrate the sustained importance for several weeks during the campaign of a social movement that sprung at a university but then widened quickly to a constituency that shared a predilection for the use of social media and an antipathy to the Peña Nieto candidacy. The use of social media to organize, motivate, and sustain a group of political activists for a period of weeks is, of course, neither original nor unique to Mexico. The so-called Arab Spring, in particular in Tunisia and Egypt, shows the effectiveness of such a communicative instrument in quite different countries. But #YoSoy132 was new to Mexico, and chances are that social media is here to stay for future Mexican elections.

Also for the first time in these elections, the formal duration of the campaign was set and shortened by law (Magar, chap. 3), with the Federal Electoral Institute enforcing the rule. The shock of the new rule enforcement fell especially on the precampaign period, which disadvantaged candidates who lacked a public presence and advantaged well-known candidates, such as former presidential candidate López Obrador or Peña Nieto, who had been governor of the State of Mexico, facilitating his appearance on Mexico City–originated national mass media television and radio broadcasts. Along with the prohibition of negative advertising and private purchases of mass media time, these rules compelled parties to find alternative means to reach the electorate. As noted, social media access was one and, as we shall see, clientelism was another.

There were also important analytical continuities. As noted above, partisanship, candidate traits, assessments of the outgoing administration, and economic policy preferences remain the workhorses for explaining Mexican voting behavior in 2012, as in 2006 and 2000. These four variables explain the bulk of voter preferences at the start of each campaign (Greene, chap. 6). Mexican voters thus resemble voters across the democracies that straddle the North Atlantic region.

As in past elections, demographic factors mattered relatively little in voting behavior. In looking at Díaz-Domínguez and Moreno's findings (chap. 10), the anti–Peña Nieto social media movement called #YoSoy132 began at the Ibero-American University and was broadly associated in news reports with young and fervid Internet users. Yet analysis of the #YoSoy132 movement shows that age was never statistically significant in explaining voter choice, attitude toward the presidential candidates, or policy preference. The #YoSoy132 movement mattered, but precisely because its impact was not just on the young.

Also as in past elections, positional issues—attitudes on specific policy issues—did not explain the voting choice. Lawson, Bruhn, McCann, and Greene (chaps. 1, 2, 4, and 6, respectively) show that the presidential candidates blurred their policy disagreements and actively avoided differentiation along most positional issues. The various models across the chapters confirm that positional issues were never statistically significant. On the contrary, and also as in past elections, valence issues—Peña Nieto's projected immense competence—remained statistically and substantively significant explanations of voting behavior (chaps. 4 and 6).

More strikingly, chapter 7, by Edgar Franco Vivanco, Jorge Olarte, Alberto Díaz-Cayeros, and Beatriz Magaloni, shows that a clearly significant impact of the prevalence of criminal violence was to decrease voting turnout in the country's most violent localities. The impact of criminal violence on the voting outcome requires a nuanced analysis, however. First, Peña Nieto was the candidate most adversely affected by the prevalence of violence. Second, López Obrador captured a larger share of the votes in violent areas. Third, the partisan identity of the state governor in violent areas had a significant impact on vote outcomes. There may have been retrospective voter punishment related to violence targeted at state governors. Thus, in violent zones of states led by PAN or PRD governors prior to the elections, voters favored the PAN's Vázquez Mota; in violent zones led by PRI governors, citizens voted against the PRI's Peña Nieto, the incumbent governor's candidate. This complexity made the positional issue—violence—difficult to discern in its impact on public opinion. Voters may have held state governors, not the Calderón presidency, as more responsible for the maintenance of public order in their communities, casting their votes differently depending on geographic context. Peña Nieto won the 2012 election for reasons unrelated to violence or the war on drugs.

A final important continuity, as Lawson notes in chapter 1, is that "campaigns matter much more in Mexico" than in the longer-established North Atlantic democracies, even if on many dimensions Mexican voters are similar to voters in the United States or other North Atlantic democracies. The 2012 campaign mattered, but so had its predecessors (Domínguez 2009, 303), although the ways in which campaigns have mattered, as noted above and discussed below, have changed.

Analytical Rebalancing

In each of the concluding chapters on two collective studies of Mexican elections by the same core scholarly team (Domínguez and Lawson 2004; Domínguez, Lawson, and Moreno 2009), I highlighted findings that may be new, or new to my own understanding of Mexican elections, thereby correcting either mistaken analyses or prior poorly specified findings. That is the purpose of this section—self-criticism. I focus on three questions: the relative strength of partisanship in the context of strong election campaign effects, the aggregative impact of positional issues as measures of public mood, and the impact of clientelist strategies on voter decisions.

Partisanship in Mexico may look impressive in comparison to other Latin American countries such as Peru or Venezuela, where the party systems have collapsed and political leaders have found it challenging to build new and enduing political parties. But, Greene argues forcefully in chapter 6, Mexican parties are not as strong as the scholarly literature and popular coverage may imply; they are also not as strong as our own team's prior research and my own writing may have portrayed it. Voters change their voting intentions during the campaign, which should not happen if partisanship were unchanging and more powerful. The net campaign effect varied between 10% and 15% in the 2000, 2006, and 2012 presidential elections, in each case to the benefit of the eventual winner. "Net effect" implies that some vote shifts may cancel each other out. Greene also found that about a third of the electorate in these three elections became convinced during the campaign to support a candidate who was not in line with their precampaign dispositions. Partisanship in Mexico is therefore still a significant building block for the analysis of electoral behavior, but in comparison to past characterizations there is a much greater role of political independents—"voter converts"—who help to shape the outcome of these elections.

The public mood matters as well in Mexico, as it does in other Latin American countries. This is Andy Baker's important and persuasive finding in chapter 5. Our research team's past work had shown that broad ideological perspectives help to structure Mexican public opinion, even if survey questions using words such as "left" or "right" do not capture them well (Domínguez 2009, 301), but the past research had not explored public mood as Baker has done. Moreover, the collective impact of past research, and for this book, deemphasized positional issues.

Public mood, as Baker explains, is a metadimension, built on responses to questions regarding positional issues, but in its aggregation it is quite different from attitudes about any one positional issue. He shows that the public mood on the economically liberal versus statist dimension oscillated considerably in Mexico across the 2000, 2006, and 2012 presidential elections in ways roughly consistent with their outcome. The analysis of public mood explains especially well why the PRD has failed to win the presidency or a larger number of governorships; voters prefer officials who on economic topics are significantly to the right of the PRD. The public mood also explains the PRI's victory in 2012, while it also shows that the PRI had squandered its ideological advantages in the electorate in the 2000 and 2006 presidential elections. This is an important correction to the view that positional issues "don't matter." Rather, the aggregation of positional issues into Baker's construct of public mood sheds significant light on the attitudes and behavior of Mexican voters. It may be best understood in the context of opportunities and constraints for parties and candidates during campaigns.

"Clientelist strategies (i.e., handouts) had become much less effective at generating voter support" in the 2000 and especially the 2006 presidential elections, I once wrote hopefully (Domínguez 2009, 298). We lack the evidence and analysis to show whether that conclusion was simply wrong for those elections. Nevertheless, clientelism mattered in the 2012 election—perhaps as many as a fifth of the electorate in the postelection wave of the Mexico 2012 Panel Study may have received handouts. Given the work by Ana De La O (chap. 8) and Simeon Nichter and Brian Palmer-Rubin (chap. 9), clientelism probably mattered in 2000 and 2006 as well.

De La O shows why past analyses were prematurely enthusiastic regarding the alleged decline of clientelism in Mexico: less than 3% of Mexicans in the first wave of the Mexico 2012 Panel Study reported, in response to a direct question, receiving a gift, a favor, or access to services in exchange for their vote. Relying on a list experiment that was part of both waves in the 2012 survey, De La O detects much more clientelism than the direct survey question. The list experiment and the direct question may give us the upper and lower bounds for the likelihood that voters accept a handout, 21% and 3%, respectively. De La O also finds a clear relationship between perceptions of corruption and the practice of clientelism. People who strongly agree that corruption is widespread are forty-one percentage points more likely to sell their vote compared to respondents who totally disagree with the statement that corruption is widespread. She also shows that aggregate changes in corruption are important determinants of vote buying. Voters most exposed to corruption are also the voters most likely to be exposed to, and to experience, clientelist practices.

In the same vein, Nichter and Palmer-Rubin present in chapter 9 robust quantitative evidence of the link between declared support and vote buying.

Citizens who declare their public support for a party, with political posters on their homes, are significantly more likely to receive partisan offers of reward. However, the panel survey does not allow us to determine whether the support is declared in order to obtain a handout, declared only following the receipt of a handout, or declared simply as an expression of genuine allegiance that happens to coincide with the transmission of money. But there is likely a strong connection between the declaration of support and the receipt and acceptance of handouts. The survey evidence indicates that politicians from all parties engaged in some clientelist behavior (see also Müller 2012), yet the analysis also shows that the PRI engaged in disproportionately more clientelist practices in the 2012 election, interacting with those voters ready to express their support publicly.

The campaigns' reliance on political posters at homes and the use of clientelist practices respond to the changes in the electoral law, which Magar reports in chapter 3. Banned from certain practices using mass media, anti–Peña Nieto supporters resorted to social media while pro–Peña Nieto supporters (as well as to a lesser extent supporters of all parties) resorted to clientelist practices. Mexico's 2012 election was not bought, but the stench of clientelism soiled the process.

Conclusion

Writing about the United States, Alesina and Rosenthal (1995) have argued that "divided government is not an accident, but the result of the voters' desire for policy moderation" (2). In Mexico, this argument applies with even greater force. As shown in table 11.1, many more millions of Mexicans voted against Enrique Peña Nieto than had voted for him in the 2012 presidential election. Similarly, many more millions of Mexicans voted for deputies and senators from the PAN, the PRD, and various small parties than for the PRI's congressional candidates. The PRI increased significantly its representation in both chambers of the federal congress but obtained an outright majority in neither chamber. Voters seemingly wanted to compel PRI politicians to draw into their tool kit as pragmatic negotiators to make deals with other parties to enact legislation.

Voters got their wish. At the start of his term, President Peña Nieto unveiled the Pact for Mexico, supported by the PRI, the PAN, and the PRD, which committed the parties to support significant legislation regarding various areas of public life. Mexico's past coalescent tendencies would blossom during Peña Nieto's first year in office as significant laws were enacted. Peña Nieto, a candidate who sought to say as little as possible on positional issues during the campaign, as president focused impressively on enacting policy change. But the voters' insistence that the PRI must look for allies also installed the opposition, thanks to the PRI's alliances to govern, as watchdogs over the PRI in congress and in executive branch appointments. Mexican citizens were ready to return the PRI to the presidency but through divided government they also secured an insurance policy against renewed authoritarian lordship.

In my reflections about Mexico's pivotal 2000 election, which ended seventy-one years of one-party rule, I wrote that "the hero of Mexico's democratic transition has been the voter" who behaved "prudently, cautiously" by supporting reform through the PRI and then electing two consecutive PAN presidents, neither of whom had a majority in either chamber in congress (Domínguez 2004, 341). In 2012, the voters concentrated greater power in the PRI, but deprived it of the capacity to govern Mexico simply on its own. The 2012 election is still a story of the admirable Mexican citizen—a prudent democrat.

Twice in this century Mexicans have witnessed a shift in the political party controlling the presidency. Therefore honor in constitutional democratic behavior also belongs to the presidents—Ernesto Zedillo in 2000 and Felipe Calderón in 2012—who handed over power, peacefully and professionally, to their opposition successors who had defeated their party on Election Day. May President Enrique Peña Nieto earn the same respect as a constitutional democrat as his predecessors, and may he best them as a successful policy wonk.

ACKNOWLEDGMENTS

This chapter draws extensively and explicitly from other chapters in this book. The author is deeply grateful to all his colleagues. All the good ideas belong to them; all the mistakes are the author's alone. In particular, he thanks Anna Grzymała-Busse and Eric Magar for their comments, and Alejandro Díaz-Domínguez for his improvements to table 11.1. Chappell Lawson provided especially helpful comments on an early draft of this chapter. Harvard University's Weatherhead Center for International Affairs and the David Rockefeller Center for Latin American Studies have supported this research, and Kathleen Hoover all of my work.

NOTES

1. López Obrador did not acknowledge his 2006 election defeat and instead proclaimed himself Mexico's legitimate president. For analysis, see Loaeza (2007).

REFERENCES

Alesina, Alberto, and Howard Rosenthal. 1995. *Partisan Politics, Divided Government, and the Economy.* Cambridge: Cambridge University Press.

Camp, Roderic Ai. 2010. *The Metamorphosis of Leadership in a Democratic Mexico.* Oxford: Oxford University Press.

Casar, María Amparo. 2008. "Los gobiernos sin mayoría en México: 1997–2006." *Política y gobierno* 15: 221–70.

Domínguez, Jorge I. 2004. "Conclusion: Why and How Did Mexico's 2000 Presidential Election Campaign Matter?" In *Mexico's Pivotal Democratic Election: Candidates, Voters, and the Presidential Campaign of 2000,* ed. Jorge I. Domínguez and Chappell Lawson, 321–44. Stanford, CA: Stanford University Press.

———. 2009. "Conclusion: The Choices of Voters during the 2006 Presidential Election in Mexico." In *Consolidating Mexico's Democracy: The 2006 Presidential Campaign in Comparative Perspective,* ed. Jorge I. Domínguez, Chappell Lawson, and Alejandro Moreno. Baltimore: Johns Hopkins University Press.

Domínguez, Jorge I., and Chappell Lawson, eds. 2004. *Mexico's Pivotal Democratic Election: Candidates, Voters, and the Presidential Campaign of 2000.* Stanford, CA: Stanford University Press.

Domínguez, Jorge I., Chappell Lawson, and Alejandro Moreno, eds. 2009. *Consolidating Mexico's Democracy: The 2006 Presidential Campaign in Comparative Perspective.* Baltimore: Johns Hopkins University Press.

Fell, Dafydd. 2013. "Impact of Candidate Selection Systems on Election Results: Evidence from Taiwan before and after the Change in Electoral Systems." *China Quarterly* 213: 152–71.

Gibson, Edward. 2012. *Boundary Control: Subnational Authoritarianism in Federal Democracies.* New York: Cambridge University Press.

Giraudy, Agustina. 2013. "Varieties of Subnational Undemocratic Regimes: Evidence from Argentina and Mexico." *Studies in Comparative International Development* 48: 51–80.

Grzymała-Busse, Anna. 2002. *Redeeming the Communist Past: The Regeneration of Communist Parties in East Central Europe.* Cambridge: Cambridge University Press.

Hernández Rodríguez, Rogelio. 2009. "Una competencia sin reglas: La candidatura presidencial de Roberto Madrazo." Volumen temático, *Política y gobierno*: 15–49.

Hernández Rodríguez, Rogelio, and Will G. Pansters. 2012. "La democracia en México y el retorno del PRI." *Foro internacional* 52: 755–95.

Ho, Karl, Harold Clarke, Li-khan Chen, and Dennis Lu-chung Weng. 2013. "Valence Politics and Electoral Choice in a New Democracy: The Case of Taiwan." *Electoral Studies* 32: 476–81.

Hsieh, John Fuh-sheng. 2002. "Whither the Kuomintang?" *China Quarterly* 168: 930–43.

Lacy, Dean, and Emerson M. S. Niou. 2012. "Information and Heterogeneity in Issue Voting: Evidence from the 2008 Presidential Election in Taiwan." *Journal of East Asian Studies* 12: 119–41.

Linz, Juan. 1975. "Totalitarian and Authoritarian Regimes." In *Handbook of Political Science,* vol. 3, ed. Fred Greenstein and Nelson Polsby. Reading, MA: Addison-Wesley.

Loaeza, Guadalupe. 1994. "¿Será?" *Reforma.* August 23, 11A.

Loaeza, Soledad. 2007. "La desilusión mexicana: Populismo y democracia en México en el 2006." *Foro internacional* 47: 817–38.

Lupu, Noam. 2013. "Party Brands and Partisanship: Theory with Evidence from a Survey Experiment in Argentina." *American Political Science Review* 57: 49–64.

Meyer, Lorenzo. 1994. "Y al despertar, el dinosaurio seguía allí." *Reforma*, August 25, 7A.

Müller, Markus-Michael. 2012. "Transformaciones del clientelismo: Democratización, (in)seguridad y políticas urbanas en el Distrito Federal." *Foro internacional* 52: 836–63.

Pacheco Méndez, Guadalupe. 2009. "El PRI: Relación interna de fuerzas y conflictos en la víspera del proceso electoral de 2006." *Política y gobierno* 16: 157–90.

Paolino, Philip. 2009. "La posición del PRI en la política mexicana." *Política y gobierno* 16: 321–48.

Prud'homme, Jean-François. 2010. "El sistema de partidos." In *Los grandes problemas de México: Instituciones y procesos políticos*. Mexico City: El Colegio de México.

Reynoso, Diego. 2011. "Aprendiendo a competir: Alianzas electorales y margen de victoria en los estados mexicanos, 1988–2006." *Política y gobierno* 18: 3–38.

Slater, Dan, and Joseph Wong. 2013. "The Strength to Concede: Ruling Parties and Democratization in Developmental Asia." *Perspectives on Politics* 11: 717–32.

Solinger, Dorothy. 2001. "Ending One-Party Dominance: Korea, Taiwan, Mexico." *Journal of Democracy* 12: 30–42.

Tan, Alexander. 2009. "The 2008 Taiwan Elections: Forward to the Past?" *Electoral Studies* 28: 502–06.

Tan, Alexander, and Jun-deh Wu. 2005. "The Presidential Election in Taiwan, March 2004." *Electoral Studies* 24: 519–24.

Index

258; and voting behavior, 16–18, *98–99*, 233–34, *235*, *237*; and #YoSoy132 movement, 227–28, 231–32, 239–43, *241*. *See also* leftism; statist-liberal divide

IFE (Instituto Federal Electoral), 20–21, 28n18, 39, 55–58, 149n8, 177n12, 214, 252; and campaign duration, 263; and candidate media access, 64, 66, 70; and censorship, 64, 80; and clientelism, 222–23; discretionary powers of, 64, 67–68, 78, 80–81; and Internet monitoring, 42–43, 60nn7–8; and media content, 42–43, 64, 66, 78–79

image, candidate. *See* candidate traits

Imai, Kosuke, 211

incumbent performance, 86–89, 107, 118, 135; and Calderón, 11, 16, 35, 39, 59n2, 90–91, 94, 97, *98–99*, 103n2, 146, 155, 229, 236; and PAN, 2, 12, 23, 35–36, 59n2, 90, 146; and voting behavior, 10, 23, 39, 88–89, 91, 93–94, 104n8, 229, 233, *235*, 236, *237*, 261, 263; and #YoSoy132 movement, *241*, 242

independent voters, 81, 96, 147, 265; and age, 239; and campaign effects, 130, 132, 142, *143*, *230*, 231; and ideology, 234, *235*; and López Obrador, 38, *230*, 231, *235*, *237*, 242; and media use, 245, *246–47*; and Peña Nieto, 14, 18, 146, *230*, *235*, *237*, 242; and PRI, 234; and social media, 239, 245, *246–47*; and Vázquez Mota, 12, *230*, *235*, *237*, 242; and voter volatility, 130, 132, *230–31*, *237*, 239, 242; and voting behavior, *230*, 231, *235*, *237*; and #YoSoy132 movement, *241*

India, 157

infrastructure, 43, 55

Institutional Revolutionary Party. *See* PRI

Internet, 42–43, 60nn7–8, 232–39, *235*, *237*, 244–45, *246–47*; voter access to, 166, *168*, *170–71*, 175; and #YoSoy132 movement, 33–34, 227–28, 240–43, *241*, 263. *See also* social media

Israeli-Palestinian conflict, 156

issues. *See* positional issues; valence issues

Iztapalapa debacle, 59

Jalisco, 160, 163, 214

jobs, *11*, 33

Katzenberg, Jeffrey, 75

Kibris, A., 156

Kitschelt, Herbert, 112, 213

Klor, E., 156

Korea, South, 87

Kuomintang Party (Taiwan), 258–59

Labastida, Francisco, 7, *8*, 13, 21, 253, 257, 262; and campaign effects, 128, 134, 137, *138*

Latin American politics, 34, 81, 107–12, 120, 128, 147, 149n1, 245; and corruption, 183; and public mood, 109–10, 124, 125n8; and social media, 228, 239

Latin American Public Opinion Project (LAPOP), 99–101, 104n10, 114

Latinobarometer survey, 113, 114

Lawson, Chappell, 1–31, 79, 81, 109, 207, 261–64

leftism, 2, 4, 18, 35, 162; and media use, 245, *246–47*; and voting behavior, 234, *235*, *237*; and #YoSoy132 movement, 231–32, *241*, 242–43

legislative elections, 32, 94–97, *95*, *99*, 109, 146, 267; and campaign spending, 73; and PAN, 39, 253; and party subsidies, 67, *69*; and PRD, 51, 253; and PRI, 2, 7, 22, 27n7, 27n16, 28n21, 80, 253, 254

liberalism, economic. *See* statist-liberal divide

Loaeza, Guadalupe, 252

local politics, 82, 162, 166, 195n3, 204; and clientelism, 190, *209*, 210, 219–21, *220*; and corruption, 173, 190; and declared support, 216–18, *217*, 219–21, *220*; and voting behavior, *168*, *169*, *170–71*

López, Carlos, 100

López Obrador, Andrés Manuel, 1–2, 7, 21–22, 97, 108, 182, 252, 263; and 2006 election, 9–11, *10*, 21, 26n6, 51, 128, 133, 145, 262; and 2006 election results protest, 2, 9, 13, 19, 37–38, 64, 136; and 2012 campaign, 13–18, *15*, 27n13, 37–38, 44–45, 73, 136, 144–48; and 2012 election results contestation, 200, 205–7, 222; and campaign effects, 134, 137, *138*; and candidate traits, 9, *10*, 13, *17*, 18, 37–38, 125n8, 142; and clientelism, 204; competence of, *17*, 22; and drug violence, 144, 169–73, *170*,